MEMOIRS

Mike

THE MEMOIRS OF
THE RIGHT HONOURABLE
LESTER B. PEARSON
PC, CC, OM, OBE, MA, LLD

VOLUME 3
1957-1968

EDITED BY JOHN A. MUNRO
AND ALEX.I.INGLIS

University of Toronto Press
TORONTO AND BUFFALO

© University of Toronto Press 1975
Toronto and Buffalo
Printed in Canada

Library of Congress Cataloging in Publication Data
Pearson, Lester B
Mike; the memoirs of the Right Honourable
Lester B. Pearson.
Half title and on spine: Memoirs.
Vol. 3 edited by J. A. Munro and A. I. Inglis.
Includes indexes.
CONTENTS: V. 1. 1897-1948.
1. Pearson, Lester B.
2. Canada—Politics and government—20th century.
3. Canada—Foreign relations. I. Title
FI034.3. P4A36   971.06'43'0924 [B]   72-88037
ISBN 0-8020-1913-7 (V. 1)
ISBN 0-8020-1999-4 (V. 2)
ISBN 0-8020-2198-0 (V. 3)

⚜

FOREWORD

The editors explain in their introduction the circumstances of the preparation of Volume 3 of my father's memoirs. It was not an easy decision for the executors of his estate (my mother, Senator John Connolly, and myself) to agree to publication. We did so on the grounds that, given L.B. Pearson's intention to complete his memoirs, enough first-person material was available and was sufficiently representative of the ten years he spent as leader of the Liberal Party to justify publication now rather than putting it aside for use by historians. Moreover, about half the material was already in the public domain, and we were completing a process begun shortly after his retirement in 1968. I consulted a number of people who had worked closely with my father when he was Prime Minister or who knew him well. Some gave me general encouragement, others specific critical advice. One or two believed that the manuscript was an inadequate reflection both of the record of these years and of his own part in them. I explained that this was memoir, not biography, and that one did not exclude the other. Some thought that too much was made of the politics of the period, which in retrospect would appear to be secondary, and that the tone was defensive. There was concern about references to persons, many still active in public life, and to events which still remain controversial.

The editors and I took account of these reactions. Christopher Young and Blair Neatby, who again performed an invaluable advisory function, helped with revision. Publication was delayed for a year to give more time for reflection. While we could not add material about subjects which my father had not treated himself, we could and did refine the existing material to conform with our best judgment of changes he might have made, and we checked his recollections of important events with those who had better knowledge than we did. If mistakes of fact remain, we take responsibility.

I am grateful to my mother and to Senator John Connolly for their willingness to accept the view that publication of Volume 3 would be justified, and to those friends who read some or all of the manuscript, whatever the conclusions they drew. I was encouraged by my sister's opinion that the story should be told. Once again the Canada Council, the Molson Foundation, and the International Development Research Centre helped to defray expenses. The editors, besides their usual skill, showed patience and restraint in the face of delay and indecision.

This enterprise is now concluded. I hope it will contribute to a better understanding of Canadian public policies at home and abroad and to a better sense of proportion about the motives of public men – for the most part neither gods nor rascals, but ordinary men who find themselves for brief periods at the head of the parade.

GEOFFREY PEARSON

CONTENTS

❦

ILLUSTRATIONS

INTRODUCTION

This third and final volume of *Mike: The Memoirs of The Right Honourable Lester B. Pearson* was begun by Mr Pearson in the early part of November 1972. At that time Mr Pearson knew that the cancer which had led to the removal of one eye in the summer of 1970 had spread and that the probability of medical treatment arresting the disease's advance was uncertain. He therefore set aside the second volume of his memoirs for the editors to complete and concentrated his attention on the last and most important volume, dealing with his career as national leader of the Liberal party, Leader of the Opposition, and as Prime Minister of Canada. During the six or seven weeks in which he remained well enough to write, he produced in his own hand some 30,000 words of manuscript. This draft provided a basis for this third volume, in terms both of material and of direction. Inherently it also expressed a last literary and political wish – that, if at all possible, the work be completed.

In addition to his uncompleted manuscript, there was a small amount of material originally prepared by Mr Pearson for the first chapter of Volume 2, but not used because it extended beyond the chronological limits of that volume. Without these materials prepared by Mr Pearson himself, Volume 3 of *Mike* would not have been possible. His uncompleted first draft, however, was not in itself sufficient for this book. Fortunately, the editors had available, as they had for Volume 2, the transcripts of lengthy interviews done by the Canadian Broadcasting Corporation for the television programmes 'The Tenth

Decade' and 'First Person Singular.' The editors have had to rely on these interviews to provide much of Mr Pearson's reflective judgment on the issues and personalities under discussion; often, they have had to rely on the transcripts to provide a basis for the narrative structure as well. Fortunately, much of this transcript material had been looked at by Mr Pearson with a view to its incorporation in these memoirs and had been corrected by him. The interviews none the less remained a television product, more often than not dependent for their full meaning on the inflection of the voice and the facial expression of their author. Thus, especially in dealing with the uncorrected portions, the question arose, 'Well, of course Mr Pearson said that, but would he have written it in those same words?' There is no satisfactory answer to this question. The editors can only hope that their decisions have not distorted the truth of what Mr Pearson would have written had he been alive to do so.

Another important source for the volume was the material referred to in the text as 'diary.' Mr Pearson did not keep a regular diary for the years 1957 to 1968. (We might add, as a matter of clarification in relation to Volume 2, that Mr Pearson's diary for the years prior to 1957, while more extensive, was also kept irregularly. It was occasional and episodic.) For the period of Volume 3, his diary took the form of 'memoranda for file': contemporary, first-person accounts of various important events and decisions. These have been used extensively in the preparation of this volume. Finally, the editors had Mr Pearson's correspondence, papers, and a close working relationship with him during the last years of his life to provide necessary detail and conceptual framework.

Volume 3 of *Mike*, like Volume 2, is the result of the editors' weaving together these various sources. As with Volume 2, the editors have exercised every care that contemporary judgment should not be confused with later reflective judgment in relation to any event, decision, or personality. They are conscious of the fact that the full story of L.B. Pearson in politics is not told within these covers. One of the major criticisms of those consulted during the preparation of this volume has been its areas of omission, particularly its lack of reference to the high achievements of the Pearson government and its cursory treatment of some colleagues and assistants. The editors make no excuse for these omissions. The subjects they could treat were strictly limited by the availability of first-person sources. Thus, if the Canada Pension Plan is not discussed in detail, it is because there was no suitable first-person Pearson material from which to tell the story. The reader may draw whatever conclusions he thinks appropriate in relation to the absence of this material. Nevertheless, we considered the material available sufficient to justify this volume's completion and publication.

While the editors had to assume a greater responsibility for this volume than they did in Volume 2, they were convinced that the material warranted presentation in the first person, as the memoirs of the Right Honourable L.B. Pearson. They have courted the risk of third-person interjection and the reader must be aware of this. Every safeguard, however, has been taken to ensure that the judgments of this volume are those of Mr Pearson and not of the editors. In addition to their Advisory Committee, comprising Mr Geoffrey Pearson, Mr Christopher Young, and Professor Blair Neatby, the manuscript was circulated to a number of Mr Pearson's political colleagues and advisers. The editors have considered it their duty throughout this process to protect the integrity of the volume against any advice, however well intentioned, that would have made it untrue to the materials from which it was derived.

In detailed breakdown, Chapters 1 through 4 are based on Mr Pearson's own manuscript, supplemented where appropriate by material from his diary, excerpts from Hansard, and CBC transcripts. The supplementary material in the first four chapters was used to complement the original manuscript, to flesh it out, and to make it as complete a reflective commentary as possible. The bulk of Chapter 5 came from diary which Mr Pearson wrote after his various contacts with American leaders. Additional material was used from the CBC transcripts and a lecture given by Mr Pearson at the Couchiching Conference in August 1968, soon after his retirement. Chapter 6 is based on a few pages of original manuscript, transcript material, plus that file of documents (memoranda, diary, letters) made available by Mr Pearson to Messrs Wilson and Westell for their series of articles in 1969 on the alleged scandals in the Pearson government. Material dealing with earlier security matters was incorporated here, in keeping with Mr Pearson's intention to treat these subjects in his memoirs. The material of this chapter was in many ways the most difficult to handle. It was made easier by Mr Pearson's ability to give others the benefit of the doubt and by his sensitivity to what might affect men's private and public lives. Chapters 7 and 8 are based on original manuscript, highly detailed contemporary memoranda, transcript material, and correspondence. Chapter 9 drew largely from the CBC transcripts supplemented by small portions of manuscript, a good deal of diary, and other memoranda and correspondence. Chapter 10 is based on diary, transcripts, and lecture material. Chapter 11 is almost entirely based upon a lengthy diary piece written by Mr Pearson soon after the 1968 Liberal leadership convention. Its judgments are somewhat tempered by the CBC transcript material and its detail expanded by the inclusion of contemporary documentation.

In performing the tasks required of them, the editors appreciate highly the support, guidance, and advice of their Advisory Committee and those of Mr Pearson's contemporaries whom the trustees of the Pearson estate chose to consult. The editors further appreciate the advice and reassurance provided by Messrs Bruce Hutchison and Anthony Westell. In particular, they must cite Mr. Geoffrey Pearson for his care and attention to the detail of this volume and of his father's memory, and for his decision to see this work to fruition. Without his efforts, there would be no third volume of *Mike*. To Miss Lois McIntosh, Mr Pearson's secretary when he was Secretary of State for External Affairs, we owe another immense debt. Her diligence in typing the many drafts of this manuscript and in preparing the volume's index cannot be exaggerated. Miss Clair Hetrick and Mrs Paulette Popowick also contributed generously of their time and effort. Mr Mark Collins served the editors faithfully and well as their research assistant. Miss Annette Perron, Mr Pearson's private secretary, was constant in her encouragement. Again the editors are especially indebted to Dr Archibald A. Day who has acted as stylistic consultant in the preparation of all three volumes of *Mike*. Mr Rik Davidson and Mrs Rosemary Shipton of the University of Toronto Press, as always, have been as beacons of welcome light on stormy seas.

Finally, there has been the trust and confidence of Mrs Maryon Pearson. She could have said 'No' to the volume's production and publication. She chose not to do so. The editors hope that she will enjoy this account of the years she knew so well.

JOHN A. MUNRO
ALEX I. INGLIS

THE LIBERAL CONVENTION 1958

the image and the real

with Louis St Laurent and Paul Martin

congratulations from his family to the new leader

CHANGING FORTUNES

'on the mound

after our first Cabinet meeting 1963

"WE MUST DISCHARGE OUR DEMOCRATIC RESPONSIBILITIES"

AS SEEN BY DUNCAN MACPHERSON

THE OLD SMOOTHIE

with L.B. Johnson, signing the Auto Pact 1965

with Walter Gordon

TROOPS OF FRIENDS

retirement dinner at Rideau Hall 1968

Klondike Days

MOMENTS IN OFFICE

at Mr Diefenbaker's 75th birthday celebration
in the Parliament Buildings

outside Buckingham Palace with the Order of Merit 1972

MEMOIRS

❧1❧

DEFEAT AND LEADERSHIP

My father's advice to me was always: 'If you do your very best, sincerely and honestly, you will never have anything to worry about.' I must add that his warm and understanding encouragement was a wonderful incentive to do well in the schoolroom or at short-stop. My mother's advice was also based on a warm heart and a wise mind: 'Be a good boy and keep your feet dry.' But I do not recall much interest in political questions during my early years in our household – except where temperance was involved. I was more concerned with getting good marks, playing shinny, or catching fly balls, and even more with becoming the greatest all-round athlete Canada had ever produced. I did see Sir Wilfrid Laurier once, however, and do remember vividly the election of 1911. There were two main issues: domination by the United States and separatism in Quebec (which we called 'nationalism' then). *Plus ça change, plus c'est la même chose.* But before the First World War Canadians in general shared a feeling of security with a tinge of smugness, a feeling largely based on unawareness of the outside world. We were, after all, protected by the Royal Navy and war only meant the Charge of the Light Brigade, scarlet tunics, and Victoria Crosses. Then came the explosion of 1914, from which the pieces have yet to settle. Today's world will never be as calm and clear as the world of my youth and few can now escape an awareness of what is going on; modern communications bring the world and all its problems and dangers and tragedies right into our living-rooms.

It was my good fortune, after my retirement in 1968, to have time and health to do the things I chose, to say what I wished to say (subject only to my own sense of responsibility), to write and to think without pressure. I can cheer for the Ottawa Rough Riders or the Montreal Expos without being accused of political motivation – or kiss a baby or even a young lady for purely personal reasons. I have learned all over to dial a telephone and put out the garbage, even if not to grow roses. My wife is the best cook on our street and I am the best dish washer.

My own experience demonstrates that in Canada the top is possible for anyone. But the summit is lonely. The pressures are unceasing, the demands continuing, and the work unending. Nevertheless, service to the state through the civil service and politics has rich rewards and great compensations to make up for the load of responsibility. In retirement, as 'Lester B. Pearson – PM off duty,' I have had time to look back and remember. I can watch contemporary electoral activity, cruelly exhausting both physically and emotionally, and say, 'There but for the grace of a wise decision go I'; and once again I conclude that popular democracy is the worst form of government ever devised, except for all the others.

ॐ

My period as Leader of Her Majesty's Loyal Opposition and as Prime Minister is part of what has come to be known in Canada as 'The Tenth Decade.' This period in fact begins in 1956 with one of the most dramatic episodes in our parliamentary history, the pipeline debate. I had hoped, at the time, to keep out of it, largely because I did not know much about it. My direct ministerial responsibilities were not involved and, although I was present during the relevant Cabinet meetings, this matter was particularly within the field of activity of C.D. Howe, Minister of Trade and Commerce. He had obviously gone over the whole question with the PM and this did not encourage much Cabinet discussion. I said little, and my feeling, which was more instinctive than considered, that this natural gas pipeline should be built and financed not by Texas millionaires but by the government or governments of Canada with public control and ownership, would have received, I think, support from only one or two of the Ministers.

I was perhaps more a proponent of public ownership and public enterprise at that time than a little later on because of the manner in which uranium was then being developed in my own constituency.

Algoma East had the largest deposits in the world. I had concluded that if we were going to develop resources where continuing operations depend so much on political and international factors, and where marketing is controlled, then we should not allow exploiters to take out millions in quick profits without regard for the future. Mr Howe, a great public-ownership man when so inclined (witness Air Canada), did not judge the pipeline to be an enterprise suitable for public ownership.

Howe had become increasingly powerful in the government. Though a most modest and engaging person, he was fully aware of and accustomed to the advantages of personal decision-making, and his impatience grew at the delays and frustrations of parliamentary debate which to him appeared an annoying obstruction of good work. This attitude was reinforced by the power he had acquired and by the able and loyal organization he had created (both with the approval and appreciation of the people of Canada) during the Second World War. CD was our economic organizer of victory and had a deservedly high reputation. But the war was over, and Parliament and politics in Ottawa had returned to normal by the 1953 election. The long debate in 1955, which CD treated with ill-concealed impatience, over a government amendment to the Defence Production Act, when the Opposition succeeded in limiting to three years a proposed indefinite extension of the powers over the economy which Howe had regained during the Korean War, was a symptom of the changing times. I began to wonder, as other people did, whether Howe had not had enough of politics. He often expressed a desire to leave and I think he would have welcomed the chance; but he was not one to run away when the tide was turning. From that first dent in his good fortune and prestige in the House and his respect in the country, we went on to the pipeline debate.

I had been fortunate in my personal contacts with CD. They were always friendly. I never crossed him. I did not have to. I had represented him once or twice during the war and afterwards in Washington when I was Ambassador. Later, when I was External Affairs Minister, he was very co-operative in those foreign economic policies with which I was concerned. Further, it was hard not to be impressed by his reputation, particularly in the United States, where they regarded him as a very great man. One of the reasons, I think, for his high reputation was not only his tactical common sense, but his ability not to say much when other people were making long speeches. He was known for his silences. 'Les silences de M. Howe' were very impressive. But when he did speak, he spoke with great authority, the authority of achievement and reputation. In consequence, there were not many in the Cabinet who were prepared to get on the wrong side of Howe on policy matters. With Mr King's departure (King, very much Howe's senior, dominated everyone in the Cabinet), Mr St Laurent as a relatively new man deferred like everyone else to Howe's authority on trade and economic matters. I do not recall that Howe ever interfered with other ministerial business in Cabinet, but I suspect that privately he may have greatly influenced the Minister of Finance and the other Ministers concerned with trade and economics.

When the pipeline came before Cabinet in 1956, Howe naturally and immediately took charge and rather assumed that there would be no differences of opinion on how this project was to be arranged and organized. Mr Howe, as everyone knew, did not do business in the usual political manner. He liked to pick up a telephone and say: 'Let's have a pipeline.' He would talk to a few people who would convince him that this was, of course, a splendid thing. I had a feeling when the matter first came before Cabinet that he had already made commitments on government guarantees to the proposed financiers – not formal commitments, but personal guarantees, because he was so sure of himself. Our early discussions were not controversial. We agreed orally that the pipeline would be a constructive project in a vital aspect of our national development and that it would be advantageous to build it so as to open up the American as well as the Eastern Canadian market. Only when the Texas oil crowd appeared in the wings did the discussion in Cabinet become somewhat more vigorous. Although I must not write about Cabinet discussions in any way that would violate their secrecy, it is public knowledge that some of CD's early proposals to finance the line were not acceptable to Cabinet. From a business point of view his suggestions might have been the best, but politically, had they been adopted, we would have been in even greater trouble than we later were. After CD had changed some of his original views on financing the pipeline, there was no disagreement in Cabinet.

Mr Howe then began to talk about getting the bill through Parliament at once since otherwise we would lose an entire year of construction. In retrospect, to lose a year would not have been catastrophic, but at the time I remember there was a general belief that he was right. Thus, when CD introduced the bill he announced, as a consequence of deliberate government decision, that closure would be moved to limit debate. The project may have been sound in itself, but the procedure adopted in 1956 to get parliamentary approval of the $80 million loan to Trans-Canada Pipe Lines in time to permit construction in that same year turned out to be disastrous for the Liberal party.

It is possible to make a good case for closure, that there remained ample opportunity for discussion and decision. But this point was lost in the appearance of things, to say the least. The manner in which closure was applied and the anger thus created in the Opposition (some of it merely political, but much of it genuine), together with difficulties over certain rulings of the Speaker, made it look as though there was to be no debate at all. And in the House, the more violent the attacks by the Opposition on our procedure and on us as a government and a party, the more extravagant their criticism became, the more our position hardened. We were bound to suffer from this in public opinion, especially in the changed political atmosphere which had developed. Also, Howe's manner did not help. At the time, he was pretty arrogant; he hated this kind of debate and told our opponents in the House exactly what he thought of them. But when they argued bitterly against him as a dictator, a fascist, and a destroyer of Parliament, when they said that no matter how we did this they were not going to let this bill go through, everything collapsed into complete chaos. It became a wild and irrational struggle, a parliamentary débâcle.

I did not want to take part, but I simply felt I had to. I remember attending a dinner given by President Sukarno of Indonesia for the Governor General at the Royal Ottawa Golf Club on the last night of the debate, 5 June 1956. This was a very formal occasion, very *protocolaire*, all very subdued and quiet, in stark contrast to the rest of my evening. I had to leave early to get back to the House where I was to speak at 10:30. I made my speech in my evening clothes, pretty rumpled by the end since that night I became a real tub-thumper. This was the first truly partisan political speech I had made in eight years in the House of Commons, certainly the first outside the area of foreign affairs. The Hansard record of it reads as follows:

Hon. L.B. Pearson (Secretary of State for External Affairs): Mr Speaker, this afternoon the hon. member for Eglinton (Mr Fleming), in a speech part of which at least I hope he will regret, suggested that we on this side, and especially we in the government, were putty in the hands of the Minister of Trade and Commerce (Mr Howe).

Mr Lennard: Aren't you?

Mr Pearson: He went on to say, with that fine disregard for accuracy which he so often displays—

Mr Nowlan: He studied under you.

Mr Pearson: The hon. member was a disgrace to my teaching. 'Where are all those members of the government? There is not one of them who has stood up here'—I am proud to be the eighth member of the government to speak on this bill.

We are now, Mr Speaker, ending a debate which began, and we often forget this, on May 14th.

Mr Fulton: It began on May 17th, and you know it. Why persist in falsifying the record?

Mr Pearson: In the immortal words of the hon. member for Prince Albert (Mr Diefenbaker), I ask the hon. member for Kamloops (Mr Fulton) to maintain silence and listen to the truth. We occasionally forget also that this is a debate on a pipeline. The opposition to this bill has been long and vigorous.

Some hon. Members: Hear, hear.

Mr Pearson: At times it has been frenzied. It was forecast many years ago, the tactics that should be followed by a Conservative opposition in such a discussion.

Mr Nowlan: That was when you were a Tory.

Mr Pearson: I can stand heckling, but I do not like to be insulted in that way. A great Canadian, Mr Speaker, the late John W. Dafoe, in his book 'Clifford Sifton in Relation to his Times,' had this to say in describing the tactics of the opposition of 1897 to a railway bill introduced by Mr Sifton. From his book I quote the following paragraphs which have a peculiar relationship to the debate we have been having in this house. He said: 'If any Canadian satirist wishes to write an oration for the use of an opposition resisting a government proposition to build or assist in building a railway'—or, if you like, a pipeline—'he can readily find his material in that vast repository of talk, the Canadian *Hansard*. The lines of the attack are defined by usage and sanctified by tradition.' This was written many years ago. 'First it must be urged that the building of the road is too early or too late . . . then the route is all wrong; it either starts at the wrong place or follows the wrong course. The parties to whom the building of the road'—or the pipe line—'is given are not the right parties.'

Then, Mr Dafoe put in quotes some of his own reflections on this.

'Is not the government aware, Mr Speaker, that the bankers of London, New York, Paris and Kalamazoo, in alliance with the engineers of Great Britain, the United States, Germany and Kamchatka are eager to build this railway, and given the opportunity are prepared to make a proposition which will save this country millions and rescue the people from the hands of the exploiters whom the government delight to honour?' Then, Mr Dafoe went on: 'Since the government cannot tear up the contract any alternative offer can be put in the most attractive light; while conversely, the arrangement to which the government is committed, is to be painted in the darkest colours.

Flagitious, corrupt, improvident, perfidious, knavish, faithless are words very suitable to be used. Any member of the opposition can be trusted to say that the treasury of the country is being robbed in order that means may be obtained for the debauching of the electors;'—

Mr Nowlan: That is obvious.

Mr Pearson: I continue the quotation: —'but only those most skilful in the art of innuendo should be permitted to hint that there is a private and sinister explanation of the favouritism displayed by the minister. By the use of some such formula an opposition running to interminable length can be offered.'

Well, Mr Speaker, the opposition has undoubtedly run to an interminable length, but there has not been as much discussion on the bill during this interminable length as on things external to the bill. This is probably a good reason why the Minister of External Affairs should take part.

The opposition, of course, claim, and they claim very often, to be gagged. If that is true, Mr Speaker, they are the noisiest group of gagged men in history. They have talked, gag or no gag, endlessly on the bill, around the bill, above the bill and below the bill. They have ranged far and wide from Alcibiades, through Shakespeare down to poor old Guy Fawkes and then on to Hitler. They have raised endless points of order, questions of privilege, especially from one or two members.

A charge, and it is a serious one, has been levelled that what we are witnessing in this debate is the end of our parliamentary freedom.

Some hon. Members: Hear, hear.

Mr Pearson: Well, that is the charge, Mr Speaker.

Mrs Fairclough: Absolutely right.

Mr Pearson: What in reality are exaggerated and excitable statements cannot destroy the facts any more than carefully contrived scenes in the House of Commons can obscure them. Parliamentary government is in danger when the government elected in a democratic way is prevented from carrying on the business of government by a minority using and exploiting the rules of the house. To prevent that, Mr Speaker—

An hon. Member: What about closure?

Mr Pearson: I wonder if some of the apostles of free speech would allow me to continue my speech. To prevent this, there are rules of closure recognized in every deliberative assembly, and in most of them the rules are far stricter than they are in this assembly. That rule has been applied here, not to stop debate but to limit it. In that connection, reference has been made very often to the use of closure in the mother of parliaments, about which we have heard so much in the discussion. Let us see what happens in the parliament at Westminster. From 1945 to 1951, which was the period when the Socialist government was in power in the United Kingdom, the maximum time actually devoted to the consideration of any government money bill by the House of Commons during that period of six years was 21 hours and 25 minutes.

Mr Dufresne: It was defeated since.

Mr Pearson: And of that total time, including 44 minutes on the resolution preceding the bill, 7 hours and 18 minutes were given to second reading, 10 hours in committee, 22 minutes on the report and 2 hours and 35 minutes on third reading.

In the six Socialist sessions covered by this period, 55 money bills became law in the United Kingdom. Altogether, they took up 260 hours, 9 minutes, of parliamentary time which would suggest—

Mr Knowles: Good legislation.

Mr Pearson:—that the average time spent in debate on a bill over there during that parliament was 4 hours and 44 minutes. That country, Mr Speaker, the home of parliamentary freedom, also understands the necessities of parliamentary government, the responsibilities and rights of the government as well as of the opposition.

There is going on tonight in Paris, Mr Speaker, a debate on which the government of that country has staked its existence. Before that debate began a period of three days was allowed for it. Is that the end of democracy in France?

Some hon. Members: Pretty much.

Mr Pearson: Or is the real danger to democracy in France from the extremists in that country, right or left, who delay, obstruct, provoke scenes, shout down the presiding officer, or walk out? Extremists in those countries know, Mr Speaker, that the best way to destroy democratic government—and in some of them they have succeeded—is to prevent it from governing; that the way to destroy freedom is to promote licence and confusion, and the best way to destroy democratic authority is to bring it into ridicule.

'Mr Hees: Is this your pitch for the leadership?

Mr Lennard: No; it is his swan song before leaving.

Mr Pearson: This hon. member for Broadview, whose interruptions in this debate are as vociferous as they are vacuous, must remember that all members are not consumed with the political ambition that seems to consume him.

Mr Sinclair: Back to the bush leagues.

Mr Pearson: The people of this country are not going to believe that a Liberal government headed by the present Prime Minister is going to destroy the liberties of parliament.

Some hon. Members: Oh, oh.

Mr Pearson: There is no one in this country who is also going to believe that the Minister of Trade and Commerce (Mr Howe), who has done so much for Canada in peace and war, is—to use, Mr Speaker, the shameful phrase that came from the other side—the tool of United States interests.

Mr Hees: Do you think you can catch Walter? [Harris, the Minister of Finance and a possible leadership candidate]

Mr Pearson: The hon. member for Broadview is a physical heavyweight but a mental featherweight.

Mr Hees: You were ahead last year but not this year.

Mr Pearson: If we could have a little free speech for once I would appreciate it. I now come to a very important aspect of this discussion which has been referred to by a good many speakers, and that is the international side of the question. It has been suggested in the debate that our relations over this bill with the United States have been humiliating; that this bill represents a sell-out to United States interests.

Some hon. Members: Hear, hear.

Mr Pearson: Mr Speaker, there is no reason for not speaking very frankly on our relations with the United States of America on any subject. I have done it in the past and I hope to do it in the future. But it is no service to our country or to the United States to indulge in unfair references to Americans, to make destructive and insulting comments on United States investment; to use coarse epithets and charge that our resources are falling into the hands of United States buccaneers.

Mr Nowlan: What does the *New York Times* say today?

Mr Pearson: It is humiliating and degrading to suggest that we are becoming hewers of wood, drawers of water and diggers of holes for our United States neighbours.

Mr Hees: That is your Montreal speech.

Mr Pearson: That is a defeatist attitude. It is as defeatist as some of the references on the other side to 54-40 or fight, or to suggest that we are becoming a banana republic. I know the members of the opposition get quite violent in denying that they are unfriendly to United States investments in Canada. Well, if they are so friendly to United States investments in Canada why scare them away with this kind of talk?

Mr Lennard: Oh, rot.

Mr Fleming: Hand it to them on a platter.

Mr Deputy Speaker: Order.

Mr Hees: Where else would they invest it?

Mr Pearson: Their attitude, Mr Speaker, reminds me of the old English music hall ballad: 'I forgive you, my dear, for dissembling your love, but why did you kick me downstairs?' There is no danger of our losing control in Canada of any investment in Canada in connection with any project under Canadian control, federal and provincial, as this one is.

A good deal of talk has occurred in this debate about the analogy of the Canadian Pacific Railway. There was a case of a Canadian enterprise being controlled, not in theory, but in fact, out of Canada, in London, and at a time when Canada was not a self-governing free country as she is now, but at a time when Canada was a colony ruled from Downing street. Did it stop our growth, politically and economically? It did not. Who says, then, that this Trans-Canada pipe line project will stop our growth politically or economically, or sell us to any outside country?

Mrs Fairclough: Now I have heard everything.

Mr Pearson: It is just as well that we should stop talking, even the hon. lady from Hamilton, if it is not too much to ask, in a way which is going to disturb the inflow of needed capital into this country.

Mr Hees: You were ahead last year.

Mr Pearson: I take the hon. gentleman's interruption as a tribute to the fact that I am getting under their skin. Next year, $7,500 million will be invested, capital investment, in Canada, 23½ per cent of our gross national product. We shall not be able to find all that money in Canada. We must get some of it from outside, especially from the United States, if we are to maintain the development which we have begun—

Mrs Fairclough: Let us get the $80 million, too.

Mr Pearson:—unless we want to slow down the development; but let there be no suggestion, because we have had this $600 million worth of capital come into this country last year and maybe more next year, that that makes us a satellite.

This country, Mr Speaker, Canada, in the councils of the world has won a reputation for frankness, for independence, above all, for courage in facing the problems of development and for energy to conquer them. Therefore, let us get ahead and pass this bill and take one more step in national development.

I have a feeling now, with no evidence to support it, that some of our members may have thought when I sat down amid jeers and hoots and cheers that perhaps this fellow might make a good leader of the party after all. At that time, however, this was beyond my imagination. I had simply got caught up by emotion while speaking. I remember thinking to myself as I went up to my office afterwards: 'What a hell of a way to run a railroad. This has been going on for seventeen days, and now I'm in the middle of it too, and I'd hate to have to justify in cold reason with statistical evidence some of the things I've said tonight.' Now, had I been a really good politician all this would not have occurred to me at all. My ideal politician, in the parliamentary debating sense, was a former deskmate. In a similar debate he had me almost in tears, so moved was I by his remarks. Indeed, I thought that he was going to collapse from emotional strain; but when he sat down he turned to me and coolly asked: 'How did I do?' Here was the reaction of a true professional. Another story also illustrates this kind of political virtue. One cold and blizzardy February night, four Liberal MPs were returning to Ottawa from a town up the valley where they had been curling against local rinks. They had won their matches and enjoyed the hospitality. The conditions for the return journey were terrible. When they left for Ottawa the wind was blowing, the snow was falling, the roads were icy, the going was difficult and dangerous. A slippery hill with a turn halfway down was too tricky to negotiate. Just as they left the road and seemed headed for a big tree, one of them, in what might well have been his last words, said to his parliamentary colleagues: 'I hope we win these four by-elections.' That is the spirit of the true politician. Fortunately, there is a happy ending to this story. There were no by-elections; the car missed the tree, got back on the road, and reached Ottawa safely.

I do not recall during the pipeline debate any general feeling among our members of being unbeatable, whether in the House or on the hustings; but there is no doubt in my mind that everyone on our side, however doubtful he may have been at the beginning, was caught up with the fury of the competition, the fury of the attack. Indeed, I had never seen the morale of the party so high. When one is involved in political battle, however, I do not think one can be a good judge of the feeling in one's own caucus, and there may have been a few thought-ful, objective members in the corner saying: 'Well, a general election is coming or they're digging their own graves,' but I did not come across any of them. Inevitably in our minds, I suppose, was the thought that since we had gone to the country and won before so many times and, in spite of our mistakes, everybody said that we were going to win again, we would do so. Certainly, we took rather lightly some of the extravaganzas of the Opposition: draping the flag around Donald Fleming's seat we thought a big joke; George Hees's speeches were entirely unimpressive; the indignation of George Drew, then Leader of the Opposition, was laughable; and Mr Diefenbaker's wild showmanship prompted ribald comment over our coffee cups. The pipeline bill was passed as we expected, but we did not realize at the time the consequence of all the exaggeration and histrionics.

It was during this period of parliamentary crisis that I accompanied Mr St Laurent to the Commonwealth Prime Ministers' Conference which opened in London in June 1956. It was a gloomy visit; St Laurent was completely exhausted and dispirited after the violence of the parliamentary struggles. During the past year or two he had lost some of his old resilience in the House; he did not enjoy the give and take of debate and became more easily irritated. People forget he was Irish as well as French; the Irish side came out more often in quick and irritable reaction. But he never treated the House with the appar-ent contempt of CD; in fact, he never treated the House with con-tempt at all. As I have pointed out more than once, he was the least arrogant of men. Occasionally, however, he would grow impatient; this was a sign of fatigue. Perhaps it is also true that, had he felt stronger and more vigorous, he might have been less reluctant to stand up to Mr Howe. The pipeline debate had become so sordid towards the end that I felt very sorry for him. And I suspect that his depression was increased by a feeling of guilt that he, as leader, had not prevented such a dishonouring of the parliamentary process, and of apprehension at soon having to face the electorate on this issue, rather than on the record of the government.

I attended all the meetings at Downing Street with the PM and even these, presided over by Anthony Eden, and the attendant social occasions, far from being a release for him, failed to remove his brooding depression. Indeed, he often asked me to speak for the government when remarks were required. It was an unhappy prelude to the forthcoming campaign, made even more unhappy by the message we received as we left for home that the Speaker of the House of Commons, René Beaudoin, wished to resign. During the pipeline debate M. Beaudoin made a procedural ruling which could have delayed the bill, and then the next day reversed himself, allowing it to pass as scheduled. The Opposition claimed that the reversal resulted from government pressure and M. Beaudoin never recovered that reputation for impartiality which a Speaker must have. He was a tragic victim of events.

If George Drew, with all his good qualities, was not the man to exploit with maximum effect the feeling against government arrogance and complacency that was developing, John Diefenbaker, the Prairie populist, the eloquent evangelist, was. The Liberals, with very few exceptions, did not realize this, as was shown by their relieved reaction when he was chosen Tory leader in December 1956. Personally, I did not then have nearly so much respect for Mr Diefenbaker's parliamentary and political appeal as I acquired a year or two later. He was not in my opinion a dominant influence in the House.

My first exposure to Mr Diefenbaker on the hustings had come during the 1953 election campaign, when his path and mine continually crossed. By accident, I found myself at least once a week speaking in some place either just before or just after him. I remember in Moncton we both made speeches on the same night as the circus. The next morning the Moncton *Transcript* published the score board: Circus first, Diefenbaker second, Pearson third. As I was nearby so often, he began to attack me in his speeches as a nondescript, unimportant person, trying to make a great name for himself through diplomacy at the United Nations and by spending the poor taxpayers' money on striped pants and white tie parties. He had two wonderful examples to show how I was wasting money on these faintly immoral diplomatic extravagances. He talked about a dinner I gave in Rome for the NATO Council when I was its chairman in 1952. It was a great dinner, catered by the best hotel in Rome and served in a beautiful mediaeval palace. Dief had heard about this and he played on it to his audiences: 'Can you imagine how much this must have cost you poor fishermen?' and so on. In response I wired to Ottawa for the exact figures which were on record. The dinner came to just over $10.00 a head for everything, which was about half as much as it would have cost at Ottawa's Chateau Laurier. So I read the costs at my next meeting and thought, 'Well, we'll hear no more about this.' It did not work that way. We kept on hearing about that dinner and also how I was trying to curry favour with the Liberal back-benchers to secure the next leadership of the party by sending a delegation of them to Paris each year to attend a NATO meeting. Mr Diefenbaker did not point out these were all-party delegations and that he himself had been on them. I had great fun making play with Mr Diefenbaker's exaggerations, but I might as well have saved my breath. These were his two pet stories about me for the rest of the campaign. Nevertheless, he could be, and was, discounted. He was thought then, as still in 1956, to be merely a talker. The PM and CD were the doers. We did not realize that the time for talking, for swaying public opinion against the government, was then beginning. The full lesson of the pipeline debate was not understood.

I have often felt that that crisis would not have developed as it did if time had not been running out for us; if it had not been the pipeline, it would have been something else. We were coming to the end of our career as a Liberal party in power. We had been the government for over twenty years; people were getting tired of us, which was inevitable and natural. Nevertheless, we unwittingly handed our political opponents some very dangerous ammunition in that pipeline debate. We were vulnerable to any pressure against us; we were more likely to be hurt by our mistakes than if we had made them ten or fifteen years earlier. I remember at the time getting a letter from a public relations man I used to know in London during the war. He wrote: 'We will be going to the country in a year or two and I've thought of a slogan for the next election. Let's call it the Silver Jubilee election.' I wrote back: 'You may not think that I'm much of a politician, but surely nothing could be worse than to remind the people that if they elect us once more they'll have had us for 25 years.'

ॐ

Walter Harris's 'six buck budget' in the spring of 1957 added to the
negative effect of our public image. We thought that to increase old-
age pensions by that amount was a pretty generous thing to do.
Instead, it merely strengthened the suspicion, already fairly widespread, that we had become cocksure and arrogant and needed to be
taken down a peg. This impression was not reduced, once the election was called for 10 June 1957, by the campaign speeches and
tactics, especially in the West, of C.D. Howe and some others who
radiated confidence. They treated the feverish activities and old-time
political orations of that Prairie Savonarola, John Diefenbaker, who
was conducting an almost one-man campaign, with something approaching amused contempt.

Opposed to the Tory leader in this campaign, eager, exuberant,
extravagant, non-stopping in word or movement, was the quiet, restrained, reasonable Prime Minister, too tired to repeat the 'Uncle
Louis' success of the previous two elections. The intervening years of
crisis and problems had taken their toll. I feel sure that more than
once during the campaign he wished that he and CD had been able to
carry out their wish to retire together before the 1957 test began.

I took an active part in the campaign, speaking from coast to coast,
which did not give me much time in my own constituency. This time
foreign affairs was an issue, at least in some parts of the country.
Attacks were made on our Suez policy at the UN where, according to
some but not all of the Tory leaders, I had 'stabbed the Mother Country in the back'; I had acted as a tool of the United States from whom
in this and other respects we pro-American Liberals, myself especially, got our instructions.

The most vigorous criticism of this kind came from British Columbia, especially from Howard Green, a veteran front-bencher who was
as strong in his language on this issue as he was sincere in his views. I
thought, therefore, that the place to meet this charge head-on was
not in Quebec, where I would have faced a strongly favourable audience, but in Victoria, where it has been alleged they are more British
than the British. I closed my speech and clinched my argument with
the following remarks and quotations:

Then, finally, we were anxious to do everything we could at the Assembly to
bridge the gulf between Commonwealth members over Middle Eastern policy, as well as that equally dangerous gulf between the United States and the
United Kingdom. Our efforts in this regard may or may not have been suc-

cessful. Personally I think that they were useful, and I know that our motives were worthy ones. There can be no more important cause than healing divisions inside the Commonwealth and inside the Western coalition. Would those divisions have been less or greater by now if the United Nations had not intervened, or if the United Kingdom and France had been successful in preventing that intervention or had rejected its resolutions?

In following this policy last autumn, we have been accused of 'knifing our best friends in the back.' Some of those who have attacked us in this way have, however, also strongly supported the United Nations Emergency Force and efforts to bring about a political settlement in the Middle East through the United Nations. But if we had supported the United Kingdom by voting against UN intervention in the first place, then these other results could not have occurred or even have been attempted.

In this connection, the governments whom we are supposed to have 'knifed' don't seem to have realized what we did to them. The victim has been curiously unaware of our unfriendly action. This is what Mr Harold Macmillan, the Prime Minister of the United Kingdom, said in March of this year about our policy last autumn: 'I think the service [the Canadian Government] gave to finding good solutions and helping us at critical moments [at the United Nations Assembly] was one of a most remarkable kind and will always be remembered by us with gratitude.'

The Prime Minister of France, speaking somewhat earlier, said: 'Whatever may have been our disagreements at one moment, I must underline the positive character and extreme usefulness of the initiative taken by the Canadian government, how its interventions, always animated by the most friendly spirit, have often been decisive.'

Also, the Israeli spokesman at the United Nations had this to say: 'Our admiration goes out to the delegation of Canada for constantly focusing the attention of the General Assembly upon its affirmative and constructive tasks.'

The test of the success of a nation's foreign policy is its willingness to accept and discharge responsibility for the maintenance of peace; its success in protecting the national interest, and its prestige and position in the world.

The present Government has not, in my view, failed in its effort to meet this test. Canada stands today respected among nations, as a country which has played a good part in the search for peace and good relations between all peoples.

I hope we will continue to play that part as a strong, united, and forward-looking nation.

I cannot say I made many, if any, converts at this crowded meeting, but I got a good hearing with only a few hecklers to enliven things.

Quebec tours were particularly trying. I did most of my speaking in French, which was even more of a strain on me than it may have been on my audiences. But they were charitable and kindly people and I

was always made to feel very much at home. My only complaint was
that most of the big evening meetings went on too long. In Quebec
they still honoured the nineteenth-century tradition of many lengthy
and eloquent speeches. This could warm up the audience before my
more sober French cooled them. But once when I was Prime Minister,
I recall, so overflowing were the tributes paid to the Liberal party, the
Quebec ministers, the local candidate, and to me, so much scorn was
poured on the Opposition and all its minions that the hour the party
had taken for television and radio, forty minutes of which were to be
mine, was exhausted before I even began to speak.

As I moved around the country, I became worried about the swing
of opinion against the government, at the feeling that we had to be
taught a lesson. I felt, as did nearly everyone else, that the government would be returned, but I sensed the loss of many seats. Indeed,
the feeling that it would be possible to vote against the Liberals,
without thereby defeating the government, caused many switches
from the previous election.

The support the Liberals got in the 1957 election was the basic,
fundamental support to be expected for the Liberal party. And you
never win an election on that support. You have to get the floating
vote. If you fail, you are finished. Not only did we not get the floating
vote, some of our Liberal vote floated away. I remember the wife of a
man who later, when I was Prime Minister, became a powerful
Cabinet minister, saying: 'Of course I voted for Mr Diefenbaker. I
thought he was a voice crying in the wilderness against the corruption and arrogance that comes from long holding of power in office,
and I thought I would just vote Conservative this one time. Of course
I had no idea they would ever win any seats.'

My anxiety was confirmed by the big wind-up rally at Maple Leaf
Gardens in Toronto on Friday, 7 June 1957. That was a day I shall
never forget. It began at Chapleau in my constituency of Algoma
East, where I campaigned during the morning. Then I was to fly with
my wife to Sault Ste Marie, 150 miles or so south, by a small float
plane, and then on to Toronto by commercial flight in time to introduce Mr St Laurent to the rally. The journey was more exciting,
however, than this indicates. The take-off from the river at Chapleau
was very tricky because the weather was so bad. It got worse, and we
found ourselves flying in a fog. It seemed to me we were too low, and
once or twice I could see outlines of trees on one side of the plane or
the other. I expressed some alarm to the pilot, an experienced northern flyer, and he assured me that there was no cause to worry, that

we were flying down a valley which would soon open into the flat country just north of the Soo. At that particular moment a hill appeared right ahead of us. We must have chosen the wrong valley. Up and away – barely. The Soo airport was fogbound, so we decided to continue to Sudbury, refuel there, and on to Toronto Island Airport in our little plane. The weather became very stormy as we reached Toronto and we had an uneasy landing. Air-sick, battered, and a shade bewildered (my wife was in better condition), we were rushed by motor to the rally, and I was plunked on the platform just in time to introduce the Prime Minister.

The meeting, which it was hoped would be the triumphant climax to the campaign, turned out to be discouraging, almost disastrous. The faithful had turned out in their thousands, but there was also organized hostility, unpleasant heckling, and one or two nasty incidents. Nearly everything went badly. This was three days before the election; St Laurent was so tired that he did not read his speech well. His reception by the audience was unfriendly. And finally, in an attempt to break up the meeting, there was a parade of young people down the centre aisle. They had banners reading: 'Throw out St Laurent' and that kind of thing, and they began to chant: 'Throw out the old man; down with the old man.' It was quite unpleasant. When they got to the platform, two or three of them tried to climb up with their placards. One of our Toronto organizers rushed forward to push one of the young boys off. The boy fell back on his head in front of the platform. He appeared to be unconscious (in fact, he was not) and a howl of anguish went through the crowd. They thought that he might have been killed. Poor Mr St Laurent went white. He was such a humane person, such a gentle, kind person, especially with children. From that point on the meeting was awful. I left almost in tears.

I was emotionally overwrought but felt that, if this was what goes on now in Toronto, something has gone wrong in this party. In 1949 or 1953 the crowd would have reacted against the demonstrators. My wife and I had to rush away to catch the night train for Sudbury so I could spend election day in my constituency. I felt a gloomy foreboding of failure, not to be explained solely by the kind of day we had had.

The results of the 1957 election seemed to surprise everybody except John Diefenbaker and his organizers. I could hardly believe my ears when the results came in that Mr Howe had been beaten by someone I had never heard of, one Douglas Fisher. The final standings were:

Progressive Conservatives	112
Liberals	105
CCF	25
Social Credit	19
Independents	2
Independent Liberals	1
Liberal Labour	1

It was a despondent Cabinet that met a few days later to survey the situation with the Prime Minister. Mr St Laurent was strongly of the view that he should resign and ask the Governor General to invite Mr Diefenbaker to form a government. The majority supported him but there was a minority, led by Jimmy Gardiner, as always a doughty fighter, especially against a Saskatchewan Tory, who thought we should remain in office, meet Parliament, and try to manoeuvre with the support of the CCF. I was emphatically on the side of resignation, for reasons which I summarized in a letter to a friend, Professor Clifford Curtis of Queen's University, who had urged me to take the other course. I wrote him on 17 June:

Frankly, I think you are wrong in your view that we should meet Parliament but, whether wrong or right, the Prime Minister has very firmly decided (and the decision is primarily his) that the other course should be adopted.

I do not think that the analogy with Mr King in 1925 stands up. Mr King had had four years in office, while we have had twenty-two. He had only one group, the Progressives, with which to make the necessary arrangements, and they were glad to co-operate with him. We have two groups who have made it quite clear to us that they will not take any action which would keep us in office. Therefore, the only result of our remaining in power until we met Parliament in the autumn would be to be accused of hanging on to the last minute after twenty-two years of power; after an election where we were certainly given a vote of 'no confidence' by the electorate, even though many of them did not apparently know what they were doing. Having hung on until the last minute, we would then be thrown out in the first days of Parliament, unless we were able to produce a Parliamentary programme which would be in such startling contrast to the one we produced during the last election campaign that we would also be accused of unprincipled bribery, while Diefenbaker, once again, could be the pure and honest evangelist against a grasping group. A second election under those circumstances would seem to me to be quite disastrous.

There is another factor. About eighty of our one hundred and five Members are from predominantly French-speaking and Catholic constituencies. I would hate to be part of a government which attempted to survive on that basis. Furthermore, what would we do in the reconstruction of our Cabinet, with a French-speaking Member as the sole representative from Alberta and a new French-speaking Member as the sole representative from Manitoba?

Above all, however, and I think this is decisive. Mr St. Laurent is not Mr King, and he would be quite unable to manoeuvre and direct things in a situation of this kind in the way that Mr King was able do to.

Mr St Laurent announced his decision to resign on 17 June. The day before the actual transfer took place on 21 June, I met with Mr. Diefenbaker to brief him on the forth-coming Commonwealth Prime Ministers' meeting in London. I noted afterwards:

I found him in a state of mixed exhilaration and exhaustion which made it difficult for him to concentrate on any single subject, let alone the forthcoming meeting. He was almost embarrassingly grateful for my offer to brief him on the subjects of the meeting, and also the other international matters with which he will have to deal. I also told him that I would be glad to discuss any departmental questions, personnel, organization, etc., about which he might like to talk.

A good deal of the time he reminisced about the election but, to my surprise, he also took me into his confidence about some of his immediate difficulties, especially in regard to Cabinet appointments.

He told me that he had received more than 40 messages and 2 calls from Conservative MPs to the effect that I should be persuaded to join his Government as the Secretary of State for External Affairs. He thought that this was an unprecedented tribute to me, but I found it somewhat difficult to take seriously.

He then told me that he was thinking of taking on the job of External Affairs himself, and he asked me what I thought about it. I said that it might be possible for a short time, but not for long, as the pressures would be so great. I strongly advised him (I did not expect to be put in the position of advising the new Prime Minister on anything!) to appoint a first-class, experienced Parliamentary Assistant for External Affairs as he himself would not be able to go to the UN, NATO, and other meetings. He asked me to suggest a name on the basis of my experience with Conservative MPs, and I said that I could think of no one better for the job, unless there were other plans for him, than Roland Michener. I mentioned Nesbitt as a young Member who had made thoughtful speeches on international affairs, and John Hamilton as a very bright person, though not in the past concerned with External matters.

Mr Diefenbaker then wanted to know all about how the Prime Ministers' meetings were conducted; how you acted when you called on The Queen, what you did in London on these occasions, etc., etc., etc. He said he was thinking of taking one of his colleagues with him to London and wondered what I thought of bringing General Pearkes. I said that Defence matters would not loom very large in the discussions, but that the General knew a lot of people in London and would be a comfortable person to have around.

Then I was asked what I thought of George Drew as High Commissioner. I said I thought the Drews would be admirable, but I got the impression that this was not the kind of reaction that John Diefenbaker desired. He wondered whether Mr Drew, having been an important public figure in his own right, might not be inclined to take a somewhat independent line in London. I admitted that this was possible, and pointed out that this danger was one of the main reasons why we liked to appoint professional diplomats to important posts . . . [as it turned out, he appointed Drew].

He also surprised me by saying that he had been considering bringing in someone from outside Parliament to be Secretary of State for External Affairs, but had run into too many difficulties to make this a practicable proposition. I wonder whether he was thinking of Sidney Smith? . . .

The next day I was out of a job, except that of a member of Parliament in opposition. My wife was wont to complain that she and the family saw little of me as I was so much away on official duties from our home. Now, for a few weeks at least, she could reproach me for hanging around the house too much and getting in the way without the compensating advantage of being a good domestic helper. In 1954 she had decided we should buy a duplex in Sandy Hill for our old age – little did she know how many changes there would be after that! We lived there four years – until 1958 – when we moved again, this time into the house of the Leader of the Opposition, 'Stornoway.'

Mr St Laurent was most anxious to retire immediately after the election. His health alone would have justified this, quite apart from the fact that he had served his country well beyond the call of duty. No one would have reproached him for retiring and there were some, most of them for reasons which reflected nothing but the highest respect and affection for him, who felt that he should do so in his own best interest. But the old leader was tortured by the feeling that, in leaving the party at this low period in its fortunes, he would be defaulting on his duty and be guilty of cowardice.

On Monday, 2 September 1957, Labour Day, I received a telephone message from Renault St Laurent at St Patrick where the St Laurents had their summer home, asking me whether I could visit his father as soon as possible and bring Lionel Chevrier, a former Cabinet colleague, with me. He seemed agitated and despondent.

On Tuesday I arranged transportation to Quebec for Wednesday morning. I also managed to get Chevrier on the telephone in the afternoon at his summer place. I thought it essential that he should be with me. He agreed to meet me at the station the next morning. I then telephoned Renault who said that he and his brother-in-law, Mathieu Samson, would meet us on arrival in Quebec and drive us to St Patrick.

We talked politics most of the journey and speculated on the reason for our summons. We felt that by far the most likely reason was Mr St Laurent's desire to tell us he could not carry on beyond the autumn session of Parliament. We both agreed that this decision, in view of his condition, was to be welcomed. The sooner it took effect the better in order to put an end to the speculation which was spreading and becoming embarrassing. At all costs we would have to try to prevent any public controversy or unpleasantness. Our leader, whose greatness in person and achievement had been obscured by the events of the previous June and his own physical decline, deserved a better political ending than this. The whole thing could have developed, had we not been careful and he not wise in judgment, into a tragedy. My own position on a mission of this kind was made much more difficult by a general assumption which prevailed that I might be his successor. I was very glad to have Chevrier along, to help remove any wrong interpretation from our visit if, as was likely, it was said that I had prompted the visit for my own purposes.

The drive from Quebec to St Patrick was pleasant but the conversation revealing and distressing. Our hosts told us the whole story. Mr St Laurent was in a low, depressed condition, without vigour or strength, and obviously quite unequal to the demands of leadership. His family had been trying hard to convince him that he should announce at once that he would not contest another election. They had hoped against hope that, after a couple of months' rest at St Patrick, he would snap out of his low state of mind and body, but realized now that this was not going to happen as long as he continued to carry the burden of leadership. St Laurent agreed with his family that he was unfit to carry on but was possessed with the idea that people would think he was running away from his duty after a defeat, that he could not take it. He knew that he had lost his energy and his interest in politics, and especially his skill in public relations, as certain recent contacts with the press had shown. But he could not seem to make up his mind to take the final step and announce his withdrawal.

Renault was most anxious that we should tell his father that public opinion, far from criticizing, would fully understand and approve a decision to resign before, during, or immediately after the autumn session, the decision to be announced now. His father had seemed anxious, however, to get confirmation of the wisdom of this course from Chevrier and me, and for this reason they had sent for us with his full approval. They were all most grateful we had come. We realized, from what we had heard, that our visit was not going to be easy.

At five o'clock, in heavy rain, we reached the very pleasant guest house where we were to stay, opposite the St Laurent home, a lovely old white brick place with beautiful gardens sloping down to the river. At six we walked across, had a drink and then dinner. Madame St Laurent, very domestic and cordial, and Miss Lora, his sister, were also there. His sister impressed me as a very nice, sensible, and calm person who, I gathered, had been a strong influence for good while she was there. Mr St Laurent was, I thought, in shocking condition, dejected, and looking much older.

After dinner, a very good meal, with talk mostly in French, we five men got together for the business of the evening. Mr St Laurent made it easier by announcing at once that he agreed he was no longer physically fit to retain the leadership. But he had three worries. Would he be considered as letting the party down if he dropped out now? Should he not go to Ottawa, see his colleagues, and face the music there? How could he reconcile the announcement of his retirement now with the regrettable opposite impression he had given to the press, as recently as two days earlier? It was our task to reassure him on all these points and we made some progress in this, though the going was hard. He made it difficult to carry on the discussion by his lack of responsiveness; he seemed too tired to show much interest, the interest indeed which we knew he actually felt. It was a pathetic situation.

Renault finally suggested that I should try my hand at drafting a statement for the press, announcing the decision not to go through another election but willingness, if health permitted, to continue as leader until a new leader had been chosen. I agreed to try this, though only on the clear understanding that he had already made the decision and merely wanted me to put it into words. Mr St Laurent seemed very relieved and grateful that I would take on the assignment and have a draft ready for him next morning.

I worked on a text in my room until after midnight. It was not easy to get it right. Next morning before breakfast I showed it to Chevrier, who was very pleased and suggested only one or two minor changes. At ten we met Mr St Laurent, who looked even older and more tired than the previous night. He stared uneasily at the draft, at times reading, at other times merely brooding, for what must have been some minutes. This reaction seemed to suggest that he did not think much of my work or even of the decision it announced, and I rather expected him to throw it into the wastepaper basket. However, after two or three more readings, he looked up and said it was just right. Then there was more silence until we urged him into a discussion of the timing and manner of release. I had hoped that this could be postponed for a week, so that it would not be associated directly with our visit. Nasty people would say that Chevrier and I had gone to St Patrick and had pushed him into resignation for our own purposes. The others all felt, however, that it would be better to get the document out at once to prevent speculation and leaks; and we agreed to release it Friday evening.

As to the manner, Mr St Laurent wanted to go to Ottawa, see the press there, and submit himself to questions. We persuaded him that this was unnecessary and undesirable, that it would be quite enough to release the statement through his office, and that he need not add anything to it if journalists phoned him. He was also worried that his former colleagues should learn of the decision through the radio and the press. So we arranged to have Pierre Asselin (his Executive Assistant) phone all concerned an hour or two before giving out the statement. Then we translated my English into French, and our work was done. I have never had a more difficult, indeed more distressing two hours, or taken part in a more painful task. But it was certainly required and this perhaps was the best way to do it.

Mr St Laurent seemed to cheer up after the work had been finished and the decision taken. He thanked me privately, and in a very moving way, for my help. I do not think I have ever felt more sorry for anyone; but I know I would have felt even worse had he decided to try to carry on. To resign was sad, to continue would have been tragic. Madame St Laurent, meanwhile, had been busy in the kitchen showing her cook how to deal with an eleven-pound roast and apple pie. She was very happy. She felt that the danger was over and that her husband was safe. Renault and Mathieu were also pleased at the way everything had gone; indeed, they were much more than pleased.

We did full justice to an enormous meal; the four of us, again through heavy rain, then motored back to Quebec. We had tea there with the other members of the family anxious to hear the news. They were all relieved and happy and warmly thanked us for our help. We then got the 6:15 train to Montreal. It seemed only fitting that our journey should keep its depressing character to the end, for our train hit and killed a motorist on a level crossing.

After our return to Ottawa on Friday, 6 September, Mr St Laurent issued the statement we had drafted:

After carefully considering medical advice which I have now received, I have decided that I have no longer the energy and stamina required to lead the Party through another general election campaign.

From participation in four elections, I know the physical demands they make on one's strength and physical resources and I am convinced that I could not do full justice to those demands in another campaign.

· Health permitting, however, I will be happy to continue to serve as Liberal Party Leader in the forthcoming session of Parliament until my successor has been chosen.

My regret at having to make this decision is equalled by my conviction that it is the right one and that any other would not be fair to the Party through whom I have had the honour – and there can be no greater one – to serve my country for so many years.

ॐ

With St Laurent's resignation and the call for a convention, the succession became a burning issue in which I became directly involved. Even before the 1957 election, indeed soon after the 1953 election, there was increasing speculation on who would succeed St Laurent as leader of the party. The Prime Minister's age and his unconcealed desire to retire as soon as possible to private life made the question more than academic. There was a widespread feeling after 1953, which I shared, that the Minister of Finance, Doug Abbott, would be the next leader. When some of my friends pressed me to consider the matter, I made it quite clear that I would not compete in any contest between Abbott and Paul Martin, then Minister of National Health and Welfare, whose intentions were well known. This situation changed when Abbott left politics in 1954 on his appointment to the Supreme Court of Canada.

It was at this time also that Mr St Laurent, while not expressing then or later any preference for me as a possible successor, spoke to me, after consulting C.D. Howe, of a transfer to another ministerial post so that I would gain that broader experience of Canadian affairs a potential leader should have. I told him I had entered the government as Minister for External Affairs and wished to remain there. If he wished to move me to some other department that, of course, was his prerogative, but I hoped he would not do so, much as I appreciated his thoughtfulness, with the leadership in mind. I heard nothing more of the idea.

The pipeline crisis, followed by the election, postponed consideration of the leadership question. But, as I have said, that ended with St Laurent's resignation and the call for a convention. There was much speculation and manoeuvring but, at first, only one announced candidate, my old friend Paul Martin. His claim to the leadership by virtue of long service to the party, great experience in government, and shrewd political judgment was strong. He was handicapped, however much one might deplore it, by the fact that he was Catholic and half French Canadian, while the tradition of our party was that an English-speaking Protestant succeeded a French-speaking Catholic.

The pressure grew on me to stand for the leadership and I was caught up in a turmoil of contradictory emotions. I had very real doubts about my fitness for party leadership, for operating successfully the management side of politics, where I had so little experience. My training for political leadership, to say the least, was unusual. A life that had taken me from student to professor to diplomat was a better preparation for government than for politics. I had never anticipated politics as a career, even when selling newspapers. I had had no on-the-job instruction as a back-bencher, the best way to learn about politics and Parliament. What I knew, I had learned from Messrs Bennett, King, and St Laurent, the three Prime Ministers whom I had served; from my experience as Secretary of State for External Affairs (not particularly good training for bread-and-butter politics); and as MP for Algoma East I learned, from the age of fifty, the little I knew about politics in the House of Commons and in the caucus and counsels of the Liberal party. I was also given lots of advice, by pros and amateurs, players, managers, and spectators – some of it even good advice. Despite my doubts about my qualifications, however, it seemed to me that a member of a party who had benefitted from the years in power in the sense that he had been given a post of responsibility, authority, and privilege, unless he had an unassailable reason, had no right to reject the invitation of his friends to allow his name to go before the convention. Whatever his personal feelings, his public obligation was overriding.

This feeling of obligation on my part, paradoxically if you will, was increased by the low state of our party fortunes. John Diefenbaker and the Tories were obviously on the way up, while, if chosen, I would inherit the leadership of a party in opposition whose great years were behind it. Yet, having enjoyed ministerial responsibility in those great years, it seemed churlish now to run away from the difficulties of the new challenge facing us. Moreover, I was not accepting, or even seeking, a new position for which, frankly, I had no particular desire. I was merely allowing my name to go before the convention which would make the decision. I agonized over this problem for days and discussed all the pros and cons with my wife and a few intimate friends. Then, one night at Sudbury, accosted by the press after a hockey game, of all places, I announced that I would be a candidate for the Liberal leadership at the forthcoming convention. At least, and at last, the fateful decision had been taken.

The leadership contest was an easy one for me. Indeed, it was no contest, in the sense that I made few personal appeals, by canvass, letter, or visit. This does not mean that I did not have a very active group of friends and supporters who worked hard to organize and advance my claims. But I kept out of the contest myself. A cynic might say that this was merely good tactics on my part, to leave the campaigning to my friends but make myself available to all who wished to see me. In fact, this was not a matter of tactics at all, so far as I was concerned, merely my insistence, for personal reasons, on following that procedure.

In any event, it was clear before the convention opened that I had acquired a great deal of support, mainly, I believe, because of my work as Minister of External Affairs, culminating in the glamorous award of the Nobel Peace Prize. Certainly I had become very well and, on the whole, favourably known throughout Canada in consequence of my External activities; this, no doubt, was a strong point in my favour. Further, I had never taxed anybody, given inadequate pensions, failed to keep wheat prices up or labour disputes down. Nevertheless, I prepared three speeches for the convention: one, my appeal for support; two, my acceptance speech; and three, my speech to make the nomination of Mr Martin unanimous.

I was anxious not to exploit any achievements in External Affairs because I had made a point of emphasizing, in and out of Parliament, that foreign policy should be kept on a non-controversial basis and that its successes were national, not partisan. I was especially sensitive about using the Nobel Peace Prize for any political purpose and found it most embarrassing when well-meaning friends, introducing me, or referring to me at meetings during this period, used this award as the final and conclusive evidence of what a very great man I was. I never could have received this distinction if the government I represented had not laid down the policies of which I was the spokesman and which were almost invariably backed by all parties in Parliament.

The convention was exciting and for me successful, since I was chosen leader by 1084 votes against Paul Martin's 305. He was naturally disappointed and I could not help but share some of his disappointment because I knew how he felt, and he was a friend. He was also a trouper in the political arena and became my right-hand man, the indispensable party tactician in the House of Commons. I needed all the support I could get.

OPPOSITION YEARS

My parliamentary debut as Leader of the Opposition is a less pleasant subject. I might preface this by saying that I was not much impressed by the new Cabinet or by Prime Minister Diefenbaker's approach to the problems facing his government. Further, there was a marked decline in the Canadian economy. There were sharp contrasts between Mr. Diefenbaker's statements, at the time of the election, and the hard reality of our growing trade imbalances and spiralling unemployment. My party had plenty of ammunition in the House of Commons and we made the most of it.

We were eloquent on the theme: 'If only we had C.D. Howe again. There was a man who knew how to handle trade matters. Look at you people, babes in the woods. You don't know what's going on.' Further, Diefenbaker had made a very silly statement, or so I thought (it was part of his 1957 campaign), that he was going to divert trade from the United States to Britain. He repeated this at a great rally in the Albert Hall during his first appearance in Britain, where it appeared to many that a new imperial messiah had been born. To me this was a lot of nonsense, a return to the old empire and all that. As it turned out he soon had to abandon the whole idea. In sum, I had not been overwhelmed by the first months of Conservative government in 1957.

This situation formed, in part, a psychological framework for my first speech as leader, without doubt one of the most disastrous debuts of any political leader, certainly in this country. I was a neophyte; I knew really nothing of political tactics in Parliament. I had learned a little in opposition in autumn of 1957, but not very much. So when the experts, our professional politicians, gathered around to decide what we ought to do to launch me as the leader of the party, I was much influenced by their advice. They said that this was the time to make a real impact and to contrast what was happening now with what had happened under the past Liberal régime, to blame the new government and yet to save the country from a second general election in one year. We would follow the practice, established in British parliamentary history, of defeating one minority government to replace it with another—a variation, if you like, of our own 1926 experience. Had I had a couple of years of experience as leader, I think I would have been more careful. However, most of my advisers with whom the idea was discussed thought it very clever. Only two people, my wife and my Executive Assistant, Mary Macdonald, cautioned me against it.

A suitable speech was accordingly prepared which I carried into the House on Monday, 20 January 1958. It should have been a day memorable for the pleasant tributes paid me by the Prime Minister, by other party leaders, and by St Laurent as I assumed my position as Leader of the Opposition. Memorable it was; pleasant it was not. I have never regretted anything in my political career so much as my proposal that day. My speech began with the normal sort of attack on the government's record:

We do not know very much about the national budgetary picture. We do know that expenditures have not been reduced as promised, but vastly increased. We do know that the course of national production has been levelled off and is probably declining, that revenues are declining, that there will almost certainly be a deficit in the present fiscal year and that there is a prospect of a huge deficit in 1958 to 1959. I suggest, Mr Speaker, that this is a dismal contrast in seven short months to the Liberal financial record of preceding years and what a contrast it is to the promises of half a billion dollars in tax reductions and half a billion dollars in reduced expenditures.

No wonder this government apparently is not anxious to disclose the facts to the Canadian people and in the light of this situation it is not perhaps so hard to understand why the Minister of Finance (Mr Fleming) failed to bring in the budget he so gaily promised last July and why he may wish to avoid bringing in a budget this spring.

Then there is the field of defence and security. There is no need for me, nor shall I attempt, Mr Speaker, to dwell on the confusion existing in this field. The utter confusion and contradiction over NORAD, for instance, with no parliamentary discussion or decision in regard to that vitally important step.

Indeed, so far as we know up to this moment, there has been no inter-
governmental agreement on which a discussion could be based. I will leave it
at that—the confusion in this particular matter is one of baffling bewilder-
ment.

We have the right to say from the record of these months that in every
field, this government lives from day to day with hand to mouth policies, a
yielding response to one pressure, a concession in another quarter with no
consistent pattern, no attempt to fit particular projects into a national design,
no vision for the future but a ceaseless preoccupation with the politics and
publicities of the day. . . .

The hon. gentlemen opposite call this deterioration a pause, a word they
may come to regret. It is a deterioration of a kind which makes us believe the
Canadian people would welcome a return, and an immediate return, of a
government which would apply Liberal policies to our national administration . . .

I then moved (seconded by St Laurent):

That all the words after the word 'That' be struck out and the following
substituted therefor:

In view of the fact that, in the seven months His Excellency's advisers have
been in office, Canada's total trade has ceased to expand, export markets
have been threatened, and proposals for freer trade have been rebuffed;

That investment has been discouraged and unemployment has risen drastically;

That farmers and other primary producers have been disillusioned and
discouraged;

That regulations with provincial governments have deteriorated into confusion;

That the budget is no longer in balance, revenues are declining, expenditures are rising and parliament has been denied a national accounting;

That there is growing confusion about defence and security;

That day-to-day expedients have been substituted for firm and steady
administration;

And in view of the desirability, at this time, of having a government
pledged to implement Liberal policies;

His Excellency's advisers should, in the opinion of this House submit their
resignation forthwith.

When I took my seat, I knew immediately that my first attack on
the government had been a failure, indeed a fiasco. There was some
applause from our side for my speech, not for the resolution, but only
hoots and jeers from the government side of the House. When
Donald Fleming, a student of mine at the University of Toronto years
before and always a good friend, groaned: 'Mike, it is sad to see you

come to this,' he was trying to be kind. I had made a spectacle of myself by coolly inviting the government to turn over their seals of office to those of us who had, a few months before, been rejected by the electorate. One of our back-benchers came up to me afterwards, as I was sitting alone in a state of some depression, and said: 'That was a magnificent speech, Mr Pearson. It's too bad you didn't stop before you ended it.'

I was saved from brooding too long by having to appear on television to explain my motion. This was one of the hardest political tasks I ever undertook, but I think I did it better than many less demanding broadcasts. When I returned, Jimmie Sinclair (a doughty parliamentary fighter who, unhappily for the party and for me, did not return after the next election) hauled me off to his office for a drink with a few colleagues. He told me that my broadcast had been magnificent, that it had cleared up all doubts about the motion. Those were sweet words, though I knew they were designed more to encourage me than to voice real conviction. I have never forgotten Jimmie Sinclair's encouragement at that dark moment in my new political career. Fortunately, however, I am a resilient person and, even though the immediate political prospects were not bright, I refused to be buried in gloom for long.

In the House of Commons the Prime Minister tore me to shreds. He had a better opportunity that day than ever subsequently. His was the speech of an Opposition leader, not a Prime Minister. The economy was weakening, unemployment was going up, and Mr Diefenbaker wanted to blame the economic recession on the previous government. To prove his point, he quoted from a confidential report entitled 'The Canadian Economic Outlook for 1957,' prepared in March 1957 for the Minister of Trade and Commerce. The Prime Minister must have know that this was a serious breach of parliamentary convention and the established relationship between ministers and officials. I thought it a sorry performance. However, the careful selections from the report that he made public accomplished what he desired – to create the impression that St Laurent's government had known that a recession was imminent, had done nothing to prevent it, and were now blaming it on their Conservative successors. Doubtless Mr Diefenbaker was manœuvring for an early dissolution. The momentum was in his favour. He argued that, as leader of a minority government facing an obstructive opposition, he could not do the exciting things that he had promised in the 1957 campaign and that he must ask the people for a decisive vote of confidence.

I remember well the day of 1 February 1958. In an operation as
secretive as the landings on D-Day, the Prime Minister disappeared
from the Commons. There were all sorts of false alarms that he had
gone west, or that he had gone south, or had gone to the North Pole.
It was pretty clear, however, that he had gone to Quebec, where the
Governor General was in residence, to secure the dissolution of Parliament. He arrived back just at 6 o'clock. This was the only quarrel I
ever had with my good and old friend, Roland Michener, who was
then Speaker. At 6 o'clock he should have left the chair and recessed
the House. Instead, he allowed Mr Diefenbaker, who was a few minutes late, to come in. We were furious. With a smile the Prime
Minister announced that Parliament was no more. In retrospect, the
Speaker probably had to extend that courtesy since he had been told
that Mr Diefenbaker was on his way. All we could do was to hurl cries
of defiance at the government and go off to fight the election.

Thus I faced my first campaign as leader. After only a few days to
settle into my new responsibilities, I had now to conduct and help
organize a national election campaign, about which my experience
and knowledge was minimal. No doubt, if we had been ready for the
election, the Prime Minister would not have called it. My office staff,
with additional but not nearly enough recruits for the campaign, was
largely new, though they made heroic efforts to make up for this by
hard work, intelligence, and complete dedication to carrying out the
complex and exhausting programme that faced us each day. Most
important, we were a happy and congenial group, and managed to
get whatever personal enjoyment was possible from an ordeal that
cannot be amusing. This was also true, I might add, for the subsequent national campaigns I waged in 1962, 1963, and 1965.

Initially, I thought we might win. It is very easy to be deceived in
these things, especially when there are so many kind people who do
not want to tell you what is in fact going on. One of the problems of
political leadership is that you are so often isolated from the facts,
from the truth. For the best of reasons and with the best of intentions
people tell you: 'Oh, you're doing all right, you're picking up, you're
learning your job and things are improving.' But, of course, I sensed
as I went along that while things may have been improving a little for
me, they were improving a great deal more for Mr Diefenbaker, who
was putting on a ferocious campaign. As I have written earlier, I was
by no means a natural-born vote-seeker, and I disliked intensely
some elements of campaigning. I could never really feel comfortable
with those enormous two- or three-hour political jamborees before

five or ten thousand people. But as I proceeded across the country, I got to know my role, to learn my job. I certainly worked as hard as anybody could, from breakfast until midnight. I began to handle the campaign rather better and even began to enjoy the small meetings where I could reason with people and answer questions. The last week or two I was really feeling quite optimistic about the impact I was making. We had a good rally in Kingston. What I now remember in particular about that meeting, however, was our cavalcade through the streets of the city. As we slowed down for a light, a gentleman offered a friendly but rather discouraging observation: 'Mr Pearson, you are a very nice man, but go home, you're wasting your time.'

Our last meeting, in Pembroke, was one of the best I ever attended. We really raised the roof. I thought,'Well, maybe this isn't going to be as bad as it seems.' John Connolly, our chief organizer, encouraged my hopes by bringing me cheerful reports from the final round-up across the country. Perhaps he was just trying to make me comfortable and happy over the final weekend, I do not know and I have never asked him. He said: 'You're going to do better than you've dreamed.' It did not work out quite that way; but we did win in Pembroke.

Personally, I did not think we had a chance of getting a majority, though I also did not believe we would get fewer than between sixty and seventy-five seats. Quebec would stay loyal, even if our pickings elsewhere would be slim. The newspapers, as it turned out, were fairly accurate in their predictions. Nevertheless, on the Sunday before voting, I was enjoying that wonderful feeling which comes from the knowledge that tomorrow and tomorrow and all the tomorrows ahead for three or four years I would be free from:

8:30 AM	Liberal business men's breakfast
9:30 AM	Talk with local candidates
10:30 AM	Main-streeting
Luncheon meeting	At next rendez-vous—a town 40 miles away
2:00 to 4:00 PM	Rest—ie, discussions, drafts of speeches, and arrangements for following days
4:00 PM	Main-streeting or selective visits; bishops, ministers, editors, or ancient Liberals
5:00 to 6:30 PM	70 mph to the city for the big parade and rally
6:30 to 7:30 PM	A quick dinner and orders for the evening
7:30 PM	The Big Show and the aftermath

That Sunday my wife and I were enjoying our grandchildren and their parents in their backyard in Manor Park, Ottawa. I remember being very pleased with a new pair of brown shoes I was wearing and basking in the thought that the results tomorrow might not be so bad after all. Our son, Geoffrey, a cool and realistic young man, interrupted these pleasant reflections by observing: 'Dad, has it ever occurred to you that you were called on to preside over the liquidation of the Liberal Party?' I crushed him with a fixed and haughty stare, but, oh, how nearly right he was!

လ

Before discussing the election results, I must add that if the leader and his staff generally lacked something in experience and preparation for the campaign, this did not apply to our party headquarters people in Ottawa. There we had a good mixture of veteran political hands who knew the mechanics of running a campaign and of eager volunteers who had only recently become part of the Liberal team. We suffered from no lack of skill, energy, or resources under the leadership of Walter Gordon, Chubby Power, John Connolly, Duncan McTavish, Bob Kidd, Keith Davey, and Andy Thompson. I do not think any group could have put on a better campaign than they, for they made the most of the party's organization and policies.

This was the election that marked Walter Gordon's debut in politics. In part, he became active in consequence of his personal friendship with me, and I owe him a special debt of gratitude. We had become friends in the days of the Royal Commission on Price Spreads in 1934. I was the commission's Secretary. Walter had come down to Ottawa with Grant Glassco; their firm had been appointed to look after the statistical and accounting research for the commission. We became very close, as did our wives, and we retained that friendship over the years. He was one who encouraged me to leave External Affairs for politics and helped make it possible. Once I made the decision, he became interested in helping to keep the party both national and liberal, and for that purpose began to take an active part in its councils. I know also that he felt strongly that I should succeed St Laurent, and worked hard to bring that about. During the period in opposition, he became a principal in our party organization and a chief architect of its rejuvenation and reorganization. No leader had a more dedicated, untiring, and unselfish lieutenant, or a more helpful and generous friend. Not once during those years did I make a demand of him which he did not cheerfully and effectively carry out; and my demands were only a small part of the service he gave. There was nothing he would not do or could not do in building the organization. His was a wonderful, unselfish work of political service.

Naturally, there was more to it than personal friendship. He was interested in public affairs. He had acquired over the years a good many friends in the Liberal party. He liked us as a managerial party, I think, and felt (he was a strong Liberal himself) that we were still a liberal party in his terms, and that we would remain so while I was leader. Further, by 1960 he had acquired a very deep and strong feeling that Mr Diefenbaker was going to ruin the country. During the early period of our opposition, however, he was not publicly identified with the party and was almost exclusively involved in managing behind the scenes, where he was deft and invaluable. But if he thought I was a man who would keep the Liberal party liberal, when the results of the election came in on the night of 31 March 1958 there was hardly a party left to keep liberal.

On that night my wife and I watched the results as they came in at our national headquarters in Ottawa. Within a couple of hours it was all over but for the shouting, or rather, with our company, the groaning. There was a large electoral map on the wall and, as a result came in, a blue or red star was stuck on the relevant constituency. After the initial and encouraging returns from Newfoundland and some later from Quebec, the blue stars began to dominate the scene in a thoroughly dismaying manner. It was my first big setback since Hamilton Collegiate Institute where I had been defeated by three votes for the presidency of the Literary Society by a red-haired chap named McClellan who was very good-looking and got the girls' votes. We were reduced to forty-eight seats. My own constituency, Algoma East, was, for some reason, one of the last to report. My wife, who until that time had stood up bravely to the evidence of a great defeat, finally broke down. 'We've lost everything,' she moaned, 'we've even won our own constituency!' No devotee of political life, for a moment she thought there might be an honourable if not flattering exit through an adverse decision by the voters in Algoma East. That exit was closed.

There was now the challenge to recover and reverse the verdict of that day. For the moment, however, I wanted to go home and hide. But that was not to be. First, I had to telegraph congratulations to the Prime Minister, then meet the press, radio, and TV to give a few philosophical observations about the glory of our democracy, the people having spoken, and the comfort that came to public men in being able to 'treat those twin imposters, triumph and disaster, just the same.' There is a ritual on these occasions, for vanquished and victor, to be discharged with all the grace and sincerity that one can command. Next, to a victory party for George McIlraith, who had overcome the national tide and defeated that redoubtable and colourful Mayor of Ottawa, Charlotte Whitton. I had then to hurry home, as I had invited all the press, radio, and TV men who had been with us on the campaign to join the Pearsons in a celebration or a wake. My luck held. It was snowing and slippery outside and, while hurrying back to our house, my brakes failed to hold on a red light and I skidded into a crossing car. The damage was inspected by both drivers, I accepted responsibility, and was able to limp slowly the rest of the way. The party, happily, was a success and finished a memorable day of defeat on a note of goodwill and good cheer. By 2 in the morning the Pearsons were asleep, dreaming of red stars for the next contest and of all the problems and difficulties the Diefenbakers would have to face until then. A couple of days later we went to Florida to recover. The first item I heard on the news after arriving in Palm Beach was a short analysis of the Canadian election in which it was said John Diefenbaker had overwhelmingly defeated the Liberal leader, 'Mr Liston Parsons.'

The five years in opposition, were, strangely enough, a most productive, rewarding, and stimulating time. From a decimation at the polls, we not only rebuilt our party and operated as an effective and constructive opposition but also became the government in the election of 1963. In this I was much helped by the experienced politicians in Parliament and by able new recruits we were able to attract to our party. For my chief lieutenants, I had three very experienced Privy Councillors in Lionel Chevrier, Paul Martin, and Jack Pickersgill.

Chevrier was my deskmate in the Commons. A French-speaking Ontarian from Cornwall, he had become, under St Laurent, leader of the Quebec caucus. This was a position of great importance in our party's hierarchy especially when I, an Anglophone, became the national leader. Indeed, even with Mr St Laurent as leader, it seemed unfair to expect, at that stage in our federal history, that Mr Chevrier be accepted as Quebec lieutenant when his birth and background were in Ontario. Fortunately, Lionel was an old parliamentary hand, able, respected, and well liked by his Quebec colleagues. He may never have felt that his background handicapped him once settled into his new riding of Laurier in Montreal. Yet I remained convinced, despite the fact that Chevrier was a good and loyal friend, that the Quebec leader should be a *Québecois*. The Conservatives, of course, had far greater problems in this regard than I ever experienced.

On my other side in the House was Paul Martin. He knew every trick of the parliamentary trade and was able to intervene with effect and without notice in any parliamentary imbroglio. Once, after the 1958 electoral débâcle, we had so few members that Paul found himself acting as the Liberal agricultural critic, a duty which he performed with aplomb. On yet another occasion when I rose as Leader of the Opposition, the Speaker betrayed our old friendship and strengthened his reputation for expertise and objectivity by ruling me out-of-order on some technicality. While the point was being argued, I told Paul to get the Speaker's eye at the first opportunity and give my speech, which we wished to get into *Hansard* that day – and into the press. I had a full typed text – those 'notes' which, under the rules, we were not allowed to read but could 'consult' – so as soon as he got on his feet I fed him the script, page by page, underlining what I wished him to emphasize. He performed magnificently, as if he had spent hours writing and memorizing the speech, and even the 'ranks of Tuscany,' who could see, naturally, what was going on, could 'scarce forbear to cheer.' How I envied Paul his parliamentary debating skill – never using one simple word when fifty were needed to confuse and frustrate our political foes – as well as his ability to detach himself from the fray once the battle was over! He had politics in his blood and was one of its finest practitioners during my time in public life. I was the beneficiary of his skills as well as his friendship.

The third of these well-tried and able veterans whom I wish to mention is Jack Pickersgill. He was an old friend from civil service days in the East Block who had entered politics in 1953, under the combined pressures of Mr St Laurent and Joey Smallwood, as Secretary of State and member of Parliament for Bonavista-Twillingate in Newfoundland. That may have seemed a strange political resting place for a Manitoban and Ottawan. It proved, however, to be a good arrangement for Jack and an equally good one for the rugged fishermen of that province. No one could have identified himself more closely with their interests than the transplanted Prairie bureaucrat.

Pickersgill was a dedicated and enthusiastic political warrior. Further, he could reinforce his moves with an unparalleled experience of government operations through his long service as Mr King's secretary and close confidant and his even closer association with Mr St Laurent. There were many who wondered why he left this position of power and security for the vulnerability and risks of party politics. If they had known his zest for combat and his eagerness to be involved openly in political change, they would not have been puzzled. He had an excellent mind, an insatiable curiosity about everything, and a genius for the in-fighting of the House of Commons, although his speaking manner was calculated to irritate rather than impress our opponents. Above all, he was a friend of unshakable loyalty.

℘

Most of those who were close to me when I took over the party leadership did not survive the disaster of the 1958 election. One who did, but who left Ottawa shortly afterwards, was Jean Lesage. Though still young, he had several years' experience in the House, as a private member, a Parliamentary Assistant (for a time to myself in External Affairs), and as a Minister. With his quick intelligence, skill in debate, and personal charm, he was considered to have a bright future in federal politics. There was nothing to prevent his rising to the top. But he had other plans. A few weeks after that election, when I was recovering in Florida from the rout, Lesage, who was not far away at Miami, came to see me. He wanted me to know that a great deal of pressure was being brought to bear on him to announce that he would seek the Liberal Leadership in Quebec. He was assured that if he gave the word, he would be chosen; but he knew how hard-pressed I was and did not wish to leave the House of Commons unless I approved. I did not hesitate (though some of my colleagues indicated to me later that I should have) and told him that he had my full approval for the move, much as I would miss him. I believed that a main road to office in Ottawa was through Liberal victories in the provinces. Lesage was the man to do this for us in Quebec, and so it happened. As we listened to the results from Quebec on 22 June 1960, all of us in Ottawa got our first lift since March of 1958. Even though the sweeping Liberal victory was purely provincial, our morale was greatly improved and this was what we needed. I might add, parenthetically, that this victory did not make Quebec any easier to deal with. Jean Lesage turned out to be a pretty tough provincial leader and on this I shall have more to say later. A Liberal victory in New Brunswick five days after that in Quebec, with a new, young, and forceful leader, Louis Robichaud (I had gone to the convention that chose him), gave us further encouragement.

For our parliamentary purposes, though we were certainly short in numbers, we had some good and experienced debaters and developed some good new performers. Our ranks as well as our morale were soon somewhat strengthened by success in two by-elections. Paul Hellyer, defeated in 1957 and 1958, won a seat in Toronto on 15 December 1958 and proved to be a strong debater, especially on defence subjects. This was an area in which he already had some experience as a Parliamentary Assistant and Associate Minister. Judy LaMarsh, our new war horse, came to the House from Niagara Falls on 31 October 1960. She had been prominently identified, sometimes controversially (she was naturally controversial), with Young Liberal politics. She seemed at home in the Commons from the day she was sworn in and it was not long before she made her presence felt. An effective, rough-and-ready speaker, she could, without even trying, infuriate her opponents and delight her friends, while never allowing her criticisms to descend to lady-like generalities.

ॐ

On 12 May 1958 the new Parliament met for the first time. We forty-eight Liberals (not one from the three Prairie provinces, Nova Scotia, Prince Edward Island, or British Columbia), eight CCF, and one Liberal Labour were faced, indeed surrounded, by 208 Tories (including fifty from Quebec, our own special preserve) and a triumphant front bench. They were led by a sure and confident Prime Minister who had reached the pinnacle of power and glory in spite of many ups and downs. He was a man who had always been certain of his destiny. He had every right to take pride in that moment and to look forward to challenging Mackenzie King's years at the Canadian summit.

It was a time for Liberals, after such a defeat and under a new leader–untried–to sit back, be quiet, reasonable, and co-operative; to get busy with the work of regrouping and rebuilding; to be alert but not aggressive in opposition; and to see how things developed. Certainly those were the right tactics for the first session. I tried to express that viewpoint in my opening speech:

We shall try to be guided by something more than mere partisan considerations as we approach our work. While vigorous and alert in carrying out our responsibilities to oppose, we will try to do this in a constructive way and co-operate with the government in all those endeavours which in our view further the national interest.

Like members opposite, of course, we on this side are influenced and perhaps at times oppressed by human prejudices and other emotions. We shall endeavour to prevent opposition degenerating into mere negation or criticism into mere obstruction.

The absence of a strong opposition means a one-party state. A one-party state means an all-powerful cabinet.

Those were very wise words uttered by the Prime Minister some years ago when he was in opposition. Well then, Mr Speaker, it is our duty in parliament to oppose, and that will mean causing divisions of this house on occasions. We do not forget that we are united in a sincere desire to serve our country and that the influences that draw us together in that ideal of national service are much stronger than the influences that separate us into political parties.

After the 1958 election, attention naturally was focused on the Prime Minister and the Leader of the Opposition. There could not have been two more different parliamentary opponents. Perhaps I should write something of these differences which are now becoming distorted in many respects by gossip and legend. This is no easy task, to write about one's self in relation to one's chief political adversary before the dust of political controversy has settled and history has had a chance to correct personal feeling and viewpoint.

Contrary to some stories from Ottawa, there was never any problem in our personal relations. This was fortunate because the Prime Minister and the Leader of the Opposition are bound to see each other frequently, notably on those social-official occasions to which the Leader of the Opposition is by custom invited. Mr Diefenbaker was always amiable and of good value as a fellow-guest or host on these occasions. His story-telling and anecdotal abilities were famous. He was also very sensitive about observing the courtesies of official and social life: a note if you were ill, had lost a close relative, or on a birthday or some other personal occasion.

My differences with Dief were political and official. This was bound to be so in a normal and healthy Parliament. Certainly that has been true in Canadian history. These differences can lead to bitterness and suspicion when party feelings run high and, in the heat of a bitter debate, things are said that would seem to preclude indefinitely any further normal relationship. But this is rarely so. Also true, in contrast with the past, is that the communications media, which can report all the details of a political debate or conflict in a matter of minutes, tend to do so in terms of personality and conflict, often at the price of confusing the real issues. This is bound to sharpen personal differences and result in comparisons with a past which has fallen into perspective and whose leaders have been transformed into calm and gentlemanly statesmen. In fact, the confrontations of the tenth decade of the Canadian Parliament and politics showed much less notorious behaviour and personal criticism than the clashes marking our House of Commons in earlier times.

The approaches of Mr Diefenbaker and myself to politics and government were as different as the backgrounds and the personal attitudes that influenced, if they did not determine, those approaches. My entry into politics, after many years of official and diplomatic work, and my subsequent accession to the leadership of my party were unsought, unplanned, almost accidental. In my whole life one step followed another in, for me, satisfactory if often unrelated succession, without any final goal ever in my mind. 'I do not ask to see the distant scene. One step enough for me.' But I tried to make each step a good one and in a right direction. Mr Diefenbaker has told us that he had decided as a boy what he wanted to do: enter politics and become Prime Minister of Canada. He had his goal, he kept his eyes fixed on it, he overcame obstacles and rose above reverses on the way, with courage and determination. Refusing ever to admit final defeat, he achieved ultimate triumph, as he knew he would.

My background of official and diplomatic duty, along with my own nature, tended to make me more interested in issues, in finding agreed solutions to problems, and in trying rather to convince doubters by an appeal to reason that my answers were right than to make sure they were politically feasible as well as right in themselves. I was far less interested in defending or attacking a proposal for political reasons alone. Naturally, I became more aware with experience of the necessity for that kind of compromise which makes politics the art of the possible. I learned to defend measures and proposals by a debating speech rather than by a lecture, thereby strengthening my own position and weakening my opponent's. I learned how to exploit the mistakes of those opponents, remembering that governments are defeated by themselves, not by their adversaries. But I never could be a good 'cut-and-thrust' parliamentary debater, and I was just not built to 'go for the jugular.' I might have been more effective had I been a politician from the beginning, working my way up from the backbenches, learning on the way to curb my weakness to find something worth supporting in nearly every proposal of an adversary, and remembering that in party politics all is black and white: the other chap is black because you have so coloured him, even if it had to be done by demagogic diatribes, unfair and malicious insinuations and distortions and by playing fast and loose with facts.

I have said enough, I think, to show that the two party leaders who were to face each other across the House of Commons and in the country in the years ahead were not cast from the same political mould. This may have added piquancy to the confrontation; it added nothing to my comfort or confidence as the first session of the new Parliament opened. Opposite me was a seasoned and secure parliamentary performer, with his horde of supporters cheering his every word. He was an explosive, emotional orator and actor, even if his style made no appeal to me. He was equally at home in defence and denunciation, in both of which he could soar without effort or inhibition into flights of fancy which we, on the other side, often scorned as based on no foundation of truth or fact.

My earlier training as an academic and official had impressed on me the importance of accurate research before public declaration or criticism of policy. But I admit that in the heat of political conflict I made statements on occasion which I might have found difficult to justify by fact; or I drew exaggerated and even distorted conclusions from the facts I used. Again, I might have said something factually wrong from a lapse of memory. This last transgression used to worry me particularly, since it could be so easily interpreted as calculated deceit. I can only say that never at any time in the Commons did I ever deliberately deceive the House, no matter what pressure I might be under.

ॐ

To return to the first post-election session, I do not think that the Prime Minister could have been much impressed by the Opposition; certainly not by its leader whom he had already demolished in the House and in the country as an ex-diplomat and professor, now an inexperienced and insecure political leader. We must have looked pretty weak. It was, however, our responsibility, as it already was our fixed determination, to reverse that scheme of things and bring down this political giant who, on the face of it, looked as though he had many years of power and office ahead. We did bring him down. Parliament opened on 12 May 1958. Almost exactly five years later I moved across the aisle to the Prime Minister's seat, and now it was his turn to look at me from the seat of the Leader of the Opposition.

Many friends have commiserated with me on what they regarded as those unproductive and frustrating years in opposition. I do not agree; in many ways, those were the most productive and satisfying years of my political life. Personally, they were comfortable years; they were busy without the crushing burden of ministerial, let alone prime ministerial, responsibility. Our children were now away from home; our son was making progress in his chosen career, the foreign service; our daughter was happily married to her doctor who was making a name for himself in Toronto as an obstetrician and gynecologist. More important, they were producing children (in whom their grandparents took an inordinate delight) at a rate to defy the consequences of a population explosion. My wife and I lived most comfortably at Stornoway, the Opposition leader's residence. It was a homey place in Rockcliffe, with spacious and lovely grounds, but rather too large for two. In any event, I became determined to move out before long, into an accommodation even larger.

Politically, during the sessions of 1958 and 1959 we were not aggressive in the Commons, though we discharged our duty to oppose, I believe, with increasing confidence and competence. We were very few in number, but still we needed time to become a cohesive, organized group. Moreover, the people had given the government an overwhelming vote of confidence and naturally would be impatient if our opposition were captious or obstructive. So we supported, in principle, many of the government's measures, trying to improve bills by amendments without delaying them unnecessarily. The Bill of Rights is a good example. This was a long cherished dream of Mr Diefenbaker's and a major promise in his election campaigns. As a charter of human rights, as an objective to be reached, we thought it could be of great value. Thus, when it came before the House we supported it. We did attempt, however, to remove the public misunderstanding that this bill had constitutional authority. It was, after all, a piece of federal legislation having no force over those important areas of our society falling under provincial jurisdiction. Further, Parliament could alter or rescind it at any time. If the Bill of Rights was to protect all Canadians in all circumstances, there would have to be a constitutional amendment concurred in by the provinces, and this, when in office, I tried and failed to bring about. Apart from pointing out the bill's constitutional limitations which were often submerged in the flood of government oratory surrounding it, we succeeded in improving its language, especially its preamble, to make it a more inspiring document.

There were, of course, government policies and decisions during those early years that demanded and received much stonger criticism. Some of them resulted from Mr Diefenbaker's more colourful and high-flown campaign promises. For example, he had held forth a vision of the North as a new frontier humming with economic development. It was to be a frontier opened and sustained by government expenditure and to result, he hoped, in a massive upsurge in employment. His programme of Arctic road-building was an example of how this was to be accomplished. As a cure for unemployment, it was of little value. I scornfully rejected his scheme for building roads 'from igloo to igloo,' a quip I lived to regret. The Conservatives would delete my reference to unemployment and forever brand me as a narrow-minded, effete easterner who had sneered at the 'vision of the North.' Well, their cleverness in debate did not prevent their chickens, especially unemployment, from coming home to roost in the government benches, and we did not fail to remind them of their presence. Even though such reminders are an inevitable and an agreeable part of Opposition duties, I never, in any speech in the House, blamed the government for all the unemployment during these years. Even in the heat of debate I cannot do this sort of thing since it is so transparently silly. A government can mitigate the effects of economic troubles but cannot completely remove their causes. Nevertheless, we in Canada suffered more than we should have because of a growing lack of confidence in the ability of the government. The disagreements within the government, which affected this confidence, gave the impression that no one was fully in charge. The financial and economic systems in all democratic countries now rest so largely on confidence, on a foundation of belief rather than of fact, that if the people lose confidence in a government, the misfortunes that might have happened in any event are magnified and aggravated.

This is not to say that the Conservatives did not make mistakes in their economic and financial policies. I have already made reference to a promise by Mr Diefenbaker, as flamboyant as it was ill-considered, to divert to Britain 15 per cent of our imports from the United States. The British took him up on this at once, but a Commonwealth Finance Ministers' meeting at Mont Tremblant in 1957 and a Commonwealth Economic Conference at Montreal in September 1958 confirmed what was obvious to anyone but a campaign orator—that a transfer on so massive a scale was quite impossible. We made the most of this failure, and this must have been particularly galling to the Prime Minister who was a fervid and emotional monarchist, anxious to retain and strengthen economic and political ties across the Atlantic with the 'Mother Country.' His government even went so far as to warn Britain to beware of joining the European Common Market. This led to considerable embarrassment when statements by Mr Fleming and Mr Hees, opposing Britain's efforts to join, were given to the press at the annual meeting of the Commonwealth Economic Consultative Council at Accra in 1961.

After serving as his own External Affairs Minister for three months, Mr Diefenbaker chose in September 1957 the president of the University of Toronto, Sidney Smith, to implement the foreign policies of his government. As one of my Tory friends gleefully remarked to me, 'He'll soon make Canadians forget all about you, Mike.' It did not work out that way for reasons which, as a good friend of the new minister, I deeply lamented. Sid had some difficulty in adjusting himself to the House of Commons, particularly in handling questions from Opposition members. He had nothing of the parliamentary combativeness and unqualified aggressiveness which characterized his leader in dealing with us. He even said at an informal press conference after being sworn in as minister that he generally approved of what I had done at the United Nations over Suez. This was particularly unfortunate for him since he was sharing the spotlight with Mr Diefenbaker, who intervened and took over the interview to ensure that no further heretical observations were made. Sidney Smith was just beginning to find his way, and perhaps would have become a good and successful External Affairs Minister, when he collapsed suddenly and died on 17 March 1959.

It was not in the area of foreign affairs, however, but in domestic administration that we were able in these early years to exploit mistakes made by the government. Notable among these was the decision to abandon the Canadian-built and designed fighter, the famous Avro Arrow. The decision to build it had been made by the St Laurent government. The research and development work, done almost entirely in Canada, had been completed and the first plane had been successfuly flown when Mr Diefenbaker announced that the whole project was to be shut down. There were reasons of defence and economics that could have been advanced to justify this decision but none to justify the way it was done. Suddenly, on 20 February 1959, without any effort to keep together the fine professional team of scientists and engineers which had been assembled, Mr Diefenbaker pronounced his government's policy. There was even an apparent vindictiveness in the decision to scrap the five completed planes and the others half completed so that no museum of science and technology would ever be able to show what we could design and produce. It was on this irrational element in the decision that we centred our attack, thus reflecting the feelings of most Canadians.

In consequence, by 1960 we had a great deal of ammunition to use against a government becoming more and more vulnerable, especially in its economic policies; these had done little to stimulate growth, maintain price stability, or prevent massive unemployment. We were becoming more effective as an opposition and became even more so as a result of the government's tactics. Because the Prime Minister and most of his Cabinet colleagues had been so long in opposition, or because Mr Diefenbaker could not resist his temptation to attack, to answer any question by trying to score points off the 'Grits,' to inflame a controversy rather than reduce it, whatever the reason, he at times began to act more as a Leader of the Opposition than a Prime Minister. He appeared more concerned with putting us in the dock than in keeping his government out of it. This, of course, made our task all the easier.

Hence, from 1960, after we had crossed that political divide between post-election and pre-election which invariably quickens the parliamentary atmosphere, the House of Commons became a much livelier and more contentious battle-ground. The most dramatic of our clashes on which we scored heavily was what has now become known as the Coyne Affair, during the summer of 1961. James Coyne was the Governor of the Bank of Canada. The government disapproved of his monetary policies as too tight for a situation of economic recession. He was invited to resign. He refused unless and until he had an opportunity to explain his policies and to defend himself before a House of Commons Committee. This he was not permitted to do and the government, to overcome what they considered to be unreasonable obstinacy, brought in a bill to remove him. There is no doubt that in a dispute between the government of the day and the Governor of the Bank the will of the government must prevail; the Governor should resign. But the legislation establishing the Bank did not make this clear (when I became Prime Minister, we corrected that). Coyne insisted on his right to be heard, and the government on its right to be rid of him. Coyne was a tough and obstinate character and the government showed a singular ineptitude in dealing with the matter.

I had no doubt about what my own position should be. While not in any sense supporting Coyne's views on tight money, of which we questioned the wisdom, I insisted that he must have his day in court. How could a Prime Minister and a government which was praising from coast to coast its Bill of Rights as a new Magna Carta so contemptuously remove the Governor of the Bank of Canada from his position without a hearing? I could do more. I could ensure that he got a hearing before the Senate Banking and Commerce Committee. Although the Liberals had a large majority in the Senate, we were always cautious not to use our strength there to impede legislation approved by the Commons. But when the Coyne bill reached the Senate, we decided to refer it to the committee and to prevent final action until Coyne was given full opportunity to state his case. This he did with force and skill, and with great dramatic effect issued his resignation ten minutes after the full Senate defeated the bill to fire him. The affair attracted national interest and the government's reputation was severely damaged. We were elated, and from this point on our opposition became more and more vigorous. We had more confidence in ourselves and correspondingly less respect for the skill and wisdom of the front-bench opposite. Moreover, we had reason to believe that the tide in the country was beginning to move in our favour; disenchantment had set in with the Diefenbaker government, which had been elected with such high hopes and a terrific majority and yet by February 1961 was faced with 700,000 unemployed – 11 per cent of the labour force.

And so while we were doing constructive and creative work in the re-making of a strong and energetic party, we also had to take advantage, if we were alert, of the opportunities the government gave us to cut them down. I have mentioned the cancellation of the Arrow project and the Coyne Affair. There were other issues to arouse resentment in the country or in parts of it. Newfoundland was deeply angered by the government's refusal to accept the recommendations of the Royal Commission established by Mr St Laurent, in accordance with the terms of union in 1949, to reassess the financial needs of that province and the adequacy of federal grants in meeting those needs. Newfoundland was further distressed by the refusal of the federal Cabinet in March 1959 to meet its request for RCMP reinforcements to assist those already there, as provincial police, in dealing with a loggers' strike that had erupted into dangerous violence. Among other things, this led to the resignation of Commissioner Nicholson of the RCMP. A Columbia River Treaty was signed with the United States, even though opposed by the government of British Columbia, the province affected; later we had to revise the treaty. The government interfered with a CBC radio programme, 'Preview Commentary,' for, as it certainly seemed, partisan reasons. It was an open secret that relations with Quebec were not good, while, for a variety of reasons, relations had deteriorated also with the United States and even with Britain. There were the beginnings of division in the Cabinet. Uncertainty in the country over defence policy was countered by a flat refusal on the part of the Prime Minister to allow that policy to be publicly discussed by his colleagues. It was obvious, then, that we would be in a much stronger position for the 1962 election than for that of 1958. So I looked forward to the approaching contest with anticipation and with as much pleasure as any election ever inspired in me.

To be fair, there were achievements by the Conservatives. One was the South Saskatchewan dam, a project that had been under consideration for many years. In St Laurent's time, we had hesitated because he refused (I think he was wrong in this) to approve it until its cost-benefit ratio could be established. When Mr Diefenbaker came in it was begun immediately. There were other initiatives whose benefits were greater than material: regional aid for development, winter works and other projects designed to relieve unemployment. These were good. We used to say, with evidence, that most of these things had originated with the St Laurent government. But that was part of the give-and-take of party politics. The government had also given steady and strong support to the United Nations. Howard Green, who had taken Sidney Smith's place as External Affairs Minister, proved a determined and devoted fighter for peace and disarmament at the UN, more so than I would have expected in view of his earlier attacks on our Suez policies. While Mr Green seemed more interested in the UN than NATO (I do not quarrel with him for that), Canada remained a strong partner in the Atlantic organization.

ॐ

The improvement of our position in Parliament, or perhaps I should say the deterioration of the government's position, formed only part of our growing confidence. As a party, we had to strengthen our organization and broaden the base of our support. We had to recruit new men and women to work for us and to seek nomination as candidates in the forthcoming election. We had also to propose constructive and progressive policies which would appeal to a broad section of the people. On the organization side, we had a fine, competent group of men and women. I took an active part in their work, both at headquarters in Ottawa and in the provincial structures.

The principal body through which the federal party operated was the National Liberal Federation, with headquarters in a fine old residence on Cooper Street in Ottawa (the house has since acquired a more relaxed atmosphere as the home of the city's University Club). The federation was in capable hands under the presidency of General Bruce Matthews from 1958 to 1961 and of John Connolly from 1961 to 1964. The title of the man in charge of its day-to-day operations changed frequently, but the performance was consistently high. From 1949 to 1960 H. E. (Bob) Kidd was General Secretary, followed by James Scott as Director of Organization. In 1961 Keith Davey became Executive Director, occasionally also wearing the mantle of National Organizer.

One of the central organization's most important sub-committees was its Communications Committee (later, the National Advisory Committee on Communications). Under the chairmanship of Keith Davey, this committee included, among others, Walter Gordon, Jack Pickersgill, Tom Kent, and Dick O'Hagan. Their responsibility was to determine the best ways of making known the policies and the candidates of the party.

Working alongside the National Federation were organizations designed to reach and embrace special audiences within the Canadian community: the Young Liberals, the Canadian University Liberals, and the National Federation of Liberal Women. Each of these groups was important, giving the party vitality and character. They undertook essential organizational tasks and often proposed valuable additions to party policies; indeed, I made it a point to take part personally in their meetings. Particularly stimulating and free-wheeling were the University Liberals. Amongst them controversy was, as it should be, far more evident than conformity. To complete this brief outline of the party's structure, I must mention the semi-official Leader's Advisory Committee, of which I was chairman and Walter Gordon, co-chairman. We got together about every two weeks on matters relating to party organization, finance, and strategy. The committee's chief members included Jack Pickersgill, John Connolly, Maurice Lamontagne, Bruce Matthews, Keith Davey, Allan MacEachen, Tom Kent, and Andy Thompson.

I was ever anxious that the party, in its organization and activities, should above all incorporate that essential source of political success, the grass roots. For that purpose, I encouraged the holding of party conferences, working groups, and so on. In 1960 we decided to convene a gathering of public-spirited, informed, experienced Canadians to give us their views on the most important questions of the day, with discussions based on papers submitted by experts. This was not to be a Liberal conference. Although many prominent Liberals would be present, invitations would also be sent to non-Liberals and even to anti-Liberals who might enrich our deliberations. There was to be no party limitation on these discussions. The chairman and organizer, Mitchell Sharp, was not a member of the party at that time, and the active participation of men such as Professor Frank Underhill, whom I once described as 'a perceptive if somewhat astringent commentator on the Canadian scene,' ensured that the virtues of the Liberal party would not be exaggerated. I hoped, in short, for what would now be called a thinkers' conference, and I was gratified when 'The Study Conference on National Problems' held at Queen's University in Kingston from 6 to 10 September 1960 proved to be a great success.

In many ways, this conference marked the beginning of our comeback. The progress made from the election of 1958 to the elections of 1962 and 1963 stemmed, among other things, from our recruiting many new people into our party, people not before identified with party liberalism. Our aim was to bring together a fine group of young men and women interested in politics as intellectuals and well-informed citizens. We hoped that some of them would seek election, not for personal ambition, but as a public service. The Queen's Conference began this process; in fact, when I chose Mitchell Sharp to organize the Kingston Conference, I had hoped that this would lead him to a political career, although I was not certain that this would be his decision. I did not regard him as either conservative or left wing; from my knowledge of him as an official in his Trade and Commerce days, I thought of him rather as a political technician than as a party person.

This process of attracting new people culminated in those opposition years with our great National Rally in Ottawa from 11 to 14 January 1961. Here local committees, after weeks of preparation, were encouraged to produce and debate resolutions on policy. These meetings created a sense of participation by the rank and file and established a broad popular basis for our party. This sort of thing has its dangers, of course, in that it often exposes differences of viewpoint and objective within the party, differences to which the media invariably give extensive publicity. Further, there invariably emerge resolutions not only controversial but also impractical to the point of absurdity. The other political parties always exploit and distort these proposals, especially if they have won any kind of majority, even of eight to seven, in some committee or sub-committee. I made it clear, therefore, that the party when in office would not be bound by conference resolutions; that was the responsibility of caucus and Cabinet. I did assure these meetings, however, that all their views would be considered before legislative action was taken.

In my opinion, the advantages of public forums for discussion of policy outweighed the disadvantages. I also advocated the publication of all proceedings, a practice which did not often commend itself to the Tories. I did not advocate general and open policy conferences more frequently than once every two years, the period our party later formally adopted, but I let it be known that at these conferences the leader would give an account of his stewardship and that the party leadership would then become a proper subject for open discussion. I might add that this was a continuing process. Our 1966 convention rejected a proposal for an automatic leadership convention every two years. But at the same time it adopted a resolution that at future policy conventions there should automatically be placed on the agenda the question of whether a leadership convention should be called during the next twelve months. It also resolved that there should be a Biennial National Policy Conference. When I addressed that convention, I experienced no wariness in urging it to deal 'with subjects as modern as the next century.' I also urged it to 'widen and deepen the democratic basis of our party's organization and struc ture' to give the 'grass' a real feeling of involvement and participation to review the actions and the leadership of the government and 'put heat on it.' I assured the party that 'I have never believed in the Divine Right of Governments, or of Prime Ministers or of Party Leaders,' and it was a conference that truly operated in this spirit. In six workshops every aspect of party policy was discussed with no holds barred. They supported unification of the armed forces, recommended a Department of Consumer Affairs, and vigorously debated the question of US control of our resources and industry.

The Liberal party, then, as always, in opposition or in government, included one group anxious to move to the right and a second group eager to steer to the left. This dichotomy is an essential characteristic of Liberalism, even though the terms 'right' and 'left' no longer retain their former precision. For example, at the time of the Queen's Conference, one would have called Bruce Matthews a conservative. This he was by nature, although his family were Liberal by tradition. He was a businessman of high reputation, the youngest of our divisional commanders in the Second World War, and a man of great value to the Liberal party. In 1958, with our party fortunes so low, I asked Bruce Matthews to step into the breach when Duncan MacTavish left the party's national presidency. Such unselfish actions began to make me feel much more buoyant about our prospects.

People began to rally around and to support our efforts in building a new party. My desire was to forget about the old party, to stop looking to the past. New men, young men, were brought into my office, the party organization, and the constituencies. Keith Davey began to take over our party management and Bob Fowler was extremely useful in proposing new ideas, whether for policy or organization. Most of our recruits were what I would call progressive. Of this quality, Walter Gordon was a very good example, as were the new people in my own office. I had begun in 1958 to create a small but excellent staff of advisers. I had only three, my experts on research, politics, and policy: Maurice Lamontagne, Allan MacEachen, and, later, Tom Kent. These were idea men, with ideas very much in harmony with my own. In the terminology of 1960, they would have been regarded as left-wing Liberals. I would not have been so comfortable with them at hand, however bright they were, had they not agreed with me that the Liberal party must keep in step with changing economic and social conditions both in our country and in the world. We no longer believed in the old-fashioned nineteenth-century doctrine of *laissez-faire* liberalism. We could not be successful unless we were a truly liberal party, progressive enough to attract people who might otherwise turn to the New Democratic party.

The Kingston Conference, as I mentioned, was designed to provide ideas, liberal ideas, for Liberal policies. In other words, the political and academic excitement generated there was meant to help produce a scenario for the party rally in January 1961. We had, of course, to sell ideas from the Kingston script to our party workers before they could complete the play, and this they would be expected to do when our election campaign began. If I do say so, the programme developed in those first two or three years was adroitly planned and successfully executed. The rewarding if difficult task of rebuilding the party's organization was virtually completed on 9 December 1961 when we were able to announce that our Campaign Committee had been formed to fight the next general election. Walter Gordon, Lionel Chevrier, and Keith Davey were respectively (and appropriately) appointed National Campaign Chairmen and Campaign Director.

By 1962, then, we were well organized for the election, though, as always, our treasury was sadly lacking in funds. When I took over the party in 1958, I was idealistic enough to hope that our expenses, including a substantial part of our campaign costs, could be met from membership dues and annual donations from the party faithful. I had hoped to escape our financial dependence on the larger grants from business corporations and to make all donations open to public examination. I soon discovered, after certain efforts to bring about these changes, that there was no way in which the party could be financed between elections, let alone during campaigns, without corporate help. Politics is indeed the art of the possible.

The financing of elections is becoming a more and more serious problem, both for the party and the candidates. Each candidate is given an amount from headquarters which varies with conditions and with the effectiveness of the candidate in securing more. It is a recognized ploy, toward the end of a campaign, to send a desperate message to headquarters: 'Wire me another thousand or I will be beaten.' In one case, I recall, a plea was made by a candidate who a week later was to win with a majority of around fifteen thousand. In Algoma East I managed on the basic allocation, plus a few donations from personal friends. I did not solicit personal donations but could not deny a few close friends their wish to help in this way. (Certainly none became an ambassador or a senator.) I was not pestered by big corporations or millionaires eager to help finance my election or the party's. If anyone whom I did not know personally as a friend wanted to send me a contribution, I told him to send it to headquarters. I know that stories go around that favours must be done for the big contributors to a party. I did not have detailed information about specific contributors and I was never subjected to any such pressure, directly or indirectly. I draw no general conclusions from my own experience, I merely cite it. Perhaps I should add (for I have heard charges and innuendoes to the contrary) that our party did not accept funds from the United States. Nor were we offered any other help (which would not have been accepted had it been) from Americans of high or low degree who, it has been alleged, were anxious not so much to make me Prime Minister as to have Mr Diefenbaker defeated.

I feel strongly, however, that if parties cannot be financed in a broad-based democratic manner, then some practical way should be worked out for public financing. I know how great the difficulties are in making any such arrangement effective and equitable but it is becoming increasingly necessary to find a way, now that the costs of national elections reach astronomic and intolerable heights. I hoped to do something about this when in office, and I set up a commission to report and make recommendations. Unfortunately, by the time it reported, other priorities, as well as parliamentary difficulties and delays, prevented legislative action.

As we rebuilt the party, I worked hard and steadily in associating myself with all its activities, as was rightly expected of me. In 1961, the pre-election year, I travelled more than 60,000 miles from coast to coast on party activities and I also took advantage of any occasion that could be arranged to speak on non-political subjects, both national and very often international, at citizens' groups, service clubs, schools, and universities. During that year I addressed sixty-six Liberal meetings outside Ottawa.

Of my Canadian journeys in 1961, fourteen were made to the West, to all four provinces, for a total of thirty days. This was no reluctant duty. There was and is no part of Canada that I prefer to visit than the exciting expanse of prairie and mountain, stream and forest west of my own province of Ontario. There was no part that I tried harder to understand, since its problems, its difficulties, and differences were often brought about by, or were due to a feeling of alienation from, the industrial east. The West and its northern reaches are Canada's hope for the future; the variety and quality of their races and peoples warrant confidence that this future will be great. I do not wear my heart on my sleeve in this basic feeling of love of country. I have often wished that I had the easy and flowing eloquence of Mr Diefenbaker when talking about Canada, especially about his beloved Prairies. But the feeling has been deep within me and I have never returned to Ottawa or Toronto from a journey to the West, to Quebec, or the Atlantic provices without a deeper realization of love for my country in all its variety of strength and beauty and majesty.

But whatever I may have felt and however much I tried to understand, the Liberal party was nonetheless at a great disadvantage in the Prairie provinces, as became distressingly clear in the next three elections. In the first place, our political power base had become centred in Quebec and Ontario. This seemed to make us predominately an Eastern industrial party, hence too concerned with the protection of economic interests not shared by the West or the Maritimes. The stronger we became in the centre, the more aloof we might seem to be from the other regions. Then, of course, there was Mr Diefenbaker, the voice of the West, its evangel and its champion—and at this time, in a very real sense, the Tory party. Who was I, an Easterner, to match his appeal even if I spoke with the tongues of angels, which I did not. He had, in addition, managed to become the leader of Western progressive radicalism. Dief was no Bay or St James Street Tory out there, nor perhaps a Conservative in any place at all! I should add on my own behalf, however, that never on my excursions from the capital, political or non-political, did I receive more personal kindness and a warmer personal welcome than in the three Prairie provinces. Once while my wife, who was born in Winnipeg, and I were driving through cheering crowds in a Western city where I was guest of honour at a great municipal fiesta, she turned to me and, with her matchless capacity for reducing any subject to its basic elements, observed: 'Why do they cheer you when they don't vote for you?' I was too busy waving back to answer.

VICTORY AT THE POLLS

The 1962 election was called for 18 June. We had expected it to be in the autumn but the Prime Minister presumably hoped, as we learned later, to get it over before growing financial problems created a crisis requiring drastic measures. So the pretext of Opposition obstruction, on this occasion more transparent than usual, was trotted out and Parliament was dissolved on 19 April. We were ready. We had fielded men like Walter Gordon, Mitchell Sharp, Jack Davis, John Nicholson, Bud Drury, Red Kelly, and Hazen Argue; Mr Argue had joined our party a short time before, after serving as House Leader for the New Democratic party. Two of the men in my own office, on whose advice and assistance I had relied so greatly, Allan MacEachen and Maurice Lamontagne, were also standing. All in all we ran a very good slate of candidates, many running for the first time, both young and energetic.

We struck as hard as we could against the government's record of failure, confusion, and indecision. In 1958 the five big government promises on the domestic front had been:

1. no one would suffer from unemployment;
2. the budget would be balanced;
3. government expenses would be cut;
4. taxes would be lowered;
5. tight money would be ended;

all of which could be embraced in the phrase 'prosperity and work.' It was easy to set these bright promises against, as we saw it, a dismal record:

1 average unemployment during these five years, 420,000, against a postwar average of 179,000;
2 continuous deficits;
3 federal expenditure up by one-third;
4 tax increases of $36 per family;
5 highest interest rates in our history.

We had a strong case and made the most of it. Our theme was firmly set: Canada needed a stable government to restore confidence in the country at home and abroad and to implement, stage by stage, a new development policy. 'It is not that we are hungry for power, but hungry for an opportunity to do something for Canada in a way which has not been done since 1957.' Our tactics were to be largely repeated the next year.

The course of a campaign, however, can never be fully planned in advance. Adjustments have to be made as public reaction develops and as new issues emerge. One such new issue appeared toward the end of the campaign in the financial crisis to which I have alluded. In immediate terms, this led to the devaluation of the Canadian dollar to $92^1/_2$¢ US on 2 May. In his budget speech of 10 April the Minister of Finance had maintained that all was well with the dollar; that his policy of letting it float marginally downward against the US dollar had substantially helped our balance of payments. Now, a few weeks later, we had devaluation, obviously not carefully planned but grasped in circumstances of pressure and panic. Quite a commentary on government policy! Our campaign managers, not at that point concerned with the economics of the situation, considered this as manna from heaven: 'Your dollar,' we told the Canadian electors, 'is worth only $92^1/_2$¢. See what Conservative policy has led to.' We then flooded the country with 'Diefenbucks,' quickly printed imitation dollar bills with the 'One Dollar' crossed out and replaced by '$92^1/_2$¢.' Since a picture is worth a thousand words, our election strategists felt that this was the kind of thing everybody would understand, and they were right. It was idle for Mr Diefenbaker to boast, 'It was a bold and imaginative decision and they said we couldn't do it,' or for his party to broadcast just before the voting, 'The people of Canada are moving into one of the greatest eras of expansion in their history.' To the PM's assurance on the eve of voting that there was no cause for alarm, we pointed to the sudden and unexplained $92^1/_2$¢ 'Diefendollar.' It had a considerable influence on the voting and is part of a story that I should complete before going further.

During the campaign, on 8 June, Alvin Hamilton, the Minister of Agriculture, off-handedly suggested that there was no crisis. Six days after the election the PM was forced to confess that the country, Alvin Hamilton to the contrary, had been close to financial disaster on 20 June. This had been brought about, so he claimed, by the Liberal campaign of pessimism, gloom, and doom. The fact is, of course, that our monetary position had been deteriorating for months. From the government's point of view, this obviously had to be concealed or minimized during the election campaign. Devaluation occurred only when pressure on our dollar removed their hope that nothing need be done until the votes were in. However, the run on our dollar did not stop with devaluation, and the magnitude of the crisis had finally to be admitted on 24 June. Emergency measures were taken to restore confidence in our currency. The *Winnipeg Free Press* in its analysis of the crisis on 25 August 1962 offered these comments:

If Mr Diefenbaker, with all the latest secret figures available to him, had suspected no trouble he was not fit to be Prime Minister. If Mr Fleming had failed to understand the long-developing crisis, or had failed to inform his chief, he was unfit to be Minister of Finance.

In fact, it was perfectly clear on June 24 that the government had been quietly preparing for an emergency well in advance of the election. The proof of that will be found in the internal evidence of the emergency program itself: credits of a billion dollars could not have been negotiated in the six feverish days after June 18; preliminary approaches to the [International Monetary] Fund and the British and American governments must have been made before then. Nor could the tariff regulations issued on June 24–exhaustive in detail, immensely complex in figures and all laid out in neat schedule–have been prepared in this brief interval; obviously they had been previously drafted because the government knew they might be needed–knew that even while it assured the public that all was well.

Neither I nor my party criticized the government's short-term post-election emergency measures. They were necessary in the national interest, whatever may have been their cause. But it was obvious that something more than austerity was required for the long term. This was a national crisis requiring the co-operation of all parties in the House. I expected the Prime Minister to see me and to request my co-operation as the Leader of the Opposition. Instead he sent an emissary, Louis Rasminsky, the new Governor of the Bank of Canada. I made note of this visit and of subsequent developments at the time. In view of later criticism in the House of Commons that I had tried to play politics over the government's difficulty, I am including this note:

On Thursday, June 21st, Mr Rasminsky telephoned me to find out if he could see me alone and privately at my home. I asked him to come out and spent most of an hour with him late that afternoon. He said he had been authorized by the Prime Minister to convey to me information regarding the alarming deterioration of our dollar position and what the government proposed to do about it.

The facts as he gave them to me were certainly alarming. He indicated that almost $100 million had been lost from our exchange reserves on Wednesday and almost the same amount on Thursday. There was indeed a run on our dollar and, at the present rate of loss, the exchange reserves would be exhausted in a matter of seven or eight days. There was a flight of dollars out of Canada, which denoted a loss of confidence.

I was very much impressed by this information and agreed that the situation was serious; in its own way comparable to a wartime emergency.

Mr Rasminsky expressed the hope that the Liberal Party would forget Politics, irrespective of the immediate past, in its approach to this problem and would give the government its support in the measures which the Bank had recommended. (This, of course, was a hope that should have been expressed to me by the Prime Minister, then, or during the next two days, not by an official of the Bank.)

Mr Rasminsky added that, if these measures were not accepted by the government, he would resign. He then outlined what they would be (substantially as they appeared later in the PM's statement issued on Sunday). I told Mr Rasminsky that this was much too serious a matter for partisan political considerations and that, as Leader of the Liberal Party, I would want to support the program in its objective of protecting the dollar and, indeed, of restoring confidence in our currency. I added, however, that the action I would take—as Leader of my Party— would depend on the contents and form of any statement issued by the Prime Minister and the way in which the government put forward its programme. In a non-partisan approach, the government could count on our support for the emergency measures as such; and on the same attitude in Parliament if it were to be summoned as soon as possible in emergency session. We would put the national interest first.

I told Mr Rasminsky that, if he could get me an advance copy of the PM's statement announcing the programme, I would then be glad to go over my own proposed statement with Mr Rasminsky. He said he would try to do this.

Later I learned from the press that the Prime Minister's statement would not be issued until sometime on Sunday and that it would be followed by a radio and television appearance by the PM on Monday at 9 PM.

That is all I heard of the matter from Mr Rasminsky, the PM, a Minister, or anyone else authorized to speak to me on behalf of the government, until Sunday evening.

I was never at any time given any advance information concerning any statement to be given by any government spokesman. I was given a copy of the Prime Minister's statement Sunday afternoon at the same time that it was given to the press; and only after my office had asked for a copy.

I had drafted a statement of my own but, after learning that there were to be two prime ministerial statements and after reading the Sunday statement, I decided merely to issue a short, interim statement Sunday evening based on what had been given to the press by the PM that day.

Statement from Honourable L.B. Pearson – June 24, 1962

'The Prime Minister's statement now recognizes that the country is facing serious financial problems.

'I share with all other Canadians the hope that the emergency steps announced today will be effective in dealing with these problems.

'The proposals now made public, and any others that may later be made by the Government, will be considered by the Liberal party solely from the point of view of what is best in the public interest.

'I expect to make a further statement after the Prime Minister has given his explanation of today's proposals.'

Sunday evening, Mr Rasminsky phoned me, expressing great disappointment and some chagrin at the nature of my interim statement. He said that it was political in character in the first line, and that it did not give the actual support promised to the government programme.

I reacted strongly to this. I pointed out that the Prime Minister had already issued one statement, with political undertones, and that I had learned from the press, but not from him, that he was about to give another public statement Monday evening. In the circumstances, I said that I had gone as far as I could in giving support, in my interim statement, and I refused to go any further at this time. I insisted that I had discharged any obligation I was under in respect of support for the programme dealing with a national, financial emergency.

I assured Mr Rasminsky, however, that my Sunday statement was only an interim one and that I would be issuing another statement; but only after I had received the text of the PM's television and radio statement or had listened to it. I added that I would be glad to discuss the whole matter with the Prime Minister himself if he so desired, which I thought would be better than dealing through an intermediary. This suggestion was subsequently ignored and I was given no advance information regarding the PM's Monday broadcast.

My caution in this matter proved to be wise. The Prime Minister's television appearance seemed to me to be misleading and partisan under the guise of a national appeal. Therefore, while rejecting advice from many quarters that I should issue a strongly-worded reply, I drafted a statement which was given to the press on Tuesday morning June 26th.

In my view, the PM, by his television broadcast, removed from me any obligation of any kind to issue a second statement giving any Liberal Party support to his government in this matter even during the emergency. However, I felt that such emergency support should be given on national grounds, insofar as that was possible. I attempted to do this in the June 26 statement while answering some of the PM's misleading statements in regard to a matter which I had been assured was so critical that it would and should be considered by the government as above all Party political considerations; an undertaking which I claim was violated in the PM's broadcast.

Mr Rasminsky phoned me today, Wednesday, June 27th, at 2 PM, expressing further disappointment in my second statement and hoping that one of positive support would be coming from the first Liberal caucus which was to meet today.

I told Mr Rasminsky that there were no grounds for his disappointment, that I had nothing further to say and that I felt the caucus would take a correct stand in this matter.

It was, to say the least, disappointing that throughout this crisis neither the Prime Minister nor the Minister of Finance felt it necessary, in seeking support of the Liberal party, to have a single direct word with the leader of the party or to send him in advance a copy of the statements which the Prime Minister had decided to issue; and these were partisan enough to make our support more difficult. It was an unhappy augury for any kind of co-operation in emergencies between government and opposition in the years to come.

ॐ

I had worked hard to ensure that after 18 June we would have a Liberal government. I covered about 30,000 miles by air, train and car, with very little time for rest, even on Saturdays and Sundays. While this was the same kind of ordeal as in 1958, our organization throughout the country was better. We were more experienced and our morale was higher than during the previous election. We believed that we had a reasonable chance to win, even though this would require an unprecedented turnover of seats.

I had only one real break during the campaign, and that in its early stages: a trip to Washington on 29 April in response to President Kennedy's invitation to a gala dinner for all the Nobel Prize winners in North America (only two were not United States citizens). I was treated in a very friendly way by the Kennedys, and had an interesting talk with the President before dinner (he had asked me to come early). Indeed, it was an evening long to remember. I did not expect, however, that my presence at the White House would be publicly interpreted by some Tories as United States intervention in our election and as proof of their suspicion that Kennedy was hoping Diefenbaker would be defeated.

On the evening of 18 June, my wife and I joined some of my staff, campaign managers, and a few friends to follow the election results in a suite at the Château Laurier Hotel. The first returns to arrive, because of time differentials, were from Newfoundland, and they could hardly have been better, 6 out of 7 for us. The rest of the Atlantic provinces were not so good, 17 Conservatives, 8 Liberals. Quebec raised our hopes again with 35 to the Conservatives' 14; the Social Credit party were the spoilers here with 26. We were encouraged by Ontario where we won 43 seats to 35 for the Tories. The outcome clearly would depend on the West. It soon became obvious that the Prairies were remaining faithful to Mr Diefenbaker. We won only two seats, Argue in Saskatchewan and Teillet in Manitoba. Our hope for victory disappeared in the Prairie night and British Columbia did nothing to restore it. The final results were:

Progressive Conservatives   116
Liberals 99
Social Credit   30
NDP 19
Liberal Labour   1

Nevertheless, this was a crushing if not the final blow to the Diefenbaker government; they were down even if they were not out, losing 92 of the 208 seats they won in 1958, and ending with not many more than in the 1957 election.

I remember phoning my mother around ten or eleven o'clock on election night to tell her that I was not going to be Prime Minister. She expressed no great distress over this and said: 'Well, I've been watching the campaign and there seems to have been an awful lot of talk about the dollar and financial matters and all that kind of thing, and I notice you've been taking part in these discussions and I was thinking, you know, that perhaps it's just as well that you haven't been asked to take on the Prime Minister's job at this time because you were never very good in arithmetic.'

We had gained many able new members to strengthen us in debate. Walter Gordon, who had been such a tower of strength in reorganizing the party and in helping work out plans and policies in the lean years, was now a member from Toronto. Mitchell Sharp, also a candidate in Toronto, lost but reduced to 760 Donald Fleming's 1958 majority of 19,097, a good sign for the next round. Others entered Parliament at this time who would soon be on the government front-benches: Bud Drury, Bryce Mackasey, Jack Nicholson, and Jack Davis. To my special pleasure Allan MacEachen regained the seat he had lost in 1958 and was now one of our two Nova Scotia members. Maurice Lamontagne, equally valuable as an adviser, was unfortunately defeated by a Créditiste in Quebec; but he would be elected in 1963.

I summed up my feelings in a letter to my son and his wife a week after the election:

The reward of this campaign for me is that I have paid my debt to the Liberal Party – and now I am on my own. But 'my own' keeps me here – where I am – for the present – as the work is only half-completed. If the next round is within 12 months – I'll go through it all again – hard though it is. If, however – and this is unlikely – he [Mr Diefenbaker] works out a coalition arrangement with Social Credit – and hangs on for 3 or 4 years – then – after one session – I withdraw – if not with much honour at least without scars.

If it were not for SC in Quebec – our complacent party managers muffed that one – we would now be forming a minority government. And *that* would be a real headache – in present circumstances. Imagine – with a combination of Dief & Caouette in opposition against you – with a combined majority! With a turnover of a few votes in 15 constituencies (where the Tory majority was under 500) & a 'reasonable' Quebec, we would be forming a majority government. *That* would be better – but – if we don't make silly mistakes – it will come next time.

The campaign was very rugged and exhausting – but I am in good condition. Your mother was magnificent – especially as it doesn't come easy for her. But she was a real trouper and I was proud.

The problem now was to bring on and win the next election. We would have to work even harder, with better policies and better communication of them to the people, if we were to convert improvement into victory in an election bound to come soon with a discredited minority government trying to carry on. However, to defeat the government in the House, we would need help from the other opposition parties. For Mr Diefenbaker the situation was very different from that of 1957 when he had won a great though not decisive victory. His aim then was to bring about an election at the earliest possible moment to convert his minority into a majority. After the 1962 election the tide was rolling against him. His aim now was to hold off an election as long as he could, hoping to strengthen his position in the House and in the country. Since he himself would not ask for dissolution, our aim was to force him by defeat in the House on an issue of confidence; this would require both NDP and Social Credit support. There was some danger in this course. Elections are not popular; a party forcing one too quickly risks turning public opinion against it. We were saved from this danger by a widespread belief that just as the Tories in 1958 were entitled to seek a majority mandate, now we were entitled to complete our success by asking the electorate to throw out a disintegrating and discredited administration.

Not one of our members had any reservations on our tactics of attack without quarter on every front. They were eager and excited for the battle and sensed victory ahead. I am not by nature a belligerent person, but during the first and only session of this Parliament I took special pleasure in seeing the government compound its difficulties and in watching it fall apart, a process completed when three Ministers—Harkness, Hees, and Sévigny—resigned (with others rumoured to be seriously considering resignation) because of lack of confidence in their leader. I had respect for and friendly relations with many of the Ministers and back-benchers on the other side, but little for the government which, I felt, was now reaping the harvest of its mistakes and failures. It had to be replaced. But it was some months after the election before we were able to confront the government in the Commons. Notwithstanding the financial and monetary problems I have already described, the PM did not summon the House until 27 September. The session lasted, uneasily and bitterly, until 5 February 1963. The next day Parliament was dissolved.

I should add that during these months I was assailed by advice from all sides, political and non-political, on the tactics best designed to bring about a change of government. Some of this advice came from Conservatives, including one or two high in the ranks of the party who, without ministerial obligations for the time being, were willing to lend me their assistance if needed. I thought it better not to need it.

During this session, apart from the political opportunities we faced and the tactics to exploit them, there were two subjects especially on my mind; indeed, they had been for some time. Now was the time to do something about them. The first and the most important problem the country faced was national unity; more particularly, the relations between the two founding language groups in our federal structure. Strains had been increasing since 1960 as a result of Jean Lesage's 'Quiet Revolution' and the reluctance of much of English-speaking Canada to respond in a constructive and understanding way to that revolution. In a sense this problem was tied in with the general problem of federal-provincial relations. Indeed, it was a very special and vitally important part of those relations. On its successful handling would depend the future of our country. During the autumn of 1962 I decided to make a speech, entirely non-partisan in character, advocating a formal and comprehensive investigation, through a Royal Commission, of the whole question of bilingualism and biculturalism as the officially recognized basis for our national development. I believed that the problems emerging could not be solved unless they were understood throughout Canada. The first step toward general understanding was to reveal the problems, to examine them, and make them known in a way which would ensure maximum attention. Maurice Lamontagne, wise and broad-minded in his understanding of the issues, had drafted my speech when I first publicly broached the problem in Quebec in November 1961. He now undertook to write a draft which became the basis for the speech I made in the House on 17 December 1962. The very good reception I got from both sides in a sense inspired and initiated my later activities in the area of national unity. I include a portion of that speech here:

...Confederation was our declaration of faith in the destiny of a united Canada. It was also our declaration of independence from the United States. We would go it on our own on this continent from coast to coast, first as part of the British empire and later as an independent nation of the Commonwealth of Nations. We knew at that time that such a declaration, based on such a faith, would involve an economic price. We were ready then in Canada to pay that price—and I hope and believe we are still ready to do so—namely, the price of being Canadian.

Confederation, however, also involved another price which too many of us either forget or do not wish to pay because perhaps it is inconvenient for us to pay it. Confederation meant the rejection not only of political and economic annexation by the United States but also of the American melting-pot concept of national unity. Confederation may not have been technically a treaty or a compact between states, but it was an understanding or a settlement between the two founding races of Canada made on the basis of an acceptable and equal partnership...

Outside Quebec, and as Canada grew from coast to coast, this understanding was more often honoured in the breach than in the observance and for reasons which any of us who know about the development of Canada can understand. As a result, there has grown up in this country two different interpretations of confederation...

To French-speaking Canadians Confederation created a bilingual and bicultural nation...

English-speaking Canadians agree, of course, that the confederation arrangements protected the rights of French Canadians in Quebec, in parliament and in federal courts; but most felt—and I think it is fair to say this—that it did not go beyond those limits, at least until recently. This meant that, for all practical purposes, there would be an English-speaking Canada with a bilingual Quebec. What is called the 'French fact' was to be provincial only...

Perhaps we needed shock treatment to make us appreciate the full significance of what had happened, of Quebec's social revolution. That shock was given in recent years by separatism, by the agitation in some quarters, which got so much publicity, for what was called political liberation...

It is now clear to all of us, I think, that French-speaking Canadians are determined to become directors of their economic and cultural destiny in their own changed and changing society... they also ask for equal and full opportunity to participate in all federal government services, in which their own language will be fully recognized. This right flows from the equal partnership of confederation.

... This means, I believe, that we have now reached a stage when we should seriously and collectively in this country review the bicultural and bilingual situation in our country, our experiences in the teaching of English and French, and in the relations existing generally between our two founding racial groups. In this review there should also be, in my view, every opportunity and every encouragement for Canadians, individually or in their associations and organizations to express their ideas on this situation. If they find it unsatisfactory they should suggest concrete measures to meet it and to reach a better, more balanced participation of our two founding groups in our national affairs.

Are we ready, for instance, to give to all young Canadians a real opportunity to become truly bilingual? If the answer is yes, as I am sure it would be, what concrete steps should be taken at the different levels of our educational system to bring about this opportunity, having regard to the fact that constitutional responsibility for education is, and must remain, exclusively provincial? What further contribution to this end have we the right to expect from radio, from television and from films in both languages? How can we encourage more frequent contacts between young Canadians?

Then, there is the question which has already been mentioned in this debate, one of specific and inescapable federal responsibility. What are the reasons why there are relatively few French-speaking Canadians in the professional and administrative jobs of the federal civil service, including crown corporations and federal agencies? How can that situation be improved as it must be improved? Would it be desirable, for instance, to have a bilingual school of public administration operated by the federal government in Ottawa?

There are a great many more questions that we might ask ourselves. These questions are now very much in the minds of Canadians, more so I believe than ever before in our history. They deserve concrete answers because they are vital to our future as a united country. They should be thoroughly examined and Canadians should be given an opportunity of expressing their views about them. There could not be any better preparation for the celebration of the centenary of confederation than to seek and find these answers. The federal government, as I have already stated and as is obvious to us all, has a special and exclusive responsibility to do something about the federal service and the crown companies. But an inquiry here, Mr Chairman, and even necessary changes, will not in my view go far enough. Many of the most important problems to be solved fall within provincial jurisdiction, especially those arising out of the teaching of both languages. Therefore, if this wider inquiry into the means of developing the bicultural character of Canadian confederation is to be undertaken, the provincial governments would have to be associated with it.

I suggest that to this end the federal government should consult with the provincial governments without delay. If these consultations—I hope this would not happen and I cannot see any reason why it should—do not result in a positive response or if they are delayed, then of course any federal government would have an obligation to go ahead with the inquiry into matters which fall within its own jurisdiction. One additional advantage, Mr Chairman, of the joint inquiry, that is with the provinces, is that it would show the importance of the contribution to our national development made by Canadians other than the founding races, which has been of special and indeed exciting value since World War II. This contribution of new Canadians from old races has added strength, colour and vitality to the pattern of our national life. It has enriched Canadianism by qualities inherited from old and noble traditions and cultures of other lands.

What better way could we prepare for our centenary than by taking effective steps now to deepen and strengthen the reality and the hopes of confederation so that all Canadians, without regard to race or language or cultural backgrounds, may feel with confidence that within this nation they can realize, without discrimination and in full partnership, a good destiny for themselves and for those who follow them? In that spirit of hope and confidence we can all work together and build a greater and more united Canada.

The other subject on my mind was national defence and the tragic confusion government policies had created. This was especially so on the question of nuclear weapons; Canada's position was intolerable, or rather the fact that we had no position was intolerable. Two things happened to bring the matter to a head. The first was the Cuban missile crisis in October 1962, bringing into direct confrontation the Soviet Union and the United States over Soviet missile sites in Cuba in what has been described by many as the most frightening event of the Cold War. Canada was bound by the NORAD agreement with the United States, accepted and signed by the Diefenbaker government in 1957, to co-operate in continental defence. The Americans had supplied us with air defence equipment in Bomarc missiles and Voodoo interceptors. Despite our commitments for co-operation and our acceptance of the equipment to implement that co-operation, the government refused to act when the crisis came. Our bases were not put on emergency alert until almost two days after the joint Canadian-American NORAD Command in Colorado Springs requested it. This appears to have shocked some people across the border into the belief that Canada was an unreliable ally. Even when our bases were put on alert, we discovered that we were impotent to use them since we had failed to make arrangements to acquire nuclear warheads for our defence systems; there was no warhead possible for the Bomarc except an atomic one, and without nuclear-tipped rockets the Voodoo lost much of its effectiveness as an interceptor. Many Canadians were indignant that we could not efficiently carry out our defence commitments in a crisis of this kind. On the nuclear weapons question, the argument of the government was: 'Let's not make this decision now; let's make the decision at the time when the weapons may be required. We'll make this decision in the future.' This was not a very impressive position to take, especially after Cuba where, from the very first minute, we would have been included in a USSR-USA conflict. Mr Diefenbaker claimed that Canada had co-operated with the United States and always intended to co-operate fully. He complained that we had not been consulted sufficiently by the Americans about what was going on, and that this was the only reason our collaboration had been less than perfect. But the fact was, even if co-operation had been perfect, the necessary formal arrangements had not been made with the American government for the completion of our weapons systems.

After Paul Hellyer, our defence critic, returned from a NATO parliamentarians' meeting in Paris in November 1962, he reported to me the hopeless position of Canada's forces in Europe. They, too, had the equipment. Our air force squadrons were receiving CF-104s and our army brigade had Honest John missiles. But neither had the nuclear ammunition to make these weapons effective. Morale was very low and our men were fed up. So were our allies. In the light of the lessons of the Cuban crisis, and with the information from Mr

Hellyer and others, I concluded that our position was entirely unacceptable. We had taken on obligations; we had made a very large investment, over 600 million dollars, in equipment; now we refused to take the decision which would make it possible to use the equipment in an emergency. Once I was quite clear in my own mind that there would be no question of sole Canadian responsibility for the use of atomic warheads, that they would be under joint Canadian-American control, and that our NATO relationships would not be affected by their acquisition, I was prepared to take a decision on the nuclear question. After a good many months, indeed a couple of years of hesitation, and despite our earlier criticism of the government for accepting these new roles in the first place, I judged, as the leader of my party and in the light of changing circumstances, that a Liberal government would discharge the commitments regarding nuclear weapons accepted by Canada under NATO and NORAD. That done, we would then begin to negotiate Canada into more appropriate roles, ones which would not require Canadian forces to use nuclear weapons. In contrast with Mr Diefenbaker's position, mine was at least a decision. I think it was the right decision, although I deplored the circumstances which made it necessary.

Over the 1962 Christmas holiday period I concluded I must make a speech in January to announce our position. The fact that it was obvious the government had split on the issue, and this would soon be revealed; the fact that the Gallup poll showed the majority of Canadians believed that the decision should be the one I had come to–these factors certainly did not inhibit me. I discussed this with one or two of my colleagues, but the responsibility was mine. I made my speech in Scarborough on 12 January, with consequences both controversial and far-reaching. This was never in my view a moral question. However, some very bitter letters were sent to me, accusing me of shameless immorality. I was told that I was making Canada worse than the United States, that we were American toadies, and that we were going to drop nuclear bombs on innocent people. This sort of thoughtless criticism never disturbed me unduly. We were members of NATO. NATO had an arsenal of nuclear weapons for collective defence, even if these were under American control. These weapons formed part of NATO strategy. We had accepted that strategy and hence accepted responsibility for the use of nuclear weapons as part of that strategy. Even more, we supplied most of the uranium to make these nuclear bombs. If we were immoral, we had been immoral from the beginning.

The impact of my Scarborough speech on the government benches, when the House resumed in January, was obvious and helped to widen the divisions within the Tory government. It was clear that Mr Diefenbaker would not be able to carry on much longer. I suppose the series of events leading to the collapse of the government really began with a press conference in Ottawa on 3 January given by General Lauris Norstad, the retiring NATO Supreme Commander. I knew Norstad well and had a great admiration for him. I thought, however, that he was going quite far in coming to Canada and telling us publicly that we were not fulfilling our NATO commitments and that our government's delay in concluding a bilateral agreement with the United States to make available nuclear weapons prevented even the training of Canadian crews in the use of these weapons. But the General had been the NATO Commander and he judged it his duty as our Commander, as well as the American Commander in NATO, to express his views. This he did in no uncertain terms to the great discomfiture of Mr Diefenbaker.

The next step on the government's road to defeat was the famous press release issued by the United States State Department at 6:15 PM on 30 January, half an hour after it had been given to our Ambassador in Washington and to External Affairs in Ottawa. On 21 January the Prime Minister had sought to counter General Norstad's comments by emphasizing the non-nuclear implications of the December Nassau discussions between President Kennedy and Prime Minister Macmillan. Then, on 25 January in the House, Mr Diefenbaker went further in his attempt to quell public and parliamentary criticism, to say nothing of that within his own Cabinet, by denying that Canada was in default of her undertakings to NATO, asserting that he was maintaining Canadian sovereignty in NORAD, and revealing (without prior United States consent) the existence of secret negotiations to provide Canadian forces with nuclear weapons 'in case of need.' He then went on to maintain, again, that the strike-reconnaissance role of our CF-104s in NATO had 'been placed in doubt by the recent Nassau declaration concerning nuclear arms, as well as other developments both technical and political in the defence field.' Mr Diefenbaker held forth the prospect that our defence role in NATO would be clarified when the NATO Council met in Ottawa that May. Finally, he stated that 'More and more the nuclear deterrent is becoming of such a nature that more nuclear arms will add nothing material to our defence.'

Mr Diefenbaker's disclosure and assertions resulted in the United States choosing the tactless method of replying by public press release. Their statement noted that:

Shortly after the Cuban crisis in October 1962, the Canadian government proposed confidential discussions concerning circumstances under which there might be provision of nuclear weapons for Canadian armed forces in Canada and Europe. These discussions have been exploratory in nature; the Canadian government has not as yet proposed any arrangement sufficiently practical to contribute effectively to North American defense.

In 1958 the Canadian Government decided to adopt the Bomarc-B weapons system... The Bomarc-B was not designed to carry any conventional warhead... The installation of the two Bomarc-B batteries in Canada without nuclear warheads was completed in 1962.

In addition to the Bomarc-B a similar problem exists with respect to the modern supersonic jet interceptor [the Voodoo] with which the RCAF has been provided. Without nuclear air defense warheads, they operate at far less than their full potential effectiveness...

During the debate in the House of Commons various references were made to recent discussions at Nassau. The agreements made at Nassau have been fully published. They raise no question of the appropriateness of nuclear weapons for Canadian forces in fulfilling their NATO or NORAD obligations...

Conventional forces are not an alternative to effective NATO or NORAD defense arrangements using nuclear-capable weapons systems.

Immediately after the release was issued our Ambassador in Washington was recalled for consultations, a fairly drastic step in diplomatic terms.

I considered that the State Department should never have issued this statement, that questions of Canadian policy should be left entirely for discussion and decision by Canadians. Regardless of provocation, it was wrong for the foreign office of any government, however friendly, to so intervene in a matter before the House of Commons. But if it was improper for the United States to issue this release, it was equally improper for the Prime Minister to make public the fact that there were negotiations going on, without first getting approval from the other party to the negotiations. The press release, however, was particularly interesting because of the light it threw on the confusions and contradictions of Canadian defence policy.

Needless to say, when the House met the next day, Thursday, 31 January, the State Department's communiqué caused a furore. Mr Diefenbaker rose as the House met to denounce this 'unwarranted intrusion in Canadian affairs' and to claim that the press release bore 'a striking resemblance to the statements made here last Friday' by myself during the defence debate. This latter charge was unworthy of the Prime Minister; it was a cheap and false insinuation. A few minutes later I moved that the House adjourn under Standing Order 26 to discuss the communiqué as a definite matter of urgent public importance. The Speaker, Marcel Lambert, ruled that the subject did not warrant a special debate. I appealed. The Speaker ruled that his decision could not be appealed; but when Paul Martin challenged this, all three opposition parties voted together for the first time to overrule the Speaker. My appeal against the Speaker's original decision was then sustained, and the House decided to debate the State Department's communiqué.

There was a real split in the government ranks on the nuclear warheads issue. We had read about it and heard about it, but now we could see it happening before us in the House of Commons. Whenever any question on defence was asked and the Prime Minister answered, it could be seen from Mr Harkness's face that he was not in agreement. George Hees, if watched carefully, was clearly restless about what was going on, and others with him. As their disunity increased, so our excitement and our energy mounted. We had them on the ropes and would not let them escape.

This was a period of intense uncertainty and confusion, not only over defence policies. There were other important matters to cause division. And with knowledge of this, we did everything we could to convert the government's confusion into defeat. This we were entitled to do. I have often been told that when, as Prime Minister, I later complained about Mr Diefenbaker in opposition (where he really cut us to pieces), I should have remembered my earlier role. I disagree. I consider that I have nothing with which to reproach myself in those four years. The Liberal Opposition from 1958 to 1962 was very different from the Conservative Opposition after 1963. We had our cut-throats, of course, but we went along with the government on a great many issues and did try honestly to put forward serious alternative proposals. It is quite true that during the two or three months at the end of 1962 and the beginning of 1963 we were as vigorous, and, I suppose, from the Conservative point of view, as vicious as any Opposition could be. This was, in part, because we had just fought an election in which the government had suffered a vote of No Confidence. They had lost almost half their strength. I would have been a very inadequate Opposition leader had I not gone after them in every possible way.

The crucial blow to the Diefenbaker government was Douglas Harkness's resignation as Minister of National Defence on Monday, 4 February. Harkness's public letter of resignation to Mr Diefenbaker stated: 'For over two years you have been aware that I believed nuclear warheads should be supplied to the four weapons systems we have acquired which are adapted to their use... It has become quite obvious during the last few days that your views and mine as to the course we should pursue for the acquisition of nuclear weapons for our armed forces are not capable of reconciliation.' Here was irrefutable proof that the government's condition was critical.

We were determined to take the opportunity of a Supply Motion to move no confidence. I think a good many of the Conservatives were reconciled to defeat. We were satisfied in our own minds that with the right kind of motion all the Opposition parties would vote against the government. And when the Social Credit members decided to support us, that was the end. In a situation of this kind everyone is lobbying everyone else, and I am sure that we did our best to co-operate with the other parties or to get them to co-operate with us. I was not personally involved in the lobbying. There were, however, plenty of tales that we had promised this or that to certain people during that crucial dinner hour on the eve of the vote. Although I am not aware of any specific promises, I would not be much surprised if there was a good deal of talk between some of our front-bench members and the leaders of the other two Opposition parties.

Thus, on that Monday afternoon, 4 February, when I moved 'that this government, because of lack of leadership, the breakdown of unity in the Cabinet, and confusion and indecision in dealing with national and international problems, does not have the confidence of the Canadian people,' I thought that it might fall very quickly. I had enough of a political nose not only to smell their defeat but our electoral triumph. After nearly winning in 1962, we were now to get a second chance. We were ready. Our organization which had performed so splendidly in 1962 had been kept in good condition. We were short of money, but so were the others.

So there it was. February the fifth was one of the most exciting nights in parliamentary history, certainly within my experience. We defeated the government. By 'we' I mean all the Opposition parties. Mr Diefenbaker characteristically fought to the last minute, making his plea to the Social Credit party not to force an election, but he lost. The vote itself was not entirely a surprise, 142 to 111. We were off to the hustings once more.

I consider government mishandling of the defence issue and the resultant disintegration of their ranks was the main reason for their downfall. But there was more to it than that. The policy I put forward on defence did not commend itself to the NDP, and they would not have voted against the government on that score. Confidence in the government had not been restored after their narrow escape in the 1962 election–indeed, quite the contrary. No budget had been brought down. There was a growing belief that Diefenbaker was largely to blame for the deterioration of our relations with the United States and Britain. Also, his government was held responsible for the serious situation in Quebec, where a rather violent form of extreme left-wing separatism was appearing and the Quiet Revolution showed signs of becoming not so quiet. The government never had a strong position in Quebec. Even in the 1958-62 period its fifty Quebec members were not able to establish positions in authority in Ottawa or control the situation in Quebec, where the provincial government had serious differences of opinion with the federal régime. I think all this had much to do with the weakening position of the government. At the same time I do not think Mr Diefenbaker's growing emphasis on Canadian nationalism and Canadian identity, arising perhaps from some of his difficulties with the United States and his consciousness of a growing American penetration of our economy, hurt him in any way. Indeed, I think it may have helped him in the country.

So we were once again on the election trail, criss-crossing the country, exhilarated and exhausted, worrying and wondering and, above all, waiting for the final day to come when the people would speak. The routine was very much like that of 1962. Once again a normal day's programme:

Thursday, February 28

9:30 AM	Depart Fredericton by car
OROMOCTO	
10:00 AM	Arrive Oromocto Hotel, reception.
11:00 AM	Depart Oromocto
11:20 AM	Depart Fredericton airport, charter aircraft
12:00 noon	Arrive Moncton
1:25 PM	Depart Moncton CNR #2 (lunch on board)
TRURO	
4:20 PM	Arrive Truro, daytime accommodation Stone House Motel
7:00 PM	Depart Truro by car
8:00 PM	Arrive Milford, public meeting Milford High School
10:00 PM	Depart Milford by car
HALIFAX	
11:00 PM	Arrive Halifax, Overnight – Nova Scotian Hotel

As in 1962, we had a plenitude of policy which we pledged ourselves to implement when we formed a government. Some of our
commitments were to reforms that had been talked about for years
but postponed by successive governments as too difficult or too controversial to implement. In the economic field we proposed basic tax
reform and a revision of tax-sharing arrangements between the
federal and provincial governments; special incentives to foster
economic development in slow-growth areas; and the establishment
of an economic advisory council. We intended to redistribute parliamentary constituencies and establish non-political machinery for
future redistributions. To improve the conditions under which Canadians worked and lived, we pledged to bring in a new federal labour
code, collective bargaining in the federal civil service, and to institute national health and contributory pension plans. In order to
strengthen national unity and affirm our Canadian identity, we were
committed to forming a Royal Commission on Bilingualism and Biculturalism; to considering with the provinces constitutional changes
and other ways of strengthening 'co-operative federalism'; and, finally, to putting before Parliament within two years of forming a government a distinctive national flag.

These and many others that appeared in our electoral programmes
of 1962-3, as well as some, such as unification of the armed forces,
which were not specifically mentioned in campaign programmes,
were our commitments when we took office in April 1963. The record
of the subsequent five years will show that, in spite of our minority
position and many unfortunate and delaying mishaps along the way,
our achievement through legislation of the important things we set
out to do was substantial.

Meanwhile, we had to win the election. The best policy proposals
in the world will not ensure success unless enough electors can be
informed and convinced that the leadership and the men are available
and competent to make election promises effective. Negatively, but
perhaps even more important, if the reputation of the government in
office has declined in the country, the possibility of success for the
Opposition is greatly advanced. We certainly had these assets. My
background, however, was still in some measure a handicap to me. I
remember seeing in 1962 an unsigned, undated memo to Walter
Gordon, the chairman of our National Campaign Committee, from
what must have been our publicity experts in the field; looking back, I
think I placed too much confidence in their wisdom and judgment,
and especially in some of their honest and well-meant efforts to improve my 'image.' If, in what is quoted I include certain panegyric

references to myself, I do this realizing that these were exaggerated to advance new tactics for presenting me to the public. The memo began:

The problem, simply stated, is to devise means of improving Lester B. Pearson's public relations position.

That there should be a need for such planning is in itself an anomaly because Mr Pearson would seem to be the embodiment of all that is most desirable in the popular political leader; he has intelligence, warmth, sincerity, flexibility.

Moreover, he is eminently successful: perhaps no Canadian of our day is better known; none has been more honoured abroad and is more deeply respected at home.

Yet, ironically, the very source of his celebrity – world statesmanship – would appear to have been at least partially transmuted into a cumbersome political liability . . .

The disturbing conclusion we have reached is that, in spite of the forceful and penetrating speeches he has made recently in the House, a dangerously large and influential body of opinion holds that Mr Pearson is really not interested in domestic affairs and, as a consequence, is not now and is never likely to become a genuinely effective Leader.

There is further consideration: Mr Pearson must contend, in Mr Diefenbaker, with the most formidable and intuitive kind of political animal.

Since he himself can never be expected to become everybody's idea of the clawing, single-minded politician, it is our task to help shape and direct the projection of what must be, by any set of standards, an altogether superior political personality.

Our job in the coming months must be to help project a clearly defined image of the real Lester Pearson – a man firmly wedded to the Canadian scene, a man determined to be the Prime Minister of his country.

In applying ourselves to this objective, maximum-exposure publicity must be actively sought for the Leader. This cannot, however, proceed on a piecemeal basis. A blueprint of action should be blocked out and a co-ordinated effort initiated.

The memo then proceeded to make a number of proposals to show that I was a genuine, down-to-earth shirt-sleeve Canadian, quite as concerned with the problems of our farmers, fishermen, and factory workers as with the United Nations. Most of these proposals were sensible. One or two were not; they would have transformed me into something I was not.

My difficulty was that most Canadians, I think, notwithstanding what I have quoted above, wanted me to continue to wear the mantle of international statesmanship. At the same time, they wanted me to show guts and strength in domestic leadership. They wanted a fighter in the political struggle, inside and outside Parliament, but not to the point of becoming 'just another politician' interested only in votes and office. This created for me a dilemma I was never able to resolve. A letter I received from a friend, dated 13 February 1963, put the problem well:

Perhaps little of this has got through to you, with even your best friends reluctant to tell you of the unpleasant odour. But I assure you it is the case as I find it. 'All parties are alike' and 'one is as bad as the other' and 'just a bunch of cheap politicians' are common expressions one hears from people of all kinds: old ladies, students, taxi drivers, bankers, waiters, dentists, doctors, lawyers, elevator operators, dinner guests, car washers, or any kind of person you care to think of. I have heard this view from each of the examples I have mentioned and rarely now do I hear any different view or expression of confidence in any party or any leader.

When I say that this feeling appears to be attached to you only in less degree than to Diefenbaker I am referring to you as a public figure. Most people seem to put you well ahead of Diefenbaker as a man but rate you much the same as a party leader; they now rate you with other politicians in appearing to think mainly of winning votes and scoring points in a silly party shinny game which politicians seem to treat as got up for their benefit rather than for management of the country's affairs with competence.

It may have been with this in mind that in the 1962 and 1963 campaigns our emphasis was on The Liberal Team, whereas the Tories spotlighted The Chief. I suspect that in modern democracies the average voter is more interested in the leader than in the team; the voter tends to focus on the star rather than on the troupe of supporting performers. In 1963, of course, it would have been embarrassing for the Tories to concentrate on the team since so many of its members had left it shortly before the campaign opened.

An unfortunate aspect of this campaign for us was the failure of our gimmicks designed to call attention to how bright and smart and 'with it' we were and to get big black headlines. I suppose this kind of electoral gadgetry, however much I might dislike it, has its place in elections today and, if used wisely and with restraint, may gain votes by attracting favourable attention. One or two of ours were successful in 1963 (or so I was told); but the circulation of 'colouring books' which, when filled in, ridiculed the Tories, or the release of homing pigeons to precede and to signal my arrival some place (they simply pushed off) were merely silly, even if they did not do us much harm. The 'Truth Squad,' as it worked out, was both silly and harmful, though I still think the idea itself had merit.

As the campaign began, the Tories, and especially the Prime Minister, began to make false and inaccurate statements. As we saw it, these statements went far beyond the normal exaggeration expected in the heat and emotion of an election battle. When I read the reports of these Tory distortions I was reminded of an observation made by Winston Churchill during a debate in the British House of Commons: 'I should think it hardly possible to state the opposite of the truth with more precision, but the Right Honourable Gentleman feels keenly that his return to office is a necessity and you know what necessity is the mother of.' Our idea was to have one of our people trail Mr Diefenbaker and make note of every statement he made which seemed of doubtful factual accuracy, check it that night, and then issue to the press the next morning a correction, giving the source from which the correction was made. Whether this could have proved effective or not I do not know, but it certainly backfired in the way we carried it out. It was felt, mistakenly, that we should have a prominent Liberal do this task so that more publicity could be obtained from the 'Truth' reports. Judy LaMarsh was suggested, and I asked her to take it on. She demurred, because she did not think much of the idea; further, it would disrupt her own campaign. When pressed, however, stalwart that she was, she agreed to become part of the 'Truth Squad.' The first time she appeared in that capacity, at a Diefenbaker meeting in New Brunswick, she was greeted with hilarity, she was offered a place at the press table to take notes, and Mr Diefenbaker, in his own inimitable way, welcomed her to the fold. The whole project dissolved in national laughter and jeering. We at least had enough sense to call the whole thing off quickly.

One incident in this campaign might have had worse consequences than our gimmicks. I was visiting Northern Alberta on 28 March and had three separate meetings scheduled for Edmonton that evening, at 7, 8, and 9PM. I had just reached the last one, in a Legion Hall, had taken my place on the platform amidst the cheers of the faithful, and was about to be introduced when the chairman whispered that there was a long-distance call for me from Washington, urgent. Would I take it in the basement room where the phone was? Mystified, I said, 'of course,' and was taken to the phone by the janitor of the hall who was much impressed, he told me. He had answered the call and it was from the White House. My mystification turned to alarm, as one of Mr Diefenbaker's most strident criticisms of me in the campaign was that I was a tool of the Americans and, if the Liberals were elected, the country would be dominated by Washington. I could see without effort what he would do with the news that, so anxious was

President Kennedy to get me elected, he had phoned me from the White House with advice, assistance, and comfort. When I reached the phone, I found that it was a Canadian journalist friend of mine stationed in Washington phoning from the White House Press Room, where he had been discussing the Canadian election. So he thought he would call to see how we were doing. The switchboard in Ottawa, with great and dangerous efficiency, found out, from our central organization, where I was supposed to be and switched the Washington call to Edmonton. This was a narrow escape since I knew that there were people abroad in the land who would never believe my explanation of the incident and insist that it was a deep dark American plot to take over the country via Pearson and the Liberals. To my relief, it never was reported; the janitor said nothing about the call.

Our campaign got off to a good start but bogged down after the first month. Campaigns have their peaks and valleys, and so it was with us. We decided that something must be done to get it moving again. This was to be done by bold, decisive, confident, and convincing statements in the last two weeks; we proposed to drive home the contrast between the last month of a divided and indecisive government and the bright days ahead of decisive and determined Liberal action. I had been emphasizing the need for a clear majority so that a new government could put its policies into effect 'steadily, stage by stage.' Then I began to put less emphasis on the policies themselves and more on 'action vigorous, forthright, and intelligent action,' while repeating my warning that 'there will be no miracles. There are no simple, cure-all promises for our troubles.'

I remember Walter Gordon and others coming to me and saying, 'This is the time to strike hard on the note of decisiveness.' We decided that this should be the note that would push us over the top, this note of action. Some of my friends thought I had been going too far in seeking the high level of 'no miracles—no simple cure-all solutions,' so on 28 March in Edmonton, at those evening meetings, I became more dogmatic about our determination to act. I pledged 'more constructive things will be done in the first sixty days of a new Liberal government than in any similar period of Canadian history.' I repeated this pledge in Vancouver and Winnipeg and in Montreal, where fortunately I was tired and only spoke for twenty minutes. Since the others on the platform had not spoken for as long as expected, we left the hall early. Later a bomb was found under the platform. Then at the great wind-up meeting on 5 April at Maple Leaf Gardens, I put the seal on the pledge. That was one of the finest political meetings I have ever attended. There was a tremendous crowd of fourteen or fifteen thousand, and I was confident that night that we were going to do well in Ontario.

But out West I knew we were not making any headway. The Vancouver meeting on April 1st had also been a terrific affair in terms of crowd and excitement. I was told in advance that there would be some noise and interruptions. Although admission to the meeting was by invitation, a thousand cards had been forged. As soon as I got on the platform I knew there was going to be trouble. The chairman was howled down and very wisely cut short his introductions and called on me to speak. There was pandemonium. The front people hooted and hissed and called me 'yankee stooge' and 'Washington slave.' Then, with thousands of people in the arena they set the Stars & Stripes alight in front of the platform. Fortunately it did not set the building on fire. It was a careful burning! Meanwhile a couple of people in the gallery were aiming pea shooters at me. While I spoke peas were bouncing off the side of my head. I went on speaking for about forty-five minutes while my wife sat in tears. Later, I went back to my luxury suite in the hotel. As we sat there feeling depressed, commiserating with ourselves and bemoaning our fate, my wife and I resolved never to go through this sort of thing again. As we drank to that, our provincial organizer and a couple of his assistants charged in, filled with satisfaction, almost gleeful. This made me very angry. I said, 'Hugh, what are you so happy about? You told me this was going to be a good meeting and it was a disaster.' 'Disaster?' he said, 'this was a triumph. The way you stood up there for forty-five minutes was magnificent. We won three extra seats to-night, and if they had only drawn blood, we would have won two more.' There was a loyal politician, one who puts seats ahead of everything–even ahead of soul. Party loyalty is a very strong thing. If it gets into your blood it becomes a dominating influence. After a while he convinced me it had not been so bad.

Election night, 8 April, was almost a repetition of the year before. We did very well in the East. Then 41 conservatives to 3 Liberals in the Prairie provinces prevented our getting a clear majority. However, our 129 Liberals to 95 Conservatives gave Mr Diefenbaker no alternative but to resign. It was now clear that my wife and I would soon be moving from Stornoway to the Prime Minister's residence on Sussex Drive. My mind soon turned away from the election to the problems, opportunities, and privileges ahead.

Shortly after he became Prime Minister in Britain, Harold Wilson

visited Ottawa. This was in December of 1964, during those trou-
blous first days of the Rivard scandal. During lunch at Sussex Drive, I
told Mr Wilson that my 'sixty days of decision' had recoiled on me
and that I now wished I had been somewhat less decisive in my
commitment. He disagreed. He pointed out that you can make no
decisions unless you are the government and that it was, as he saw it,
our unqualified, confident stand that won the election for us. Present
difficulties, he asserted, were a small price to pay and, furthermore,
one could always link the sixty days to a majority in Parliament,
pointing out that a minority has to take a little longer. He did suggest
that we might have given ourselves a little longer, say a 'hundred
days' (a slogan he was to adopt in his next election). I replied that one
hundred had been our first choice but that I, as a historian, had
reminded myself of Napoleon's 'hundred days' which took him from
exile on Elba to Waterloo, and on to final exile on Saint Helena.

4

SIXTY DAYS

I should have slept long and happily on election night 1963. But I did not. There was much to think about. I was aware of the new responsibilities which would soon be mine, and wondered if I would prove equal to the heavy burdens of governing without a majority. There were so many things I wanted to accomplish: to provide work for all in a context of financial stability; to complete the structure of social security with national pension and health plans; to bring about better relations between the levels of government so that our federalism would be strong and united; to make a new deal for French-speaking Canadians so that they might play a strong but distinctive part in Canada's development; to establish the symbols of a proud Canadian nation, above all a national flag; and to move steadily toward a greater Canadian and lessened American control over the economic development of our nation.

I did not go away on a holiday but instead relaxed for only a day or two before getting down to business. I had indicated during the election campaign that we were going to be a very energetic government during the promised first sixty days of decision and, as the record makes clear, no government could have been more active. I had also indicated that I would call Parliament at the earliest possible date. Looking back, I wish I had interpreted that pledge to mean the first practicable date when we would have new legislation and the budget ready. This would have required two or three months of preparation. Instead, I felt obliged to call Parliament as soon as this was constitutionally possible. That proved to be 16 May, leaving us little time, especially as I had announced that before Parliament assembled I was going not only to visit London but also to meet with President Kennedy. There were, in addition, many other matters to be taken in hand. My first job, however, was to form a Cabinet.

Of course, before I could do anything, I had to be summoned by the Governor General and invited to form a government. For this to happen Mr Diefenbaker had to resign and, since the House of Commons would again have a minority government, he waited thirteen days before taking that step. After Mr Diefenbaker had made his decision, he got in touch with me to offer his assistance in the change-over, as I had done before the Commonwealth Conference in 1957. Thus, the transition was all very civilized and orderly and, at least for me, quite painless. Incidentally, I did not move into 24 Sussex Drive until a few weeks later. I had told Mr Diefenbaker to take all the time he needed. These things are dealt with much more quickly at Downing Street; apparently the moving vans arrive almost on the same day the Prime Minister has audience with the Queen to resign. The Prime Minister's delay in resigning prevented my summons to Governor General Vanier until 22 April. By then I was ready to present my first Cabinet and we were sworn in at Rideau Hall with all the traditional ritual.

During the two weeks preceding that event I had learned, at first hand, some of the rather agonizing realities confronting a head of a government in the complicated task of forming a Cabinet. I had given this matter a good deal of thought over a long period of time. There were certain people I wanted. A few had been members of the St Laurent government and it was only a question of which portfolios to give them: Lionel Chevrier, Paul Martin, Senator Ross Macdonald, Jack Pickersgill, and Paul Hellyer. However, the composition of a Canadian Cabinet depends on many other considerations in addition to the preference of the Prime Minister. By tradition, each province is represented (unless you have no member from it as was true with us in Saskatchewan). Therefore, if the man most fitted for a portfolio comes from the wrong part of Canada, he may not get it if his province has already received its quota of Cabinet places. There are also limitations within this limitation, though not so compelling. A certain number must come from Ontario, and these have to be balanced by a certain number from Quebec, customarily including at least two English-speaking Protestants. There should be at least one woman, an Irish Catholic from Ontario, and one or more representatives of our ethnic communities. Although restrictive, this system has served us well since Confederation by producing a good cross-section of able people in our governments. After all, what Prime Minister wants a government of all the talents, which usually embraces all the temperaments as well?

I remember reading at this time *The Holmes-Laski Letters*. The book contained a letter of 1 July 1924 written by Harold Laski to Mr Justice Holmes of the United States Supreme Court. The letter gave an account of Ramsay MacDonald's views on the difficulties of a Prime Minister, and on the nature of Cabinets:

... a dinner at Haldane's with Ramsay MacDonald – almost entirely political talk, but to me most interesting. MacDonald told me that the job takes, on an average fifteen hours a day; that he had to make decisions on seventeen subjects totally unconnected with each other; that if he read all the papers sent in to be read he would go through a thousand foolscap pages a day. Even Haldane, whose own job [Lord Chancellor] is no sinecure, was appalled at the sheer volume of work revealed. MacDonald said that if you stopped to go much beyond the surface of things, you got caught up in doubts that were like nightmares and that the only thing to do was to plunge boldly in the knowledge that the next man would have to do the same.

Both he and Haldane were most interesting on the types of men you get in a Cabinet. There are some who literally cannot do any business at all and merely repeat the advice of their permanent officials. There are some, again, who do their own work most competently but refuse to budge an inch beyond purely departmental questions. There are others who carry their weight on all subjects. There are others who insist on butting in with the clearest inability to understand. I gathered that in a cabinet of twenty you can expect four or five who are really generally useful; that ten will bear their own burdens so long as they are not expected to go beyond their province; and the remainder are deadweights who are there for political reasons not justified in the event.

MacDonald told me that the interesting things to him were first the absolute loyalty of the Civil Service which had worked in amazing harmony under entirely novel circumstances [the first Labour Government in British history], and secondly the degree to which the Prime Minister is the general maid of all work in the cabinet. In that respect we seem to come nearer to presidential government than the strict classicists would like to admit.

I was soon to learn that by and large MacDonald's reflections, though too harsh if directly applied to my Cabinet colleagues, were valid.

For a week or so there was a steady stream of visitors to my office as I interviewed about thirty-five of my parliamentary colleagues, both those whom I wanted to see and those who insisted on seeing me.

Some I wanted to interview because I had already made up my mind they should be in the Cabinet; others, to help me make up my mind. Eventually, after a good deal of soul searching (and leaving some of our members bitterly disappointed), I formed my Cabinet. It was a pleasure to inform those I had chosen, but a difficult and unhappy duty to tell those I had not, and to urge upon them patience and hard work until their day arrived. I was anxious to keep my Cabinet as small as I could (this is true of every incoming Prime Minister), and I failed.

With the scarcity of Liberal MPs from Alberta and Manitoba, I was unusually fortunate in my Cabinet representation from those provinces. An obvious man to be Minister of Agriculture was our one member from Alberta, Harry Hays, Mayor of Calgary and, more important, a very successful farmer and rancher. In Manitoba the problem was interesting and well illustrates how some Cabinet ministers come to be appointed. We had Mrs Margaret Konantz, an old friend of mine, and we had Roger Teillet, who had served in the Manitoba Legislature and also with me in opposition. His experience made him my choice as the Cabinet Minister from Manitoba, and I found, to my pleasure, that he had a very distinguished war record with the Royal Canadian Air Force, had been captured, and had escaped from a prisoner-of-war camp in Germany. Further, he was a Métis with a French-speaking background. He subsequently became, I thought, an extremely good Minister of Veterans' Affairs.

If I had no trouble about Saskatchewan (where we had no member), and little about Alberta and Manitoba, the difficulties of selection were very real in Ontario and Quebec. There we had fifty-two and forty-seven members respectively; they were a highly qualified group of men, most of them quite capable of administering a department of government and all of them, naturally, hoping to be given the chance to do just this. With Ontario in particular I had a very difficult time. Indeed, if the first team had all resigned, I would have been quite happy to have picked a second Cabinet team from Ontario. Some choices were very clear. Walter Gordon, Mitchell Sharp, and Bill Benedickson, the last a staunch supporter with lengthy experience in the House of Commons. I had no difficulty in selecting Jack Garland, the member from Nipissing in Northern Ontario, for whom I had great admiration. Another obvious candidate was Judy LaMarsh. She had learned a great deal in opposition and was, it seemed, well qualified to be in charge of Health and Welfare — and, as a not unimportant consideration, she was a woman.

Quebec presented its own difficulties. Even in our days of minimum strength we had quite a good group from Quebec, some of them members over a long period. I was anxious, however, to get some newer men in the Cabinet. Some of those I had in mind had never served in the House before, such as Maurice Lamontagne, Guy Favreau, René Tremblay, and Jean-Luc Pépin; in fact, the last three had all been pressed into being candidates. Another new man, Maurice Sauvé, was, I think, anxious to get into political life. He had a particular aptitude for the rough and tumble of politics. Our English-speaking Ministers from Quebec also required the appointment of a new man. I regretted deeply that my decisions on the Quebec section of the Cabinet caused a good deal of heartache among some of the more experienced members from that province.

Arthur Laing was the obvious choice for the first British Columbia post. He was an old parliamentary hand with great experience and ability, and was the senior Liberal in BC. It was much more difficult to choose Jack Nicholson over Jack Davis (both were first elected in 1962) for the second Pacific minister.

Although the office of Parliamentary Secretary did not work out entirely as I had hoped, it was one factor which made Cabinet-forming a little easier than in earlier times. I could soften the disappointment of some who were not made Ministers by saying: 'Well, shortly you will be a Parliamentary Secretary and that will be a recognition of your ability, at least in my view. It will give you some encouragement to go ahead.' Once or twice I got somewhat impatient, I admit, with members who made no attempt to conceal their conviction that they should be in the Cabinet. Some of them had given up a good deal to go into politics and believed that, since they had been highly successful in what they had been doing in private life, they should by right enter the Cabinet forthwith. I used to point out to my more ambitious members that a parliamentary apprenticeship was traditionally considered almost essential for a Cabinet post. Not only that, it was invaluable; nothing really was so important as experience. I always mentioned Ernest Lapointe, who was a backbencher for many long years before he became a Cabinet Minister and Mr King's Quebec lieutenant. Of course, it was a little difficult for me to press this line too far because of my own experience before becoming Secretary for State for External Affairs in 1948, and because I had chosen as members of my Cabinet some who had had equally little parliamentary background. Indeed, I had gone out myself to look for first-rate candidates, some of whom had never been in politics. In earlier days that was not necessary, at least not often. But the sacrifice a man makes in coming to Ottawa is much greater now; he must be there most of the year and he likes to feel that he is doing important, responsible work – 'responsible' in the sense of executive responsibility.

In choosing my Cabinet, the decisions were mine and I did not ask anyone to share that responsibility. I did, however, talk things over generally with two men who had been in my office as advisers during our days in opposition and with whom I was very close – Maurice Lamontagne and Allan MacEachen. I was very careful, however, not to consult any of my close friends who had remained in the civil service. I never brought them into my political problems, however tempting the prospect. Very conscious of the fact that I had been a Deputy Minister myself and that no other government in Canada's history had ever included so many ex-civil servants, I wanted to make sure that I did not associate with them in any way which would leave me open to accusations that the bureaucracy was advising me on purely political matters. Early in my administration I called a meeting of all those of Deputy Minister rank to speak to them about the change of government; to thank them for their impartial service over the past years, including those of the previous régime; and to encourage them to continue in that fine tradition. I have heard a lot of talk in recent years that the civil servants dominate the politicians. It was not so in my time in the civil service, and it was not so in my day as Prime Minister. I know they have great power but, in my experience, they also have a very real sense of the meaning of parliamentary responsibility. The danger is that, in spite of themselves, they may usurp functions which are really parliamentary and political. This danger has increased, not by design but almost by accident or default. Cabinet Ministers have to be very careful in this regard and it is important that a Minister and his deputy have a proper understanding of each other's roles.

I also discussed Cabinet appointments with Walter Gordon, though not in any formal or final way. There was no one at this time who had greater influence in the party than Walter and no one whom the party had greater cause to thank for its success, even though ours was not a majority success. I have dealt with the fact that he believed I would keep the party on the path of social, political, and economic reform and would pursue ends close to his own heart: greater social welfare, increased Canadian control of our economic destiny against pressures from the south; and a stronger, more vital Canadianism.

During the opposition days, Gordon used to send me memoranda on these and related subjects as we worked on policies for the new Liberal party and the next election. On 9 March 1960, for instance, he wrote that, while he could visualize, 'if the international situation were serious enough,' complete Canada-US political and economic integration, nevertheless, 'I am unhappy about the gradual economic and financial take-over by the United States, or rather by the owners of United States capital, that is taking place, and if I were in public life I expect I would wish to urge *some modest steps* to counteract what is presently going on in this direction. As I have said at other times, I would prefer us to go in one direction or the other knowing what is happening and what we are trying to do about it . . . ' He wrote about absentee ownership on 26 December 1960: 'This kind of question cannot be answered precisely or in any dogmatic way. It depends on the circumstances and how much absentee ownership we are talking about.'

On this subject and on social security I found myself in full sympathy with Walter Gordon's views. Later, when he was Minister of Finance and I was Prime Minister, these sympathies caused me some difficulty. Mr Gordon became impatient for quick and decisive action. I was anxious, in contrast, that no economic action should create controversy in our relations with the United States which could lead to mutual economic retaliation. Such retaliation could only sting the United States but could be disastrous for Canada. Similarly, in completing our social security programme, I was only anxious not to move beyond the limits of our economic resources, while he became increasingly emphatic in the expression of his views, especially after he left office in 1965. If I was more cautious than Mr Gordon, it was because, as leader, I had a duty to keep our party together, especially when an important section of it began to go against his ideas. Any successful Liberal party leader cannot align himself openly with either his left or right wing, but must keep urging both toward the centre. This is even more true when a Prime Minister has only a minority in the House of Commons and a split would be fatal, Nevertheless, my objectives were instinctively and always those of the reform and, if I may use the word here, nationalist wing of our party. This was particularly true since I could see no conflict between that kind of rational Canadian nationalism and the internationalism in which I continued to believe passionately as the only ultimate hope for the world and for mankind.

I had thought at one time that Walter Gordon would be better suited as Minister of Trade and Commerce than as Minister of Finance, because I considered his statements had alienated many people in the financial community and this might make it difficult for him in Finance. I remember mentioning to him that he might perhaps be more comfortable in another portfolio. Mr Gordon replied that it had been understood between us that he should have Finance, that he wanted it, and so it was.

I should also say a word here about the man who was to become within the year my Quebec lieutenant, Guy Favreau. I have mentioned my view of Lionel Chevrier's difficulties as Quebec leader. Some Quebec friends had urged me to try to get Guy Favreau, a former Associate Deputy Minister of Justice in Ottawa and now a highly respected and successful lawyer in Montreal, to run. I asked a mutual friend to sound him out about entering politics but he was reluctant; I was told that only I could persuade him. Therefore, many weeks before the 1963 election, I spent a Sunday morning with him in Montreal. I was tremendously impressed but soon realized that the only way to get his agreement to run was to appeal to him on the highest plane of public duty, to stress the part which he could play in retaining Quebec within an improved federation. I did not press him hard or directly. I prefer reasoning to rushing. Thus, I was quite satisfied when he said he would let me know in a few days. His reply, when it came, was a sincere but not enthusiastic acceptance. I felt a special responsibility in his case since I know that, had I not made the appeal I did, he would not have given up his very attractive life in Montreal for all the uncertainties of Ottawa. No man made a greater sacrifice in leaving private life and no man brought greater qualities of intelligence, integrity, and selflessness to public life.

All in all, I was very happy at the result of my Cabinet-making. There were five experienced former Ministers: Lionel Chevrier, Justice; Paul Martin, External Affairs; Ross Macdonald, leader in the Senate; Jack Pickersgill, Secretary of State; and Paul Hellyer, Minister of Defence. Of the newcomers there were Walter Gordon, Finance, and Mitchell Sharp, Trade and Commerce; George McIlraith, an old parliamentary hand, as was Bill Benidickson; my two colleagues in the Liberal leader's office, Allan MacEachen and Maurice Lamontagne; Guy Favreau, Bud Drury, Harry Hays, Judy LaMarsh, and others. Thus, we had our cast of players for the parliamentary drama soon to begin. Of the twenty-six Cabinet members, seventeen perforce came from Ontario and Quebec. Among them, eight had been civil servants or officials of whom four, including the Prime Minister, had reached deputy minister rank. It seemed to me that the superior quality of our Cabinet stemmed in part from the fact that we had so many experienced in government on the administrative side. Moreover, the Cabinet included a wide variety of political thought and conviction, from ardent progressivism to the most cautious approach to reform. This Cabinet was a cross-section of our society, as a Liberal Cabinet should be. That its members worked so well together is a tribute to their essential reasonableness.

At our first meeting around the Cabinet table in the historic room in the East Block we were a highly confident and cheerful group, looking ahead to a bright and productive future. Presiding from the high-backed velvet-seated, awe-inspiring chair, more like a throne, on which prime ministers had perched, or sat, or lounged since 1867, I made one innovation. I asked Mr Chevrier in French what he thought about something or other. He replied in French. I was anxious to establish at once that every French-speaking member had the right to use his own language in Cabinet if he so desired. There remained, of course, the old difficulty of converting desire into practice; if someone spoke French, only a few of the English-speaking members would understand; we certainly did not want translators for Cabinet discussions, even if this had been constitutionally permissible. Hence, though French was used more frequently in my Cabinets than before, English remained the normal language for our meetings.

I had many ideas firmly established in my mind on what I was going to do, quickly and efficiently, to organize my office and to give it a particular character. I had, of course, no real awareness at this time of the problems I had to face in trying to move forward with a minority government, especially when we became entangled in controversial legislation. I came up against a situation which, I suppose, confronts all heads of government on projects they plan to do but are not matters of immediate urgency. One tends to put these questions aside, especially if they are likely to result in any general criticism, until there is a little more time and room for manœuvre; but there is never a little more time; something else invariably crops up. For example, I wanted to reorganize the Prime Minister's and the Privy Council offices. The two work very closely together and the latter, in much of its work, is practically an adjunct of the Prime Minister's Office. When I first came to Ottawa in 1928, the Privy Council Office was small in size and clerical in its operations; it kept records of meetings, looked after Orders-in-Council, and presided over certain formal activities. The Prime Minister's Office, including stenographers, file clerks, and messengers, could not have comprised much more than a dozen. If the PM wanted special assistance he would get it from departments on an *ad hoc* basis, usually from External Affairs, of which he was also the Minister and which occupied the same building, the East Block. With the growth of government business, and its increasing centralization in the Privy Council and Prime Minister's offices, the numbers have grown considerably. I know that an increase was needed. I suffered a good deal myself by keeping my office staff to a minimum. I did make some changes in the sense that I brought in one or two more people, but I had planned to do much more than that. I never did; and there was in fact no real change in the structure of either office. Looking back now, one of the things I should have done first was to double the strength of my office and to organize it carefully. This would have saved me from some later problems and I would not have had to work quite so hard on matters of detail. No doubt with broader experience in government I might have realized the urgency of what I had in mind, but my experience had been entirely in External Affairs. Thus, although I had a very efficient and loyal staff who worked perhaps twice as hard as they should have had to, we were always swamped and were never really able to keep up with the work confronting us.

One of the most important and hard-working members of my staff was Tom Kent. He had come from England to edit the *Winnipeg Free Press* in 1954 and in 1961 joined me in opposition as a policy adviser. I also recruited, from the world of advertising, Dick O'Hagan as press officer. He served me well through trying times. Jim Coutts, a brilliant young man, was in charge of the outer office; he had been the youngest candidate to stand for election in Alberta but was wise in the ways of politics. Annette Perron was my private secretary and was invaluable, bilingual in French and English and with long experience in government. She had worked for Mr St Laurent and stayed with me in opposition. (To my good fortune, she continued as my personal private secretary when I left office for the happy wilderness of retirement.) Mary Macdonald, my Executive Assistant, had been with me since 1947 and looked after my constituency together with a good many other things, and became indispensable as my Girl Friday. Nobody ever served anyone with greater devotion. That was our office.

In the Privy Council Office I came to rely more and more on Gordon Robertson, who became Clerk of the Privy Council soon after the election. We have been very fortunate over the years in having first-class men in that job. So much depends on the Clerk of the Privy Council. He is, in a sense, head of the civil service, the key man in East Block administrative work. Indeed, I saw as much of Robertson as I did of any other person in the civil service. Certainly, I valued his advice. He attended the morning meetings in my office, and whenever I wanted anything done, anything investigated, anything reported, I could depend on him to get the relevant department to produce the information needed. However, there was never the kind of relationship between the Privy Council and Prime Minister's offices which I had hoped to bring about. That did not happen until after I left office in 1968, when these offices became more or less a team, working very closely and allocating duties between each other.

Yet, while I approve of the strengthening of the Prime Minister's and the Privy Council offices, it is disturbing to see the relative position of the civil service in Ottawa decline in relation to new administrative practices. I know that it should always be possible, as it often is wise, to insert into a civil service establishment men and women from outside, not merely because they have special qualifications but because they can bring to bear fresh insights. But if this trend becomes too pronounced, it may lead to the concentration of all power in the hands of the Prime Minister and of a few chosen Ministers and advisers. Advisers and experts can work in the security of anonymity. They can also acquire a sense of power, and even delusions of grandeur, by close and continuous contact with the political leaders, without the chastening influence of exposure to fellow MPs and, inevitably, to the electors. This is a new problem of government, more complicated and more difficult than ever before, and it requires careful examination to keep it under control.

There are one or two other things I should like to mention about the organization of government. There were special problems of which I soon became aware, problems special to a minority government. We intended at first just to carry on and to bring in the necessary legislation as though the party had a majority of twenty-five or thirty. That is what we said we would do; but we found the reality not so simple. Almost instinctively and unconsciously a minority government looks for legislation likely to get at least some support from the other parties because, naturally, if that support is not given, defeat and an election will result. For example, I very much wanted to launch at once a comprehensive and drastic scheme of parliamentary reform. What I had in mind was no mere tinkering with the existing rules. Nothing is more important in the technique of government and democratic in-

stitutions than to modernize their practices. I believe that this can be
done without destroying the spirit or the traditions of parliamentary
rule. We have all been taught at school and in our history books that
our parliamentary system, patterned on the Parliament at Westminster, is the finest flowering of human political genius. So it is, in a
sense. But it will disappear if it is unable to take care of the business of
the country. This business demands a speed-up of procedures in the
House of Commons, an extension of responsibilities of committees,
and an increase of work for private members to do. Very early in my
career as Prime Minister I set up a committee under Allan MacEachen
to bring in recommendations to these ends. But we found in this, as
we found in so many other matters, that without a majority these
changes were simply not practicable. Nevertheless, we made some
progress. We managed to get a few minor reforms accepted on a
provisional basis.

More important, we changed the whole electoral system to take
constituency redistribution out of politics. We moved to recognize in
a practical way that being a Member of Parliament is now a full-time
occupation. We decided that members should be paid accordingly.
Unfortunately, this last proposal became a matter for division in the
House although it should have been accepted unanimously. I do not
mind saying now that we were let down by Mr Diefenbaker who
decided to oppose us after we had been led to believe that all the
Conservatives would support the measure. I used to find it ironic that
our right-wing traditionalists would oppose change, especially if it
involved attempting to allocate the time of the House in some proportion appropriate to the importance of the measure (while still ensuring full debate), as a violation of the sacred rights of Parliament
handed down to us by the Mother of Parliaments at Westminster,
when that Mother, far more progressive than this child, had made
these essential changes long ago. It is not difficult to discover why, at
the end of a session nowadays, the roll of unfinished or unintroduced
legislation is longer than the legislation accepted.

The other way to tackle our problems as a minority government
would have been to work out formally or informally an arrangement
with an opposition group. There are two kinds of coalition. There is a
real coalition where positions in the Cabinet are shared and there
occurs an amalgamation of the parties for parliamentary and administrative purposes. Some in our party thought that we should try to
achieve this arrangement with the New Democratic party, and some
informal approaches to a tentative coalition between the NDP and the

Liberals were made between 1963 and the 1965 election. But nothing came of this. Again, there is a type of coalition where Opposition members will work with the party in power and attend caucus but are unwilling to take the responsibility of ministerial office. We liked to think that we were a left-of-the-road party and that most of the NDP would have been comfortable in our party, and that most of our party would have been comfortable with them. But if a coalition accepted to create a majority causes enough loss of the original party to destroy that objective, then that coalition would hardly be worth the trouble, even were it practicable. I think that the NDP would also have split over a proposed coalition. In any event, we never got down to anything beyond preliminary discussions. There were also those from the right wing of our party who approached me with regard to the other minority party in the House of Commons: 'Look, if we could get eight or nine Social Crediters over, we'd be safe.' Indeed, I talked to some of the Social Credit members about the desirability of providing this country with a period of stable parliamentary government. As with our discussions with the NDP, however, there was no concrete result.

But there were individual changes. I have already mentioned that Hazen Argue, a former NDP House leader, came over to our side before the 1962 election. He had held his seat in Saskatchewan against the Conservative tide in 1958, had gained victory as a Liberal in 1962, but was defeated by narrow margins in 1963 and 1965. When H.A. (Bud) Olson, a Social Credit member from Alberta, decided that there was no future for his party nationally, he came to see me. This was in September 1967. I encouraged him in his decision to cross the floor of the House and seek admission to the Liberal caucus. I also expressed the view that, with his experience and ability, and on the basis of his fine record in the House, he could look forward to achieving a responsible position in the Liberal party, especially since he came from Alberta where we had by then neither Cabinet representation nor members. I told him, however, that I could not make any specific commitment. He did not ask for one. I knew that he looked forward to a Cabinet post, and I told him that I saw no reason why he should not expect this eventually. In fact, it was not until after I had retired that he joined the Cabinet; in July 1968 Mr Trudeau appointed him Minister of Agriculture.

Fortunately, during my régime no member expressed a desire to leave the Liberal party (although there were one or two whose desertion I would not have deplored). This is all part of the fascination, to say nothing of the drudgery of politics. A great deal of time is expended in trying to assess the relative advantages of recruiting this member or that group. But it did not much appeal to me.

Thus, we simply carried on as a minority government and made the best of our position. I gave much thought, naturally, to the tactics we should adopt. I was not really worried about a defeat in the House during the two years after 1963. I knew that, if the combined opposition brought us down on anything but a major national issue where we were obviously acting foolishly or dangerously, they would be heavily punished by the country for forcing another election. They knew it too. One of my front-bench friends was invariably worried before each vote. He would constantly fear that we would lose it by one or two. After some hasty mental political arithmetic, I could always soothe him by assuring him we would win by two or three at least, and that his fear of losing the vote was nothing compared with the fear of some of the opposition members of winning it. And so it always turned out, except on one snap vote in 1968, on no great issue of confidence. I had often thought what I would do about such a trick vote, and shall be discussing this later.

A minority status made it important to arrange our priorities and House tactics with equal care. I was extremely fortunate in my House Leaders, the wily veteran George McIlraith, the expert Jack Pickersgill, and the 'old smoothie' Allan MacEachen. Guy Favreau was House Leader for a short time only and in circumstances unfair to him, or he would have been equally good. With the complexity and quantity of parliamentary business, the House Leader is one of the most important members of the Cabinet and should have no other ministerial responsibilities. I was in much closer touch with House business than perhaps appeared, but I left the day-to-day contact with the Opposition entirely to our House Leader, although I sometimes saw him every few hours, certainly as frequently as I saw any one else.

In addition, as Prime Minister I had the responsibility of keeping in close contact with the leaders of the other parties, particularly with the Leader of the Opposition, whose position is officially recognized, so that he would be fully informed of developing national or international crises. In the worst kind of crisis, the PM is bound to try to get parliamentary, not merely governmental agreement to a course of action. I used to meet with the Leader of the Opposition and the leaders of the other parties whenever a crisis seems to be developing. Although we never had what might be called a major crisis, we had

other kinds of crises. For example, we consulted over the flag issue to
determine whether we could work out an agreed procedure; but I
must confess that my experience of interparty consultation was not
very satisfactory. I will deal with this in more detail later; it is enough
to observe here that it was not easy to establish the kind of relationship between party leaders which one sometimes reads about and
which sometimes does exist. I think there is always a suspicion that
the PM may be informing the Opposition to blunt their criticism.
Thus, our relations with the Opposition parties were neither continuous nor very close politically. Nonetheless, I was always available
when necessary and, of course, my door was open at all times to
members of Parliament. I spent a great deal of time with members.
Naturally, the great majority of my parliamentary visitors were my
colleagues, but on occasion members from the other side would come
to see me. I felt very close to our private members and my meetings
with caucus were among the happier aspects of my political life.

During the election campaign I had criticized the Conservative
government for the mismanagement of Canada's foreign policy. I
remember saying that, if elected, I would, as a matter of first importance, visit London and Washington to re-establish good relations
with the governments of those countries. I went to London first, and
for good reason. Had I gone first to Washington, which would have
been more convenient, some would have said: 'Well, of course, he
has gone to get orders from his master.'

To go to England was thus politically sound but, quite apart from
this, I felt so much at home in London that I wanted to go there first.
So on 30 April 1963 I arrived to see Mr Macmillan and members of his
Cabinet, at least half of whom I knew personally. I had known Mr
Macmillan since my years as Secretary of State for External Affairs
and had much to do with him at various times. I have mentioned in
Volume 2, for example, our long conversation about the Suez crisis in
December 1956. I spent five days in London and had some very good
general talks, but nothing of great substance. We had not as yet been
engaged in policy decisions in our new government, and there was
little specifically to discuss. My diary for the trip reads as follows:

The atmosphere was very friendly and relaxed; especially when I was with
the Prime Minister alone.

Mr Macmillan was more concerned with talking over international and
'cold war' questions than those more specifically of United Kingdom–Canadian concern. He showed little disposition to raise trade and
economic matters in a UK–Canadian context; but only in relation to international economic affairs generally . . .

The Prime Minister was very anxious to bring about a break-through on the 'test ban' front and briefed me in detail on the approaches he and the President had made to Khrushchev. He wasn't very optimistic however. He thought Khrushchev was more or less indifferent and felt he, Khrushchev, had been out-manœuvred by the Americans in the matter of inspections.

I told Mr Macmillan that we would do everything possible to help because we considered progress on the test ban front absolutely essential if we were to get anywhere at all in disarmament negotiations . . .

Mr Macmillan was worried about the whole disarmament business being sent back to the United Nations, of whose capacity to deal with anything he seemed sceptical. He certainly is no admirer of the UN.

I tried to give him a better picture of the United Nations, pointing out that, in its present form and in spite of its faults, it reflected pretty accurately the kind of world in which we lived in 1963. There was no use in longing for the 'concert of Europe' of 1823.

The Prime Minister was concerned about the deterioration of the situation in Laos and the possibility of the United States becoming even more deeply involved in conflicts in that part of the world. He felt that Khrushchev wished to act as a brake on Chinese ambitions but he realized that Soviet freedom of action was limited by the divisions in the Communist world.

Macmillan's sympathy, of course, was all with Khrushchev in his trouble with the Chinese Communists. In fact, he thought that Khrushchev was about as reasonable a Russian leader as we were likely to get.

The Prime Minister was very appreciative of Canadian help on the Commission in Laos.

He was impatient with both India and Pakistan over the Kashmir dispute, now so closely linked to military aid to protect India against China. Lord Home [the Foreign Secretary] was even more impatient and annoyed with both the Indians and the Pakistanis. He, Home, was quite pessimistic of anything being done for better relations between the two as long as Nehru was in charge.

We discussed Jordan and the danger that a collapse of the King's position would result in an Israeli defensive-offensive occupation of the west bank of the Jordan. I put out the possibility of a United Nations move—possibly on an initiative by Canada—to extend its existing supervisory authority in this area, to prevent serious Arab-Israeli trouble.

Mr Macmillan was interested in this but not as alarmed over the situation as I was . . .

We had a good deal to talk about ways and means of strengthening NATO; and especially of NATO nuclear matters . . .

I suggested it would be desirable to avoid an open split with France on the nuclear force issue at the forthcoming Council meeting in Ottawa; that a formula should, if necessary, be found to postpone any decision and conceal a real breach. The Prime Minister seemed to agree, but Lord Home on Saturday was more aggressive and thought NATO should push ahead for an immediate decision and ignore any negative French attitude. I demurred, as I was not convinced of the necessity for an *immediate* decision of any kind – unless there was unanimity.

Macmillan was very friendly; relaxed and unworried; 'unflappable.' He anticipated lots of trouble domestically and internationally but thought that things would work out all right; that there would be no war; and that he might even win the next election!

During this visit I also took the opportunity to meet with the Queen, who kindly invited me to spend the night at Windsor Castle. That evening, as I was leaving the dining table with her, I was handed a telegram. We stopped and I asked permission to read it as it was doubtless of tremendous importance. It read: 'URGENT SAVE OUR VILLAGE WE ARE TO BE DEMOLISHED FOR PARKING GERRARD VILLAGE ASSOCIATION TORONTO.'

Following my return, I went to see President Kennedy for two days. He had asked me not to come to Washington but to Hyannis Port, where we could have a more relaxed time and still get through the same kind of business. As it turned out, the surroundings were very informal and most agreeable. Hyannis Port is a pleasant place at any time, and particularly in May.

It was a stimulating experience to be exposed to the charm of Kennedy's personality and to the toughness and clarity of his mind. When talking business with our advisers around the table, he did not waste any time but went right to the heart of the problem, a very satisfying procedure when decisions have to be made. I had, of course, met the President before, at the Nobel Prize winners' dinner in 1962 and once when he asked me to have a talk with him while I was in Washington about his impending trip to Vienna to meet Khrushchev. Apart from these occasions, there was his 1961 trip to Ottawa when, as Leader of the Opposition, I was invited to the official dinners at Government House and the United States Embassy and to the Prime Minister's luncheon at Sussex Drive. I had never corresponded with him when I was in opposition. This would not have been proper, nor would he have wanted me to write to him on policy matters. I might add, however, that I had been long attracted to John Kennedy. In 1959 he had written an extremely complimentary review of my book, *Diplomacy in the Nuclear Age*. It seemed to me that anyone who valued my literary efforts must possess some special quality.

This trip, as that to London, was not meant to establish anything beyond a good personal relationship, and in this it succeeded. I think one of our less serious chats (I will deal with the business side in the next chapter) may have had much to do with it. The President had been told by the American Ambassador, Walton Butterworth, that baseball was a great hobby of mine. The President may have treated this information sceptically, knowing as he did that politicans must throw out ceremonial balls from time to time. Perhaps my hobby was 'political' baseball rather than the real thing. In any event, he had on his staff a personal confidant, a shrewd Boston Irishman named Powers. Powers was famous not only for his statistical infallibility on past election returns but also on baseball. I suspect that John Kennedy must have primed him to bring up the subject at dinner on our first night at Hyannis Port. I love to talk baseball and so we tossed batting and earned run averages back and forth, with Powers throwing a few curves at me and my answers showing that I knew something about the sport. Then he mentioned a game played in Detroit the year before in which, he claimed, the pitcher had thrown a no-hitter and nonetheless lost, an almost unheard of event. I was able to fill in some of the details: the pitcher had not allowed any hits but he was pulled in the seventh inning, and the relief pitcher had let in the winning run in the tenth. I was able to add: 'As a matter of fact, the reliever was Ken MacKenzie.' Powers was somewhat incredulous, so at my invitation he sent someone to check it. I was proved right and my reputation was established once and for all in that group, although the only reason I knew this particularly obscure fact was that Ken MacKenzie was a Canadian who lived in Gore Bay on Manitoulin Island in my constituency. Indeed, I had helped to get him into professional baseball. I am not sure whether or not President Kennedy was impressed by my grasp of North American and international affairs, but I certainly know that Powers was impressed by my knowledge of baseball.

It is a great advantage for a Canadian Prime Minister to be on such good and informal terms with the American President that he can, if necessary, simply pick up the telephone and call him. It is here that our relationship with the United States is unique, though no doubt the Prime Minister in London may phone the President occasionally. But this kind of closeness has its dangers; it may appear to domestic critics that we are too close. After all, the United States is our problem. There is also (and I do not want to be misunderstood in saying this) another disadvantage: to have the President of the United States telephone to ask you a favour can be rather startling, as I found out later with Lyndon Johnson.

As I was leaving Hyannis Port, Kennedy walked with me down to

the beach, where a helicopter was waiting to take me to our plane at
Boston airport. It started to rain. Though I wore a raincoat, he had
neither coat nor hat and was getting soaked. I suggested that he take
cover, but he said: 'No, I want to give you something when we get to
the helicopter.' At the end of the driveway the Presidential flag,
flown wherever the President is in residence, was at the top of a
flagpole. He lowered it while the rain pelted down, rolled it up and
handed it to me as a gift. I thought this a very agreeable gesture,
though it may have surprised a few of his staff, and I am not at all
sure that it was accepted protocol to hand over the Presidential flag to a
foreigner. It was a good start to a very warm relationship, ended too
soon by the tragedy of his death.

On my return from Hyannis Port, four days before Parliament
opened, I was much concerned with the Speech from the Throne.
This was to be a short first speech, bilingual by alternate sections – an
innovation – outlining some of the things we would undertake in the
first sixty days of the session and beyond. Part of that speech read:

... Unemployment, on the serious scale of recent years, is therefore the most
urgent of our domestic problems. To provide the many new jobs that are
needed every year, we must create new industries. The fiscal and monetary
policies of the government will give priority to the encouragement of soundly
based industrial expansion.

Provision will be made to assist labour and management to make manpower adjustments required by technological and other industrial changes.
The special assistance for technical training will be extended in co-operation
with the provinces.

Other measures will be put before you to assist in increasing production
and employment in Canada.

You will be asked to provide for the early establishment of a department of
industry, which will foster industrial expansion and provide a central point to
which industry can look for consultation, a stimulus and assistance. It will be
proposed that, within the new department, there will be established an area
development agency. This agency will work with the provincial governments
and other organizations to co-ordinate programs for parts of the country
where, because of chronic unemployment, a special thrust for development is
needed.

Amendments to the Atlantic Development Board Act will be proposed, to
strengthen the board and to provide for a capital assistance fund through
which it can promote basic projects in the Atlantic region.

You will be asked to establish a municipal development and loan board,
through which municipalities may obtain, with the approval of the provinces,
loans and grants to carry out projects which will increase employment and

improve services. Amendments to the National Housing Act will also be proposed.

A measure will be placed before you to establish a Canada development corporation, by means of which Canadians can more readily direct their savings to the building of new Canadian industries and to increasing the Canadian ownership of existing industries, which is one of the important objectives of the government.

A measure will be placed before you to establish an economic council of Canada, in order to assist the government, industry and labour to develop means of ensuring in Canada the highest possible levels of employment, of efficient production, and of sustained growth for our economy . . .

Towards the end of May, I outlined my feelings of that time in a letter to my son Geoffrey at the Embassy in Mexico City:

. . . Things are going well with us in Parlt & Govt – but, of course, it is still a honeymoon and the drab conflicts of housekeeping are only beginning. But one thing I know, that I am going to be happier, more comfortable and more effective in government – than ever I was in opposition. The problems are agonisingly difficult and complicated but we have a chance to do something about them – instead of criticising others for not doing anything or doing the wrong things. Psychologically, this makes all the difference to me. It means that though I started in right after the election and have had no let up, I feel fine, full of energy and without any need of a holiday; yet if I have had any success so far it is in the field of intangibles, creating a better climate for Canada both at home and abroad. Morale really is higher now – especially in the civil service. We have a very efficient managerial govt – and we will not lose touch – as in 1956 and 57 – with public and parliamentary opinion. There will be no arrogance in this administration if I can prevent it . . .

Most important among our early decisions was that we fixed June for the presentation of the budget. As soon as he was appointed Minister of Finance, Walter Gordon conferred with me about the budget. He set 13 June as the earliest date to bring it down. Though the Minister of Finance recommended this date, it was my responsibility to approve or reject it. In fact, we needed much more time and we should have taken it. I might add here that, before moving on to our own fiscal measures, we first had to pass the supply or appropriation bill for the last year of the Diefenbaker administration, 1962-3. I agreed that there was no point in our being recriminatory over these administrative expenditures. Our position was, 'Let what was spent in the last year of Conservative government be approved and done with.'

Naturally, I did not know how Walter Gordon was going to accomplish the financial task he had set himself; that was his job. He worked on our budget almost exclusively during those weeks. He was working hard against time, and to help him he brought in three technical financial experts from outside the government. I was not aware that these men had been engaged, yet do not think I would have questioned Gordon's action if everything had been done correctly. Unfortunately, although he had his special advisers sworn to secrecy as temporary officials, he allowed two of them to remain on the payrolls of their companies. To recruit outside assistance was not in itself improper, although unusual. This was not, however, the best way to show confidence in the budgetary establishment of the Department of Finance. To have these three outsiders come into the holy of holies in the department and work closely with the Minister on the budget caused, I am sure, a good deal of fluttering in the civil service dovecotes. Perhaps Gordon would have been more content to work with his permanent officials had I been able to make Bob Bryce immediately available to him as Deputy Minister of Finance. Bryce's transfer from the Privy Council Office had been promised Gordon during the election and was made effective as soon as we could. However, these things cannot be done overnight (to say nothing of Bryce's reluctance to change jobs). I now wish that his move had been sooner since he did not approve of some parts of that first budget and no doubt would have been forthright in bringing his views to Gordon's attention. Still, I had no knowledge of any trouble.

The time came, about a week or so before the budget went to Cabinet when, in accordance with normal procedure, I was shown in the course of two meetings the important aspects of what the Minister of Finance was proposing. It was then that I learned he had these outsiders, whom I knew to be good men, to assist him. I did not attach any great importance to this since I assumed that the procedure followed had been thoroughly correct and that officials of the Department of Finance were working normally with the newcomers. I could not foresee that the Opposition would later cast the darkest of suspicions around the engagement of these men who, they claimed, had been recruited in deepest secrecy. When I went over the budget memoranda with the Minister of Finance, I had some doubts about one or two of their provisions. Although I am not a great financial expert, I wondered whether the proposed 30 per cent takeover tax was not too harsh, might cause a great deal of trouble, and that perhaps its administration would not be practical. Together with other measures, the takeover tax was intended to begin the process of reversing the trend to United States domination of the Canadian economy. In this instance, a 30 per cent tax was to be levied on the sales of shares in listed Canadian companies to foreign corporations and individuals. My reservations prompted me to ask: 'Do you mind, Walter, if together we see the Governor of the Bank of Canada and perhaps the Deputy Minister of Finance?' I did not press the matter of the Deputy Minister of Finance since that could have been regarded as a lack of confidence in the Minister himself. In any event, the Deputy Minister would never have said anything with his Minister present, nor perhaps should he. In contrast, the Governor of the Bank of Canada has a more autonomous position, and I was anxious to get Mr Rasminsky's views on the draft budget proposals. Mr Gordon seemed quite content to have this talk with the Governor of the Bank, and showed no reluctance that I should ask the Governor about these matters in his presence. At lunch on 31 May, therefore, we went over the draft budget with Mr Rasminsky, who knew all about it. His advice had presumably been sought earlier. I asked the Governor if he would let me have a copy of the *aide memoire* he had prepared for his own use at the meeting.

He wrote that the economy would continue to expand over the next year, aided by growth in the United States, devaluation, increased investment, and business confidence in our government. The magnitude of unemployment and the unused capacity of the economy justified, in his view, the size of our proposed deficit—indeed, the essential task, given the government's concern with unemployment, was to keep the economy expanding. Although he was in basic agreement with the general accounting of our budget, Mr Rasminsky was seriously worried about three proposed measures.

He did not like the proposal to reduce from 15 to 10 per cent the tax on corporate dividends paid to non-residents by companies over one-quarter Canadian owned, while increasing it to 20 per cent for companies with greater foreign ownership. Such a move might be regarded as hostile to foreign investment and could cause withdrawals of foreign capital which the balance of payments could not stand; a new exchange crisis could arise which would be harder to deal with than the one in 1962; and a reduction in investment by foreign controlled corporations would adversely affect the growth of the economy. For these reasons he advocated that we not raise the withholding tax on corporations with less than 25 per cent Canadian ownership, but that we lower it to 5 per cent for corporations over one-quarter Canadian owned. Mr Rasminsky preferred the carrot to the stick, as he put it.

The proposed increase in the corporation tax, he considered, would discourage private investment and encourage unnecessary and wasteful expenditures at a time when our goal should be to promote the efficiency of industry, provide jobs, and improve the balance of payments. Rasminsky also disapproved of our intention to levy a surtax on income, largely because this could drive young Canadian executives and professionals to the US where rates were substantially lower.

These were the main points in the Governor's *aide memoire*. He went on to criticize other features of the budget which he disliked, including our proposed 30 per cent tax on certain foreign takeovers. The business community regarded the government as competent and business-like; such a move as the takeover tax risked changing that assessment.

This was the kind of honest, central-bank economic appraisal that I would have expected, with one exception. In view of the fury of opposition that the takeover tax aroused and, as I learned later, the unanimous opinion of the financial establishment in the civil service that it was ill-conceived, wrong, and impracticable, I think those views should have been expressed strongly to the Minister by those who were advising him and felt that way or, in this case, to the Minister and me by the Governor of the Bank. There comes a time a civil servant (Mr Rasminsky was not one) should oppose his Minister to the point of resignation if he feels a matter of principle and national importance is involved. This did not happen in consideration by the civil service experts of Mr Gordon's budget. This may be due to the tradition of civil service propriety: advise and, if it is rejected, implement what your political chief has decided to do. In this case, reticence may have been encouraged by Mr Gordon's recruitment of the three experts.

Mr Gordon stood firm on his budget and it was introduced in the House on 13 June. I remember that night so well. This was his first budget, a great and dramatic occasion. He was given a tremendous ovation, I recall, from our side when he rose in the House, and so he should have. This, therefore, was a very special day for him. It is the custom of the Minister to invite to his office those who were engaged in the budget's preparation and a few friends to drink the health of the budget just launched. Our party was elated as befitted the occasion, even though there was an under-current of uneasiness over the first major move of the new government. We were right to be uneasy. Next morning the first hint of the storm broke upon us. The Opposition were able to make the recruiting of the three financial experts seem pretty sinister. They claimed that this was contrary to all constitutional practice and that it would have been quite easy for these men to leak budget secrets. Two of them were members of financial businesses in Toronto and, while they were never charged with wrongdoing, their connections were built up beyond all proportion, an unfortunate development especially when the budget itself came under fierce attack a week later.

Seldom has a budget been so universally condemned, with the thrust of the attack against the tax designed to protect us from American takeovers. It was not the purpose that was attacked but the amount of the tax, which was castigated as impracticable and unfairly discriminating. I do not think I have ever known in my years in Ottawa anything quite so violent and so bitterly hostile to a particular clause in any budget.

We knew that we were in trouble, although trouble is nothing novel for a government. This was the end, however, the quick and almost catastrophic end of the honeymoon; usually there is a little more time to adjust than we had. Walter realized at once the crisis confronting us. As the responsible Minister, he had been the principal target of the counter-fire. I remember his coming to see me soon after to discuss what should be done. I said: 'Well, we'll have to think it over but it seems to me some changes are going to have to be made if we're going to get out of this.' We were a minority government and could not ride out the storm without making concessions. There were telephone calls, letters, telegrams, people clamouring to come and see me. It is not true that we allowed our policies to be dictated by the open letter from the President of the Montreal Stock Exchange, Eric Kierans. His was just one rather hot-headed Montreal reaction. I do not recall that his letter was of any greater importance than many others. Nevertheless, it was clear that we had to do something about the budget: withdraw or modify it.

After a full Cabinet meeting one evening at Harrington Lake to consider what budget changes should be made, Walter came to see me in my office and stated: 'I want to offer you my resignation.' I had seriously considered its acceptance, if offered, and asked: 'Have you lost confidence in yourself?' In spite of having endured a pretty shattering experience, he replied: 'No, I haven't.' I responded: 'Well, just carry on. We'll get over this by making the changes that have to be made.' And so we did. But all this made Walter's dealings with the financial communities much more difficult thereafter. Indeed, I suspect that Walter's main anxiety about staying on stemmed from his belief that he had completely alienated the confidence of Canada's financial communities, many of whose members held him in slight regard and had not at all wanted him to be Minister of Finance. Some would have taken any opportunity to get rid of him; thus, they seized on the budget, exaggerated its impact, and tried to get me to agree that my government could not survive with him in Finance. To that I paid little attention. In fact, one reason for our esteem of him at that time was that he had shown himself a very progressive member of the financial establishment. I thought, however, that if this incident was an insuperable handicap, he should be given an opportunity to change to another ministry. He was a truly progressive liberal, who had long before the budget offended the financial community with some of his views.

I have been accused of not adequately supporting Gordon. In fact, in the House of Commons I told George Nowlan, the Conservative financial critic, that, as Prime Minister, I took full personal responsibility for the budget. On 9 July 1963, in response to a letter from Senator Tom Crerar in which he was highly critical of Walter Gordon and the budget and in which he suggested Mr Gordon be removed from Finance, I wrote:

... With much of what you write, I am in complete agreement, though I would not go as far as you suggest with regard to the position of the budget or of the Minister of Finance. Mr Gordon, notwithstanding the way in which the budget was handled and certain of its provisions, has a very strong position in the Caucus and in the Party and a forced withdrawal from the government at this time, under pressures which reflect on his personal integrity as well as on his ability, would bring about a serious split in the Party.

Mr Gordon admits that certain of the budget provisions have to be altered and his statement in the House of Commons last night embodied that admission. This was not an easy thing for him to do but it is the right thing to do and the changes, I believe you will agree, are good ones.

I think you will also agree that the budget has, at least, achieved the 'shock' purpose which you mention in your letter. It has underlined the fact that, if we are to reduce the deficit, we will have not only to reduce or eliminate unnecessary expenditures, but also increase taxation. It also has underlined the fact that it is easy to talk about saving the Canadian economy from American control but that, once concrete measures are put forward to that effect, some of those who talk the most, oppose most strongly any action proposed.

I think we will get out of this budgetary difficulty and I earnestly hope that we have learned something from the mistakes we have made. The basic mistake for which I take full responsibility, was to have attempted to produce a budget at all in such a short time. Adequate preparation was simply not possible and Mr Gordon, new to his job and to parliamentary politics, suffered accordingly . . .

It has been argued that had I kept a tight and disciplined rein on my colleagues, our government would have been much more effective. This may be so, but a man does these things in his own way. More often, from my own experience, it is preferable to exercise a loose and flexible control, to rely on consensus rather than on compulsion, except in those rare emergency circumstances when one man must act, and act quickly. I do have a weakness or a strength, whichever way you look at it (and that is perhaps one reason why I first went into the diplomatic service), of examining every side of a question before coming to a decision. I am no Lord Beaverbrook. He used to pick up the phone, as it is no doubt accurately alleged, during the Second World War when he was Minister of Aircraft Production and say, 'Yes, go ahead and do it,' before he was told what it was the person wanted done.

I gave my own views on leadership to a party gathering in 1966;

I have never believed that the political arena is primarily a place for blood sports, nor do I believe that political greatness is to be measured by a capacity to create debating confusion. I do not think that results, and those are what we are seeking to achieve, flow from rhetoric, but from facing up to facts and acting according to requirements those facts impose upon us. This does not mean that you should see things only as they are, not as they can be.

I have no illusions about my infallibility or my indispensability. I have not the divine certitude that I am always right or that I am one who has been called on by God to save the country. I even admit that I can see both sides of a question when, as is usually the case, there are two sides, unless there are four or five. That, I admit, is a great handicap for a political leader. John Kennedy once pointed out that it is the politician who sees more than one side of a question who has a depressing and a worrying time. On the other hand, a politician who can see only one side of every question, and who stubbornly digs himself in on that side, can, if it is wrong, lead his party and his country to disaster.

Remaining firm and immovable in a bucket of hardening cement is nothing to boast about.

Political leadership is to be steady, not stuck. In politics, as in any group activity, leadership is persuading people to work hard and loyally with you, and for you, in a good cause. It is getting the right things done, even at the price of conflict or controversy.

So, I hope you will pardon me for saying that I hope my leadership will not be judged by the excitement generated by partisan conflict and controversy, but by a record of achievement; by what I have helped to do to increase the unity and the well-being of the people of this country.

I have learned—I suppose it goes back to my parsonage origins—that the triumphs and the failures of political life, the hottest partisan debates that command the top headlines, are seldom of enduring importance. The real trends and the big changes that determine human events flow too slowly, too far below the surface, to be readily marked by day-to-day reporting or to be affected by day-to-day political in-fighting. It is a man's relation, and it is a party's relation, to these enduring trends and changes which advance or retard the progress of a nation, that really count. And it is by this that we should all be content to be judged.

I knew well the continuing fascination, as well as the occasional folly, of politics. I knew that it was no ivory tower and that it meant working and fighting in the human arena, where there was often dust and dirt, but always action. I was no mere spectator exhorting others to score. I could be as competitive a performer as anyone, and I did play hard to win. While I believed, and often said, that to deserve success was more important than to achieve it, I could fight hard for that achievement and be bitterly disappointed over failure. I knew that in politics, as in sport, and indeed in life, there is no substitute for true success, honourably gained.

5

CANADA-UNITED STATES RELATIONS

Before we took office in April 1963, there had been some measure of personal alienation between Mr Diefenbaker and President Kennedy and, in consequence, some mistrust between the two capitals. This was a breach illustrated by the now famous 'Kennedy Memorandum' of May 1961, prepared for the President on tactics to be followed during his visit to Ottawa. The memorandum came to Mr Diefenbaker's attention and attracted wide publicity, not to say notoriety. When I was at Hyannis Port, the President brought up the matter, and I recorded the following on 17 May 1963, after my return to Ottawa:

The President remains deeply disturbed by the action of the Canadian Prime Minister in keeping this document and even more disturbed by the publicity given to it and the misrepresentations made about it. The latter have gone so far as to state that there was an abusive reference initialled by the President in the margin.

The President assured me that there was no such writing in the margin by him and he finds it difficult to understand how this story could have been circulated.

Our meetings at Hyannis Port, of course, ranged over many topics. Canada's Ambassador, Charles Ritchie, and the United States Secretary of State, Dean Rusk, came up from Washington. The American Ambassador in Ottawa, Walton Butterworth, was also there. Since there were some outstanding difficulties to consider, an informal agenda was prepared for our meeting; although this was not an official State visit, we were able to cover a lot of ground. I particularly remember our discussions of the Columbia River Treaty. I had been advocating the renegotiation of the treaty for some time. In a political telecast to British Columbia while still Leader of the Opposition, I stated our position as follows:

It's either a question of renegotiating or letting the Treaty lapse. Surely the former would be a good thing for the Canadian government to initiate, because the American government is not likely to do it, to initiate renegotiation of a Treaty which in its present form I think is too favourable to the United States.

I think there are two respects in which the Treaty could be renegotiated. One, there should be an alteration in the time schedule of the construction of the dams which I think is too favourable to the United States. The Mica Creek dam or the Arrow Lakes dam should be postponed.

The other respect in which a change should be made before ratification is that the price of downstream power should be established in the Treaty before ratification.

Now I let the President know that we would not submit the treaty to Parliament in the form signed by the previous government. There would have to be changes. The President agreed, and I left a memorandum suggesting what alterations might be incorporated in a protocol. Of course, the Columbia River Treaty negotiation is a long story and need not be told here.

The variety of topics covered in our discussions can be seen from the agenda prepared for Friday afternoon:

Prospects for disarmament and the abolition of nuclear weapons tests

US-Canadian defence matters

Defence production sharing

Proposals for development and further utilization of channels of communication and consultation between the United States and Canadian governments

Forthcoming trade negotiations in Geneva

Inter-allied nuclear force and multilateral force

Great Lakes shipping dispute

and for Saturday morning:

East-West relations

Latin America

Columbia River

Oil

Lumber

Fishing (including Law of the Sea)

Campobello Island

Laos

Communiqué

We also agreed that other topics could be raised either during the working sessions or at meal times.

I am happy to say there was no breach in our relations with the United States during my period as Prime Minister (although, once or twice, I would have been glad to have had a little more elbow room). There were, of course, difficult issues, but our governments remained on good terms.

The problem of Canada–United States relations is always with us, and in consequence requires both historical and contemporary international perspective. Today's relations between countries have to be considered in the context of the devastating changes that have taken place, and will continue to take place, in man and his world. It is not easy to draw the right conclusions from events which, almost before we know of them, are made irrelevant by new and further events. But some factors appear almost to be constant. I have recently been reading my notes and speeches from over the years on Canada-US relations. In January 1932 I wrote:

The relations of few countries are as intimate and important as those between Canada and the United States. It is certain, furthermore, that these relations will become even more intimate and more important as the Dominion grows in population and power, and as the United States becomes more conscious of that growth than at present. It is, of course, true that they loom far larger in the eyes of a Canadian than of an American. That is natural. The United States is a great power with interests and contacts in every corner of the globe ... Canada, on the other hand, as an international unit, is at the very beginning of her career.

The obvious influences in our relationship such as our common language, our common inheritance, geography, history, trade, those things which are the inevitable ingredients of every public utterance on this subject, may be dismissed with mere mention, along with the four thousand miles of unguarded boundary and the hundred years of peace. . . . That said, it would be unwise to imagine, because Canadians are similar to Americans in so many respects, either that they are similar to them in all or that this similarity is going to make relations any easier in their day-to-day conduct.

May it not be true that American influence on Canada, far from really Americanizing the Dominion, is one of the strongest forces making for a Canadian national consciousness? One must, of course, fully recognize the tremendous force that one hundred and twenty million cannot fail continually to exert on ten million and realize that Canada must react in some way to that force. But it can be argued that she more often reacts against it than in favour of it. Canadians have, to put it crudely, Americans right on top of them and so constantly about them that if they would survive as a separate people, with their own definite characteristics, they are forced to emphasize the fact of their own existence and of their own separateness . . .

It may be expected that the relations between the two states will become increasingly important and that the problems arising therefrom will grow in number and in magnitude. The very similarities of the two people and the intimacy of their contacts will promote such problems, while making easier, it is to be hoped, their peaceful solution . . .

Today, as then, the United States is our obsession. In earlier colonial years our obsession was Downing Street, and for the same basic reason: concern over domination by, and dependence on, another government. Today this concern is even more disturbing and frustrating. We like to think of ourselves as strong and free and are worried that we may have gone merely from the colonial frying pan into the continental fire.

This is a natural enough preoccupation, and unhealthy only when we allow it to degenerate into morbid self-doubt and fear. Worry about the Americans and their friendly pressures is still probably the strongest unifying Canadian force. At a time when some of us are in doubt about the nature or even the reality of a separate Canadian identity, whether we are one nation or two or more or none, we can stand shoulder to shoulder, one thin but unbroken red line facing Washington and proclaim: 'No surrender,' even if there may be no certainty about what we are not surrendering. The Americans have no idea of the psychological help they have given us in the resolution of our national problems merely by being there, big, powerful, and overwhelming. This may at times, however, lead to inconsistencies bordering on the absurd. I once read a stirring editorial call to arms against United States penetration of our Canadian way of life, while on the same page there were contributions from three American but no Canadian columnists.

We should, to use the words which got me into controversy in 1951, accept the fact that 'the days of relatively easy and automatic relations between our two countries are over.' Back in January 1943, in a Town Hall radio programme in New York, I put it this way: 'As Mr Churchill would say "we're all mixed up together . . . and this mixing up will . . . increase . . . This increasingly close relationship will be of increasing mutual benefit if it is based on sound principles."' The first principle I mentioned in that radio programme was one we still have to recall to Americans: 'The recognition of Canada as a nation in its own right—one that is not merely an extension northwards of the USA or westward of Great Britain; one equal in status with the USA, controlling its own policies, as free as any sovereign state can be in an interdependent world but one which has no intention of confusing co-operation with absorption.' These many years later, while I would not change the substance of what I said in 1943, I might put it differently. I would point out that while states are equal in status, some are more equal than others, that in any event the "most equal" has not complete control of its own policy nor is it completely free. I might also admit that the confusion between co-operation and absorption is not always the fault of one side alone.

There are certain principles in our relationship which apply more particularly to Canada. One principle is that we should exhibit a sympathetic understanding of the heavy burden of international responsibility borne by the United States, not of her own imperial choosing but caused in part by the unavoidable withdrawal of other states from certain of these responsibilities, or, if you prefer, from imperial power and privilege. Above all, as American difficulties increase we should resist any temptation to become smug and superior: 'You are bigger but we are better.' Our own experience, as we wrestle with our own problems, gives us no ground for any such conviction.

In recent years the risk of all-out world war seems to have lessened. As one result, we have become more critical of some aspects of US foreign policy. It is natural to wish to talk and act differently from the dominating power. This is to be expected and should not be resented on one side or abused on the other. Often, however, our criticism of specific American policies reflects our worries and frustrations about our general relationship, and our schizophrenic love-fear attitude. We have to reconcile a friendly intimacy toward the Americans (and the admitted and cherished benefits of our special economic relations) with our indignant rejection of political union or cultural oneness, and with our anxiety that increasing dependence could lead to absorption. Worse still, we might finally become Americans who have a vote only in Canada. If we can be charged with being charter members of the International Order of Sidewalk Superintendents, in everything the Americans are constructing or demolishing, this is understandable. We have good reason to know that almost everything they do will affect us, whether our attitudes or our well-being.

Canadians should be clear on what independence can mean at this time, on this continent, in this world. Independence clearly cannot mean our complete determination of our own destiny. It cannot mean freedom from United States influence or pressure. For us, indeed for any country, independence must be restricted if there is to be international co-operation and peace. As I have already noted, it is relative and limited, even for the most powerful. For us, independence can mean only the right to take decisions in our own country, through our own procedures and institutions, not only by governments, but by unions, companies, professional associations, and even by the Canadian Football League. Within these limits, we are in some measure independent, but other decisions, if taken by us alone, would be futile, as on global or nuclear war, and they would be dangerous and unwise if they ignored the facts of geography and power and the legitimate security concerns of our neighbour.

For example, we have the right to become a neutral or uncommitted state, but this would ignore the implications of our geographical and strategic position for the defence of this continent, including the United States half, as well as our interlocking economic relations. Neutrality would not give us a stronger voice for peace in the world nor greater security against war. I cannot see any adequate compensation for the disadvantages of neutrality. This does not mean that in the 1963-8 period we did not take a hard and searching look at our defence and foreign policies, especially in their bearing on the United States and the Atlantic Alliance. While we moved immediately to conclude a bilateral agreement with the United States covering the acquisition of nuclear warheads for the Bomarc, Voodoo, CF-104, and Honest John equipment of the Canadian forces, we also established a non-partisan House of Commons Committee to review the whole structure of Canadian defence policies. We had pledged ourselves to acquire these warheads to make our weapons systems effective, but we were also pledged to negotiate a non-nuclear role for Canada in NATO and NORAD, if that seemed best for our future. I remember my satisfaction when I visited the Canadian forces stationed at Marville, France, in January 1964 and I was able to assure our forces that this government would never ask them to do a job and then withhold the means of doing it. I also remember wondering whether we should be there at all, and if there were not some more effective contribution we could make to peace and the common defence.

Canada has its own role to play in the world, which it could never play as a satellite. We have our own values to develop and to offer, our own identity to realize as something worth preserving. These things can be done, but not by mirrors or miracles, or by considering our relations with the United States as a matter for rhetoric rather than realism.

The world of 1963 was not the world of 1948. But it remained a dangerous world for the weak, the unwary, and the unwise, even if policy for security had no longer to be based on the over-hanging and immediate threat of a powerful, aggressive, monolithic communist conspiracy, centred in Moscow and controlled by Stalin. Unhappily, while collective arrangements could now be based on something more constructive and lasting than fear, fear remained the strongest incentive to effective international co-operation. As fear diminished, so did the pressures for effective international organization for peace; and so did the willingness to accept without too much questioning United States leadership of the alliance for collective security.

Fortunately, during my prime ministership there were no international alarms comparable, in terms of Canadian concern, to the Korean War or the 1956 Suez crisis. Certainly, we could not and did not ignore the situation in Cyprus or the Arab-Israeli Six Day War of 1967. And always, there was the war in Vietnam. But my principal preoccupation in foreign affairs was with our bilateral relations with the United States.

I have already mentioned my trip to Hyannis Port and this was the beginnings of my friendship with John Kennedy. Our joint communiqué at the end of that important meeting concluded with these sentences:

Our two countries will inevitably have different views on international issues from time to time. The Prime Minister and the President stressed the importance of each country showing regard for the view of the other where attitudes differ. For this purpose they are arranging for more frequent consultation at all levels in order that the intentions of each Government may be fully appreciated by the other, and misunderstandings may be avoided.

These preliminary discussions between the President and the Prime Minister will lead to a good deal of additional activity for the two Governments over the next few months. It is expected that there will be almost continuous exchanges of views during that period as work progresses in resolving many matters of concern to the two countries. Then, in the latter part of the year, meetings will be held of the Joint Cabinet-level Committee of Trade and Economic Affairs and on Defence.

The Prime Minister and the President look forward to a period of particularly active and productive co-operation between the two countries.

It was only six months later, on 22 November 1963, that I rose in the House of Commons to express the feelings of shock and grief that accompanied the news of the attack on the President's life. I was expressing our sympathy and conveying our prayers to the wives and families of the President and the Governor of Texas and was just about to express our fervent hope for their recovery, when I received a message that President Kennedy had died at 2 o'clock. It seemed almost unbelievable. We could only share in the outpouring of grief throughout the world for this young man and for all he meant to us.

During the next four and a half years while I was Prime Minister of Canada, Lyndon Baines Johnson was President of the United States. I did not know him before his succession, but afterwards I not only saw a good deal of him, but heard a good deal from him. Our first meeting, at John Kennedy's funeral, was brief. Following it, on 3 December 1963, I sent him a handwritten letter:

Dear Mr President:

I have been wanting to write you since my return from Washington – it was a sad visit on a sorrowful occasion – to thank you for your courtesy in receiving Mr Martin and myself, for giving me the opportunity of talking with you and of establishing from the beginning, as I am sure we did, that kind of friendly relationship which is not only so agreeable in itself but will, I know, help us both to maintain and to strengthen the friendly relationships between our two governments and peoples.

I know it had been a long day for you, exhausting both physically and emotionally, which makes my appreciation of your kindness and consideration all the greater.

May I confirm in writing what I tried to say to you then; my warmest good wishes and heartfelt prayers as you take on the heaviest and most responsible governmental burden in the world. With this goes my sincere wish to co-operate and be of help in any way I can, not only in respect of relations between our two neighbouring countries, but in international affairs generally.

In a very real sense you are the leader of all the free democracies as well as President of the USA and we who have also positions of responsibility in our own countries should be only too anxious to assist you in any way we can in discharging your wider responsibility.

I would like to add, if I may, an expression of my deep admiration for what you have said and done since becoming President. Your words, and even more the spirit behind them, gave to me as they must have given to multitudes, outside as well as inside your own country, faith, hope and encouragement at a time when it was so greatly needed after the tragic loss of your predecessor, a loss which had an impact so heavy and so universal.

May I repeat the assurance of my good wishes and my admiration at the way you have 'taken over.'

My next encounter with the President was in January 1964 following my visit to Paris and General de Gaulle, of which I shall write later. The friendly, easy, and comfortable atmosphere of Washington and the White House was as different from Paris and the Elysée Palace as Lyndon Johnson was from Charles de Gaulle. On the evening of our arrival we attended a dinner with the Johnsons and the Rusks at the Canadian Embassy. There was the usual exchange of gifts — too many I felt — including an RCMP saddle and blanket for the President. He looked at the saddle sceptically and indicated he preferred the western variety, but perhaps 'Lady Bird' might use it. The President was preoccupied throughout the dinner and not too forthcoming; he seemed worried. I noted: 'Perhaps it was Panama [the Americans were having serious troubles over the Canal Zone] or Bobby Baker [a political scandal then breaking around one of his associates].' The toast he proposed indicated how little he really knew about Canada, as he merely repeated what he had said in his welcoming speech at the White House: that our border was undefended, that there had been 150 years of peace between us, and that our good neighbourliness gave an example to the rest of the world. Perhaps these were the only facts about Canada in the Texas school books. But the President did not pretend. He admitted he knew nothing about us, which, I thought, was perhaps the better way to begin knowing.

After dinner, he relaxed. We got together in the corner of the library with coffee and brandy — he liked both — and the others left us alone for a few moments. He wanted to know about the trip to Paris, about de Gaulle, and particularly what I thought about France's intention to recognize the People's Republic of China. I told the President that de Gaulle had made up his mind and was not one to change it; the United States should accept the decision and play it down. I told him they would be making a big mistake if they made it a subject of conflict, even though I knew how much they disliked it. I had told de Gaulle he must expect the US reaction to be strongly critical and, therefore, if he was going to act, he should do so quickly before the American presidential election campaign was really under way. Recognition was bound to be a political issue, but less so in January 1964 than if the French acted three months later. I was very relieved when President Johnson agreed that the thing to do was to accept the decision and minimize its importance, if possible. He asked me why I thought de Gaulle had taken this action. Was it merely to irritate the Americans? My diary records my reply and the rest of our conversation:

I said I was sure this wasn't the reason. He claimed he liked Americans, appreciated their power, accepted their leadership, though he was going to be no satellite.

But in the China matter he was simply recognizing facts— being logical. He had told me he was certain that there was a deep dispute and distrust between China and Russia, far deeper than ideological differences, and surely it would be helpful to have a French Embassy in Peking to follow events.

But why now? insisted LBJ.

Partly because France wanted to restore her influence in China and especially in South East Asia – at a time when the Americans, he thought, were making a mess of things in Viet Nam. General de Gaulle thought genuine neutrality was the best future for the new states there and that France might be able to influence Communist China to accept this and keep out.

I agreed with LBJ that de Gaulle would soon be disillusioned on this score of Communist non-intervention. But I also felt that recognition was not an irrational act and we should not react too strongly against it in North America; especially if, as seemed the case, he had persuaded Peking to accept recognition without France breaking with Formosa.

LBJ was, of course, very worried about the political consequences of French recognition but took it much more calmly than I expected. More so than Dean Rusk did.

They are worried about a chain reaction from French recognition and wondered what we would do in Canada. I made no commitment but said that we would take no action without consulting them, as we appreciated the importance to them of the issue.

The Americans had come a long way in their attitude towards Red China. I recall an incident that perhaps illustrates this change. It occurred during the Geneva Conference of 1954. There, the Americans wished neither politically nor socially to recognize the Chinese delegation. At the first tea break there was some fraternization among the delegations. The Chinese, however, were off by themselves. Not even the Russians were with them, though at that time there was no breach between them. They looked rather sad, isolated. Chester Ronning, who knew them all from his days at our Embassy in China in the late 1940s, said: 'Come, let's go over. I want to introduce you to Chou En-lai who's a friend, and some of the others.' I agreed, and the Chinese seemed very grateful that somebody recognized they were there. I had a pleasant talk with Chou En-lai, in the course of which he invited me to the great villa that they had taken for the conference (we were staying in the old Hôtel de la Paix). My later call on him was greeted by the Americans with consternation. They did not like it at all. And General Bedell-Smith, who was the American delegate, let me know that I was letting the side down badly by such normal fraternization. He felt it was wrong to let the Chinese feel they had any friends at all in the Western camp. This was the conference where the Vietnam settlement was worked out and the International Control Commissions for Vietnam, Laos, and Cambodia were set up. We were asked to be a member of all three commissions. Incidentally, as a small footnote to history, when I left to go back to Ottawa, Chou En-lai sent me a beautiful book of Chinese brush-paintings on rice paper; it has remained one of my most cherished possessions.

A discussion at the 1956 Commonwealth Conference (not mentioned in the official communiqué) further indicates how unyielding American opinion on China had been in those days: this was on the recognition and acceptance in the United Nations of China's Peking régime. I recall that Mr St Laurent, in responding to an effective and balanced statement by Nehru in favour of the seating of Red China, pointed out that little progress could be made because of the position taken by the United States, and that this was particularly so in an American election year. He went on to describe the strong views which President Eisenhower had personally expressed to him against recognition on moral grounds. While Mr St Laurent could not explain the feelings of the American people on this subject, he was certain that they did exist and that a too hasty effort to force a change on them would meet with a reaction so great that the United States might actually withdraw from the United Nations. For Canada, the possibility of the United Nations existing without the presence of the United States was a matter of greater significance than the incongruity of having the vast majority of the Chinese people represented at the UN by the Nationalist government. We could only hope that the attitude of the administration, Congress, and public opinion in the United States would not persist indefinitely. It was a matter of waiting until after the American election and then proceeding very carefully in seeing what could be worked out. And none of us knew how long that would take.

To return to my visit with President Johnson, one thing that particularly upset the Americans was the discourtesy of de Gaulle in neither discussing his China policy in advance nor in bringing it before the NATO Council. I noted in my diary:

De Gaulle and Couve de Murville [his Foreign Minister] both insist, however, that the Americans had been warned before that something was likely to happen. The Americans say they were not so warned.

This is the kind of misunderstanding that arises with allies who hint but don't inform. Later, when action is taken, the hint is considered on one side to have been information and, on the other, to have been nothing. So bad faith is alleged.

Another example of this was in the suggested meeting between de Gaulle and the President.

There is no doubt whatever that the President is convinced that he had received a specific assurance from de Gaulle, when he was in Washington for Kennedy's funeral, that he would pay an official visit to Washington in the spring. Therefore when de Gaulle curtly indicated a few weeks ago that LBJ could meet him in Martinique en route to or from Mexico, Johnson was surprised and annoyed. But perhaps de Gaulle never felt he had made any such commitment to visit Washington. Who knows?

LBJ assured me that he was not a touchy man and never stood on protocol (that certainly is true) but that he could only meet de Gaulle in the USA this year. This is due to the fact that, without a Vice President and with the requirements and responsibilities of atomic action in a grave emergency, only the President could act and therefore he *had* to stay at home. This was also the reason he gave me for his inability to accept my invitation to visit Canada during 1964, much as he would like to. This explanation rings true but I wonder if they have given it to the French or have merely indicated a negative and annoyed reaction to what is considered rather arrogant discourtesy on the part of the French President.

The formal meeting on the next day, 22 January 1964, had hardly begun in the Cabinet room at the White House when the President announced he was going to let the experts settle all our mutual problems while he took me next door to his office for a private chat. That talk lasted over an hour, part of which was spent walking in the garden on a lovely spring-like January morning. Our conversation covered the length of the agenda and more. I do not think the President was too well briefed on some of the items and therefore may have thought it better to talk alone. I kept the following record of our conversation.

He began by asking my views on the international situation generally, and China and South East Asia in particular, and I gave them along the lines of our policy already laid down – and which, as a matter of fact, we had discussed the night before.

I was impressed by the President's calm and moderate approach to cold war problems, except Cuba and Sukarno [then President of Indonesia].

He was really irritated about the British sale of buses to Castro, especially at a time when they were asking him to cut off all economic aid to Sukarno because of his aggression against Malaysia. He was inclined to do this because he thought Sukarno was (here he used some very rough and profane words, really let his hair down, treating me as if I were a friendly Congressional visitor). The 'boys in the State Department,' who were supposed to be experts, were strongly advising him against cutting Sukarno off as it would just drive him into the arms of the Communists and facilitate a Communist take-over. But just as he was arguing the British case with State, then the British 'slap him down' by helping Castro. He didn't think much of this and he would like my advice on what to do. I suggested I didn't have all the facts but perhaps he should reduce Indonesian aid, but not cut it off completely—and see what happens.

We then got on US-Canadian economic problems: [such as balance of payment problems, trade and tax measures, GATT negotiations, etc.] . . .

I warned him that we were going to have lots of problems and difficult ones in the days ahead. I mentioned especially the trouble in the Great Lakes over the SIU [the Seafarers International Union, and its president, Hal Banks] . . . I thanked him for the help they had already given, mentioned the new AFL-CIO-CLC discussions that were beginning and expressed the strong hope that a solution would be found. But any solution must admit our right to clean up our SIU without harassment from the parent labour union in the USA.

In our talk on economic and balance of payments difficulties, I discovered he was very keen to get a working group set up to see if we couldn't agree on some principles as 'guide lines' to our economic relations with each other. George Ball [then US Under-Secretary of State] is pushing this but there is no doubt Johnson is behind it too.

I expressed approval in principle but thought there would be difficulties in finding the right formula; one that would be certain to do more good than harm.

There were two other matters I brought to his attention, the undesirability of restricting our exports of oil and the desirability of removing the restrictions on imports of our base metals.

The first, of course, interested him particularly and he told me of the sad plight of the Texas independent oil producers! I told *him* of the dire plight of the US Venezuelan oil exports to Canada if, as a result of US restrictions, we had to divert oil to Eastern Canada at the expense of US Venezuelan oil. This was an aspect of the matter that hadn't been brought to his attention.

The President expressed concern over our automobile parts arrangements. He said this would get him into difficulty with a lot of small manufacturers of motor parts and cause unemployment. He seemed to think that the closing down of Studebaker and its transfer to Canada (which astonished him) had something to do with our action. I set him straight on this and on the nature and purpose of our action.

We also had a few words about the forthcoming Kennedy round talks and I gave him the Canadian policy on this. I was encouraged by his own views.

It was a good talk. Once or twice the President flattered me by throwing away diplomatic proprieties and using language which showed he felt very much at home!

On the whole, however, he was quiet, confident and relaxed, in spite of the current difficulties.

The talk we had around the table later with the others lasted only a few minutes, but I took the opportunity of mentioning particularly our resolve to go ahead with a twelve-mile fishing zone and made clear our hope that there would be no opposition from Washington.

The White House luncheon was a very pleasant affair; the American guests were mostly Congressmen, many of whom I knew. It amused me to watch LBJ politicking. He stopped most of the Congressmen who were passing through the reception line to gossip about some bill or to invoke their support for something or other. I noted later: 'He doesn't miss a trick. But how long can he work so hard at being head of the state, head of the government, head of the party and its Congressional manager? He works about 16 hours a day now and will not be able to keep it up. But it is in the political manoeuvring that he excels. Here he is more effective than Kennedy was, at least vis-à-vis Congress.'

We said goodbye to the President at 4 o'clock and later in the day had a drink with Dean and Alice Acheson. Dean was in great form. He was an admirer of Johnson, who, he thought, would be another Truman: a 'man whom you can trust, who keeps his word, and has shrewdness and courage.' He certainly preferred him to Kennedy, whose apotheosis made Dean cynical and annoyed. He was wrong about Dean Rusk (whose appointment by Kennedy was on Acheson's recommendation) when he said that the problems were getting Rusk down and that he was not tough enough to last. Personally, I thought Rusk seemed happier with the new President than with Kennedy.

That evening we had dinner at the Embassy with our Minister, Basil Robinson, and wife and my old friends, the Restons. Scotty was, as always, fascinating on the Washington scene. He agreed that the President was living and working at too fast a pace and, if he was not careful, would wear himself down. There was obviously a real danger as there was nobody, as Vice-President, to share the burden. My last diary entry for the trip was for Thursday, 23 January. It read: 'To Florida—and did I ever look forward more to a holiday? No!'

My next major meeting with President Johnson was a year later when we visited his ranch in Texas. In between, however, I saw him twice in New York when I was there on speaking engagements. Before one of these occasions we had an hour or so together in a hotel room while he was dressing for dinner, the President speaking in that sulphurous language he used when talking confidentially. If he was on good terms with you, he might use you as a sounding board for whatever was on his mind that day, give you hell or praise you, all in equally strong and unconsidered language. He was certainly a very earthy and very vigorous man. We met again in September 1964 at Great Falls, Montana, for the formal ratification of the Columbia River Treaty; after this I had the pleasure of taking him from Great Falls on an aerial tour of the Columbia River Basin. This was a very interesting plane ride, as he had brought along some Senators, among them Bill Fulbright. Talk about smoke-filled rooms, the way they spoke to one another! I was aware of that sort of thing up to a point; but I had never been exposed to quite that kind of relaxation of the presidential aura. Then we went on to Vancouver, where we both enjoyed sharing a platform with Mr Bennett for further ratification ceremonies. We soon found out that, while I was the head of the Canadian government and Mr Johnson was the head of the American government, in British Columbia Mr Bennett was the head of all he surveyed.

Then came my visit to the famous LBJ Ranch deep in the heart of Texas. We landed on a new runway right on the ranch, exactly at the appointed hour, 4:00 PM on Friday, 15 January 1965. The rambling old ranch house was surrounded by planes, jeeps, trucks, communications towers, and security people, with the Pedernales River running past the front door. President Johnson and Lady Bird were awaiting our arrival. As we mounted a little podium before a battery of TV cameras, the President and I were a study in contrast. I was properly ceremonial (dark suit complete with a boutonnière) because I was officially visiting the President of the United States; he was the Texas cattleman, splendid in ranch clothes. But the President welcomed me very warmly and greatly enlivened the ceremony by ending his remarks: 'and we are so happy to have Mr Wilson here with us.'

Before anything else, the President insisted on giving us a tour of the ranch. I did not get to my room to unburden myself of my black Homburg for two and a half hours. What an experience, from the microphones to golf carts, and from the carts to a helicopter for a fifteen-minute flight over typical Texas hill country, to see deer, armadillo, and anything else that might be about. Meanwhile, though it was only 4:15, we had to have a drink on the helicopter. When we landed, we transferred to a cavalcade of cars. Five of us—President

Johnson, Paul Martin, Dean Rusk, 'Mac' Bundy, and I—were in the first car driven by our guide, the President's friend and financial manager, Judge Morrison. The second car was filled with security chaps and staff, who had the liquor as well as the guns. Then came the ladies, followed by a photographer riding with Lady Bird's own secret service man.

It was a desolate but strangely fascinating country, dry, rocky, with some trees and enough grass for cattle and sheep. There were deer all right, dozens of them, although I fear they could not uphold the Texas reputation for bigness, only one-third the size of the deer in Algoma East. So on went our cavalcade. We had constant telephone communication between all the cars, with the President making certain Lady Bird did not miss anything.

It was nearly six o'clock when he phoned his wife on the spur of the moment to say 'Lady Bird, let's have the Connallys to dinner with the Pearsons.' Governor Connally was in Austin, the capital of Texas, about a hundred miles away, so Lady Bird suggested, 'Well, don't you think it's too late, dear?' Time and space proved no barrier to the President, who told the operator to get the Governor: 'John, I want you to meet the Pearsons. I'll have a helicopter there in twenty minutes. Bring the wife, OK?' I could not hear what the Governor was saying, but he obviously was not enthusiastic. LBJ settled it with what, in effect, was an order: 'You've lots of time.' More phone calls to helicopters, wife, kitchen, and it was all arranged, while we continued cruising through the countryside, with three pit stops for drinks, and one or two to admire the scenery.

The dinner at the ranch was as informal as a farm meal back in Ontario's Chinguacousy Township. More drinks; the arrival of the Connallys, obviously great friends of the President; yarns about politics (the President was an incomparable political raconteur); men coming and going, although whether they were valets or Congressmen or assistant under-secretaries was always doubtful; the phone ringing, the fire burning, and finally dinner served Texas style. We had soup, followed by steak and catfish on the same plate (the blessing before the meat), and, once the meat was finished, dessert, regardless of the progress made by others. It was all very homey and unpresidential, perhaps a little too much so, even for a ranch. The President had a phone at the table and took a call there, speaking for about five minutes, which effectively prevented anyone else talking. Afterwards, we straggled out into the living-room, the President bringing up the rear, more or less. General MacArthur would definitely not have approved, nor, I suspect, John Kennedy.

We talked shop, some very important shop. The ladies sat and listened or exchanged gossip while the President and Secretary of State of the United States and the Prime Minister and Secretary of State for External Affairs of Canada dealt with Canada-US relations, the United Nations, Communist China, Vietnam, and the cold war. At ten o'clock the news came on. Mr Johnson had four television sets, so he could get every network's version. He wanted to see it all. He especially wanted to see the coverage of my reception that afternoon. I knew his gaffe was coming up as did the others, but the President did not. He was listening very carefully to his little speech, in which he called me his 'old friend,' when he saw himself refer to me as 'Mr Wilson.' He was completely bewildered, apologized profusely, and explained that Prime Minister Wilson had paid him a visit not long before. I retorted by saying: 'Think nothing of it, Senator Goldwater!' For the rest of the visit 'Senator Goldwater' was not allowed to forget his performance.

The next morning I arose early to find LBJ and Mr Martin up ahead of me. Paul looked very cheerful as he told me that he had had a wonderful talk with the President, clearing up a lot of things. He explained that he had been thirsty and had gone down to the kitchen in his pyjamas and dressing gown to see if he could find a glass of milk. In came the President, also in pyjamas and dressing gown, looking for a cup of coffee, whereupon the two of them had an hour's talk on the state of the world, sipping coffee and milk by the dawn's early light.

While Paul and I were with the President, Dean Rusk brought in the overnight telegrams. We rose to leave, but were urged to stay, look at the messages, and join in the comment. I wondered whether any other two government leaders had that kind of free and easy relationship. 'Mac' Bundy was also there, obviously a very trusted adviser with great influence. He talked very frankly to the President, which I thought was particularly good for LBJ, surrounded as he was by people who wished to please and do his will, people clearly over-awed by the 'Divinity that doth hedge a President.'

After telegrams, breakfast. And what a meal it was—hominy grits, highly spiced sausage *specialité du ranch*, toasted home-made bread with marmalade, and gallons of coffee. As I told LBJ, if I had been willing to serve my country by drinking vodka all night with Khrushchev and Bulganin, I could hardly balk at eating hominy grits for breakfast with the President of the United States.

Outside, with the temperature well below freezing, we got on with the official purpose of the visit. In front of newsmen made cold and miserable by a hundred-mile bus ride from Austin, we signed the agreement for free trade in automobiles and auto parts.

The signing of the Auto Pact raises the question of our economic relations with the United States. There was (and is) a growing popular concern in this country over American economic penetration and business takeovers. Almost 40 per cent of the over 2500 business takeovers and mergers in the sixties were promoted by foreign, mainly American, interests. I regarded this trend to American domination of Canadian resources and the Canadian market as an urgent problem that we, or any government, would have to deal with. We could have controlled United States investment in Canada in any way we wished, including total prohibition. But no responsible Canadian government would take measures which would, either directly or by the inevitable American reaction, do us far more harm than good. Independence must rest on strength and policies discouraging foreign investment could weaken us. But contrary policies, while increasing our economic strength, could also ensure that this stronger Canada would be controlled economically, and hence ultimately politically, by the United States. This does not have to happen. We can reconcile these difficulties—and in a way which should give us the best of both worlds. To do so, we need to receive the kind of special treatment that we have enjoyed in Washington, while making clear to our American friends that this is not a matter of grace and favour but something to which we are entitled by the nature of our trade and financial relations with them, and from which both countries benefit.

As for the automobile industry, I do not think the trade arrangement ran counter to our anxiety about increasing American control of Canadian economic development, because we gained considerably in an economic sense. The automobile agreement did not in any way exacerbate the problem of US intervention in our industrial affairs. This was an industry which was already 99 per cent American-controlled; there was no Canadian-owned automobile industry. The Auto Pact's real economic advantage to Canada was confirmed from the first by the way in which the Senate of the United States reacted to it. They wanted to scrap it or have it amended.

In other areas, we tried to work out principles which would govern the general problem of foreign investment. We established guidelines for American companies to follow as good Canadian corporate citizens. In our first budget we had moved to reverse the trend toward absentee ownership of Canadian resources and Canadian companies, to hold back foreign takeovers, and, in some respects, to penalize foreign investment through our tax policy. The measures put forward in that budget managed to create a great deal of irritation and anxiety in financial circles in the United States. (I have already mentioned the adverse reaction in Canada.) We had further intended to proceed with the creation of a Canada Development Corporation, as promised in our first Throne Speech. Indeed, at Hyannis Port I had informed President Kennedy of our intentions. I explained that the purpose of a Canada Development Corporation would be to help Canadians buy into industrial companies in such a way as to forestall any legitimate criticism from the United States. As I recall, the President listened attentively but refrained from comment.

Unfortunately, the difficulties over our first budget and the atmosphere of controversy surrounding it tended, quite naturally, to push the creation of this corporation down on our priority list. We had not worked out adequately in advance the details of its operation, nor had we consulted the provinces. Further, there was basic disagreement in Cabinet over the whole idea, and I have a feeling that even Walter Gordon, who throughout remained committed to action, may have felt that 1963 was not the right time to press too hard for it. (Gordon was not quite so emphatic about these things then as he is now.) Thus, this project was not dealt with at all during the first session. My own view was that the Canada Development Corporation was desirable. It could make available Canadian funds under public control to assist in preventing foreign takeovers and might be helpful for Canadian development generally. Unfortunately, it became one of those important measures that had to be reserved for future consideration.

Throughout my period in office, there was an increasing demand in some circles that we take action to discourage further the development and expansion in Canada of American corporations by limiting foreign stock ownership in Canadian companies and the proportion of directorships held by foreigners. My preference, however, was to deal with these problems as they arose, to concentrate on specific cases. We were determined to treat United States investment in Canada with scrupulous fairness, while seeking to remove any threat to our right of independent decision. But even so, we still had some very unpleasant episodes with Washington, as indeed our predecessors also had, over interference in the export operations of American-owned Canadian subsidiaries.

In determining what could be put forward as government policy to deal with American influence on the economy, all proposals had to be integrated with our commitments to tax reform and, in particular, to the recommendations of the Carter Commission on Taxation. To get the expert analysis needed and then to transform these complex considerations into legislation was no mean task, especially for a minority government. We had to be very careful every day not to be defeated in the House of Commons and we were often preoccupied with flags, scandals, and other distractions. The result was that tax reform, like the Canada Development Corporation, fell by the wayside.

We did, however, do something to protect our Canadian banking and financial institutions. The Mercantile-Citibank Bank question, a continuing problem during most of the five years when I was in office, remains in my mind as perhaps the most notable example of our problems with American ownership and our approach to them. Our difficulty was to hold a middle line between non-action and over-reaction against pressures from the south to weaken our separate identity, however friendly and even profitable to us these pressures may have been.

The Mercantile Bank affair was a proposal for the purchase by an American banking corporation, First National Bank of New York City, of a Canadian incorporated bank. The Mercantile Bank was very small, but could be transformed into a much larger and more profitable operation if owned by the New York bank in question. We had come to the conclusion that there were certain institutions of Canadian economic and financial life that must never be allowed to fall under foreign control. Citibank, or more particularly its head, Mr James Stillman Rockefeller, was made very much aware of our position in November 1963, before his bank's acquisition of Mercantile. They ignored our warning, relying on US official pressure to maintain them in Canada as a purely US bank. We, however, stood firm and forced them to sell 75 per cent of the shares in Mercantile to Canadians. I might add that seldom have I been on the receiving end of stronger representations, almost offensive representations, than those from some of the officials of this bank. As for Canadian bankers, a number stood in fear of retaliation against their operations in New York if they supported us against Citibank. On the other side, I had to resist the pressures of those who were not satisfied with forcing Mercantile's shareholders to comply with the law, to sell 75 per cent of its stock to Canadians and thus remain a Canadian bank, but wanted the Citibank interests thrown out of Canada completely.

I remember receiving David Rockefeller at dinner one night at Sussex Drive. I had known him for many years, as well as other members of the family. David, a second or third cousin of James, was also a banker, the head of the Chase Manhattan Bank. There were just the two of us at dinner that evening. He believed Canada was following a discriminatory, short-sighted, chauvinistic policy in the banking field. He pointed out that they had no trouble in their banking operations in other foreign countries. But here, with their best friends and closest neighbour, they could get nowhere. He was hoping to get some control and eventually, I suppose, total control of a Canadian bank, and had already taken certain steps in that direction. I replied: 'Well, there is no use in your going any further. Don't make an issue of this. We've already got one bank we're having trouble with.' We had legislation pending to limit the percentage of non-Canadian ownership in banks. This would have put an end to all foreign efforts to get control of Canadian banks. I continued: 'Forget it, because neither you nor anyone else is going to get us to change our position.'

Under my government a thorough examination was made of the whole area of our economic development, especially our economic and financial relations with the United States. When Walter Gordon rejoined the Cabinet in January 1967 (a matter discussed in Chapter 8), I appointed him head of a Cabinet Committee to pursue this examination. I let the Cabinet know why, in my view, such an investigation was necessary. I pointed out that our concern about the alleged threat to Canada's continued independence that was posed by the control of certain of our key industries and resources by non-residents of this country was a matter of public record, both as a government and as a party. This concern was mainly with the dominant position enjoyed by a number of large wholly-owned Canadian subsidiaries of foreign corporations. The operations of the vast majority of foreign-controlled business enterprises in Canada were relatively unimportant in this context.

In some circles it was felt that conditions similar to those imposed in other countries upon the extent to which foreigners may invest in their important industries should be introduced in Canada. In this connection, however, the division of powers between the federal and provincial authorities was not always recognized or understood. There was also a strong feeling in other circles, including members of the Liberal party, that if any action were to be taken in this matter it should be positive rather than restrictive, that the emphasis should be on incentives to prospective Canadian investors rather than measures that could be construed as penalizing foreign investors. This might be largely a question of presentation—an incentive to one man may be a penalty to another—but it was important that this be kept in mind. A further consideration I raised was the danger that legislative action, which could be interpreted as being discriminatory, would be resented both by many Canadians and by foreign investors whose governments might be in a position to retaliate against Canadian interests.

Quite apart from the question of ownership of existing Canadian corporations was the considerable misunderstanding about the importance of constant inflows of foreign capital if Canada's economy is to flourish. In some parts of the country there was a genuine and understandable fear that any restrictions on capital inflows would result in a slow-down in resource development and employment opportunities. These fears must be recognized and dealt with.

Another factor to be considered in this broad context was the concentration of the powers of ownership in single hands—domestic or foreign—in the case of large corporations which wield a leading, and in some cases a dominating role in their respective industries. This might or might not be in the public interest. But certainly the emerging structure of industry, both in Canada and in other countries, including the growth of the so-called international corporations, ran counter to classical economic theory respecting free competition in a market economy.

In view of the widespread interest in and the public concern about these matters, it was desirable that the government should study the matter thoroughly and in the light of that study take whatever action was appropriate. The resulting Watkins' Report was published early in 1968; most of its recommendations were sensible, although a few were quite impracticable.

There were, of course, aspects of United States pressures other than the economic and financial. I have always considered that in the long run a more serious danger to Canadian identity is posed by what we may call cultural pollution or cultural imperialism, although ultimately what we take from the United States in these areas is dependent on our own maturity and our sense as a people. There is no question of establishing a cultural boundary between Canada and the United States; no such boundary is possible, nor is it desirable. Yet, without limiting the free flow of information and opinion, some safeguards are necessary. We must ensure that the Canadian media are not allowed to fall under foreign control. We came up against this problem very early in our administration in connection with what I regarded as journalistic dumping of Canadian editions of American magazines. Our already troubled periodical press found it extremely difficult to compete with magazines whose editorial content was, in effect, provided free by their United States parents.

The problem was not new. In 1956 the St Laurent government introduced a special excise tax on the value of advertising material in special Canadian editions of non-Canadian periodicals. This was done to protect Canadian publishers threatened by the loss of advertising revenue to the very popular Canadian editions of *Time* and *Reader's Digest,* and to discourage other such special editions. That tax was repealed by Parliament in 1958 on the recommendations of the Conservative Minister of Finance, Mr Fleming. A Royal Commission was established in September 1960 with Grattan O'Leary as chairman to consider the whole question. It reported in May of 1961.

The O'Leary Report reached the conclusion that a genuinely Canadian periodical press could exist only by assuring it a fair share of domestic advertising. A 'Canadian' periodical was defined as one published in Canada, owned by Canadian citizens or by a company incorporated under the laws of Canada, and edited in Canada by a staff normally resident in Canada. The report made two major recommendations:

1 that the deduction from income by a taxpayer of expenditures incurred for advertising directed at the Canadian market in a foreign periodical wherever printed should be disallowed;
2 that the entry into Canada from abroad of a periodical containing Canadian domestic advertising be banned under the Customs Act.

The Diefenbaker government took no action before its defeat, although it had placed resolutions on the Order Paper in 1962 and early 1963, the latter exempting the Canadian editions of *Time* and *Reader's Digest* from the proposed measures.

When we came into office, we were under strong pressure from our magazine industry to save them from what they considered would be very early extinction. They were particularly wrathful about the Canadian editions of *Time* and *Reader's Digest* which in 1963 captured 47 per cent of the advertising placed in all consumer magazines printed in Canada. But a solution was difficult. While we might improve the chances of Canadian magazines, there was no way in which we could ensure their survival. A study of the problem, carried out at my request in the fall of 1963, indicated that given the inroads made into advertising revenue by television and newspaper weekend supplements, the magazine industry was in trouble everywhere. Further, any restrictive action was bound to affect our relations with the United States.

Nevertheless, we came to the conclusion in Cabinet that something must be done. Despite the reservations of the Department of Finance, we moved to discourage future Canadian editions of US magazines by disallowing tax deductions for advertising along the lines suggested in the O'Leary Report. In doing so, I believe we stopped the entry into Canada of several American publishers who had hoped to follow *Time*'s lead. We did consider that there was a practical distinction to be made here between the future and the past. Over the years *Time* and *Reader's Digest* had put out their Canadian editions without interference; they had staff and plant in Canada and had plans to broaden the basis of their Canadian editions. So we decided that, on balance, we would exempt them from our legislation. Contrary to some reports, the exemption of *Time* and *Reader's Digest* was a decision quite unrelated to our negotiation of the Auto Pact with the United States.

In the course of relations between countries, relative advantages and disadvantages tend to find their own balance. For example, on 12 March 1964 the President phoned me from the White House to tell me of their great anxiety over the delay in establishing the UN peace-keeping force for Cyprus. The situation was rapidly deteriorating and the UN should act quickly. Could we help? I do not like talking on the telephone about important matters but I told him we had already agreed to participate, in spite of some doubts about the way the force was being organized, financed, and administered; that we would move a battalion by air to Cyprus as soon as the force was constituted. Therefore, the situation could only be resolved at the UN, not by us.

He asked if we could move before UN formal action was taken. I said no, but that there would be no delay once Secretary General U Thant was able to act. The immediate difficulty was in securing the participation of a third and fourth nation on the force. With only Britain and Canada this would not be a genuine UN operation; with one or two others, it could be so justified. I emphasized that we would not wait until the other participating members were ready, once they agreed to participate. (It might take them an additional two or three weeks to get their troops to Cyprus.) We would have our men on the way by air as soon as we got the go ahead. I said not to worry; we knew our duty to the UN; we knew the danger of war breaking out there very, very quickly between Greece and Turkey (Turkish forces were already on a troop ship ready to leave). The President seemed reassured and very grateful.

Once the UN did move, our troops were on Cyprus within twenty-four hours. Indeed, they were en route before Parliament even authorized their dispatch, although we could and would have brought them back if we had not been given authorization that night. President Johnson was amazed and filled with admiration at our ability to act so quickly, and I think this may have changed his attitude toward Canada. He phoned me again the night we began our airlift to say: 'You'll never know what this has meant, having those Canadians off to Cyprus and being there tomorrow. You'll never know what this may have prevented.' Having praised us for our action, he concluded: 'Now, what can I do for you?' I replied: 'Nothing at the moment, Mr President.' But I had some credit in the bank.

This sort of credit caused the President to be sensitive to our interests in other areas. To illustrate by way of yet another telephone conversation, on 9 February 1965 the President called to say they had a problem about balance of payments and he was sending a message to Congress which affected us, though he hoped they had found language that could take care of our major difficulty. The President wanted to tell me about those parts of his message that concerned us before, as he put it, 'I tell my own folks here.' His proposed message to Congress included this sentence: 'To stop the excessive flow of funds to Canada under a special exemption from the equalization tax, I have sought and received firm assurance that the Canadian government will take the steps needed to hold these outflows to levels consistent with that special exemption.' My record of our conversation continued:

The President: 'I think this language merely reaffirms the existing earlier Canadian undertakings but I think it is of great importance to use it. The fact is that we will have to impose such a limit if Canadian reserves continue to grow.'

I said I appreciated his difficulties, as I hoped he appreciated ours. In a narrow technical way we may have contributed to them, but, in the broad sense, we had helped, rather than caused, their problems in this field. Any action against us would remind Canadians of our own unfavourable balances with the United States. I added: 'I am grateful to you for letting me know in advance and I will take the matter up with our people here right away so that they will know what is proposed.'

The President said he was explaining the matter to me first and then he would tell the Japanese later and might put in a sentence or two for them that they could agree to.

The President then asked me if the language of the message seemed repugnant to me. I replied: 'It may seem all right to me but I am not an expert and, as you know, language means so much in this particular matter. I will consult the Minister of Finance immediately and, if he has any feeling about the language, he will get in touch with your Secretary right away.'

The President: 'Point out to them that, if I am to avoid the enormous pressures to set a straight dollar limit for Canadian borrowings, I have to use this language. We will have to impose this limit if the reserves continue to grow. I'm trying to get by with the language. It's better for both of us. It's the best way to do it. I am going to meet my leaders at 4 pm; the message will go up tomorrow. If for any reason I shouldn't use this language, get your people to phone Doug Dillon [the Treasury Secretary].'

I immediately telephoned the most important paragraphs from the President's message to the Minister of Finance, while Gordon Robertson got in touch with Mr Rasminsky, the Governor of the Bank of Canada. We concluded that we should try to get the wording in the President's message changed as, in its present form, it could be unfair and damaging to Canada. We therefore revised the key passage to read: 'To prevent any excessive flow of funds to Canada under its special exemption from the equalization tax, I have sought and received firm assurances that the policies of the Canadian Goverment are and will continue to be directed toward limiting such outflows to levels consistent with the stability of Canada's foreign exchange reserves.' At my suggestion, Robertson then phoned Dillon to try to get our version accepted. Dillon agreed with the revised Canadian text, with a change in the last line to read: ' . . . a stable level of Canada's foreign exchange reserves.' This was quite satisfactory to our people.

These examples show something of the relations between the United States and Canada. They also show something of the use of the telephone which, to repeat, is not the best medium for the conduct of foreign policy. On balance, however, I think that in our case the advantages were greater than the disadvantages. I recall some published comments that attempted to make rather suspect my close relationship with the United States President and the Secretary of State, how I had a 'hot line' to Washington and all that. The hot line was only a technical requirement, once we had settled our nuclear arrangements with the United States. I had to be available for immediate contact with the President of the United States over one thing, and one thing only – the use of nuclear weapons on Canadian soil. These weapons could not be used without the approval of the

Canadian government. So I had to have the line available wherever I went. I even had it installed in my car.

There was a story that the only time I ever used the hot line was when I was travelling north from Ottawa one winter, when the car went off the road and got stuck in the ditch. The story goes that I used it to phone Washington to get the people there to phone somebody in Ottawa to send a tow truck, with the implication that I was so much under the influence of the United States that I needed the White House to rescue me from the ditch at Harrington Lake. In fact, I did use the hot line, but just to call Ottawa – it was the only available phone.

℘

On the broader international level, we were disturbed in 1967 by the worsening situation in the Middle East and the resultant Six Day War. Things were not as they had been in 1956 and, as I explained to President Johnson during his visit to Canada in May 1967, I could see no UNEF rabbit to pull out of the hat this time. As it turned out, following U Thant's decision to yield to Nasser's demand for the withdrawal of UNEF from Sinai, the crisis quickly resolved itself in war and to Egypt's disadvantage.

The war in Vietnam was, of course, a far different matter, with the ever deepening involvement of the United States and the resultant complication for their role as leader of the Western World. When I visited President Kennedy at Hyannis Port in May 1963, he was obviously worried about Vietnam and stated that it was the 'very place where we should like not to be. But how do we get out of there?' That, of course, was the continuing question. In the early period of my prime ministership, I could do no more than urge caution and moderation on the United States. Occasion to do this arose more than once. The following memorandum indicates the process:

Secretary Rusk phoned me tonight, August 4th, 1964 on instructions from the President, to tell me that North Vietnamese torpedo boats had again attacked US destroyers 65 miles off the Vietnam coast. The US had decided to retaliate against this unprovoked attack but would ensure that the retaliation was 'relevant' to the provocation and to the attack.

I thanked Mr Rusk for letting me know. I understood that they must feel strongly about the attack but I expressed the hope that the retaliatory action taken would not be in excess of that which the circumstances required; would be limited in scope.

Mr Rusk assured me that they would not go beyond what was required; that action would be 'relevant' to the aggression.

The following year I tried to answer the question in a more positive fashion, when I made my 'stop the bombing' speech in Philadelphia on 2 April 1965. I had gone there to receive the Temple University World Peace Award and in the course of my remarks said:

In this tragic conflict, the US intervened to help South Vietnam defend itself against aggression and at the request of the government of the country that was under attack.

Its motives were honourable; neither mean nor imperialistic. Its sacrifices have been great and they were not made to advance any selfish American interest. US civilians doing peaceful work have been wantonly murdered . . .

Obviously the situation cannot be expected to improve until North Vietnam becomes convinced that aggression, in whatever guise, for whatever reason, is inadmissible and will not succeed. I hope that this conviction is growing in Hanoi, though I admit that there are no signs of this at the moment. I hope they also realize that the only alternative to a cease-fire and a mutually acceptable settlement is chaos and disaster, and that North Vietnam would be a primary and tragic victim . . .

The dilemma is acute and seems intractable. On the one hand, no nation – and particularly no newly-independent nation – could ever feel secure if capitulation in Vietnam led to the sanctification of aggression through subversion and spurious 'wars of national liberation' . . .

On the other hand, the progressive application of military sanctions can encourage stubborn resistance, rather than a willingness to negotiate. Continued and stepped-up intensification of hostilities in Vietnam could lead to uncontrollable escalation . . .

What are the conditions for such a settlement? First, a cease-fire.

Aggressive action by North Vietnam to bring about a Communist 'liberation' (which means Communist rule) of the South must end. Only then can there be negotiation . . .

There are many factors which I am not in a position to weigh. But there does appear to be at least a possibility that a suspension of such air strikes against North Vietnam, at the right time, might provide the Hanoi authorities with an opportunity, if they wish to take it, to inject some flexibility into their policy without appearing to do so as the direct result of military pressure.

If such a suspension took place for a limited time, then the rate of incidents in South Vietnam would provide a fairly accurate way of measuring its usefulness and the desirability of continuing it. I am not, of course, proposing any compromise on points of principle, nor any weakening of resistance to aggression in South Vietnam, indeed, resistance may require increased military strength to be used against the armed and attacking Communists. I merely suggest that a measured and announced pause in one field of military action *at the right time* might facilitate the development of diplomatic resources which cannot easily be applied to the problem under the existing circumstances. It could, at the least, expose the intransigence of the North Vietnam Government...

With a cease-fire followed by political negotiations, with the countries in the area given an international guarantee of neutrality and assurance of aid for peaceful development, then the danger, destruction and distress of the present hour might be replaced by peace, hope and progress.

I know that the policy and the effort of the Government of the USA is directed to this end. Such an effort deserves and should receive the support of all peace-loving people.

I had barely finished the last sentence of that speech before I was invited to lunch with President Johnson the next day at Camp David, the presidential retreat in the Catoctin Mountains. It was a very friendly invitation and the President would, as usual, send a helicopter for me. I do not know what the Americans would do without helicopters.

The talk at lunch the next day was limited by the fact that the President was on the telephone almost the entire time. He appeared to be speaking with Secretary of Defence McNamara about the latest developments in Vietnam. It was difficult even to exchange polite pleasantries with Lady Bird while this was going on, let alone talk business with her husband. After lunch the President and I went out on the terrace, cool and sunny with a wonderful view. It was only then that we got down to Vietnam. I kept a diary of that conversation.

I began it by asking what he thought of my speech of last night. He replied quickly and decisively: 'It was bad,' and then for an hour (before and after the press conference) he told me why it was bad, allowing me to get in only a word or two of explanation and justification. If there had not been a kind of 'et tu, Brute' feeling about the assault, without any personal unpleasantness of any kind, I would have felt almost like Schuschnigg before Hitler at Berchtesgaden!

The burden of his complaint was that I had joined the ranks of the domestic opponents of his Vietnam Policy: [Senator Wayne] Morse, [Walter] Lippman, the *New York Times*, ADA [Americans for Democratic Action], the ignorant Liberals, the 'know nothing,' 'do gooders,' etc. By doing so, I had made it more difficult for him. He didn't expect that of me, etc.; that I would come into the United States and make a speech of this kind without consulting him or 'Mac' Bundy or Dean Rusk or somebody. That he was getting tired of receiving advice (and nothing else) from foreign visitors: Wilson, [Michael] Stewart [British Foreign Secretary] (whom he particularly resented), Couve de Murville, etc. None of these people really knew anything about the situation; they had no policy or solution of their own but that didn't prevent them criticizing his. When he asked them for positive proposals—alternative policies, etc.—they never had any reply.

Eventually I tried to explain to him what I really did say in Philadelphia, not what he thought I had said; and why I said it; how I was trying to make the kind of suggestion—carefully guarded—that might be of help to him in circumstances where the stepped-up bombing of North Vietnam had not achieved the desired result. I also pointed out that public opinion in my country was profoundly disturbed by the implications of certain aspects of US policy and that some of us were having difficulty with public opinion in our complete support of that policy.

He couldn't understand why. Nor could he understand why we seemed to be critical of, or fearful of, the results of every warlike action by the US, when we ignored the horrible atrocities of the Communists. The President seemed to feel a little forlorn at not being understood better by friends. 'OK, if you don't want us there, we can clear out; really clear out and then see what happens.'

He then expounded his Vietnam policy at some length, emphasizing a dozen times that all he wanted was peace. How dare 'they' consider him a war-monger, etc. For peace, there had to be negotiation. Of course, he knew this but who were you going to negotiate with? Did the Communists want negotiation? No, they wanted surrender, which they thought would soon come, especially when the friends of the USA began to criticize her.

The Americans would, however, not surrender or stop the fight against aggression.

I got in a word or two here to point out that I agreed—and had said so last night and earlier—that a cease-fire must come before negotiation and that meanwhile resistance to aggression must go on. But what if air bombing of the North, as part of that resistance, didn't succeed in bringing about a situation where the North would agree to a cease-fire and negotiation? What then? Extension of the air warfare, or what?

The President then gave me a frank and revealing exposition of US plans, told with great vehemence, many short and vigorous vulgarities at the expense of his opponents, and a few Texas illustrations.

There were three possible policies:

1 That advocated by General Lemay [former head of the Strategic Air Command], certain Chiefs of Staff, Dean Acheson (I gathered), and the real 'hawks'; namely wipe out Hanoi, Haiphong, even Peking, and other Asian Communist centres by using the Strategic Air Force; in short, all-out war. The President had been resisting this policy for 18 months and would continue to do so, come what may. 'Not bad, for a warmonger.'

2 The other extreme—get out—lock, stock, and barrel; back to the continental USA and to hell with Vietnam and Asia. A kind of escalation in reverse. Then watch, said the President, the reaction of India, Pakistan, Great Britain, Australia, and the others, when we leave them to their fate.

3 The policy that was being followed. What was that? Helping South Vietnam in spite of its political confusion and military unreliability; step up American military aid, which would mean more troops; kill more Viet Cong, really go after them; follow through on the planned bombing of the North.

On the last point, I pressed him on what their 'plans' were. What did Maxwell Taylor [their Ambassador in Saigon] mean by 'unlimited bombing'? This was the possibility causing most anxiety for the friends of the USA.

The President said their plans were *not* for unlimited bombing but for the progressive destruction, if necessary, of military installations, communications and industrial facilities important in the assistance North Vietnam was giving the South. They would not bomb within a 50-mile radius of Hanoi, the distance beyond which Hanoi MIGs cannot operate and return. They would also do everything possible to avoid killing civilians, for which restraint, the President repeated with the bitterness he had previously shown on this matter, they would get no thanks even from their friends.

The President is sincere about this limitation of air action in the North and he has removed certain military targets from the list because they are too near the Chinese border or in crowded towns.

I told the President I was relieved, as I thought everybody would be relieved, to hear of the careful character of this planned retaliation. I wished we had known of it before. He replied that he had told us and the world in numerous speeches and statements. But certainly he has not, at least in the detail he gave me.

I concluded my diary account with some general observations:

There is no doubt that the President is tired, under great and continuous pressure, and that he is beginning to show it. He is more worried about US policy in Vietnam than he is willing to show. His irritation at any indication of lack of full support for his policy; his impatience of criticism and his insistence that everything is working out in accord with a well-conceived plan; all these really indicate a feeling of insecurity about the situation, rather than the reverse. As the President said: 'It's hard to sleep these days.' 'I'm beginning to feel like a martyr; misunderstood, misjudged by friends at home and abroad.'

This crisis over Vietnam is going to be a great test for LBJ. I'm not now certain that he is going to be successful in meeting it.

This was an extremely good and very frank talk. Despite my efforts to convince him of the contrary, the President told me he did not consider my speech had been helpful and let me know he did not think much of my idea for calling off the bombing. We would have been pretty angry, I suppose, if any member of the American government had spoken, in Canada, on Canadian government policy as I had spoken in Philadelphia.

Following my return to Ottawa I decided to write a long letter to the President fully explaining my position:

... I came away feeling that, though I understand much better the plans and the purposes of your policy in Southeast Asia, I really hadn't made my own position clear enough; especially in the light of the 'peace' speech I gave in Philadelphia the night before.

I want to assure you that my Government, and I particularly as its leader, want to give you all possible support in the policy, difficult and thankless, you are following in Vietnam in aiding South Vietnam to resist aggression. I believe that the great majority of the Canadian people feel the same way.

There is also, however, a feeling of deep anxiety about developments which could lead to wider hostilities. This is understandable enough, especially when it is not possible to know all the facts at the disposal of the Government of another country. We are very much aware in Canada that we are inevitably involved in every big decision made in Washington, so we are concerned about the decisions themselves — at times, I think, quite as much as the American people themselves are. We also talk about them!

To this anxiety is added criticism of US Vietnam policy from certain quarters in Canada. A part of this is left-wing exploitation of fear; a part of it is merely a reflection of that irrational anti-Americanism which a few Canadians have as their preliminary prejudice. A part of it is based on a quite genuine feeling that current US policy in Vietnam is wrong and heading for trouble.

This vocal, if limited, critical reaction has resulted in a good deal of questioning, much of it unfriendly to the Government, in our Parliament. The burden of the criticism is that we are giving the United States automatic and unquestioning support; tagging along as a satellite rather than acting as a self-respecting friend.

A Government, especially a minority Government, cannot merely brush off these criticisms as unimportant.

This is the political background in Ottawa, though it isn't expressed adequately in a few words.

At Philadelphia, I took this background into account in making a plea for peace in Vietnam, along with two or three suggestions which I thought might be helpful for this purpose in the right circumstances.

In doing so, however, I also emphasized (I venture to attach a few excerpts from my speech to show this) the honourable and unselfish motives behind US intervention in the first place; the necessity of defeating aggression even if it meant stepping up military power in South Vietnam; the necessity of a cease-fire and a cessation of aggression from the North before there could be meaningful negotiations.

In my proposal for a 'suspension' or 'pause' in the series of 'increasingly powerful retaliatory strikes,' I did not argue it should be done now but might be considered 'at the right time'; that it would be 'for a limited time' and that, even if it took place, it would not apply to other action against aggression in the South.

My point is that, once the destructive effects of air strikes are really being felt by the Hanoi Government, they might wish to 'cry quits' but without being accused of doing so in the face of continued air action. In other words, this 'pause' would give them an opportunity to stop the fighting in the South—if they wished to use it for that purpose. If they didn't, then their aggressive intransigence would have been exposed and it would be made very clear who was preventing a negotiated solution. I should have thought that this would have strengthened your position diplomatically, without weakening it militarily, because the suspension would only be for a short time; long enough for Northern Communist intentions to be made clear.

Surely, if and when the right time comes and, if there has been no other break in the deadlock, this suspension would be worth trying. I feel certain that it would strengthen your support in friendly and even non-committed countries. It would also make full support easier after the suspension had been done.

I assure you that my proposal, carefully guarded, was meant to be helpful; neither critical nor obstructive. I believe that in certain circumstances it may turn out to be useful though I realize that only you can judge those circumstances.

I want you to know that I appreciate, as much as any person could, the crushing nature of the problem, domestic and international, that you are facing with such courage and wisdom; that Vietnam is only one of these, though the one, I suppose, of most immediate danger and stress. I am anxious to help you in this and other matters as the Leader of the Government of your closest neighbour and friend. But Canada is a political democracy too, with an active and often divided public opinion; sensitive that its leaders do not appear to be merely echoes of the United States but anxious, I believe, to back up their neighbour when required to do so, as an independent friend should.

I had these considerations very much in mind when I spoke the other night. May I add that your exposition of the American case for planned and limited air retaliation, designed to do the job intended, with a minimum of loss of life and without provocation to China or Russia was reassuring and impressive. I am grateful to you for it, as I am for your kindness, and for your consideration in speaking to me so frankly last Saturday.

PS, *April* 7/65. I have listened to your Baltimore speech on our National Television Network. It was magnificent and deserves, and will receive, I am sure, wholehearted Canadian support; particularly for your declaration of willingness to engage in unconditional discussions looking towards an honourable settlement and for the imaginative and far reaching proposal you made for a great development programme in the South East Asia region.

When the President did halt the bombing later in 1965, it failed to bring about a negotiated settlement. On the morning of 30 January

1966 US Ambassador Walton Butterworth delivered to me a letter from President Johnson informing me of the US decision to resume bombing attacks on military targets in a day or two. The President's letter told me that the suspension of bombing had met with no constructive response from Hanoi either by word or deed. He also told me that the US had been in direct contact with representatives of Hanoi, both at the outset of the suspension and on two separate occasions during the preceding ten days. During the more recent contacts, the US has asked whether Hanoi wished to give any confidential indication that it was taking reciprocal military action, and whether Hanoi wished to discuss the apparent obstacles to negotiation. The response to each of these inquiries, he said, had been totally negative and this was taken as a conclusive demonstration that Hanoi was not ready, at least now, to move toward peace.

In handing me the letter the Ambassador explained along expected lines, why the President had been forced to make the decision. I told Mr Butterworth that I regretted the circumstances which had brought the United States to this decision, to resume bombing, the more so because I did not think that any military solution was possible. The Communists were undoubtedly counting on two things. First, world public opinion turning against the United States if they stepped up their military effort and caused havoc and destruction by bombing the North. Second, the weakness of the South Vietnam government and the lack of popular support for them in the South. I warned that, if there was another coup in the South, as reports indicated was likely, then it would be almost impossible for the Americans to convince anyone that they were on the side of the Vietnamese democracy against aggression from outside.

The President was well aware of my concern, and the Canadian government's, that the conflict might widen. In his letter he assured me that the United States had no such intention. Nevertheless, I told Mr Butterworth that I certainly appreciated the President's difficulties and the dilemma he was in. In my view he would have a more difficult time standing up to the domestic advocates of stronger military measures than to those who would make concessions to bring the military intervention to an end. He would also, however, find it difficult to secure an international 'consensus' supporting indefinite and 'escalated' military intervention.

The last time I saw LBJ was during Centennial year when the President paid an official visit to Canada, in the course of which we had an opportunity for private discussions at Harrington Lake, the Canadian Prime Minister's summer cottage. After lunch the President, calm and relaxed, and I stayed behind for coffee and a private chat. We discussed two matters at that time. One, of course, was Vietnam, on which the President gave me the usual oral *apologia pro bello meo*. He again took a good deal of credit for resisting the pressure of his military 'super-hawks' for more violent action and for the resources to carry it out. This pressure was rising, he warned me, as was popular sentiment for stronger measures. In his view the public opinion polls were increasingly in favour of present policy or a tougher one, to which I replied that that was not the case in Canada. He then expressed sincere appreciation for our government's helpful attitude over Vietnam, even though we differed about the bombing.

Because we had only a few minutes left alone, I then put very frankly to him the proposition that he should stop the bombing, without any conditions regarding time or anything else, and merely announce that he would now meet the other side without delay to discuss a cease-fire, an armistice, and peace. I told him this would put the Communists on the spot and remove their last proclaimed excuse for refusing to begin negotiations. This suggestion, which he said he would consider, did not seem to upset him too much, but when we rejoined the others he was more vigorous in his defence of the existing bombing campaign and more reluctant to consider any proposals for change which were not linked with concessions of some kind by the North. He repeated the old well-worn argument; we stop bombing, they go on killing. I admitted the logic of this position, in the military sense, but pointed out that the victory to be won had to be political, to achieve political objectives. The United States had recognized this by limiting its own use of military power. The only question, therefore, was whether a military decision to stop bombing would do more good politically than it could do harm militarily.

LBJ was not much impressed. Their boys would continue to die, some because of the restraints imposed by their own government. In any event, ending the bombing would not stop the war, the ground combat would go on. I agreed that might well be true. It was a worrying thought that perhaps we Canadians were wrong in attaching so much significance to ending the bombing as an element in ending the war. Even if it was halted the Communists could readily find some excuse or other to refuse negotiations and continue fighting. Nevertheless, I said, such a move might have diplomatic results which would more than compensate for any military disadvantages if it failed. I noted in my diary, however:

Johnson showed no sign of being convinced: so I asked him what he thought of the proposition that the USA announce not merely that they were going to stop the bombing but that they were going to stop fighting at such and such a time and ask the Secretary General or the Pope to arrange for peace talks at once. I didn't think that in such circumstances the north could continue any offensive operations, at least for a time.

I don't think, however, LBJ thought this was a very good idea either!

All I can hope from putting forward these ideas is that he may have been persuaded to ponder over them.

My feeling is, however, that he has made up his mind to continue along the present line; neither reducing nor extending it because

1 the Chiefs of Staff would raise 'public hell' if he didn't; with the backing of the Pentagon and all those who are for a decisive and quick military victory;
2 politically, he feels he would be in more trouble than he is now if he showed 'weakness';
3 he is convinced that the Vietnam elections in September, which Bunker [American Ambassador in Saigon] is looking after, will show the purity of US intentions and the strength of new democratic processes in Vietnam; and that this will help swing world opinion over to his side.

As a postscript, I can only add that the President's views on Vietnam gave no ground for optimism that any new move of any kind is likely to break the present deadlock. But with a person like LBJ it is rash to predict anything. He operates on instinct and his assessment of domestic political currents. He is more concerned with opinion polls than diplomatic strategy, or so it would seem.

One of the aspects of the Vietnam struggle which seemed to interest him most at that meeting was the progress Ambassador Bunker was making in his efforts to condition the rulers of South Vietnam to democracy and free elections. When the President first mentioned the importance of the forthcoming elections I had the sinking feeling that he was referring to the 1968 elections in the United States, that he was subordinating the threat to global peace in Vietnam to his own return to office. It was a relief to learn he was thinking of Saigon and not Washington, though I thought he was being raither naïve in his optimism about the chances for a successful transplant of democratic institutions to South Vietnam.

Also disturbing in terms of the hard realities of the situation was his constant tendency to think of every proposal in terms of how many of 'our boys' would be killed or saved by it during the next week. A bombing pause or cessation was looked at in these narrow, if very human, terms. 'One of Luci's friends was badly wounded during a halt in the bombing. What can I say to him?' The fact that the loss of fifty more 'boys' next week might save 5000 in the next few months did not seem to occur to the President.

I concluded my account of that meeting with the following summary of Mr Johnson's personality:

He has an intense human emotionalism about the conflict which does him credit as a man, but could be a great handicap in dealing with international political strategy.

He is emotional and warm but tough and obstinate. He seemed to take an intense satisfaction in the steps taken—with which he was personally deeply concerned—to ensure that the bombing was so directed as to do the minimum damage to 'civilians': spare the people even if it meant sacrificing some effectiveness and planes. This is highly laudable but has helped hardly at all in reducing criticism of the bombing as cruel and heartless. All it has meant is that the Americans are getting the worst of both worlds. The President won't stop bombing but he wants it to be humane bombing!

I wonder whether he really has control over these matters or whether—to keep the military from 'going full speed ahead and damn the torpedoes' from China or anywhere else—he has decided not to interfere in any of their existing military tactics, including bombing, in the hope of achieving good, political results.

To me the President is more of an enigma than ever, only he is now an older and more impatient and irascible enigma; feverish in his insistence on activity, verbal and physical; moving so much and so fast in the hope, perhaps, that movement is progress; that you can be jet-propelled to peace and all the good things for everybody which he has seen granted to Texans and which everybody in Vietnam and other far off places like Canada should also have.

Just three weeks before I stepped down as Prime Minister President Johnson made his famous television bid to end the war in Vietnam by stopping all bombing north of the 29th parallel, and at the same time announced his own decision not to run for the presidency again. The next day, 1 April 1968, I wrote to him:

I have issued an official statement expressing appreciation of what you said last night on Vietnam. I would like to supplement this by a personal message which can express with more feeling how deeply grateful I think the whole world should be for the proposals you have made and for the courage and wisdom you have shown in making them. It is now strictly up to the other side to reciprocate, and if they don't, there should be no doubt where the obstacle to peace lies.

I have no right to comment on your other and more personal decision not to seek or accept renomination but I hope I may convey my respect and admiration for the motives that caused you to come to a decision which must have been a very difficult one and could only be made understandable to your friends by the spirit which inspired it.

I had wanted to telephone you but I know you will be deluged by calls so I hope you will accept this personal message instead which is sent with my most sincere and warmest good wishes.

6

POLITICS IN DISREPUTE

Early in 1964, concerned with the serious problems facing our country and the world, problems to threaten our very survival, I began to emphasize the need for a new kind of politics based more on national consensus and less on party conflict. What I had in mind was the kind of politics a nation will accept if facing defeat in war, but rarely, if ever, when confronted with disaster in time of peace. On 24 March 1964 I made this sort of appeal to a large dinner meeting of Liberals and others in Toronto. Among other things, I said:

To me, the new politics does not mean the abandonment of Liberalism as a political creed. It does not mean the abandonment of Party politics, because Party politics are the very foundation of Parliamentary democracy. It does not mean diminishing the importance of dedicated and active Party work . . . the value of good Party organization, strong Party Leadership or Party controversy. These are the very essence of a free and vigorous political society. By a new politics, and perhaps that is not the best way to describe it, I mean the dropping of narrow and nasty, short-sighted and selfish partisanship; I think the times are too serious for us in Canada to afford that luxury. I think of the politics appealing to all the people made by John Kennedy in his inaugural address.

Oh, I know that in the eyes of the rabid, the blinkered partisan, this is sheer and rather silly idealism; just as in the eyes of the politically indifferent and cynical, the old politics is merely the selfish manipulation by calculating men of human weaknesses for the profit of the manipulators. That is wrong in relation to the old politics, and to talk about new politics now as rather silly idealism is also very wrong indeed. Of course, the new politics is idealistic.

But it is realistic too because it is vitally necessary today to meet new and unprecedented challenges, to face situations where old ideas and cherished attitudes cannot stand up to new facts and swift changes.

The new politics is, in a sense, merely good citizenship, a citizenship based on a deep pride in our country and its strength and its unity as one nation; one nation with faith in its own destiny. It is a citizenship more concerned with discharging duties than in proclaiming rights. It is a citizenship desperately anxious to find solutions to our social and political and economic problems and in the search is willing to rise above special and narrow interests.

Above all, this new politics requires the involvement of everyone. It does not mean separation or unconcern, a sitting on the sidelines. Unless this broad political involvement becomes part of all of us in this country, whatever Party we may belong to, we are spectators betraying our democratic responsibility and our democratic rights.

It is this betrayal which paves the way for the extremists, for their noise and for their violence, all the more dangerous because this uproar is given so much publicity; and it is exciting. Publicity is what those people crave; without it they would soon lose their importance.

The new politics then is based on the personal involvement of every citizen. It is also based on good Party organization and on Party activities through which this involvement can best become effective.

Now that means, among other things, the fullest possible democratization of our Party, in the sense that authority and policies must flow upwards from what we call the rank and file to those who have been chosen to fill positions of responsibility and authority in the Party. This requires work on the part of the members of the Party, research work, seminar work, thinking things out, keeping in touch with your Members of Parliament. It requires also, I believe, periodic national conventions, perhaps every two years, so that the involvement of the individual can be mobilized to determine and pursue national purpose through national Parties.

That is my ideal for the new Liberal Party and for a new kind of politics to meet new and difficult situations; a politics which, based on the citizen, becomes in its principles and its ideals and in its practice less partisan and more co-operative in national effort and in the promotion of the national welfare; politics which will reject sectional and selfish interests in the interests of the country as a whole. This kind of politics will help us to overcome the obstacles to our future as a strong, prosperous and united nation. This will make the manipulation of opinion by partisan rhetoric and eloquent prejudice futile and sterile. This will ensure that the passions of extremism or prejudice will not replace unselfish, careful and objective deliberation as the basis of political decision and action.

This appeal had little or no effect. The country was unmoved. My critics probably regarded this as simply a hypocritical bid for support from the politically neutral. Certainly, although I did not know it at the time, my lessons in 'narrow and nasty, short-sighted and selfish partisanship' were just beginning.

That autumn of 1964 introduced one of the most sordid and vindictive episodes in the history of the House of Commons, when debate on policy and problems gave way to accusations of scandal and of every assorted sin of omission and commission.

The Hal Banks affair provided a foretaste of what was to come. In October 1963, following an enquiry by Justice T.G. Norris, our government placed the five maritime transport unions in trusteeship. Then the President of the Seafarer's International Union, Hal Banks, while free on bail pending appeal of a conspiracy conviction, fled the country in July 1964. We were accused by the Opposition of being reluctant to take action against him, of having facilitated his departure, and of making no effort to get him back. None of this was true. We had decided to prosecute him and were quite prepared to have him extradited, but conspiracy was a non-extraditable offence. Later, the Attorney General of Ontario, with the assistance of the Department of External Affairs, requested Banks' extradition to face a perjury charge. Needless to say, we were genuinely shocked when in March 1968 the US Secretary of State in curious circumstances personally prevented Banks' extradition through some power vested in him. Dean Rusk, a man of integrity and honour, claimed that he had legal advice to justify his action, but it was hard for us to believe that his decision was not the result of union influence brought to bear on the State Department. In consequence, we protested very strongly but with no success.

The first of the so-called scandals to rock our government and the country was the Rivard or Denis case. Lucien Rivard was a notorious character, a criminal, a gambler, wanted in the United States on a narcotics charge. When he later escaped from jail in Canada, where he was being held pending the outcome of extradition proceedings for his return to the United States, and disappeared, we were absurdly accused of having facilitated, if not having brought about, his escape.

The Rivard case first came to my attention during the summer of 1964 when the Secretary of the Cabinet, Gordon Robertson, informed me that there was trouble in the Immigration Department over an indiscreet Executive Assistant (Raymond Denis). At that time I was told none of the details. Then, on 2 September 1964, on the flight back to Ottawa from the Centenary Federal-Provincial Conference at Charlottetown, when my wife had left her seat for a few minutes, the Minister of Justice, Guy Favreau, sat down beside me. He told me that allegations of bribery were being made against the Executive Assistant to the Minister of Immigration, but these had been denied. Mr Favreau and Mr Tremblay, the Minister of Immigration, had the matter under examination, and the RCMP were conducting a full investigation. Naturally, in the circumstances, I left the matter in the hands of the Minister and gave it no further thought. I assumed he would report to me, if there was anything to report, as soon as the enquiry was completed. In the press of other problems, this particular matter was forgotten.

I was wrong in my assumption that I would be kept informed. I did not hear any more about the matter until Sunday, 22 November 1964, the day before the estimates for the Department of Justice were to come before the House of Commons. At that time Mr Favreau told me that the police investigation had been completed into charges that Denis had tried to bribe Pierre Lamontagne, the Montreal lawyer who was counsel for the United States government in the extradition proceedings, not to oppose bail for Rivard. The evidence, in Favreau's view as a lawyer, did not justify prosecution. Indeed, no successful prosecution was possible since it would be simply Denis' word against that of the man who had accused him of offering the bribe. He was quite confident that he had been correct in his decision merely to let Denis resign. Favreau also told me that he expected strong criticsm of his conduct in this matter by the Conservatives during the consideration of his estimates, but believed, as he had done nothing wrong, that he could explain the matter satisfactorily.

Mr Favreau proved to be too optimistic in his assessment. He had not reckoned with the terrific onslaught by Erik Nielsen, John Diefenbaker, Tommy Douglas, and other members of the Opposition against his handling of the matter. Although I did not hear the debate in the House on the Monday afternoon of 23 November, I was told that it had gone very badly for us, and that the Minister's explanation had carried no conviction whatsoever with the Opposition. I was also informed late that evening that the name of my parliamentary secretary, Guy Rouleau, MP for the Montreal constituency of Dollard, would appear when the debate was resumed since he had been mentioned in the police report. I was now thoroughly disturbed and, that night, took action to get a copy of the police report with all the relevant information. I also called a meeting of the Cabinet for Tuesday morning, 24 November.

The Cabinet met and Mr Favreau, shaken by developments, read us the important passages from the police evidence. The report was a much more damning document than I had been led to believe, and I concluded that the government must accept immediately the Opposition's request for a judicial enquiry. We agreed that the enquiry must be announced at once and the terms of reference worked out in a general way before the opening of the afternoon sitting. While the Cabinet continued their discussion and considered the terms of reference, I left so that I could confront Rouleau in my office. It was a very difficult interview. There was no suggestion that he had bribed anyone or taken a bribe, but he had received people from Montreal concerned with these criminal activities and had made representations on behalf of Rivard. He denied any guilt and, of course, was not guilty in any technical sense. He had, however, certainly been indiscreet. I told him that he could not remain as my parliamentary secretary for another hour, and that I expected him to get up in the House that afternoon to announce his resignation. Chastened, he agreed.

I then returned to the Cabinet where the terms of reference were being determined. It was Mr Favreau who suggested that Chief Justice Frédéric Dorion of the Quebec Superior Court was suitably qualified to carry out the enquiry. I was very much in favour of the choice since Mr Dorion was not only a judge of high standing but also had been a Conservative Member of Parliament. Thus, there could be no question of our being charged with having appointed someone predisposed to help us out of what might become a difficult situation. At 2:30 PM to a hushed House, Rouleau announced his resignation. Mr Favreau then announced that the government had decided to set up a judicial enquiry into the charges levelled against Denis and matters related to these charges. Diefenbaker and Douglas, the former particularly, remained belligerent and critical, maintaining that the enquiry as constituted would be a whitewash. I denied this, but agreed to consider widening the proposed terms of reference. In fact we did widen them somewhat the next day.

Douglas Harkness asked me when I had heard about the Rivard-Denis affair and I replied (having in my mind only the fact that I had been unaware of any details before Sunday), 'the day before his [Favreau's] estimates were brought before the House.' While it is true that the earlier mention of these difficulties to me in the aeroplane by the Minister of Justice did indicate that a potentially troublesome situation was developing, I certainly had had no subsequent information and no knowledge of what in fact had happened until Sunday, 22 November.

After the enquiry had been announced to the House I went off to

Saskatchewan to begin a western tour. That night I addressed a wonderful non-political banquet at the Lloydminster High School. This
was, I recognized, a distressing time for this sort of activity. I felt that
I should not be out of the House when we were in trouble, with the
Minister of Justice under such bitter attack. However, the tour had
been very carefully arranged and my colleagues were horrified when
I suggested that I might call it off. My hope was that the announcement of the judicial enquiry would calm the stormy waters.

There was no calm. The battle in the House of Commons raged all
day Wednesday and Thursday, largely over the terms of reference
which were not considered by the Opposition to be broad enough. I
was strongly criticized for my 'lack of courage' and so on in 'running
away' from what the Opposition felt to be my duty to face the House.
I had to consider, every hour or so, whether I should not fly back
immediately to Ottawa. This problem, coupled with the very strenu-
ous and crowded programme which I was trying to carry out, gave
me two or three of the most difficult days I have ever known. Further,
Favreau had now mentioned to his colleagues that he had told me
about this affair much earlier, not just a day or two before, while
coming back from the 1964 Charlottetown Centenary Conference.

All of this disturbed me to the point where, on Thursday, 26
November, I telephoned Ottawa that I was flying back that night and
would cancel my engagements in Winnipeg the next day (including
an enormous great dinner that had been weeks in the planning).
However, on Thursday afternoon the Cabinet (Mr Martin was acting
PM in my absence) was unanimous in its opinion that I should not for
a moment consider returning. They were all firmly convinced that, as
they were broadening the terms of reference again to include the
conduct of the Minister of Justice, they were through the worst of the
affair. This would satisfy the NDP, which meant that the Justice estimates would be passed the next day and the vote of non-confidence
in Favreau, proposed by Erik Nielsen, would be defeated. If I did
return, the whole affair might blow up again. All this was in contrast
to the conflicting reports I had been getting since the start of my tour,
some urging me to continue, others to come back. In view of the
strength of opinion among my colleagues and my own belief that if I
could possibly go to Winnipeg I should do so, I again altered my
plans and continued my tour.

As things turned out, Diefenbaker could secure only thirty 'yeas' to
back him in what he considered his crusade against corruption and
wrong-doing. The vote on Friday, 27 November, was therefore com-

forting, but not so the position of the government. The Opposition had exploited the matter and the press had made the most of it. Stories were continually being thrown out that this was only the first of a whole series of disclosures which would drive Ministers, especially some from Quebec, from public life. A war of nerves began in earnest. Questions were put on the Order Paper concerning bankruptcy in Quebec, preventing the deportation of narcotics criminals from Windsor, and so on and so on.

When I returned to Ottawa on Sunday, 29 November, having spent Saturday in Toronto at the Grey Cup game, I saw Mr Favreau. Personally, this was the most difficult part of it all. He still appeared to be much disturbed at my claim to have known of this matter only just before it was raised in the House, and he reminded me of the conversation we had had at the beginning of September. His recall of this brief conversation was more detailed than mine, and later, on 14 December 1964, he gave me the following memorandum stating his recollection of it:

On August 31, 1964, after Denis had given his statement to the RCMP on the 26th, I discussed with the Honourable René Tremblay the inquiry which I had ordered in the matter. We agreed that
a Mr Denis should be suspended, or at least not allowed to exercise his functions as Executive Assistant, until the completion of the inquiry;
b that I should make you aware of the matter without delay.

I thought I could discuss the matter with you at Charlottetown, but, unfortunately, the first occasion I had to bring it to your attention was on the plane, on our return trip, on Wednesday, September 5, 1964.

I took occasion of a few moments when Mrs Pearson had left her seat next to yours. I told you, at the time, that a Montreal lawyer by the name of Lamontagne, who was acting for the US Government in an extradition case, had told the RCMP that he had been approached by the Executive Assistant to the Minister of Citizenship and Immigration, who allegedly referred to him the offer of a bribe of a large amount.

I told you that the Minister of Citizenship and Immigration, Mr Tremblay, had been advised and that, when the matter of lawyer Lamontagne's statement had been referred to me by the Commissioner of the RCMP, I had ordered a full investigation in the matter and that the said investigation was still in process.

As my mind was primarily and, I must admit, entirely preoccupied at that time with the possible existence of a criminal offence, I do not recollect having told you, at the time, of the telephone calls made to Mr Lamontagne, either by Mr Guy Rouleau, Mr André Letendre or Mr Guy Lord. [The last two were respectively, Executive Assistant and Special Assistant to Mr Favreau.] None of these three had been mentioned by Mr Lamontagne in his statement as being related to the alleged bribe offer.

You were obviously entitled to expect a further report from me on the whole matter or to expect that I would be forwarding to you a copy of the final report of the RCMP.

When the time came to assess the facts finally, and when I formed the conclusion that no successful criminal prosecution for bribery against Denis could be made, in the state of the evidence as then collected, my great concern was to discuss the matter with the responsible minister, in order that Mr Raymond Denis may be dealt with both fairly and in the best interest of the Government.

We reached the conclusion that Mr Denis should be separated from the Government. Mr Tremblay sent him to my office and I convinced him – harsh as the step could be said to be – to send his resignation to Mr Tremblay. This he did, at a date which I cannot state precisely now. At all events, he never returned to the department after the moment he was placed on leave as stated above.

Under the pressure of business, it never occurred to me to send back for the file subsequently. Had I read the file again, my perspective of the whole matter would have been more detailed and I would certainly have referred the matter back to you and, more particularly, would have discussed with you the facts as they related to Mr Guy Rouleau and my two assistants.

When I received this memorandum, I noted in the margin: 'I have no recollection of any names being mentioned or details given. We had only a minute or two on a jet plane – sitting across from each other – and part of the time we spoke also about the Charlottetown Conference we had just completed.' Certainly Rivard's name was not mentioned, nor that of Rouleau as one of those involved. In any event, with all the matters occupying my mind from September on, I had completely forgotten this conversation. I did not receive from Mr Favreau or from the Minister of Immigration, Mr Tremblay, any further communication, written or oral, until two and a half months later. These things happen. I suppose that Mr Favreau thought that he was sparing me from one more worry. Nothing in this whole period distressed me more than the accusation that I had lied to save myself at the expense of Mr Favreau. He himself never held this view, and I had subsequent communications from him to confirm this fact.

On Monday morning, 30 November, I met with the Cabinet and got a report on the events of the last week. My French-speaking colleagues were indignant, even furious, at the attacks upon us. My English-speaking colleagues were worried and frightened about the effect of the attacks on our political position. They considered that our moral position was being assailed and that it was my duty to defend it. To this end they pressed me to send a circular letter to Ministers, establishing a code of political conduct for them and for their staffs, and instructing them to convene meetings to make this code clear to those staffs. Executive Assistants were those who had got us into trouble, even though criminal charges were laid against only one of them, Denis. I agreed to this and sent the following letter on Tuesday, 1 December, which read in part:

In remarks I made in Winnipeg on Friday evening, I said there should be a moratorium on personal judgment and condemnations until Chief Justice Dorion has reported on all aspects of the matters he has under judicial inquiry. The possiblity of there having been offences that are punishable under law is now a matter for the Chief Justice and I am not going to comment on it.

There is, however, a separate question on which there should be no moratorium: whether there are, anywhere in the Government service, attitudes of mind and standards of conduct that can affect the full confidence of the people in the proper discharge of public affairs. About this the discussion in Parliament has raised doubts and uncertainties. It is an area in which doubts and uncertainties cannot be allowed even while the inquiry is in progress.

I am therefore writing this letter to ask you, as well as every other Minister, to have a meeting at once with your ministerial staff in order to impress on them the vital importance of their conduct. I am following this course in my own office.

It is by no means sufficient for a person in the office of a Minister—nor in any other position in the public service—to act within the law. That goes without saying. Much more is required. There is an obligation not simply to observe the law but to act in a manner so scrupulous that it will bear the closest public scrutiny.

It has been said that the elementary qualifications demanded of a Minister are honesty and incorruptibility. But it is not enough for us to have those qualities. Our attitudes and conduct must be such as to reflect them. In order that honesty and impartiality may be beyond doubt, members of Minister's staffs, equally with Ministers themselves, must not place themselves in a position where they are under obligation to any person who might benefit from special consideration or favour on their part . . .

The essential thing is to ensure that all appreciate the grave responsibility not only that we have but that the members of our staffs and others in positions of authority have, to maintain the confidence of the people of Canada in the probity of government in this country.

Meanwhile, I was considering what action to take about the statement I had made in the House that I had found out about the

Rivard-Denis affair only the weekend before it was raised. I did not know what to do. During the subsequent week there was technically no opportunity since we were having a difficult time over the flag and the question periods were suspended. But I do not take refuge in that: if I had gone to the Speaker and told him, he would have insisted that I be given a hearing. I was inclined to the view that I should get up in the House and make a statement of privilege, putting the thing right; but I was very strongly advised to stand firm on my earlier statement – that I, in fact, had not been informed. Finally, I decided I would have to make a statement when the flag debate was over and the House returned to its routine procedures. In the interim, on 14 December I wrote to Mr Justice Dorion to inform him of my limited earlier knowledge and sent him a copy of the statement I intended to make in the House after the flag debate. Two days later Judge Dorion read my correspondence into the record of the commission and the next day reports of my statement appeared in the Montreal *Gazette*. Before I had a chance to explain my earlier statement, I was faced with a question of privilege by Mr Harkness in the House of Commons. I explained the context of my September discussion with Favreau and assured the House that I had not deliberately deceived it. No specific charge was made that I had intentionally misled the House so the matter was dropped.

When I received the Dorion Report on 28 June 1965 I realized at once that the criticism of the Minister of Justice would make it impossible for him to continue in that portfolio. He was completely cleared of even a suspicion of wrong-doing, his integrity was not questioned nor his honour sullied; but he was severely criticized for the manner in which he had handled the affair. I discussed it with Favreau, who agreed that he must resign. I appealed to him, however, to stay on in the government as President of the Privy Council, there to take charge of federal-provincial constitutional questions, a field in which he was eminentaly qualified. At first he hesitated. He thought that he should get out of politics (he had never wanted to get in). But, in the end, he was persuaded. On 29 June he wrote to me:

As I have already stated to you, it is my view that the conclusions of the Dorion report, as far as I am concerned, are tantamount to no more than a statement on the part of the Commissioner that, had he been in my place he would have exercised his discretion in a different fashion. I wish to repeat that my resignation was tendered not out of the feeling that I'd done anything wrong, but because of the feeling that my usefulness as Minister of

Justice had been impaired by the situation which has developed. I need not say how deeply moved I am at the confidence which you, Mr Prime Minister, and my colleagues have shown in suggesting that I carry on. Therefore, while I must insist that my resignation be accepted as Minister of Justice, I would be willing to continue to serve in some other capacity.

Thus, he stayed in the government until the breakdown in his health, which led to his death not long afterward in July 1967. I do not attribute that breakdown to the wear and tear of politics or to the situation in which he found himself; certainly, however, these misfortunes aggravated the disease and brought his life prematurely to an end. I know what he went through, and I know what these misfortunes meant to him in terms of mental and emotional distress.

One reference in the report greatly disturbed me. Justice Dorion had concluded that I had been informed of Rouleau's involvement during the conversation on the plane. The day after I received the report I wrote to Mr Dorion asking him if there was any evidence of which I was unaware to support that conclusion. On 1 July Guy Favreau issued a full statement citing the relevant parts of the evidence, again affirming that I had not been informed of Rouleau's involvement until 23 November. In the face of this Mr Dorion amended his report.

In the aftermath of the Dorion Report a number of duties, both pleasant and unpleasant, fell upon me. First, I had to secure Rouleau's agreement to a statement from me that he was to resign and not stand for re-election. I succeeded in doing this. The statement, as issued, was cleared with Favreau. It was a sad and sorry business and Rouleau (who may have been weak but never evil) was broken up about it all. Then Cabinet changes had to be made consequent upon Favreau's resignation as Minister of Justice. My diary for 6 July 1965 summarizes these:

I persuaded George McIlraith to accept, with as good grace as possible, Public Works. I told him I would help him out as House Leader by giving him a special Parliamentary Secretary.

Then, at 3 PM I saw Lucien Cardin who is hesitant about his qualifications for Justice. He may be right on this as a long-term proposition but he will fill the bill admirably until after the election, at least. He is competent, and gaining confidence in himself; and is a good organizer, something that Department desperately needs.

George McIlraith would have been better in many ways but this would have been too much of a slap at Quebec. In any event, we need him as House Leader and I don't want to link this with Justice again.

Before Cardin left, Pennell arrived and I introduced the new Solicitor General to the New Minister of Justice. I told them that I wanted them to work as a team; that there was so much to be done they needed each other's help. They will do well together. Pennell is pleased; modest and grateful; a good man.

Then Favreau arrived at 4 PM and I told him about the other changes – which he likes – and what I had in mind for him in the Privy Council Office . . .

Next, I told a surprised and happy Watson McNaught that he was to be Minister of Mines and Technical Surveys. He is the beneficiary of circumstances but may do a much better job than anyone expects.

Finally, I saw Pépin and told him he was to be a Minister without Portfolio but was to assist a Minister who had one, Transport. He thought he had been summoned to become my Parliamentary Secretary and seemed a shade disappointed at being promoted to *no* Department. I told him if he preferred to be my Parliamentary Secretary, that could easily be arranged, so he quickly changed that tune . . .

I told him that he had a good future in politics if he made the most of his talents; and also if he accepted the limitations as well as the privileges of Ministerial rank. The most important of these limitations was Cabinet solidarity and collective responsibility which prevented a Minister sounding off on his own at the expense of his colleagues or his Party – even though he might have strong individual opinions on a particular matter . . .

Pépin got the point. He is going to be a dynamic and determined Quebecker in the Cabinet; without any reserve in expressing his own views, or I miss my guess.

In all the day's activities, I had little time to think about the Dorion episode – which is now working out satisfactorily. He has taken advantage of the way out offered to him by Favreau and me – and has made a kind of *amende honorable* . . .

To revert to Rivard. In March 1965, while the enquiry was going on, he escaped from Montreal's Bordeaux jail. Naturally, we were accused of getting him out, not in so many words, but things can be said in the House of Commons of which the effect is just as clear and strong as if put into so many words. I was flying in a helicopter some four-and-a-half months afterwards to attend the Highland Games at Antigonish, Nova Scotia, when I got a message from the pilot saying that Rivard had been recaptured. I heaved a great sigh of relief. At least, this showed that we were not hiding him! Five days later he was extradited to the United States where, in due course, he was found guilty of smuggling narcotics and sentenced to twenty years imprisonment and a $20,000 fine. There finally ended the first of four major and a variety of minor scandals that brought Parliament and politics in Canada to their lowest ebb in many years. I do not dismiss our own share of responsibility as a government, but we had an Opposition particularly skilful in, and passionately concerned with, this kind of debate. They were all prosecuting attorneys. This is indeed the role of the Opposition, but seldom in recent years has an Opposition been so vicious in its attacks on members of the government.

ॐ

While the Dorion enquiry was getting under way, our parliamentary debates tended to focus on new scandals, real and imagined. It was during this period that two of my Cabinet colleagues got into difficulty because of attacks made on them in connection with the bankruptcy in Montreal of the two brothers Sefkind. The Sefkinds had fled the country and, therefore, anyone who had had dealings with them could be made to look suspicious by insinuations and accusations, without evidence. The then Secretary of State, Mr Lamontagne, and Mr Tremblay, the Minister of Immigration, had had commercial dealings with them.

On 30 November Donald MacInnis, a Tory MP, placed on the Order Paper of the House the question of the involvement of 'Ministers' in the bankruptcy. Then, in early December 1964, Walter Gordon, Minister of Finance, brought to my attention a report that the press and radio were going to use a story that Lamontagne and Tremblay had been given thousands of dollars of free furniture by the Sefkinds, and that Tremblay had also received a $10,000 bribe from them for helping with an industrial loan while he was a Deputy Minister in Quebec.

I told Lamontagne and Tremblay, who were both very upset, that if these stories appeared they must take legal action at once. They agreed. When the stories did appear on Tuesday, 8 December, the libellous parts were left out. The inference of guilt by association, however, was there. In my view, after I had received all the facts, Tremblay had not committed even the mildest indiscretion. He had bought furniture and paid for it, even though some had not yet been delivered. Although he was an intelligemt and fine person, he was new at politics, and did not handle this affair very skilfully. He got himself in more deeply during a press conference on the matter, although he did not need to be involved at all. There was no scandal, no impropriety, or even carelessness on his part. Maurice Lamontagne, I think, had been ill-advised in accepting furniture on credit when he was a Minister of the Crown; he was making payments but some of his debt was still on the books. He and his wife had become close friends of the Sefkinds, whom they regarded as a fine, cultured, interesting European family. I am sure that they had no reason to believe otherwise at that time. In any event, this was a fairly minor thing. The headlines dealing with this matter, however, were enough to drive a decent public-spirited political servant almost out of his mind. I noted, after I received Tremblay's written statement: 'My indignation is now centred on those Press jackals – and even some responsible journalists – who are suggesting wrong-doing on Tremblay's part. The hypocrisy or plain unfairness of some of them is surprising and has infuriated me.' When I discussed the matter with Tremblay and Lamontagne, I said: 'You've both been the victims of unjust attacks, but these are going to persist. There is no doubt about it; and if you wish to stay on in the Cabinet you will be subjected to these.' They remained in Cabinet but the attacks continued until their resignations after the 1965 election – something that I will discuss in greater detail in Chapter 8.

When I was a civil servant, I had no feeling of constraint with the press. I was anxious to be of help to them in their work whenever I properly could. Once I became a Minister of the Crown, I began to understand and be affected by the natural conflict of interest in information matters between a Minister and the media. On the media side, the emphasis is bound to be on the right of the people to know and the duty of the newsman to discover and publish the facts. In this he has an important public responsibility and, for the most part, discharges it honestly and well. But the accepted principle can also be used to provide a good excuse if he exceeds the limits of reportorial responsibility under the pressure of competition or the spur of self-interest. To get there first with the most sensational story, he sacrifices accuracy or objectivity that might lessen the impact, or he gives the slant that sells.

The politican has his own temptation to irresponsibility in communication and does not always resist this successfully. He may wish to give out information of a kind and in a manner designed more to help himself than to inform the public. In doing this, he too can misrepresent by distortion, exaggeration, or selectivity. The reporter who is the victim of this deceit cannot be blamed for the consequences that may follow. It is different, of course, if he is guilty of collusion, something which happens too often in politics and leads not only to the misrepresentation of news, but also to an area of concern that we have not touched upon in this chapter: leaks of confidential information. On rare occasions calculated leaks, no doubt, can be condoned because of the increasing practice of government to label anything 'confidential' merely because its disclosure might be inconvenient or embarrassing politically where no question of national security or vital interest is at issue. Here again, however, abuses on the one side can be exploited to justify abuses on the other, the reporter using the principle of freedom of the press to make his own decision on whether or not the publication of a document or a story is prejudicial to the national interest. Surely it would become impossible for government to discharge properly its national and international responsibilities if any person might claim the right to decide on his own whether the details of Cabinet, diplomatic, or other confidential official discussions should be made public.

It is wrong and indefensible for government to withhold information to which the public has a right, by marking it 'secret' or 'confidential.' It is as bad, or worse, when the media or the public accept the right of every private citizen to decide for his own purposes whether information so labelled can be made public without prejudice to the national interest. Irresponsibility on either side, whether the government or the media, dangerously intensifies that conflict of interest which, as I have already mentioned, is normal between those who insist on the public's right to know and those who are concerned with the protection of the national interest and, in particular, the security of the state. This conflict can be kept within bounds only by the exercise of responsibility on both sides. There is a very real danger to democratic freedom when this responsibility is absent, when both freedom and security are abused by arbitrary decisions of the government on what should be kept secret or by the assumed right of any person to use his own judgment in ignoring these decisions.

I had often to face this problem in the discharge of political and governmental responsibilities. I know that there are no easy and permanent solutions to it. My own conclusion was to go to the maximum possible extent in public disclosure, while denouncing the operations of those who by one means or another secured and published confidential information; and I rejected their right to decide themselves whether this disclosure was justified in the public interest.

ॐ

I have not mentioned so far the situation which arose concerning Mr
Yvon Dupuis, whom I had brought into the Cabinet as Minister without Portfolio in February 1964. He had been a magnificent campaigner
for us in Quebec and one of our most effective men in politics, in
getting votes and maintaining high morale in the party; he was a fine
debater. It was not long, however, before I began to hear vague
rumblings that he had been using his political position to help his
friends to favours. These had just been rumours and no evidence had
been brought to my attention. That began to change in December
1964 when I was told of allegations that in 1961 Dupuis had promised to help someone get a race track licence in return for money. On
14 December I saw Dupuis, who said he had no worries about the
allegations and that he not only agreed but insisted that the RCMP
investigate the matter.

On 31 December 1964 when I again saw Mr Dupuis, I told him
how disturbed I was about the rumour that his connection with the
race track application was to be made public the next week. I emphasized that, if this happened, I would state that the whole matter
was under official investigation. He seemed surprised and worried,
but not unduly so. He reaffirmed what he had already told Mr Favreau; his connection with the matter had been simply that of an
intermediary between the applicant and the provincial authorities.

I next saw Dupuis at 2:30 PM on 20 January 1965. It was a painful
occasion. I asked for his resignation at once; there was no alternative,
given the information arising from the RCMP enquiry. He protested
innocence, charging conspiracy and persecution. He claimed he was
being dismissed and ruined without a chance to defend himself. I
said I was satisfied from the evidence that he was being treated fairly.
I added that with the enquiry not completed I did not feel at liberty to
give him details, but that the Minister of Justice, under whose jurisdiction the RCMP lay, might feel free to give him more information.

Having asked Dupuis for his resignation, I then had prepared two
alternative instruments of advice for submission to the Governor
General. The first advised His Excellency to accept Dupuis' resignation from the administration. The second was prepared in case the
resignation was refused by Dupuis or was unduly delayed in coming.
It advised that Dupuis 'be relieved of office.' For a time it was not
clear which instrument of advice would be formally submitted.

Before Cabinet on Friday, 22 January, I was informed that the story was going to break in the afternoon papers. It was essential therefore that I make an announcement that would, in timing and content, remove the impression that I had acted only under press pressure. After discussion with my Cabinet colleagues, I issued at 12:30 the following statement: 'On Wednesday the Prime Minister asked Mr Dupuis to relinquish his position as a member of the administration. Effective today, Mr Dupuis is no longer a member of it.' Later, Yvon Dupuis was charged with influence peddling, found guilty, and fined $5000. He was, however, acquitted on appeal.

As I mentioned earlier, when Mr Favreau became President of the Privy Council in early July 1965, I moved Mr Cardin, who had been Minister of Public Works, to Justice. It was a difficult portfolio for me to fill because it was hard to replace Favreau. I knew that Cardin had a good legal training, though little practical experience since he entered politics almost immediately after becoming a lawyer. But he had been my Parliamentary Assistant when I was Minister for External Affairs, and I knew he had a very level head. I also had much to do with him when we were in opposition, and I had a great respect at that time for his coolness and steadiness. He agreed to take on the job for a while but told me he probably would not run in the next election and would only be filling in until we could make more permanent arrangements.

One of his first problems as Minister of Justice was concerned with a security case. I had had some experience with these matters over the years and I will digress to touch upon this. The famous Gouzenko case broke during the time I was Ambassador in Washington. Mackenzie King's diary tells the story in a very detailed way, and I need not go into it deeply. In September of 1945 Igor Gouzenko, a cypher clerk in the Soviet Embassy in Ottawa, defected. He brought with him information on extensive Soviet espionage activities. I came into it when Mr King asked me to inform the US Secretary of State, James Byrnes, of what was happening. Mr King was concerned that Washington and London be kept informed step by step. The Big Three governments, especially their Foreign Ministers, were trying to work closely together on arrangements for postwar settlements. Hence our Prime Minister was anxious that the Gouzenko affair should not, in the rather exaggerated terms of his diary, destroy the peace of the world and start another war.

Mr King wanted me to get an expression of opinion from the United States government on whether we should go ahead with the prosecution of the Soviet spies. I had the feeling he was rather hoping they might say something like: 'Kill it in the interests of peace and the organization of the post-war world,' or 'You had better forget about this for the time being, or hold it in the background.' Mr Byrnes was not having any of that. I remember he was full of praise for the manner in which we had handled the matter; this was our responsibility, our business, and we could be trusted to deal with it. We should go ahead on our own and do what we thought was best.

Most of my contacts with security matters before I returned to Ottawa as Deputy Minister in 1946 had been in terms of war rather than of peace, and concerned the Axis rather than the Russians. They were still our allies and at conferences I got on very well with my Russian colleagues. Matters became quite different after the Cold War began in earnest. I became satisfied then, in 1946 and 1947, that there was such a thing as Kremlin-directed communist subversion (the Gouzenko evidence was very revealing), and that the safety of the state was involved. Members of the Communist party could well be, by that membership, a threat to our security. It is almost unbelievable what went on. We have had some of the more dramatic illustrations of this from Britain's experience, and we always used to look to Britain as the centre of wisdom in security and intelligence matters. Their experience frightened me.

It was after I became Minister in 1948 that the dreadful time of McCarthy and the 'witch hunts' began. He was one of the most horrible creatures of the twentieth century. I loathed and detested him. When I saw what was happening to the State Department in Washington because they were afraid to stand up to this man, I was determined that as long as I was responsible this would never happen to the Department of External Affairs. I remember that in 1953 the State Department sent us a request, on behalf of the Internal Security Sub-Committee (the Jenner Committee) of the Senate Committee on the Judiciary, that Gouzenko be allowed to go to Washington to testify at their hearings. The information the sub-committee was getting at that time came from former communist agents or sympathizers who had 'repented' and were denouncing people all over the place. The committee was interested, not only in evidence about United States citizens, but also about Canadians, including myself. It was a sordid business, which also became show business, with highly dramatized public hearings. We had years before turned over all Gouzenko's evidence to the FBI. We had also, in 1949, permitted Gouzenko to be examined in Canada by representatives of the US Senate Sub-Committee on Immigration. Now, they wanted to start all over again. We flatly refused to allow Gouzenko to be exposed to this committee, to be used by them for their purposes, some of which were political and not security. We could not stop Gouzenko from going to the United States, but we could inform him that if he did so the RCMP could no longer accept responsibility for his safety. The Americans were angry with our decision and a good deal of pressure was brought to bear on me to change my mind, pressure from the Senate Committee on the State Department to persuade us to allow him to testify. They said he would be treated well, that all they wanted was to get information on how the Soviet espionage services operated. If necessary, they promised to go into secret executive session. We agreed finally that if they were genuinely interested in getting first-hand information from Gouzenko they could again send representatives to Canada and hold a secret hearing with him, if he was willing, under our rules. We arranged a meeting in January 1954 at the Seignory Club, which did not suit the committee's purposes at all as this was done very quietly and confidentially. But it called their bluff; they got what information Gouzenko had without getting what they really wanted, publicity. We swore them to secrecy and had the meeting in the Manor House near the club under the chairmanship of Mr Justice McRuer. It was a most interesting experience, done with great dignity and very quietly. The judicial atmosphere was quite different from what they were accustomed to in front of cameras in Washington. They went home very unhappy about it all.

The dilemma that arose was to reconcile the security of the state with the freedom of the citizen. My attitude was very much like that of Dean Acheson, who was subjected to great pressure and some abuse when he discharged his duty to his colleagues by not allowing them to be browbeaten and accused unjustly. As Deputy Minister I felt strongly about my particular responsibility to the individual. There were one or two cases where there was unsupported evidence on the basis of which the Americans in similar circumstances would have thrown the person out. We did not. In one case where a Canadian official was accused, I was convinced that the man in question was a loyal Canadian citizen doing his duty to his country in a conscientious way, above reproach from a security point of view. But when I had read all the evidence I advised him to leave the foreign service since he might be subject to blackmail. He thanked me for the advice when I explained the reasons to him. I later helped him get a new career.

In 1951 a woman, Elizabeth Bentley, as well as some others, gave evidence off the record in Executive Session to the Internal Security Sub-Committee. In the course of her testimony she gave the names of some Canadians who had worked with a communist study group in Washington during the war. She gave one name which I managed to prevent becoming publicly known. The man became a prominent citizen in Quebec, of unimpeachable loyalty and considerable achievement. During the war he was a rather radical young man and went to some of these study discussions. But he probably did not know much about what was going on and he certainly was not an agent of any kind. I have no doubt that he talked about me, saying he had seen me at the Embassy and that I had said that the Russians were going to break through in the Ukraine, or some such thing. Thus, my name appeared in the Senatorial records, by association with this man to whom I was supposed to have fed information; that was what Miss Bentley insinuated. The committee really thought they had got hold of something, that I, as Ambassador, had been giving this group, some of whom were or became Soviet intelligence people, information through this other Canadian.

The State Department considered it their duty to pass these names on to Ottawa, including mine. I was then Secretary of State for External Affairs. I cannot quarrel with them for their decision; they were probably asked to do so by the committee. I had a call about this from a very highly placed man in Washington. He said: 'God, Mike, we've got to do it. We don't want to get into trouble with Congress. It's a political matter. Please forgive me. I'm going to have one of your friends go up with all this information so you'll know this is being done in the right way.' 'Oh,' I said, 'don't worry about it, though it's a pretty insulting thing to do. I hope we don't ever have to do anything like that in reverse. But I'm in politics now, and I know about these pressures. Just go ahead and give your list to the Prime Minister. I'll tell him all about it.'

It was not so trifling when Herbert Norman's name was singled out. They said they had evidence, which they brought to our attention, showing that he was a Soviet agent and a member of the Communist party. This was quite a shock. I had known Herbert Norman for some time and had gone to college with his older brother. His father, like mine, had been a Methodist minister and had served in Japan. Herbert was completely fluent in Japanese and had written books about Japan. When I was in Tokyo in 1950 General MacArthur said of Herbert, who was then in charge of our Liaison Mission: 'He's the most valuable man we have. We want to thank you for letting him help us.' Nonetheless, it was obviously my duty to follow up the accusation because the evidence included some specific charges. The first thing I did was to bring him back for special duty in the department. I invited him to my office and told him what had happened. It was a real blow to him. I said: 'We're going to put you through the most exhaustive investigation that any Canadian civil servant can be put through. That's what we must do.' He agreed. Then I had the man in charge of the RCMP Security Branch in for a talk with us and told him: 'Now take your time. Mr Norman, for his own protection, wants this to be a very thorough investigation. He'll tell you everything and I want reports on everything that you find.'

The enquiry went on for about six or seven weeks. The RCMP investigated in great detail and, I thought, in a very intelligent, sensible, and fair-minded way. The main charge against him was that as a student at Cambridge and Harvard he attended Marxist communist study groups. This was quite true, and he did not attempt to conceal it. The RCMP could not find anything to cast doubt on Herbert's loyalty. I went over the evidence with the chief of the Security Branch and concluded that he had a clean bill of health.

To show our confidence in him, we sent Herbert to New Zealand as High Commissioner. It had been quite an ordeal for him, though he took it very well. New Zealand was an easy post and he was not subject to much working pressure. Afterwards, we sent him to Cairo as Ambassador, a very difficult post, especially in the middle fifties. His reports from Egypt contained able analyses of the situation and the Americans were very grateful to receive digests of them. He was considered by most of his peers, I think, to have been one of the best observers there, just as he had been in Japan.

The second Norman blow occurred in March 1957 when the Internal Security Sub-Committee released to the press, without our knowledge, let alone our approval, a textual record of hearings which involved Herbert Norman, based on the earlier evidence. I sent the strongest note to the American government, to John Foster Dulles, that I ever sent as Prime Minister or Secretary of State to any country, even to a communist country. It read:

I am instructed by my government [this is Arnold Heeney, our Ambassador] to bring to the attention of the United States Government the allegations of disloyalty which have been made in the United States against Mr H. Norman, the Canadian Ambassador to Egypt, a high and trusted representative of the Canadian government. The irresponsible allegations to which I refer, and which in any event would concern matters to be dealt with by the Canadian government and not by a sub-committee of the United States Senate, were contained in the textual record of the Internal Security Sub-Committee of the Senate Committee on the Judiciary which was officially released by that body to the press in Washington at 4:30 PM on March 14 [1957]. I am instructed to protest in the strongest terms the action taken by an official body of the legislative branch of the United States government in making and publishing allegations about a Canadian official. This procedure is both surprising and disturbing because it was done without the United States government consulting or even informing the Canadian government and without taking account of relevant public statements made earlier by the Canadian government. The Canadian government examined similar allegations as long ago as 1951, and as a result of an exhaustive security inquiry, the full confidence of the Canadian government in Mr Norman's loyalty and integrity has been confirmed in all respects. The conclusions of the Canadian government were made public at that time and must have been known to the sub-committee particularly as the State Department was requested at the time, and again on December 11, 1952, to draw them to their attention. I am attaching the text of the two statements made by the Canadian government on this matter in 1951. The repetition of such irresponsible allegations in the sub-committee and the publication on the authority of this official body of a record containing such allegations is the kind of action which is inconsistent with the long-standing and friendly cooperation characterizing relations between our two countries.

The note, with the annexes, went to Mr Dulles on 18 March. Then I sent a follow-up on 10 April because they had not done much about the first note. This was even tougher. We were challenging again their whole procedure of making this information public without our knowledge, and indeed, of making it public at all: 'As the United States government knows, the Canadian government finds the procedures actually adopted by the Sub-committee with respect to Canadians difficult to understand, unfair and indeed intolerable. The Canadian government therefore requests again that these procedures be altered in so far as Canadians are concerned along the line indicated above.' We told them that in the future we did not want any Congressional Committee to ever mention a Canadian name without our approval, in any press release they made, and then we really told them what we thought of them in some pretty strong language; that we were going to protect Canadian citizens from this kind of slander. This is the paragraph that probably disturbed them most: 'In view of the conduct of Congressional investigations affecting Canadians and because of its responsibility for taking every precaution in its power to protect Canadian citizens, the Canadian government requests that in the reciprocal exchange of security information the United States government give its assurance that *none* of its agents or departments will pass such information to *any* committee, body or organization in the United States over which the executive branch of the United States government has not executive control without the express consent of the Canadian government in each case.' This was to impress the security branches to whom we were passing on information, reciprocally (as no doubt is still done), and as we did with Great Britain. The FBI was peddling that information to the sub-committee. The note continued: 'The Canadian government for its part assures the United States government that any security information on United States' citizens supplied by United States agencies to the security agency of the Canadian government would be given similar protection in Canada. Unless such an assurance can be given, I am instructed by my government to inform you that the Canadian government must reserve the right in future not to supply security information concerning Canadian citizens to *any* United States government agency.'

That really upset them. The State Department and the White House threw themselves on our mercy. They said, in effect, 'Look, you know the relations between the Executive and the Legislature, and you know the sacrosanct position of the FBI, don't ask us to give you this kind of an assurance.' It threw our security people here into confusion too, but we got what we considered to be adequate assurance that it would never happen again.

When I reported to the House of Commons there was an outburst of anti-American indignation, though the members were very pleased with the way it had been handled, even the official Opposition. It was near the end of the session. The 1957 campaign had not yet opened, but I was in Kingston talking to a Liberal assembly and meeting the people when the message came that Herbert Norman had killed himself. My feelings never reached a lower point in my public career. During the last day of the session Mr Diefenbaker asked whether I could give an assurance that all the statements made before the US Committee were untrue and unjustified. It was one of those 'Have you stopped beating your wife?' questions. I had about five seconds to decide what to do. I wish I had replied:.'I have nothing to add to what I have said, that this was an unfair and unjust accusation.' Instead I refused to say whether every single statement was accurate or not. But I told the House that every one of the allegations had been examined in detail and there was no doubt in our

minds about Herbert Norman's integrity and loyalty. It was true that
in his early days he had, as a student, been associated with Marxist
study groups. I did not say he was a member of the Communist
party, nor did I suggest that this was any reflection on his later loyalty. Mr Diefenbaker said, in effect: 'Well then, why all this indignation?' It was the beginning of an election campaign, so the Opposition
attacked, asking why I hadn't given the facts back in 1951, and so on.
This was very unpleasant.

The papers began to criticize the government, and while not accusing Herbert Norman directly of anything, the impression could be left
that I held this information back because I had some suspicion about
him. I could have made everything public in 1951 and I had considered doing so. I had disucssed it with the police, as well as with
some of my colleagues. I was urged by the security people and by
some others not to. It is a poor practice to reveal security procedures,
and it is not fair to the person concerned. It is normal procedure to
give only the results of the investigation. The story of the evidence
against Herbert Norman shows the value of our system. In 1957,
when the committee in Washington gave out the information about
him, it was that an RCMP member during the war had put Herbert
Norman's name forward as a communist agent. But that evidence
had been discredited by the police themselves. It was so mixed up, it
even had him at the wrong university. They should have burned it
but they put it on file. Some time later an official of the Security
Branch here sent it down to the FBI without any indication that it had
been discredited and was not being used. When this was found out
some months later, the RCMP informed the FBI of their error. If that
later message was sent over to the sub-committee, they never used it.
In 1951 I think we were right in not mentioning details. The fact that
the matter was not mentioned for six years would seem to vindicate
our judgment. In 1957, should I have done the same thing? It was
now a tragedy. Herbert had killed himself. There were headlines all
over the world. I am not sure, but I think I followed the right course.
The facts would have come out in any event. The people in Washington, the unfriendly people, would have produced everything. Indeed, I became the victim now that Herbert was dead. They could not
victimize him any more, so they turned against me. The stories in the
States in the unfriendly press – the *Chicago Tribune*, the Hearst Press,
and McCormick Press – were that I had admitted he was a communist.

Then an awful story appeared from Cairo. It reproduced part of
Norman's last letter to his wife explaining that he had to kill himself

because this revelation was coming. That was how it appeared in the American press. They had found him out at last. But I had seen the original letter. It was very personal and very pathetic, and bore no relation to the published version. I did not know what to do. I could not table the letter in the House, as it was too intimate. Instead, I asked the senior representative of the Canadian Press, a man with a fine reputation, Clyde Blackburn, to see me. I said: 'I can't make this letter public, but I want you to see it, and I hope you will let me say that you have seen it and that it bears no relation in any way to the fabricated letter that is appearing.' He said he would be glad to do that, and he did. His denial was sent to all the papers that had published the distortion; not one of them would publish his story. It was a sordid ending to this tragic business.

When I became Prime Minister we changed our entire security structure. I had no quarrel from my experiences of those earlier days with the general conduct of Canadian security affairs. I found the RCMP men with whom I had anything to do reasonable and understanding. They did not have the traditional secret police image. Still, I was not satisfied with the machinery, especially the procedures for appeal, and I tried to improve it. I did not like our very close association with security agencies in other countries, especially with the FBI. But we were close allies, doing intelligence work together, as well as security, and it was difficult to refuse to pass on information we possessed. I often thought, however, that this collaboration could get us into trouble. I think that the procedure was abused at times, especially on immigration questions where, again, there was not enough effective protection for the rights of the individual. The quality of the information that was gathered also worried me, but I am sure this was characteristic of all police evidence. I used to say when I was going through some of it: 'Now look, how do you know this might mean anything at all?' 'Well,' the security people said, 'we have to weigh and evaluate it. However ridiculous the information may seem, we take it all down and then we try to evaluate it.' I would hate to trust my future, in a pinch, to any security man's evaluation, no matter how honest and sincere he might be, when there is no appeal from it and when you cannot see the evidence against you.

All this may be taken as the background to my attitude toward the Spencer case. The RCMP had discovered that two members of the Soviet Embassy in Ottawa were using a post office clerk as one of their agents. He did not appear to have been of any great value to them as a spy, since most of the information he provided them could have been obtained either from an almanac or by writing to a government department. Victor Spencer was, in a pathetic way, a sincere little man, who perhaps thought he was doing the right things in betraying his country.

The Russian diplomats were expelled in May 1965. Usually we do these things quietly: 'Get out in forty-eight hours.' But the intelligence experts of the police, with the approval of the Department of External Affairs, decided to issue a statement building this case up as a warning to civil servants not to yield to the blandishments of communist diplomats. The text was shown to my by the Secretary of State for External Affairs and I was somewhat astonished at the language which implied that 'girl typists should be careful':

The Department of External Affairs today [May 8] announced that the Ambassador of the Soviet Union was requested on May 4 to arrange for the departure from Canada of two members of his mission, Mr A.E. Bytchkov, of the commercial section, and a chancery clerk, Mr V.N. Poluchkin. The Canadian Government had learned that they had engaged in activities incompatible with their official status and had, therefore, found it necessary to declare them persona non grata. They left Canada on May 7.

In one instance a Canadian civil servant was paid thousands of dollars to gather information and documentation in Canada, the purpose of which was to assist in the establishment of espionage activities in Canada and in other countries, and to perform economic intelligence tasks, including the provision of detailed information on the Trans-Mountain Pipe Line system in Western Canada.

In another instance a naturalized Canadian citizen was paid thousands of dollars to provide technical information in the electronics field related to defence industry and to compromise other Canadians, including female employees of the Government, with the object of securing their assistance in obtaining access to classified information. He was given specialized photographic training to assist him in these tasks.

The approaches made by the two members of the Soviet Embassy very shortly came to the attention of the Royal Canadian Mounted Police. As a result of this co-operation by conscientious Canadians, the police were able to establish the improper intent of the Soviet approaches and to put an end to them before any damage was done to Canadian interests.

It was exactly the kind of statement that would get a headline and I was told it was hoped the statement would have a deterrent effect. I remember saying, 'This is pretty lurid language,' and Mr Martin replying, 'Yes, it's deliberately lurid language.' But it was issued as it was.

There was some mild controversy over this matter at the time, but then it dropped from public notice until early November 1965, just before the election, when an enterprising Vancouver journalist, Tom Hazlitt of the *Province*, identified the civil servant as Victor Spencer. This revived interest in the matter, though I do not think Mr Spencer's position and background were such as would give the impression he was a spy of fictional dimensions. The matter might have been dropped – the new Parliament had not met yet – but late in the month Mr Cardin found himself on the CBC interview programme 'This Hour Has Seven Days.' Such programmes are an excellent means to get one into trouble in politics, or perhaps I should say that they prevent one from getting out of trouble, because one is confronted with current troubles and, failing alertness, these become bigger. So it happened in this incident since Mr Cardin, whom I thought a pretty experienced politician, made some unfortunate and sensational remarks, in particular about keeping Spencer under surveillance 'as long as he lives.' This put the fat in the fire. Spencer, a man who had been fired without trial, was now apparently being told that he was to be subject to surveillance for the rest of his days. It is not hard to imagine what civil liberties organizations and the Opposition did to this: 'What are we living in? A police state? If he's guilty, let him be punished. If he's not guilty, why should he be subjected to surveillance?' (Although surveillance is a nasty word, the RCMP had Spencer's own protection as much in mind as anything else.)

After the Christmas holiday, Cabinet began to review the matter, since we considered this would be a major target for Diefenbaker's eloquence when the House reassembled. Spencer had been fired under a clause in the Civil Service Act that did not provide for an appeal. After considerable discussion in Cabinet, the general opinion was that an appeal would be objectionable on security grounds and that the clause in question was put in the Act precisely for cases such as Spencer's. He was lucky merely to be dismissed, having confessed to improper association with Soviet agents.

The other question, more difficult, was whether or not we should yield to the mounting clamour for an enquiry into the circumstances of Spencer's dismissal 'as a spy.' The Opposition was virtually unanimous in demanding an enquiry and practically every newspaper in the country supported them. We were handicapped in answering through our inability to give the evidence, on security grounds, which had justified Spencer's dismissal. This evidence, indeed, could not even be given at any public enquiry or appeal. The Opposition clamour, when Parliament met, grew in volume and vigour. The NDP, and especially Tommy Douglas, were much more impressive in their criticism than the Conservatives and John Diefenbaker because they made a more reasonable appeal to justice for the rights of a 'little man,' convicted without a chance to defend himself.

In Cabinet there was a division for and against an enquiry, with a strong majority against. My own feeling was that we should have one *in camera* since the issue had been now transformed by the press and the Opposition into one of civil liberties and human rights. But since there was in fact no question of principle at stake (we had treated Spencer fairly), I accepted the view of two-thirds of the Cabinet, especially as the Minister most concerned, Cardin, took that view very strongly. He had stated it publicly and its repudiation by the Cabinet could have been interpreted as our throwing another Minister to the wolves. He would have resigned. So Cardin made his statement in the Commons on 31 January, no enquiry and why. This resulted in further attacks on the government and an appeal to me by Tommy Douglas to review, personally, the whole matter.

I was uncomfortable about the manner in which the debate had developed. I am always uneasy when accused of violating somebody's rights and freedom. So I replied: '. . . naturally when my honourable friend asks me, as he did, and as the Leader of the Opposition did, to give consideration to any matter, I will give consideration to that matter.' Having agreed to do this, the argument stopped for the time being.

I did indeed review the matter, spending hours and hours reading every police report, every bit of evidence on Spencer during all the time when he was being watched, and the entire record after he had been confronted. My conclusion was that he had been fairly treated, as he admitted himself in his signed statement, which of course we could not use since it gave so much detail about his contacts with the Soviet agents and other security matters. My study also confirmed that the press statement of May 1965, issued by External Affairs at the request of the RCMP in order to warn against dangers to our security, was a foolish procedure.

On 23 February I announced in the Commons that I had exhaustively and conscientiously reviewed the matter and saw no reason to change our attitude to an enquiry:

I have examined this situation personally. I have studied all the reports, all the documents concerning this case. I have spent a good many hours, Mr Chairman, in doing so, because I know that the issues involved are important and I know that they have aroused very real uneasiness in the minds of hon.

members. Not only did I study the details of this case and discuss them again with my ministerial colleagues who were more particularly concerned, but I examined other security cases in the last ten years which might throw some light on the justifiability or otherwise of the procedure followed in this instance – certain cases which were of very direct and immediate concern to the government of the day, which was the government preceding this government. As a result of this study and these considerations I wish to confirm the view which has been given by the Minister of Justice that an inquiry into this matter is not necessary and would not be useful.

But this did not stop the attacks. They were resumed and increased, and became more difficult to counter when the Opposition asked for an *in camera* hearing. We were accused of stubbornly refusing a reasonable request for a judicial enquiry into the dismissal of a civil servant, who had been charged with being a spy without being given any opportunity to defend himself. There was another factor in this whole problem that I could not refer to, even in private conversation. Although it was known that Spencer had been gravely ill, he appeared to have recovered; I had, however, seen a report during the previous summer that Spencer was suffering from incurable cancer and might not live more than a year, and the year was nearly up. I thought how unfortunate it would be if this poor man died without an enquiry; he would be protrayed a martyr to the cruelty and injustice of a despotic government.

Then came Friday, 4 March. David Lewis of the NDP introduced a new element into the controversy. We had previously emphasized that Spencer himself had not asked for any enquiry or made any complaint. Now Lewis read a telgram signed by Spencer and a lawyer asking for an enquiry, but, it seemed, limiting his request to an enquiry into the circumstances of his dismissal and particularly as it affected his pension. This seemed to give us a way out; to accept this kind of limited enquiry while rejecting the demand for a full review which would bring in security issues. We could save our faces and give public opinion reassurance that the dismissal was just, by the report of a judge.

A decision had to be made quickly. David Lewis also moved a motion to reduce the estimates of the Department of Justice by $17,000, the amount of Mr Cardin's Ministerial salary; in effect, a motion of no confidence, which he would withdraw if we agreed to an enquiry. If defeated on it, we would have to resign. I had to do some very quick work that afternoon to determine whether we could defeat this motion of Lewis' or not. How would the vote go? All the

Opposition groups opposed our position and we had no reason to be sure they would not vote against us. I knew that some of our members would not vote with the government, two of them had told me so. It was agonizing to think that a Liberal government could be defeated on such an illiberal position, as it would be regarded in the country; a Liberal government defeated on an issue of refusing to give a man his day in court.

I did some speedy consultation with a few colleagues during the debate (ten of my Ministers were away). I asked Cardin to come to my office. We talked over the latest developments and on the basis of our discussion, I decided that we should change front in the new circumstances. I told Cardin I would take full responsibility for the change by making the statement to the press myself but that I would associate him with it so that there would be no repudiation of him, either in fact or in appearance. So, after this hour's hurried consultation, I rose in the House and announced that I would telephone Mr Spencer to confirm that he wanted an enquiry along the lines suggested by Mr Lewis. If he said: 'Yes,' then he should have it.

I also spoke to Mr Cardin that day about the need for a Royal Commission to investigate the whole area of security. The Spencer case showed how badly this needed to be done and Cabinet now agreed. Although it was not until November 1966 that a Royal Commission on security matters was actually set up, I stated that the wider investigation would be made on Monday, 7 March 1966, when I announced the terms of reference on the Wells Commission to enquire into the Spencer affair.

The reaction to the announcement that we would set up a commission on the Spencer case was depressing. The Tory Opposition jeered 'Surrender.' The NDP were triumphant, and also co-operative in the sense that they were willing to withdraw their no confidence amendment. The tacticians in our party now became sure that, if we had stood firm, we could have won the vote. They were confirmed in their view by discovering, again after the event, that the Social Credit and Créditistes would not have voted against us (certainly we had no reason to believe this before the fact). It had been another very difficult time. There had been no opportunity on Friday, 4 March, to have a meeting of Cabinet or caucus and our members did not know that I had been discussing my announcement with some of our Ministers and, particularly, with Cardin. Many thought that, for reasons of expediency, I had cut the ground out from under the Minister of Justice. I think Jean Marchand, for instance, was furious about our reversal, especially since, while I was discussing what to do about Lewis' amendment, he had been making a vigorous speech defending our earlier position.

Cardin now decided to resign. I suspect that some Quebec members, who could be pretty volatile, reminded him that he was being over-ruled as a Quebec minister; that two Quebec Ministers, Lamontagne and Tremblay, had been allowed to resign in the reshuffling of the Cabinet; Dupuis had been thrown out, Favreau eased out of Justice, and now he himself was being tossed aside. Marchand felt that he should resign if Cardin did; so did Cadieux and Côté. Things were falling apart.

I talked to Cardin at Sussex Drive on Monday, both alone and with Lamontagne and Favreau. He was adamant. He expressed a regard and affection for me that was deep and sincere and not affected by anything that had happened; but he could not and would not remain any longer in politics. He had not wanted to run again; his home life was being destroyed; he hated the lonely life in Ottawa, just as he hated the pettiness and nastiness of politics; he was not cut out for it; and this was his chance to leave.

I discovered Tuesday evening, however, that he was really shaken by the possiblity that his resignation would break up the government and lead to my own. I passed this on to Lamontagne and we agreed that, if Cardin could be finally and firmly convinced that, if he went, we *all* went, he would stay. His Quebec friends worked on him the same evening and, as a result, he agreed to stay on and announced that decision to the Quebec caucus Wednesday at 10 in the morning and to the full caucus at 11. As a consequence, what might have been a national caucus meeting of despair and dissension became one of hope, unity, and rejoicing. Leo Cadieux was eloquent and very impressive, Cardin quiet and effective, and I made the strongest statement to caucus I had ever made on the necessity for mutual trust, confidence, discipline, and unity. It was one of the most moving and elevating experiences I have ever known with that group, particularly after the terrible ordeals we had gone through. We were all relaxed and relieved. We were entering upon a new road of unity with no scandal and no friction. This was a happy ending to a frightening weekend. Then came Cardin's press conference on Thursday, 10 March 1966, and utter chaos. Munsinger succeeded Spencer, like the relentless unfolding of a Greek tragedy.

Cardin, as I have said, had been subjected to bitter and vehement attacks in the House of Commons. Some of these were personal attacks with quite unpardonable adjectives used to describe his conduct. He was a mild and even-tempered man, but during the debate on Friday, 4 March, when these charges were being thrown at him in connection with the Spencer affair, he allowed himself to retaliate against Mr Diefenbaker and asked him to tell the House about his participation in the 'Monseignor' case. He did not even say 'Munsinger,' but I knew what he was talking about and was stunned.

My own knowledge of the Munsinger case went back to December of 1964, after the Dorion enquiry was established by the government. I had been disturbed by the alleged pressures on members of Parliament by criminals, the underworld, and dubious characters generally. So I requested, through the Minister of Justice, that the RCMP search their records and give me evidence, if any, of other cases which they had investigated in which members of Parliament, whether Ministers or not, were involved in any way. I wanted information on the nature and magnitude of this problem. To remove any impression that I was concerned only with trying to implicate the Diefenbaker government, I told the police to go back as far as 1954.

The first report I had received, the only one which produced anything startling or serious, included a brief on the Munsinger affair. It showed that a woman, who had been a Russian agent in Germany and later a call girl in Montreal, connected with the underworld, had established a close association with the then Canadian Associate Minister of National Defence, Pierre Sévigny. This matter had been brought to Mr Diefenbaker's attention as Prime Minister, but he kept Mr Sévigny (who had certainly become vulnerable from a security point of view) in his sensitive post, with, as we later learned, only a reprimand and an injunction to cease seeing the woman. When I first learned of the Munsinger case, I wrote to Mr Diefenbaker, as one Privy Councillor to another, on 4 December 1964:

In discharge of my constitutional duty as Prime Minister I am writing this letter to you as a Privy Councillor and former Prime Minister.

I have been much concerned, not only about allegations made recently in a particular case, the Rivard case, but, even more, about an attitude toward the operation of the law that certain evidence in this case discloses. This attitude is not widespread but the Rivard case illustrates the need to take thorough action to remove it.

The problem has not sprung up suddenly. In order to assess the need for corrective action, I have asked for a full report of instances in the last ten years or so in which political intervention was involved in investigations. This information will enable me to see how much matters could and should be dealt with.

One case (the Munsinger case) has given me very grave concern. It affects the security of the country. In 1960-61, a Minister who occupied a position of great responsibility in the Government was involved in a liaison which clearly endangered security.

I have been greatly disturbed by the lack of attention which, in so far as the file indicates, this matter received. The Minister was left in his position of trust.

I have decided that I cannot, in the public interest, let the matter lie where it was left and that I must ask the RCM Police to pursue further enquiries.

I recognize that the file before me may not disclose all the steps that were taken. In view of this, it is my duty to write you about the matter in case you might be in a position to let me know that the enquiries that were pursued and the safeguards that were taken reached further than the material before me would indicate. That material now indicates that the Minister of Justice brought the matter to your attention and that no action was taken.

Because national security is involved, this is the most serious and disturbing of the matters that have been brought to my attention. But I assure you that all incidents during the last ten years are being thoroughly examined, and will be followed up without fear or favour if and when the evidence requires it.

If there is further information you can provide about the Munsinger case, I will be grateful if you will let me know.

Instead of replying, Mr Diefenbaker came to my office a week later. I kept the following diary note of that discussion.

Mr Diefenbaker's office phoned to see if I could see him. I did so at 12 noon.

He had not fully recovered from his flu-cold and seemed tired and more than usually nervous.

He wished to give me an oral answer to the letter I had written about the Sévigny affair and his Associate Minister of Defence's connection with it. I indicated that I would also expect a written reply and he said it would be forthcoming.

After various remarks about the difficulties and heart-breaks of being a PM, Diefenbaker came to the point. He knew of the Sévigny case, had interviewed his minister, had satisfied himself that no security had been violated. He did this on the strength of Sévigny's passionate assurances.

I merely told Diefenbaker that this was the information I had asked for and I assumed that he would put it in writing . . .

He never did. There the Munsinger matter rested. There was no longer any question of security. Sévigny was in private life. Munsinger had returned to Germany and the report was that she had died there.

It was ironic that in the 1965 election the major issue put forward by the Conservative opposition, and to some extent by the NDP, was 'morality in government.' They charged that we had been harbouring criminals, that we had been soft on crime, that the Mafia and organized crime had penetrated the highest levels of government. I did not deal with these charges during the election campaign. Those were our tactics—to pay no attention to them.

It was only on 4 March 1966 that Cardin, goaded beyond endurance, shouted across the Chamber to Diefenbaker that he was the last man in the world to give advice on security cases, considering what he had done, or rather not done, about 'the Monseignor case.' Favreau and I, who had been following Cardin's counter-attack on Diefenbaker with some satisfaction (mixed with worry on my part) were flabbergasted by the interjection of 'Monseignor.' We seemed to be more surprised than Diefenbaker and Davie Fulton—and even Cardin did not know he was going to mention 'Monseignor' until he was provoked into blurting it out. It remained now to ignore the reference, if the Conservatives made that possible. They were likely to do this because they had nothing to gain by any revelations, quite the contrary.

So I was reasonably comfortable about what had happened until Thursday, 10 March when, to my surprise and anxiety, I learned at 10:20 in the morning that Cardin was going to have a press conference at 10:30. It was too late to cancel the conference. That would have been news in itself and I would have been charged with repudiating Cardin again. I therefore warned him to very careful in what he said about the decision to grant Spencer an enquiry, and to be even more careful not to get involved in any questions about Munsinger.

He told me that he did not want to go into the Munsinger question. I wish he had stuck to that at the press conference. At the beginning he told the press, wisely, that if they wanted any further information on the Munsinger case they should apply to Mr Diefenbaker. When asked if he had mentioned the name 'Monseignor' or 'Munsinger' by design in the debate, he said 'No' (I am sure he was right about this), 'it was provoked out of me.' The same thing happened in rather a different way at the press conference. He was continually needled and lured into saying more than he would have, or should have. In response to the question whether a Minister or Ministers were involved he replied, 'Ministers.' He added: 'All right, I said that Ministers were involved, plural. I didn't say whether they were involved romantically or otherwise.' Having said, 'Ministers,' plural, he thus threw all those who had been Ministers during Diefenbaker's prime ministership under suspicion. There was a fury of criticism in the House that afternoon and evening as former Diefenbaker Ministers demanded to be charged or exonerated. For four days the debate raged in the House, ostensibly on a question of privilege but actually by permission of the Speaker, Lucien Lamoureaux, since the proceedings were entirely out of order. The Speaker was correct in overlooking the rules because otherwise there would have been a parliamentary riot. Indeed, he acted throughout with admirable calmness, courtesy, and firmness. He never lost control, even when the House became a shambles.

I especially remember one incident. The late George Nowlan, a man who had had the respect and affection of nearly everyone in Parliament, came to be mentioned in the media as possibly being one of the 'Ministers' involved. His son, Patrick, in a short and moving speech to the House on 15 March, appealed to Mr Cardin or me to 'at least clear the dead, even though they refuse to charge the living.' I was unable to do so because I had not seen the text of all the evidence and could not possibly give details on the clearance, or not, of everyone. I knew that there was mention of two or three Ministers involved and, if I had cleared George Nowlan's name, and I dearly wished I could have, other Ministers would have demanded that I give them the same treatment, or else declare 'You are guilty.' I told Patrick Nowlan about this afterwards, but it did not make it any easier for him and it did not make it much easier for me.

I decided that we had to get this before a judicial investigation immediately, one more judicial investigation. It soon became clear that the smaller parties, and some of the Tories, particularly Doug Harkness, who raised the matter first as one of privilege, would support a judicial enquiry. I therefore spent the weekend of 12-13 March working on terms of reference wide enough to take in all of Cardin's statements but precise enough to show that Diefenbaker's mishandling of a security situation was the real point at issue rather than revelry in Gerda Munsinger's apartment.

Monday morning came. We had to get the Cabinet to agree to the terms of reference, to get the Order-in-Council signed and up to Government House; we must have a commissioner, all before 2:30, when I wanted to make my announcement. Some of the Cabinet favoured three commissioners, but we decided on one. He would have to be a member of the Supreme Court of Canada, we thought, but this presented a difficulty, since informal soundings made it clear that the Supreme Court preferred to stay aloof from the enquiry. I therefore phoned Mr Justice Spence of the Court at 12 noon and told him that it was his duty as a good citizen to take on this thankless, but vitally important, task. After thinking it over and following another telephone conversation, he agreed. We were all relieved and grateful. The Tories in the House fought hard to get the terms of reference submitted to a Committee of the House for examination and revision; but we stood firm and they gave up the struggle.

Shortly afterwards I summed up developments in my diary:

Cardin had been the hero of the Quebec Caucus earlier. Now they must have wondered what possessed him to get himself—and all of us—into another mess. Yet they—and indeed all of us—could hardly help but feel some exhilaration at seeing the Tories squirm in the gutter where they had chosen to fight. The ensuing publicity—it soon became frantic—was degrading; it debased Parliament and the country. But the issue of political contest by slander and personal attack had been joined and perhaps the result will be decisive this time. Certainly, if Cardin cannot prove, through a judicial enquiry, that Diefenbaker mishandled this case, he will have to resign and there can be no effort this time to persuade him not to. No one will want to make the effort because Cardin is the only one responsible now for the situation. If he fails and resigns, I would certainly resign too because I have backed him, at least to the extent of setting up a judicial enquiry. If he is repudiated by that enquiry, the Government is repudiated. If his charge is confirmed, by the Judge, then Diefenbaker must surely go . . .

So, in very truth, the issue is joined; in a rather sickening way on a particular matter that has personal and private implications that should have no part in politics; though they always have and perhaps always will as long as human nature remains what it is.

Mr Diefenbaker appeared before the Spence Commission for one hearing and then refused to appear again. Attacks were made on the impartiality of the commissioner, but he made his report. Although it is true that the headlines emphasized sex rather than security, I always took the position in the House that this enquiry was nothing but a security investigation. This was the only interest of the government in it; what we were trying to find out was whether there had been a breach of security. Mr Fulton, who had been the Justice Minister mainly concerned (Mr Fleming for part of the time), made the statement in the House that no question of security arose. The Spence Report showed, of course, that security had been involved and that the Prime Minister of the day had not taken the necessary action against the responsible Minister.

In sum, these so-called 'scandals' had a deplorable effect on the reputation of Parliament in the country. We spent so much time on them that they had the unhappy effect of delaying the important business of government and of Parliament and lowering the level of debate. I blame this primarily on the Opposition; they, no doubt, would have a quite different version. But to fix the blame is not so important as to realize that as a result Parliament was debased in the public mind. The House of Commons had nothing to congratulate itself for in the way the debates developed, nor had the press for the way they reported these matters (except, perhaps, Robert Reguly of the *Star*. Besides finding Hal Banks in New York on his yacht, when neither the RCMP nor the FBI could locate him, he also found the supposedly dead Gerda Munsinger, alive and kicking in Munich). It was a wretched time for Parliament and so regarded throughout the country.

Perhaps the most violent expression (whatever the precise cause) of popular feeling was the action of the man who, in May 1966, tried to dynamite us in the House. It was during the question period. An explosion was heard but we continued in debate (I thought perhaps an elevator had collapsed) until I was handed a note that a man had killed himself in the washroom with a bomb. He had been seated in the Gallery with the device under his coat when he got permission to leave his seat and go to the washroom. There he tried to do whatever you do with a dynamite bomb that will set it off; he apparently mis-timed the fuse and blew himself up. Had he been a little more accu-rate in his timing he would have blown up most of the members of the government (I assume he would have thrown the bomb in our direction). It was a terribly dramatic, terribly distressing afternoon.

One aspect of this tragedy was not generally known. The night before, while my wife and I were having dinner at Sussex Drive, the man had come to see me. (This was before the days of high security.) The maid sent him away with the advice: 'If you have anything im-portant to tell Mr Pearson, you can go to his office tomorrow morning and the staff there will take your message to him and, if necessary, you can see the Prime Minister then.' He said: 'Tomorrow will be too late.'

MID-TERM REVIEW

Politics is more than differing opinions over issues and ideas, of how best to serve the public interest. Politics also embraces power and position. Hence in politics pride is often stronger than tolerance, and prejudice more current than understanding. Conceit, even arrogance, to which the successful politician is exposed, can be a danger to those who gave him the power on which his conceit is based. A professor of philosophy, who also became a US Congressman (T.V. Smith), once wrote: 'The conceit of absolute truth is the one-a-day vitamin of political totalitarianism.' It can lead a man to believe that he is only doing what God would do if He had all the facts. From this is born the extremist, the dictator, of whom Mackenzie King observed: 'The extreme man is always more or less dangerous but nowhere more so than in politics.'

A decent humility and a sense of the ambivalence and transitory character of political triumph can help the politician to avoid both arrogance and extremism. They can also arm him against disappointment and disillusion and help him to work patiently and steadily to achieve his objectives, regardless of setbacks. Thus, I have always remembered the advice given to the rising young politician by Chubby Power: 'Always remember it is only a step from the private car to the upper berth'; or, as I later brought that up to date, 'From the prime ministerial jet to the economy stand-by.'

In trying to avoid these vices of arrogance, extremism, and over-confident conceit, the politician may tend (how well I know this!) to over-react in the other direction of caution and compromise. He will then try to rationalize what is really political timidity by explaining that he is merely following Thomas Jefferson's advice that 'No more good must be attempted than the nation can bear.' Being by nature impatient in tactics, if not in strategy, I once or twice committed what I consider the lesser evil by misjudging the bearing. When I did, I got some comfort from Gilbert Chesterton's dictum: 'Don't be afraid of getting into hot water, it keeps you clean.'

Today the politician, especially if he is a leader of government, has to deal with forces at times impossible to control, even difficult to understand. He is expected to produce instant solutions for problems that defy quick or complete analysis, to satisfy quickly expectations that can be realized only over the years, if then. He must meet tests of unprecedented complexity in an age of dissolving values, lightning change, and increasing confusion. As Professor Douglas LePan once put it:

Those in positions of seeming authority forfeit respect because they appear to be presiding over events that go as they will. The fabric of absolute beliefs and absolute values is in tatters, and in its place is a craving for absolute experiences. Power in one form or another is still necessary if society is to be held together, but power has been invalidated for many in our age by the monstrous uses to which it has been put in this century, and by its culmination in the power to destroy the species. In such circumstances, what can those charged with responsibility do to restore their credit? What can they do, I mean, beyond what the best of those with responsibility have always done in all ages and all countries – that is to go on, to go on day after day, taking decisions without full knowledge, judging in ambiguous situations and without the benefit of absolute standards, knowing that no one with responsibility can ever be guiltless and learning to live with that knowledge?

No single man, no single group, indeed, no single country can master today's challenges. A man in power does the best he can, proud of the special opportunity he has been given, hoping that his achievements will have added something to his country's real strength and its people's happiness, and that his mistakes, of omission and commission, will be corrected by his successors.

Generally speaking, I am proud of our legislative record. We welcomed the need and opportunity for reform and took on many controversial problems previously side-tracked or postponed. The record shows this. All this is the more creditable because we were a minority government which might have been pardoned for its caution. We were very conscious of the need to adapt new policies and actions to changing circumstances in all areas of federal responsibility, in small matters and in large.

There were, however, some initiatives that did not work out so well. For example, the Company of Young Canadians was fine in concept but unhappy in execution. The idea was to see what could be done to give the young people of the country, who were restless and exasperated and unsettled, an opportunity to get rid of their frustrations by service. I hope that I will not be misunderstood in writing this, but the two wars we have known in this century, while tragic and bloody and terrible, did give our young people a chance to lose themselves in a cause in which they believed. The wars channelled their enthusiasm and idealism. The new generation had not found the moral equivalent for war service and I wondered whether there was something we could do in this country to provide them with a challenge in terms of service to the state or to the international community. Thus, the Company of Young Canadians.

From the very beginning, this venture was plagued with misfortune. It was put under my direct authority, not under any separate government department; and a Prime Minister really has not time to give to that kind of project the day-by-day attention that it requires. I realized this difficulty, but I was interested in the project and was glad to take that responsibility, at least in a general supervisory way. A good board was set up which, in turn, chose the management. Then everything went wrong. The board did not turn out to have the right kind of liaison and rapport with the management, and the management turned out to be extremely ineffective, lacking the skill to combine administrative strength with an understanding of young people. Further, it became quite clear, almost from the beginning, that those who were rushing to join included far too many who wanted not so much to make their communities better as to revolutionize them. The remarkably good things achieved in some communities were obscured by news reports almost every other day about some scandal, militant demonstration, or horrible mix-up in which the Company of Young Canadians took part. I had no desire to tie them to the establishment but their freedom became pretty chaotic. They resented any effort toward administrative and financial supervision. And it went from bad to worse, to the point where I remember at one stage saying to some of my Cabinet colleagues, 'We've got to wind this up.'

Neither did our plans work out on the international service front. The legislation provided that there would be a great opportunity for those who wanted to serve abroad, and I imagined that nearly everyone would want to. I was wrong in two respects. The young militants wanted to stay at home. Second, CUSO (Canadian University Service Overseas) had already begun to operate effectively abroad, and it was argued that we should not interfere by creating a competing operation. While CUSO had its limitations in that it was largely confined to people with higher education, whereas anyone could join the Company, I accepted the argument on the understanding that, within a year or so, we would work something out with CUSO so that with more financial support from the government it could draw on members of the Young Canadians if it wished to. But it became quite impossible to make changes so that the Company could perform effectively. By the time I left office, I was sorry not only that it had failed in its original purpose but also that it had caused so much controversy. Yet, if I had it to do again, I would still support the idea and I would not make any changes in the legislation setting it up. I would make certain from the very beginning, however, that the Company was provided with effective management. I have always been interested in experimenting with things new and progressive in government, if I thought them useful.

ॐ

Broadcasting was another difficult area. I had been interested in the Canadian Radio League in the thirties and my views did not change in principle during the intervening years, though certainly they had to be modified in practice. My general view was that broadcasting should be treated as education and that there should be the greatest possible public control; that the emphasis should be on the public system and private broadcasting should be very much a subsidiary. Indeed, I used to think in the early days that the CBC should be the sole agency for all broadcasting. It soon became clear, however, that there was going to be private broadcasting and there is much to be said for the kind of competition it provides, though I still would have preferred the British system as it then existed. The CBC, however, did regulate all broadcasting until 1958, when the Board of Broadcast Governors was created.

The regulation of broadcasting in Canada is a federal responsibility where change is so rapid that there must be new legislation about every four or five years. There cannot be a single, all-encompassing Act unless the government is granted very broad authority to make necessary changes in policies by Order-in-Council. In broadcasting, no Parliament is going to be anxious to grant that kind of power. Indeed, every member of Parliament thinks of himself as an expert on the subject, on what is right and what is wrong; on what should be put on and what should not. Further, it sometimes seems that, in the public view, it was acceptable to have a strike on the Seaway or on the docks, but to be deprived of watching a favourite programme was a national disaster. Thus, there is continuous pressure on the government and on the head of a public broadcasting corporation. The President of the CBC does not have the relative independence of the head of the BBC in London, and does not get quite the same protection. For example, we actually had a political crisis over a weekly television show called 'This Hour Has Seven Days,' and this was settled only by most dexterous diplomacy.

As for our legislation on broadcasting, it had become quite clear that we were not going to be able to avoid much longer the establishment of some more effective external control commission in broadcasting than the Board of Broadcast Governors, and that a new effort should be made. We also had to take up the problems of educational broadcasting and other changes. Anxious to get the best possible legislation, we decided to set up the Fowler Commission, which reported in the autumn of 1965. We also had a Cabinet Committee on Broadcasting in which I took a great interest, presiding over many of its meetings. We received a lot of advice from a lot of people, and spent a good deal of time drafting the legislation passed early in 1968. The principal element of our new policy was the statutory statement that the airwaves are public property and that all those who use them constitute a single system, a distinctly Canadian broadcasting system in which we might ensure Canadian ownership and control of facilities and encourage Canadian creative talents and resources. I was quite pleased about the way it worked out and considered that the new Canadian Radio Television Commission, replacing the Board of Broadcast Governors, was an effective piece of machinery. Fortunately, the first appointments to the CRTC were relatively easy, whereas I would place the appointment of a new president for the CBC, in terms of the demands made on my time over weeks and months, in the same category as the unification of the armed forces.

Indeed, the post of top man in the CBC was, to my mind, the most difficult appointment my government had to make. And, to be perfectly frank, my difficulties in this regard were not made less by the fact that Miss LaMarsh was the Minister in charge of broadcasting.

She felt strongly that she should be given the responsibility and that I should accept her recommendations without question. I was not able to do that. Of course, Miss LaMarsh did not like to have her judgment questioned in any matter and this prolonged the problem until she finally bowed out with: 'All right, you choose your own man.' I was looking for somebody who would, as head of the CBC, have a feeling for and a knowledge of the medium, its potential, and its operation, but not by any means a professional or an expert in broadcasting. The best advice I got was that the second man should be a professional and that the top man should be an organization man, at least for the first year or two after our new broadcasting legislation went into effect. I thought George Davidson, for many years a Deputy Minister and then Secretary of the Treasury Board, had the governmental background and organizational ability we needed. He had a broad understanding of human and social problems and, I felt, a real appreciation of the importance of broadcasting. I thought he was the right kind of man. The Minister did not agree. For that matter, neither did George Davidson. When he was approached at the very beginning of our search, he said: 'No. I'm not going to do it. I've had enough trouble in the Treasury Board. Why should I go from one frying pan into another fire?' But I finally persuaded him.

Before leaving the question of broadcasting, I should mention that, in terms of partisan advantage, I never had any great cause for complaint. Looking back, I think the control exercised by the CBC over political broadcasting, the allocation of political time and so forth (which was worked out by an agreed procedure) was, on the whole, quite fair. When in opposition, we used to think that the government always had the greater advantage since they would have Ministers appearing constantly on the screen. Naturally, I changed my mind about that when I became Prime Minister. I remember when I was Leader of the Opposition I was one, among four or five, asked to take part in a New Year's broadcast. I was in Florida on holiday, and I went to a great deal of trouble to make the most eloquent statement of my view and then telephoned it home at great expense to the CBC. However, somebody in the network discovered that there was no one on the government side to speak in this series, so my eloquence was wasted. I was irritated at the time. But, as I say, I looked at it from the other point of view when I was head of the government.

I did come to believe in broadcasting certain parts of the proceedings of Parliament and its committees. It seemed impossible that we could forever exclude from the screen and radio information appearing every day in the press. If I had thought we could avoid this sort of thing permanently, I would have been glad to do so, because there are great dangers in it. We have seen, for instance, what happens in United States Congressional committees. The broadcasting of Congressional hearings has performed some very important public services, but at other times it has cheapened and almost debased the procedure of government. The bad must be taken with the good. There will be no cameras in a committee which is not exciting and, since excitement usually means conflict, there is a risk that the work of Parliament will be interpreted mainly in a context of conflict which, indeed, it so often is. Then if cameras are put in the House of Commons, there will be all sorts of other problems. 'Who's going to get prime time?' Well, the Prime Minister probably would have the best chance of getting prime time in a debate. Although we did not find a solution, perhaps a good way to start would be to film the question period each day; this might also improve the questions.

ॐ

Nothing, of course, could have caused me more trouble than the labour problems that beset us. Our period in office coincided with a period of labour unrest at a time of inflation and rising prices. It was almost inevitable that there should be difficulties, but problems were particularly grave in 1965-6, when we had postal, longshoremen, and railway workers on strike, each one containing within it a threat to our national economic well-being.

Although we moved with dispatch to end the postal and railway strikes, the settlements which drew most attention were with the longshoremen in Montreal and with the Seaway workers in June 1966. I have been charged with the responsibility of having set off a spiral of inflated wage demands that has yet to be concluded. I remember the details of this situation quite well. I had nothing to do with the negotiations until after the wage settlement had been agreed. Judge Lippe from Montreal was the mediator. In co-operation with our Department of Labour people he was working out a settlement with the longshoremen's union representatives and their employers' association. These had been difficult negotiations. The strike had been protracted and this had a damaging effect not only on the economy of Montreal but across the nation. Further, the strike threatened the completion of the Expo site in time for the Centennial celebrations. We were caught in a vice. On the longshoremen's side, they were relating their demands to the settlement achieved by the Montreal construction workers. I was eager to get the strike settled and, when I was told that if I intervened the small matters outstanding might be rapidly cleared away, I complied. Agreement had been reached on all major matters before I played my small role in the negotiations. After both sides met in my office, we were able to announce that the strike was over.

The Seaway workers' demands were a more direct government responsibility. This was a difficult situation because the men were working in the locks alongside Americans who for the same work were being paid about one-third more. Our men were entitled to an increase, but we thought their demands too high. A strike would have halted, among other things, the movement of grain from the West. There was a great pressure to get this settled before our economy was dealt a staggering blow. There always is great pressure. I, therefore, asked Senator Norman MacKenzie to mediate. He came to my office late one afternoon with the news that he had a proposal to which both sides, the workers and the Seaway Authority, had agreed. When I took a look at it, I thought: 'Well, we're really for it. It's his proposal now and I don't know how we can repudiate him, but it's too high. He gave them practically everything they wanted.' I called a Cabinet meeting. We had no choice and, consequently, we accepted Senator MacKenzie's proposal. We were in trouble, but it was really a matter of the lesser of evils. We would have been in even greater trouble had we not accepted the settlement and allowed a strike to occur.

We also knew by then that the 1966 railway strike was approaching since the contracts between the unions and companies had expired on 31 December 1965. But the possibility of doing anything in advance was complicated by the fact that five separate boards of conciliation were working, and the last one reported only in August.

The unions, however, were acting together and hoped to take simultaneous strike action. Thus, we had to wait for the last board to report. Knowing, however, that a strike *was* coming, we did meet and plan in July and August against that contingency. By 'we' I mean myself, the few Ministers who were in Ottawa during the parliamentary recess, and the key officials in Labour, Transport, and the Privy Council. As part of that process I asked for and got briefs on all aspects of the dispute and on the way in which a strike would affect the economy.

John Nicholson, the Minister of Labour, took almost a fatalistic view of developments. Everyone realized collective bargaining in railway disputes was a farce—a long drawn-out farce—but nothing could be done about it until we changed our labour and railway legislation. Events moved on and our plans were worked out against a strike which we expected to take place legally after Labour Day.

We were haunted, of course, by the longshoremen's and Seaway workers' increases which had been awarded in June. The government had been directly involved in those settlements and Mr. Diefenbaker began to exploit these settlements as an invitation to the unions to hold out in their disputes for a 30 per cent increase, which he dubbed 'the Pearson Formula.' I felt that he was stirring up the existing labour discontent for his own political purposes. But in doing so he also increased the agonizing doubts in my own mind on whether we had been right or wrong, wise or foolish in the agreements made in June. Should we have stood firm then and faced a national labour and economic crisis?

During the month of August, wild-cat strikes began on the railway and informal talks with the unions were started. I remember one long discussion I had with the labour leaders at Sussex Drive. They were as worried as we were about the situation and saw no hope of averting a strike unless we gave in all along the line. I let them know we would not and could not do that; that we would not go beyond the 18 per cent increase recommended by Mr. Justice Munroe as chairman of two of the boards of conciliation.

The union leaders were frank in admitting that their men were out of control and were determined to strike. They warned that if Parliament were called and a law passed to prevent or postpone a strike, it would not be obeyed. Much as they disliked governmental intervention to end a strike, they realized that this was going to be necessary. But, they insisted, the timing was all-important. It was essential that any governmental or parliamentary intervention be delayed until the men had been on strike for some days and 'had got it out of their blood.' Then, they could be legislated back to work.

This, in fact, was the major problem before the Cabinet, and the one on which there was the most acute division. Should we intervene before the strike and summon Parliament to prevent it, or intervene after the strike had been on for some days and pass a law ordering the men back to work? Opinion was evenly divided. My own feeling, at first, was that if we were going to intervene in the process of collective bargaining, we should do so to prevent a strike rather than to stop one in progress. Why incur the harm, even for a day, of a damaging strike if government is going to intervene ultimately? My view on this point changed when I heard from the union leaders that the men might obey a return to work, but in their present temper they would never obey a law which kept them at work. Even discounting the views of the leaders as based on the difficulty of their own positions, it was impossible to dismiss that advice. I was also impressed by the results of our economic studies, which showed that the effect of a shut-down for about a week would not be disastrous. In the meantime, we decided not to take any action until the unions decided whether to strike.

During all the long discussions on this point, as I have said, we assumed that no strike would be called until after Labour Day. That assumption turned out to be wrong, and the question of when to intervene became largely academic. A strike date of 26 August was announced on 22 August. The earlier date was due, I believe, to the leaders' inability to hold the line with the workers against wild-cat strikes until September. The men were becoming increasingly impatient with delays, especially since other settlements were being made at high percentage rates of increase. In a sense, the early strike date was a relief. It settled for us the argument on whether to intervene before or after the strike was called. Although we could have called Parliament to meet on Thursday, 25 August, we decided not to summon it until the following Monday.

In the meantime, we turned to the more difficult decision of what should go into our legislation to present to Parliament. In ordering the men back to work would we make an interim award of a pay increase? If so, how much? If we decided to appoint a mediator, whom would we appoint? If we decided on compulsory arbitration would there be one arbitrator or three? What would our tactics be on opening day? What if the unanimous consent of the House which was required was refused?

The most controversial of these questions was that of compulsory arbitration. Jean Marchand, our member with greatest union experience, who had been comparatively unconcerned over the problem of preventing or stopping a strike, was emphatic that we should provide in the legislation only for mediation. He disliked compulsory arbitration and believed that it should be reserved until all else had failed. He was confident that mediation would produce a settlement, and that if it did not, the men, once having been on strike, would not leave work again, especially during the winter months. Parliament, if necessary, could settle the matter at a later date. The argument was

vigorous. Some of my colleagues felt strongly that it would be considered as an evidence of weakness, indecision, and uncertainty if we
made no provision for compulsory arbitration in the event of failure
of mediation.

In the end, Marchand still protesting, the Cabinet collected around
a compromise proposal, by which a provision was put in the bill for
arbitration by Order-in-Council if, on the failure of mediation, the
government decided that this course was unavoidable. This provision
became even more acceptable when we were able to disarm Tory
criticism by using the exact wording of a similar provision in the bill
passed by the Diefenbaker government in 1958 to end a ferry strike in
Briüsh Columbia.

It was quickly agreed by Cabinet that there should be an interim
wage increase written into the legislation. In view of the outburst
soon to explode in the House of Commons and the point chosen by
the Opposition for attack, it was perhaps surprising that so little time
was spent on the interim awards in Cabinet. It was soon decided that
Judge Munroe's recommendations for increases of 4 per cent from 1
January 1966 and 4 per cent from 1 July 1966 should be accepted, as
they would now have retroactive application. Everything else would
be left for resumed negotiation and collective bargaining.

In my opening remarks when the House met on 29 August, I
pointed out that the Canadian economy is dependent on railway
transportation and that a general railway strike was a national
emergency which, if prolonged, could become a national disaster.
The debate on the bill which I introduced continued for four days
before it passed. Later that evening, 1 September, it was given the
Royal assent to become law. The railway strike was over. The fact that
we had to legislate, however, was an indication of the futility of
collective bargaining in this area. Railway negotiations are now carried out in the knowledge that if the men do go on strike, the government will inevitably intervene. The negotiation itself becomes less
important and there is not the same incentive to come to an agreement.

These strikes had come fairly close together and presented a very
sour situation, from my point of view. While I was distressed, I did
not feel apologetic about the settlements because I saw no other way
out. There is no return to the nineteenth-century *laissez-faire*
liberalism of Spencer and Mill, with government merely holding the
ring while unofficial power centres work their will on society. We
have become too vulnerable to disaster, and also more democratic, as

technology has changed the basic nature of our society. Indeed, we are in danger of becoming the victims, as we have already become in many ways the beneficiaries, of material and technological progress. Unfortunately, we continue to rely on institutions and practices which derive from out-of-date and largely irrelevant concepts. Certainly, the events described above confirmed my view that our methods of dealing with such disputes are antediluvian. In consequence, I asked the person who I was told was the ablest in the country in this field, Dean H.D. Woods of the Faculty of Arts at McGill University, to be the head of a task force on the handling of industrial disputes, to tell us how to do better in future. I refrained from appointing a Royal Commission because I thought a task force sounded more businesslike and would complete its work much more quickly. It could not. I announced in the House on 9 September 1966 that the task force was to come back with an answer in a few months. The report, however, was not made until 31 December 1968.

ℭ

One of my most important political decisions as Prime Minister was to hold a general election in 1965. We had been having a rough time as a minority facing a difficult Parliament. A vigorous, almost violent Opposition was cutting us down on every possible occasion and making our lives very uncomfortable. Whatever else may be said in comparing the two positions, the strain on a minority government is much more severe than on a majority. Goodness knows, we had enough wear and tear the year before the 1965 election; in fact, I cannot remember a moment when we were not in difficulty, every kind of difficulty. After two years of minority government I was urged by those closest to me to go to the people. Our only reason to contemplate a dissolution at that time was to secure a majority in the Commons, a 'vote of confidence' from the electorate to remove from our backs the dread incubus of never knowing when we would be thrown out. Those who felt strongly about this put it to me that if there was a chance for a majority, we should take that chance.

There were two important factors I had to weigh in making up my mind. One was my own strong distaste for elections. As I have said on a number of occasions, I was not one of those people who love to get out on the hustings, who draw strength from contact with the soil and the people. My thought after the 1963 campaign had been: 'I'm not going to go through this again if I can avoid it.' That resolve no doubt influenced me in 1965, though it also made me feel (having retained a bit of Methodist conscience) that I was allowing my judgment to be dictated by my emotions, emotions which predisposed me against an election. If they had not, my wife would have encouraged my negative attitude.

The personal factor could be overcome and had to be overcome, once the decision was made; the other and more important consideration was whether we would win if we appealed to the country in 1965. For my part, I was not at all sure that we could count on the majority necessary to inspire us with the confidence to start afresh. I was therefore opposed to the idea.

I was forced to consider the question most carefully when, at the end of March 1965, I received a memorandum from Walter Gordon strongly recommending an election that year. He argued:

1 the Liberal party organization was enthusiastic;
2 economic and employment conditions in the country were excellent;
3 the situation in Quebec was relatively quiet;
4 the polls of individual ridings showed we could win;
5 our minority government had gone on long enough and there was a great deal of work to be done – but it would take a majority government to do most of it;
6 finally, if, as was possible, Mr Diefenbaker announced his intention of retiring and a Conservative convention was called, our hands would be tied until the new leader was chosen.

There were, in his opinion, three possible polling dates that year: the end of June, the second half of July, or early November. Having ruled out June for various reasons, Mr. Gordon then went on strongly to urge an election in July. He concluded that there was no good reason to wait until fall, and many serious risks in doing so.

Although still not persuaded, I did, in mid-April, write the following memorandum on party strategy:

In the current mood of the country, what conclusions as to party strategy can be drawn?

The first is that, despite the greater likelihood now of an early election, as long as no decision has been announced, campaigning ought to be kept in a fairly low key. We should avoid personal attacks or exaggerated claims or too alluring promises. The public seems more than usually sceptical about politics and politicians. We won't achieve respect or credibility by claiming too much, or attacking too bitterly and personally.

What the public wants is to see evidence that we are not excessively partisan and that we *are* competent to run the country. It also wants solid achievement, not good intentions; and not, obviously, exaggerated partisanship or concentration on personalities.

This careful and restrained approach does *not* mean that we can go on the defensive or play things safe by doing very little. Quite the opposite. Caution means not that we become apologetic and defensive but that we know – and appear to know – what we are doing and that we do it efficiently.

Election talk

There should be no election talk from us. We recognize, of course, that an early election may be necessary because the Opposition parties could, by blunder or design, make government impossible and force an early election. We must not seem to be manoeuvring for it. But we must get ready for it as sensible people would do.

Diefenbaker

In this atmosphere, we would do ourselves no good by mounting an anti-Diefenbaker campaign at the moment. He is a real asset for us. To attack him personally reduces the value of that asset by giving him a chance to look better, not worse. We can leave it to him and to his own party to keep up the momentum of his and their decline. But we don't want *his* disappearance – yet!

What we should do, on the critical side, is to make sure that the Conservatives do not escape the incubus of Diefenbaker's unpopularity.

Again, *we* don't have to say that Diefenbaker can't get on with anyone from Quebec; what we can usefully say is that he is the Leader of the Conservative party and the *Conservatives* aren't any longer a national party. Therefore, they couldn't possibly form a national government able to act effectively.

The Socialists

Up to the beginning of December 1964, the NDP appeared to have made no progress in popular support since April 1963. But they have recently had an upswing. Certainly they have some claim to feel that they are in better shape than at any time since the bright first days of the new party. At that time we out-played the NDP. But now the 'plague on both your houses' mood is strong and, if it continues, Mr Douglas and Co may get a new start and new support.

In these circumstances, the NDP will be trying to emphasize its moderation and reasonableness. We should make that as difficult as possible. We should identify the party as socialist. We should underline its irresponsibility and its contradictions and its assumption of smug superiority.

Second, we should work hard on the theme that the one practical effect of the NDP campaign is to contribute to political instability. It isn't a national party and it can't conceivably win an election. All it can do is make an election indecisive by bringing about another minority government with all that that implies for effective administration of the nation's affairs.

Third, we should make sure that the NDP doesn't make all the running with social welfare issues. Our Throne Speech has been a great help here. We have stolen some of their clothes while they were bathing in holy water! Social Credit and the Créditistes we should try to ignore.

The power of positive action
The crucial thing for the government is to get a few more positive achievements under its belt without delay and publicize what it *has already* done. This latter is of vital importance. We have failed here.

The hard fact is that until very recently the public feeling has been that we haven't done much. This is untrue. But we won't change the feeling by words alone, or by argument. Only by good and continuous publicity in all its forms.

Our handling of some matters has looked ineffectual. The only cure is to look efficient in getting new things done. Then we will start getting more credit for the results we already have achieved.

The main achievements we should be able to get across are:

1 Better times, the economic upsurge; production up, unemployment down. We should be able to get much more credit for this. We should talk more about it. The talks will get across provided it is not mere partisan boasting and is accompanied by evidence that we are keeping up the good work; that we have a continuing practical program.
2 Greater security for all—pensions, protection for widows, and orphans; protection against disability. This has been a real achievement.
3 Better opportunities for young people—youth allowances, student loans. Also the 'Company of Young Canadians.'
4 We count again in the world—trade, common sense in defence, success in external affairs.
5 The government has successfully brought the country through a crisis that threatened its unity and survival. Nothing is more important than to deal effectively with this matter.

Nothing, however, is more difficult. It needs particularly careful handling. There is danger in talking about national unity in the wrong way as a continuing issue. Precisely because we are the only party with apparent strength in Quebec, English Canada is liable to suspect that, when we talk about national unity, we are really talking about more for Quebec.

We can be reassured by evidence that what has so far been done has not created too much resentment against us in other parts of Canada on anti-Quebec grounds. But they do expect, in the areas of concern, some positive, solid achievement.

Our immediate strategy must be to show a little more such achievement; we can then hope to be listened to when in an election campaign we talk, as we are bound to, about further achievements to come. This is why getting on with the priority measures of our Throne Speech is so important.

Evidence of a little more solid achievement is the trump we must play out before our long suit is established. That suit is the need for majority government for stability and progress in the country. Combined with this, as another good card, is Reform of Parliament. This may well become a very important issue – soon.

The next month or so may be decisive in determining the position of this government in the minds of the people as we move to an election.

The dates for calling an election in June or July were allowed to pass. But the pressure did not let up. On 13 August I had lunch with Walter Gordon, chairman of our Liberal Federation, during the course of which he pressed on me the need to call an election. His views made a considerable impact, for on 16 August I wrote:

Why an election now
An election *now* is required in the national interest. There is no need to be defensive or apologetic about it.

The technicality, that the Commons has only recessed and should be called before a dissolution is of no importance. There are no commitments to recall Parliament before an election and there is a Diefenbaker precedent for not doing so.

As for redistribution, it cannot be fully in operation before 1967. Are we to wait till then? If redistribution is of such vital importance, why did the Tories do nothing about it? We started redistribution as soon as we took office and it is not our fault that there has been so much delay in completing it.

If an election on the old boundaries is so 'immoral,' will the Opposition give a pledge not to defeat the Government and bring about an election before the new arrangements are ready; that is, before 1967? Of course not!

On the contrary, during the recess, the Opposition parties have been calling for the defeat of the Government, as soon as Parliament reconvenes. They accuse us of corruption and of dishonour; of being weak, vacillating, indecisive and wicked. Yet we are not to be permitted to take these charges, and our record, to the people; to ask for a vote of confidence; to ask for that majority in Parliament which will help give us the strength, confidence and security needed for a Government today as it faces some of the biggest and most vital problems that any Canadian Government ever encountered.

If the Opposition cry 'foul' when an election is called in these circumstances, they add absurdity to irresponsibility.

They argue that there is no need for an election, but a crying need to end this Government!

Canada is facing problems vital to its future, to its very survival politically, constitutionally, and socially!

The people must now be given – after $2^1/_2$ years of a Parliament of minorities – a chance to return a Parliament where a strong majority for one party – from every part of Canada – will back a Government of that party as it faces up to these problems.

We have a right to ask for a vote of confidence; indeed, we have a moral obligation to give the Canadian people *now* the opportunity to give us one – or reject us for some other party.

Those who oppose an autumn election fall into three groups:

1 Those who want us to win but think this is a bad time for an election. We should wait until 'Dorion' is forgotten, they say, and the 'Record' better appreciated. They fear that the result of an election now would again be indecisive. The surveys indicate they are wrong. But, even if they were right, the choice is not between October or, say, June 1966; the choice is between now and 1967 (we couldn't have an election *six months* before redistribution); or between now and the time when the Opposition will defeat us; with a new Tory leader! After October we have no freedom of action. We are hemmed in by political circumstances.

2 There are those who oppose an autumn election because they oppose us, wish to defeat us, but want to get rid of Diefenbaker first. They desperately wish for an election in which they can defeat us with Fulton or Robarts (Premier of Ontario).

3 There are sincere people, good citizens, who don't want an election *now* (some don't like elections at all) and hope that, by postponing it, we will avoid the stresses and strains on unity that the kind of campaign Diefenbaker will wage will bring about.

These people often write me to be a Canadian first and a Liberal second, by sacrificing a victory now in the interest of national unity. Wait till Diefenbaker goes, they say....

But, if Diefenbaker is able to hang on, the issue is merely postponed, not improved...

To repeat, our approach to the question of, 'Why an election now?' must be entirely strong and positive.

It is not a contradiction to include, in this positive approach, telling the public how bad the Opposition parties are as a reason for their decisive defeat at an election. This is especially true of Diefenbaker and what he is doing. We have to be aggressive – and not defensive – about this; that the character of the Diefenbaker Opposition in particular is a main reason why an election now is in the national interest; is a necessity.

To sum up, our position is:

We have been trying to do a job – a very difficult one, in very difficult circumstances.

We have certainly made mistakes, because we *do* things; we take on the tough problems, the ones that other Governments with clear majorities have talked about for years and years without result.

In spite of difficulties, and mistakes, we have a fine record of concrete achievement.

We have done much – but want to do more – and do it better.

Everyone knows what the Opposition say about us; the charges they make; the confidence they try to destroy; the divisions they create; the threats they make to throw us out.

Well, how can a minority Government continue to carry on with best results in these circumstances?

So let's have a show-down. There is much unfinished business to do. We need a mandate for it.

Having got these points across, then we can get on to the subject of what that business is (this is the really important matter); of what we propose to do once we get a clear mandate.

From 19 to 29 August I made a tour of the Western provinces to gauge feeling there; meanwhile more soundings had been taken, in the form of another of those polls that determine the fate of nations now, or at least determine the decisions that, in turn, determine the fate of nations. Personally, I could not really see how, if pollsters went around a country such as Canada and spoke to about fifteen hundred people, they could determine what was going to happen. Nevertheless, I was sufficiently impressed by the scientific approach which they espoused, to agree. So we hired the best pollster we could find, Oliver Quayle. (Of course the fact that he was an American was to be held against us when this came out.) The result of his work indicated a very good chance of our getting a majority. I will never forget a meeting on 30 August with Walter Gordon and Keith Davey, the party's National Organizer, in my little library at Sussex Drive where we discussed the implications of the poll. They strongly advised that we should have an election. In spite of what I had written a fortnight earlier, I was still not convinced, but agreed to discuss it again during the next couple of days. I spent that evening scribbling out some notes on why we should not have an election, and I remember going to sleep that night much more contented than I had been for some time.

I saw Gordon on both of the next two mornings. I recall being told that I was allowing my judgment to be determined by my feelings. I was impressed, perhaps more than I should have been, by the argument that I was being selfish and not doing my duty by the party. The party managers and the people with whom I had conferred thought the time was right for an election. The discussions were frank, the kind I like to have with people before making decisions. I agreed to think it over again; I took another look at all the evidence, swallowed hard, tore up my scribbled reasons against going to the country, and on Wednesday, 1 September, discussed the problem with Cabinet, most of whom favoured an election, though the support of some could not be termed whole-hearted. At the end of the meeting I said I would make my choice by the following Tuesday. Finally, on 3 September, I talked at Harrington Lake with my closest political advisers and decided to hold the election on 8 November. Our campaign would be based on the absolute necessity for a majority government. Four days later Governor General Vanier granted the dissolution of Parliament and that evening I announced my decision on national television.

Mr Diefenbaker had received in 1958 the majority he did not get in 1957. We knew that circumstances were different, but we did not understand how different. 'Majority government' is not the most stimulating or invigorating slogan. In fact, this was a dull appeal. It would have taken a far better campaigner on the hustings than I to rouse the multitude to 'hurrahs' for majority government (although, all things considered, I think I did pretty well in that election).

Of course, the 'scandals' became a major factor in the election. The Opposition asked, 'Majority government for what? Majority government to let Rivard out of jail? To let Hal Banks escape?' All this made the campaign an agony for me. I only mentioned the scandals once during the whole campaign, and that immediately led to a chorus of protests from my managers to leave all this alone. Looking back, I do not know whether my avoiding this issue was right or not; I should, perhaps, have met it head on and I often felt like doing so. But I did not. One can imagine how it felt to campaign for majority government when our opponents were accusing us of every political crime in the calendar, and some that were more than political. This was a very unpleasant campaign and some of the meetings were very, very rough.

In reflecting on the campaign a month after the election I wrote: 'Looking back – which is easy – I think that, while it would have been a great mistake to have accepted Diefenbaker's challenge that this was the only issue and to have concentrated on it, we should have dealt with it more effectively, I should have given two or three broadcasts on it – and spoken two or three times about it without allowing it to dominate my campaign. As it was, it looked too much as if we acknowledged a guilty conscience through evasion and silence.'

I also felt that perhaps we should have been more vigorous and positive in talking about our own achievements as a government. But here we were caught in the net of our main argument that a majority government was essential for further achievement. There was a logical answer to this apparent contradiction and we gave it, but it was too logical and not obvious enough. Election arguments have to be either obvious or emotional, and ours were, for the most part, neither. No one can really get worked up about a concept such as 'majority government.' It just does not touch the heart. You can lecture about it, as I did, day and night. But these were lectures to impress, not appeals to arouse. The argument did not arouse *me* – so how could it touch others? When I was moved, really moved, myself by my themes – national unity, the greatness of Canada, our new flag, the elimination of poverty – I invariably got a strong response from my audience. Regrettably, we made these things secondary to the appeal for a majority to get on with our job. With this approach, the things we wanted to do such as medicare became subsidiary to the mechanism for doing them.

Then there was the perennial problem of the press. Newspaper editors are always bleating about the refusal of politicians to produce mature and responsible discussion of the issues. The fact is, when we do discuss policies seriously, we are not reported at all, or reported very inadequately. Reporters do not appear even to listen, until we say something controversial or personal, charged with what they regard as news value. And audiences normally confirm the reporters' judgment by obvious boredom with reasoned argument. This may not have been true fifty years ago, but it is true today. People want a show, and the competition for their attention is savage. So a show it must be, with excitement, headlines, personal attacks, and appeals to prejudice or fear or other emotions. After the election I noted: 'The day of big meetings with big, serious meaty speeches is over, as a political asset of the old kind. If you have such meetings now, they have to be circus performances, organized as such for stimulating your own followers and depressing the opposition. They can do that on occasions but at other times they become merely expensive farces.'

I remember trying to point out in one speech the danger that economic expansion might get out of control and result in inflation. A financial newspaper had attacked political leaders for their cowardice in evading this issue. So I made quite an argument on the point. The journalists present merely reported my caution about economic expansion, without explaining the supporting argument. Within the hour I received an appeal from headquarters to be very wary of this topic; I might be accused of favouring tight money, unemployment, and stagnation, of putting the bankers ahead of the people. Headquarters were right – Diefenbaker attacked me the very next day on just these points.

We had assumed that Diefenbaker's personal position would be our greatest asset. He was an asset in the sense that, with any other

Tory leader, I think we would have done worse. But he campaigned more vigorously and more effectively than we had thought likely, while the disadvantage of his own record as Prime Minister was reduced by the shortness of popular memory and by the tactic, on which we had not counted, of the anti-Diefenbaker forces rallying around the party, and even superficially but flamboyantly around *him*, to save their party from a disastrous defeat.

This was perhaps the most nauseating feature of their campaign: the expressions of loyalty and admiration for Diefenbaker by those who had not hesitated shortly before to express their detestation of him and their determination to get rid of him after the election. In fact, that is why they 'rallied round,' as a prelude to removing him after he had failed in the election. I wrote shortly after the election:

But Diefenbaker was cunning about it and turned the tables on the conspirators. He was able to do this by claiming a great victory because he had not been annihilated. He pinned a defeat on us because we didn't get 140 seats, only 131, which was enough to retain power. He claimed a triumph because he had retained 95 seats even though that kept his party 35 seats below ours.

His triumph was to have survived and he made the most of that 'success' by riveting his control over the party, to the discomfiture of the conspirators whose position was now weaker than before the election. He did not win the election but he won a victory, for the time being, over the dissidents in his own party.

I might mention that the most frightening campaign experience I ever had occurred during this campaign. The great wind-up rally in Toronto was not to follow the traditional pattern of an assembly of the faithful in their thousands at Maple Leaf Gardens but a more popular and spontaneous gathering at the large ultra-modern Yorkdale shopping centre where, from a platform, I would talk to the cheering multitude gathered in the plaza which was surrounded by the shops. The multitude were there, packed and enthusiastic. It was all that even Keith Davey, our national organizer, could have asked for. I received a tumultuous reception but when I began to talk, the loud-speaker refused to work. Our ingenious but nasty foes had seen to that. My voice, never sonorous or powerful, was quite incapable of reaching the excitable and noisy crowd, even with the bull-horn which was produced for my assistance. So I decided to replace my dogged but unsuccessful vocal effort by moving into the crowd, greeting and shaking hands with them. That was a mistake and could have been a disaster. People, including some with small children, began to push forward from the back against those who were already submerging me. I was gradually being pressed toward the storefronts, and the pressure was increasing. It was the kind of situation where one incident or accident could have caused a panic with serious consequences. But an informal bodyguard which had gathered round me got things under control, the press of thousands of bodies subsided, and the danger passed. It was a scary few minutes and left my friends limp and myself shaken and bruised. It was my last and most memorable election meeting, and the most dramatic memory I retain of the modern technique developed by political organizers known as 'marketing our great leader.'

The major source of my unhappiness during the campaign, however, was the fact that, far back in my mind, I felt I did not have to do this after all. We were not sweeping the country, and it was not an election required because we had been defeated in the House or because our statutory five-year period in office had expired or was to expire soon. We had called the election for political reasons, and this put a greater feeling of responsibility on my shoulders. Although I did not enjoy it much, technically I was more at ease as a campaigner than I had ever been before. I was getting used to it, I was closer to the people, and received a warmer reception than previously. I was, so to speak, in the groove, even though it was not the kind of groove I would have chosen. In all, it seemed to me that the only justification would be if we got our majority.

Thus, I awaited the results with interest and excitement. The returns were very good until we reached the west, and then the familiar old story. I had never been so depressed in my political life as that evening at the Château Laurier, when it became clear that the Prairies had no interest in giving us a majority. In the end we gained seats only in Quebec and the Northwest Territories, holding our own or slipping slightly elsewhere. We came back with two extra members (131 seats) but no majority. We had gone through it all for nothing! We remained in office, surprised and chastened; our hopes and expectations, as well as the assurances of our experts on which they were largely based, were unrealistically optimistic; our immediate reaction was one of dismay and defeat. Our advantage over the Tories had stayed exactly at 34 (the NDP won 21, well below their hopes). Fortunately, we had some very good new members, whom I shall mention later.

The people of Canada were not disturbed by our lack of a majority, otherwise they would have given us a majority. As I wrote at the time, 'They were satisfied that we had retained office because of the alternatives, but were rather pleased that we had been taught a lesson for calling an election that most people didn't want. Indeed, the very calling of the election was the real reason for not getting a majority. People were indifferent to our argument for majority government, and therefore irritated by our action in trying to get it by putting them to the inconvenience of an election. I don't think any kind of campaign would have removed this initial obstacle in the way of achieving our objective. Of course, we made tactical mistakes but only a few.' Our basic strategy of a 'soft and slow' campaign, speeding up to a hard hitting climax was, I believe, right. It was certainly the best campaign I ever conducted.

My own first reaction was to resign the leadership. This was partly a reaction of disappointment but, more than that, I wanted to leave. I was never enamoured of remaining in politics. I had had enough, and would have been very happy to drop out. In this respect my own personal feelings and plans were exactly the opposite of those of the Leader of the Opposition.

But a few days of hard thinking and discussions with my closest colleagues and a few non-political friends showed me that I could not leave. If I had secured a large majority, I could have been out in a year. If there had been defeat and a change of government, the party would have expected me to resign. But we were still in office and, whatever the figures showed, we were in a stronger parliamentary and national position than before the election. Statements from other party leaders gave no support to Mr Diefenbaker's threats of an early defeat of the government. Even some of his own senior colleagues repudiated these tactics. Any party that forced another election within three years would be exterminated. My own colleagues and practically every one of the hundreds who wrote me urged me to stay on, to take heart and realize that my own position was strong. The caucus, with one or two exceptions, was unanimous in support.

I decided I must carry on. I also decided, however, that it would be only until I was seventy years of age, and this would be in 1967. I would go through the centennial year. So, even then, I knew when I was going to leave. There was no fooling this time.

If the day after the election was gloomy for me, it was even gloomier for Walter Gordon. Walter was the manager of the campaign, and had worked as hard as anybody. He had given everything and I think he felt more responsible for the decisions than anyone else, except perhaps myself. I had to take the responsibility but, apart from that, he was the most immediately concerned. He came to see me soon after the election and said that he was sending in a letter of resignation and would like to discuss it with me. This had happened once before, after his first budget, but not with the same atmosphere of finality. He felt, rightly, that he had been the strongest protagonist for an election among the Liberal hierarchy and the most optimistic as to the result. Having been proven wrong, he also felt, wrongly, that for this reason he should resign as Minister of Finance and as chairman of the party organization. He felt pretty strongly about this and I was quite agreeable to changing his portfolio because, as he himself knew, he did not have the full confidence of the financial and business community which a Minister of Finance should enjoy. However, I tried to persuade him not to resign. I thought he might like to have a change of department and I pressed him to move into another that might be less demanding for him. I indicated that he could have any department, within reason, that he wanted. But he did not want a change of portfolio, only a change from the Cabinet to private membership. Then I expressed the hope that he would stay on until I had decided on the other changes I would be making in the Cabinet so that the one announcement would cover everything. But he said he had made up his mind to resign, and he wanted to go immediately. He was leaving the next day on a holiday to Ireland. If I had told him he simply had to remain, I think he would have done so. But I deliberately did not do this, since his position would have been weaker as a conscript Minister, and so would mine, if it became known (and everything becomes known in Ottawa) that he had wanted to leave. I simply said: 'Well, I can't really argue any more Walter, if you've made up your mind. If you want my answer before you leave, I guess I have to agree with your decision.' We agreed on an exchange of letters of resignation and response.

As I recall, he had a draft letter of resignation with him. It read:

For many months as one of your senior ministers, I urged you to call an election on the grounds we needed a majority to govern the country well and to ensure the kind of stability I thought was needed.

As chairman of the Liberal party's National Campaign Committee I believed that if you conducted a good campaign we would obtain a comfortable majority. Your campaign was superb in every way. You could not have done any better or any more than you did.

The conclusion is quite clear. I gave you bad advice, both as a minister and as campaign chairman. I accept full responsibility for this and therefore submit my resignation from the Cabinet.

If there is anything I can ever do for you at any time, you know all you have to do is let me know.

After he left, I drafted a letter of acceptance, and this I did with great care. I then sent it to his office to let him see it before I signed it. He sent it back saying it was fine, and I signed one of the most difficult letters I ever had to write.

I have received your letter and I have also thought over the talk which, at my request, we had subsequently this afternoon.

I cannot accept your assumption of responsibility for the decision to hold the recent election which, while it confirmed our position as a government with considerably the largest support in the House of Commons, did not give us the majority of members we sought. You and others advised me to hold the election at this time, for reasons which seemed perfectly valid, but the decision was mine and the sole responsibility for the decision remains mine.

Nevertheless you have confirmed to me verbally the wish you expressed in your letter, to resign from the government. You know how much I regret this decision and my inability to persuade you to take another Cabinet post where the responsibilities would not be so heavy and continuous as they have been in Finance. In the circumstances, I have no choice but to accept your resignation. In regretfully doing so, I want to add this.

No single person has done more, indeed I do not know anyone who has done as much, to restore the fortunes of our party from the low point of 1958 to a position which resulted in our victory of 1963 and the defeat of the attempts of the Opposition parties to reverse that victory in 1965. I am in the best position to know what we owe you for your wholly dedicated, efficient and untiring work in the party organization.

I also want to express my deep appreciation for what you have accomplished as Minister of Finance in putting into effect fiscal policies which have done much to bring about and maintain the expansion and prosperity Canada at present enjoys; and for your effort to ensure that Canadians maintain the maximum control possible over their own economic and industrial development as essential to the development of the nation. You know that I share this objective with you.

Beyond adequate acknowledgement, is what I owe to you in friendship, encouragement and support. I know that your withdrawal from the government will not alter our personal relationship in any way, as something which has meant so much to me over so many years and which will continue.

So my closest friend and most valued colleague in the government departed. It was for me a melancholy moment, redeemed only by the hope that this severance would not affect our personal friendship in any way. This was one of the most distressing episodes in my public life, an unhappy aftermath to an unhappy election.

Some months before the election Keith Davey, a selfless and dedicated person, if ever there was one, had told me he wished to resign as National Organizer after the election, whatever the result. I had not demurred at this decision, since his political activities were taking up all his time and energy, to the sacrifice of everything else including his domestic life. He had been one of the most ardent of the 1965 election protagonists and one of the most optimistic about the outcome. The result was therefore a bitter shock to him, and confirmed his decision to leave as did Walter Gordon's departure. No party could have been more unselfishly served than ours has been by these two men.

Perhaps the best summary of my feelings about the 1965 election is contained in a letter I wrote to my brother, Duke, on 15 November 1965:

We miscalculated badly in the election, in Quebec and Nova Scotia, though the rest of the country went about as expected. I was assured, without any hesitation or qualification, that we would have at the minimum 64 Members in Quebec and that we would gain seats in Nova Scotia. If that had happened, we would have had a comfortable majority. In Nova Scotia, and in PEI, it was the Conservative Provincial machine, plus the flag, plus $100 pensions, that did us in. In Quebec it was over-confidence, plus increased NDP votes, plus the swinging of the National Union machine behind, not Diefenbaker, but the old Conservative Party which came to life. One development was quite unexpected. We though that Diefenbaker would be our greatest asset. In spite of his frantic effort during the campaign, he was neither an asset nor a liability. But what we didn't count on was the rallying of the anti-Diefenbaker Conservatives behind the Party. They apparently assumed, and rightly, that Diefenbaker would have no chance of getting a majority but that there was a danger of the Party, as a Party, being virtually wiped out in the East and in British Columbia. So they closed ranks with an effective display of unity, the superficial character of which was only apparent to those who were politically sophisticated; and that is about 2% of the population. This tactic worked but it is going to make it more difficult for the Conservatives in the House when the divisions are bound to appear again. By the same token, this will make our position, as a Government, easier, especially as the other Parties will not dare to take any action for some time which will result in another election.

My first reaction Tuesday morning was to summon the National Executive, give them my resignation, appoint an Acting Leader and prepare for an immediate Party Convention to choose a permanent Leader, holding off Parliament until that could be done. However, this proved to be quite impossible for many reasons and, once again, I had to subordinate my own personal feelings to other considerations which were more important.

But I look ahead now to the day when I can retire, after things have become stable again.

At the moment, my major problem is reorganization of the Cabinet, which is essential but very difficult in a minority Government. That reorganization began with Walter Gordon's resignation last Thursday, followed by that of our National Organization Head, Keith Davey, and there will have to be other changes. This is the hardest part, for me, of political leadership. But I have to face up to it. One of the strongest reasons for a majority in the House of Commons from my point of view was that it would have given me some ground to manoeuvre in making Cabinet changes, so that, if by-elections had to be lost because of resignations, that would not be fatal. Now the situation is different and more difficult.

So I turned my attention for a second time to the business of forming a new Cabinet.

❧ 8 ❧

MEN AND POSITIONS

Clement Attlee once said that the only task for a Prime Minister more difficult and distasteful than choosing a Cabinet was in reorganizing one. In forming a new one, as I have already said, friends had to be left out. In reorganizing an old one, friends had to move out. This made it at times a most unhappy assignment. My earlier Cabinet changes, even the major changes I made in 1964, had been relatively easy compared with the one I had to undertake in 1965.

In that first Cabinet shuffle in 1964, nine months after taking office, perhaps the most significant alterations involved the Quebec Ministers. Guy Favreau was promoted to Justice, with René Tremblay moving up from 'without Portfolio' to replace him at Citizenship and Immigration. In a three-way shift Maurice Lamontagne went from the Privy Council to Secretary of State, Jack Pickersgill moved over from that post to Transport, and George McIlraith exchanged Transport for the Privy Council. I transferred Jack Nicholson from Forestry to Postmaster General and, to complete matters, brought three new members into the Cabinet: Maurice Sauvé in Forestry, Yvon Dupuis as Minister without Portfolio, and John Connolly as Leader of the Government in the Senate.

The Quebec caucus was especially determined after the 1965 election that Guy Favreau should not become, as they saw it, another victim of Diefenbaker and Bay Street. For my part, I wanted to retain Favreau but later on to alter the Quebec leadership. We had had a run of rather bad luck. Lionel Chevrier had been our Quebec leader until he left the Cabinet early in 1964 to become High Commissioner in London. When Guy Favreau replaced him, I had hoped that he would be to me what Ernest Lapointe had been to Mackenzie King. If events had turned out differently for him politically and had his health been better, he might have realized his potential. Certainly, I was not going to have him leave the Cabinet simply because of certain reflections on his management in the Dorion Report. Most of his difficulties in the Denis case were not of his own creation; some of them were, as I have already said, my fault. In fact, as a result of the report, he had insisted, in July 1965, that he be transferred from Justice. This I had done by making him President of the Privy Council, with special responsibility for federal-provincial constitutional relations. He was a good and able man, greatly admired, and his integrity had not been questioned in the report. Had he left with Lamontagne and Tremblay there would have been not only real unrest in the Quebec caucus, where his position as leader remained strong and respected, but a serious back-lash from French Canada. I noted in my diary at the time: 'As to Favreau, we had several talks, as a result of which he stays on for the next session of Parliament, after which he wishes to leave politics for which he feels he is not suited. I am glad to have him remain because he is a fine and honourable man who had been asked by me to do too much too soon in a field for which he did not have any experience or little instinctive aptitude. Perhaps the next session will strengthen his political and Parliamentary position, in which case he may desire to remain. But I don't think he'll ever become a political leader. He hasn't the feel for it or the popular appeal.' Favreau, who was entirely unselfish, agreed that any immediate resignation on his part would have been bad for the party.

I decided at this time, however, that Messrs Lamontagne and Tremblay should leave their ministries. I hated to do this because it could look as though I were accepting the malicious and unfounded Opposition charges surrounding the so-called furniture scandals. The fact was that, though honourable and honest men of great ability, they had had difficulty in defending themselves in the House against these attacks. They had, in consequence, been so undermined as politicians that their usefulness had been practically destroyed. They had to go because they were now ineffective and could not fit my 'new look' Cabinet. Yet, as I wrote shortly afterwards, 'To force Ministers out of office in these circumstances was against my deepest instincts.'

Nevertheless, I had to meet legitimate demands in the party for

Cabinet changes, but do this so as to maintain unity between our French- and English-speaking sections. Certainly, there was a bitter reaction in the Quebec caucus against Tory persecution, and, even worse, against what was interpreted in Quebec as Anglo-Saxon persecution of Quebec Ministers. This meant going ahead carefully, taking my time, persuading Lamontagne and Tremblay to resign in their own best interests once the post-electoral excitement was over.

These were difficult conversations. I had talked to Tremblay and Lamontagne separately and then they came to see me together. Tremblay was cool and understood the difficulties of the situation. Lamontagne was understandably resentful. I could appreciate that, and would have felt as he did. Personally, I was distressed at Lamontagne's departure since he had been my first and closest colleague from Quebec when I took over the leadership and had given me great help and imaginative ideas when working in my office during the days of opposition. He was a fine and intelligent Canadian patriot with a fervent belief in a united Canada based on the partnership of our two original language groups. No one had done more for the cultural side of Canada's development. But, as he said, unless the party as a whole was willing to go on the offensive to defend him against these attacks, he would not stay on. I had to tell him that such unanimous support for him from the caucus could not be expected. So he resigned. But both he and Tremblay urged me not to make changes affecting them until the middle of December. They believed that the delay would remove their resignations from too close an association with the charges made during the election. Of course I agreed to this and the new Ministers were not sworn in until 18 December. It was all in all a sorry and a sad business.

Quite apart from these departures, there were two vacancies that had to be filled since the Minister of Agriculture and the Minister of Mines and Technical Surveys, Harry Hays and J. Watson Mac-Naught, respectively, were both defeated. Then, as I have said, the Minister of Finance resigned. I came to the conclusion that, with these changes, there must be others as well. If I was to carry on in the new Parliament more successfully than in the last, and still in a minority, I had to bring some new men into the Cabinet and transfer some of the old ones to new jobs. There had to be a new look. This was all the more necessary, and in a sense easier, because I had plans to change the whole departmental structure of government, a change which I thought was long overdue.

The task was complicated and difficult. I have discussed the normal but often frustrating difficulties inevitable in our federal system by which provinces and areas and races and religions had to be balanced in appointments. This was confused in 1965 by the fact that we had no representation from three provinces – Alberta, Saskatchewan, and Prince Edward Island – whereas we had over a hundred members from two – Ontario and Quebec. Further, since we were just short of a majority in the Commons, it was too risky to open up places in the Cabinet by compensating transfers to the Senate. To avoid by-elections, those who left the Cabinet had to be persuaded to stay in the Commons and not resign – and this would provide its own difficulties in caucus.

Before leaving for the West Indies, in December 1965, I told Miss LaMarsh that I wanted her to move from Health and Welfare. She was shaken but took it very well, saying that she would be willing to move into the back-benches for a spell. I told her she could move to Postmaster General or Secretary of State, as I would like to keep her in the Cabinet. She seemed to appreciate this but said she would let me know later, though her present intention would be to drop out of the Cabinet completely. Not having heard from her before my return, though she twice tried to reach me by telephone, I assumed that she was not concerned about my Cabinet plans. I was wrong. Back from my holiday, I found her in a rather belligerent mood, not disposed to go to any back-bench. If she could not stay where she was, she would reluctantly accept Secretary of State and concern herself with 'culture and lace curtains,' as she put it; she would certainly not want to be Postmaster General since she had not been sent to Parliament to 'lick stamps.' She could be good as Secretary of State but, a mercurial person, she might prefer to be bad.

Judy was a woman of strong views and she expressed them strongly and emotionally, often influenced more by her heart than her head. This was fine, as long as she was aiming her arrows and her arguments at our adversaries. It was sometimes disconcerting when she directed them at her colleagues. More than once when she was part of my government, she would rush into a letter of resignation to protest a policy with which she disagreed. These I would file with her other letters saying something very kind about my leadership. In each case she would be equally sincere.

There were various problems on the organizational side; Justice was certainly as complicated as any. I was anxious to make some drastic changes in organization here. The Minister of Justice had far too much to do, the Solicitor General not enough. So I took the

RCMP, the Penitentiaries, and the Remission and Corrections work of Justice and transferred these to the Solicitor General, who was to become the head of a fully-organized department of government. I was also anxious to concentrate Bankruptcy, Combines Investigation, Copyright, Trade Marks, and so on—the business end of law—under a separate minister. The Minister of Justice naturally had some doubts about this fragmentation; his senior officials had more. In the end Larry Pennell, who had become Solicitor General in July 1965 and was one of the ablest men in my Cabinet, got his new powers while some, but not all, of the other duties were put under Favreau as President of the Council. Bankruptcy for the time being, for special reasons, was left with Justice Minister Cardin.

Quebec had caused me the greatest concern. Before the 1965 election, there was no Cabinet Minister other than Favreau with the necessary experience and prestige to take over the Quebec leadership. Nor could I see the man in the Quebec caucus to fill that position, though I may have been wrong in this because we had some very able young members. I am sure a lot of them thought that they were quite capable of doing the job had they been given a chance. I considered that we needed new blood. Thus, when I first heard from Maurice Lamontagne that Messrs Trudeau, Pelletier, and Marchand might stand as Liberal candidates, I was very pleased. Maurice knew these three extremely well and was very close to them. So, I knew of them. I knew their standing in Quebec; that they were strong Quebec nationalists but good Canadians as well. I also knew that they were concerned about the pressures on federalism and believed that only the Liberal party could reconcile what they considered to be genuine Quebec nationalism with genuine participation in the Canadian confederation. The fact that they had been opposed to our party and to me as its leader in 1963 did not bother me in any way. In some ways it would be helpful to have men whose objectivity had been publicly established. In 1963 their main quarrel with me and the party was over the nuclear issue; in this I was right and they were wrong. By 1965, however, that issue had been settled. It may have continued as a difference of opinion; it was no longer a matter of political controversy. Thus, when Maurice Lamontagne suggested that these men might be prevailed upon to run in the 1965 election, I was attracted by the idea, although I knew it would get me into some difficulty, as it did, with other Quebec Liberals.

We were entering a very difficult stage in our federal relations with Quebec. I considered that these men, if they entered the House of

Commons on our side, would do a great deal for national unity, perhaps more than any of the existing members of the Liberal party who might otherwise be promoted to the Cabinet. Pierre Elliott Trudeau had a very fine reputation in Quebec as a man of intelligence and integrity. He was a good Canadian and a good radical Liberal who had stood up to Duplessis. Gerard Pelletier had made a name for himself as editor of *La Presse*, the largest French-language newspaper in the country. Jean Marchand was a fiery labour leader. (He used to come to Ottawa as head of the Confederation of National Trade Unions and tell the government where to get off.) These were the sort of men I was looking for: men of quality and standing in Quebec, men who inspired both some admiration and some fear. Guy Favreau shared my enthusiasm. Consequently, I told Maurice Lamontagne to pursue the question of their standing as Liberal candidates.

They soon made it known that, if they came in as candidates, they would have to come in as a trio, that we would have to find ridings for each of them. I might as well be frank and say that it was more difficult to get enthusiastic acceptance in the organization for Pelletier than it was for the other two because, while Pierre Trudeau had made some pretty tough speeches about nuclear arms and about myself in that context, Pelletier had been writing editorials day after day about the iniquity of the Liberal régime. He had made it very hard for some of our men to get elected in 1963, and it was not easy for them to welcome him with open arms or, for one or two of them, to welcome Pierre Trudeau with any enthusiasm.

Both Lamontagne and Favreau met with them but I did not; there was no commitment whatever, on my part, as to Cabinet posts. I did discuss with Favreau and Lamontagne and one or two other Quebec Ministers the constituencies where they would run. There was no problem about Jean Marchand. He would run in Quebec West, and he was readily accepted at the convention. There was some difficulty in getting an appropriate seat for Pierre Trudeau, but this was found in Montreal's Mount Royal riding. It was more troublesome to get a seat for Mr Pelletier, but eventually Raymond Eudes gave up his seat in Hochelaga and was later appointed to the Senate. Mr Eudes had been in line for the Senate for some time, and this provided a good opportunity. He could move out and Pelletier could move in. So it was arranged, and all three were elected. Marchand came into the Cabinet at once and, within a few weeks, Mr Trudeau became my Parliamentary Secretary. Both appointments caused a certain amount of discontent among the old hands. Later, Mr Pelletier became a

Parliamentary Secretary and, under Mr Trudeau, a Cabinet Minister. I have never had any cause to regret my role in facilitating their entry into federal politics.

Early in 1967, a few months after his illness, Favreau carried out his wish to retire. Shortly before, in January, I had decided that Jean Marchand should become the leader of the Quebec caucus. The best choice seemed to be between Marchand and Maurice Sauvé. Marchand was tough, astute, forceful, with a charming personality. He had learned to survive in the savage jungle of trade-union leadership. I had had no doubts about putting him in the Cabinet immediately after his election in 1965. My only problem at that time was where? Talks with him showed that he would have been quite content to learn his new trade on the back-benches or without portfolio. As a strong federalist, however, he was worried about Quebec's reaction if no major or prestige Cabinet job went to that province, a reaction that would be aggravated by the departure of two Quebec Ministers and the earlier transfer of Favreau. This was also very much on my own mind. I could not do anything about Finance; Sharp was the man for that job. Trade and Commerce, although somewhat reduced in importance by our reorganization, remained a prestige portfolio. Marchand would have liked it but I had promised it to Bob Winters, as a representative of the business community in Cabinet, if he would run and was successful. He, of course, did not let me forget that promise. So I had to find some other way out of my Quebec difficulty. I first thought of Health and Welfare. I had already decided to move Judy LaMarsh out of this sensitive post. But Marchand made it clear that he would be worried about taking on, as his first Cabinet job, one of such importance and complexity and one which would create immediate and difficult confrontations with Quebec. Labour was not possible because of Marchand's trade-union background and his presidency of the Quebec-based CNTU which had brought him often into general conflict with the national Canadian Labour Congress. The projected Department of Manpower and Immigration (still Citizenship and Immigration at that time) seemed the best posting. Marchand was also somewhat worried about this, but I told him that it was to be 'Manpower,' and that Quebec would have to be made to realize that this was to be one of the most important departments in government. So that was that.

Thus, Jean Marchand quickly became a very prominent member of our party. He was one of the most attractive personalities I had met in a long, long time, quick in every respect: physically, mentally, emotionally. He is also a genuine small 'l' liberal. He had a great success with the Quebec caucus, and even the old-line parliamentarians soon realized that he was the leader. Occasionally, however, we had our differences. For example, during the 1966 Policy Conference, he thought that the conservative wing of the Cabinet was taking over the direction of the party in caucus and Cabinet, and that considerations of financial stability were given too high a priority over social reform. In particular, he was disturbed by our postponement of Medicare. Certainly, he was not alone on that score. There was a clear division of opinion in the party over the question, and I spent a good deal of time trying to get the conference through those two or three days without the development of a real split. However, I think he lost his uneasiness when we were finally able to go ahead with Medicare and measures such as Area Development.

Before leaving the matter of my 'new look' Cabinet and our new members, I might complete the Marchand-Trudeau-Pelletier episode. As I mentioned, Mr Trudeau became my Parliamentary Secretary. Unfortunately, that post, and this has been my experience at least in the Prime Minister's office, is not in fact a very satisfying job. The Prime Minister is always so busy that, unless he has his Parliamentary Secretary in on everything, there is great danger that he is not in on anything. I think a Parliamentary Secretary has far better opportunities with a Minister who can delegate work to him. It is difficult for a Prime Minister to delegate his work, especially to someone not in the Cabinet. Thus, Trudeau had neither very much to do nor the opportunity to learn very much in my office. Nevertheless, I had enough contact with him to value his cool intelligence, his knowledge, and his very steady nerves.

As for Mr Pelletier, I did not see very much of him. However, I do remember one speech he made during the capital punishment debate. I thought this to be one of the finest I had ever heard in the House of Commons. I have written about the low moments of Parliament during those years; but this debate was one of the great occasions when we could throw aside party prejudices and preoccupations and say exactly what we believed and thought.

ॳ

Of course, I had, over the years, many more appointments to make than the Cabinet posts I have mentioned, appointments which only the Prime Minister can make.

These appointments varied in their range of difficulty. The Speaker of the House of Commons is an important and traditionally non-controversial appointment. In opposition, we had benefitted greatly from the Speakers nominated by the Conservative government. Both Roland Michener and his successor, Marcel Lambert, were excellent Speakers. In turn, I wanted to appoint someone who would be acceptable, fully acceptable, to the Opposition. Alan Macnaughton seemed to have all the necessary qualities. When he retired as Speaker on 18 January 1966 (he became a Senator a few months later), we were fortunate to find in his replacement, Lucien Lamoureux, who had been Deputy Speaker from May 1963 to September 1965, those same fine qualities. I had rather hoped that we could bring about the appointment of a permanent Speaker, but I did not give priority to this project and there are certain compelling arguments against it. The main consideration is that in Canada we have had, with one or two exceptions, excellent but non-permanent Speakers. Almost invariably, all is well. No one has objected to them as Liberal or Conservative partisans. However, when once a permanent Speaker is appointed who proves to be less than a happy choice, then the House is in trouble. We gave no thought to a permanent Speaker for the Senate. Maurice Bourget took on this duty, followed by the Liberal Senator from Kamloops, Sydney Smith.

Other senatorial appointments presented more difficulty. The supply of those available for appointment always exceeded the vacancies. When I took over the leadership I hoped that, once in office, we would set about what Liberal governments had been talking about for decades – Senate reform. By reform, I meant changes in methods of appointment and in the structure of the Senate. I have changed my mind on this matter. If I had the authority and the possibility of doing this now, I do not think I would make any drastic Senate reform except perhaps to abolish it. That, however, is something else because abolition, however desirable, would require a constitutional amendment with which each province would have to agree. I was soon to learn the difficulties involved in that procedure.

When I contemplated both the difficulties of amending the constitution and our minority status in the House of Commons, I soon decided to propose only those useful changes which were not contentious and would not require constitutional amendment. But I did relieve the Senate of the increasingly burdensome and anomalous work of hearing divorce cases. Again, I provided for compulsory retirement, with pension, at seventy-five, thus regrettably quenching an apparent fountain of perpetual youth for those who enjoyed the Senate's ambience and amenities.

With one or two exceptions, during my term of office I appointed to the Upper House Liberals who had been active in one form or another of party work. But I chose men well below the average age of appointment in the past and men who, I knew, would work. For I was anxious to make the Senate a much more important body in the area of examination and report than it had been and thus reduce our dependence on Royal Commissions and Task Forces. These were springing up all over the place; their expenses and the length of time taken to complete assignments were equally disturbing. The vast majority of those I did appoint, however, were not from the House of Commons, even though many of the people most desiring to be Senators were members of the House with long service. But their appointment would have meant by-elections, and I was never in a position to welcome a by-election during my régime.

It is nevertheless true that by tradition in Canada party fund-raisers and organizers become Senators. I might point out, however, that I have never met a fund-raiser who was a hack and I have never asked a man to do this job who did not merit a high reputation. Fund-raising is a terrible job, but money is necessary to run a party. I have appointed Senators who were presidents of the party organization, and I admit that this was done to give them a base in the Senate from which they could operate. This is a practice followed by both parties. But I do not know a single man appointed to the Senate during my régime who was not well qualified by ability. Those who worked hardest were those who had been most dedicated to the party, to party work, and political life.

A certain appointment to the Senate may turn out to be a mistake, but the person is not likely to do much damage there. A bad judge can do a lot of damage. Thus, in the appointment of judges, my first and exclusive concern was judicial quality and capacity. Here I relied very heavily on the advice of legal people, both within and outside the House of Commons and the Cabinet. If an appointment were to be made in Ontario, the Cabinet Ministers from that province who were lawyers would consider the matter and consult with other members of their profession from Ontario in the House. As my term of office went on, I also encouraged my Minister of Justice to assure, by informal consultation, that the nominee would be supported by the Bar in the relevant community. This procedure has now become more than a habit, it is a convention, and a very important convention. I had only two unhappy experiences after I took office. One judge nominated by Mr St Laurent suddenly began acting strangely and became quite irresponsible. He had to be told that unless he resigned at once, which he was refusing to do, action would regrettably be taken which would be humiliating to him but would ensure that he vacated the Bench. The other arose out of the Justice Minister's custom of discussing judicial vacancies with his Cabinet colleagues who were learned in the law, especially those, if any, from the same province. In this case the Secretary of State, for reasons which I need not detail, took violent and strongly expressed objection to a proposed nominee. The Minister of Justice, Mr Trudeau, looked into the matter again but concluded that his original choice, which had strong support, should stand. He therefore brought the recommendation for my consideration and explained the Minister's objection and the support of others. I accepted both the recommendation of the Minister of Justice and the hostility of the dissenting Secretary of State. I consider that, over the years, our judicial appointments have been creditable.

The selection of Deputy Ministers, or officers of equivalent rank, and the heads of government agencies is the prerogative of the Prime Minister. As for Deputy Ministers, and I based this largely on my own experience, I liked to move people around within the civil service to the top deputy posts. External Affairs was a breeding ground for Deputy Ministers. I felt, however, that if we were to have a professional civil service of high morale, every member of that service should believe that he had an opportunity to become a Deputy Minister. That is the British tradition. At the same time, I always considered we should never get into a position (which I think happens in London) where too often we are afraid to select people from outside the civil service. There are times, as I noted in an earlier chapter, when it is stimulating to bring in people from outside since this prevents an establishment from becoming excessively ingrown. I did, therefore, bring in some high ranking officials on this principle. My procedure was always to ask the Minister whether he had anyone in his own department trained to be the Deputy Minister and whom he and the retiring Deputy Minister could whole-heartedly recommend. I thought, other things being equal (and they were not always equal), that this candidate should be my choice. In the appointment of heads of Crown corporations, where the Prime Minister also has authority, I usually relied heavily on my Ministers.

Finally, it is also a prerogative of the Prime Minister to nominate a

Governor General for the Queen's consideration. Georges Vanier was the Governor General when I took office, and I could not imagine a happier relationship than that which I enjoyed with him. This was an extension of an official and personal relationship over many, many years. It is interesting that the man I succeeded as First Secretary at Canada House in London in 1939 became Governor General and I, Prime Minister; and our then High Commissioner in London had been the first Canadian Governor General. Years before, though we had been generally fortunate in our British Governors General, I remember suggesting to Mr St Laurent that we must have a Canadian in that office. The last British one, Viscount Alexander of Tunis, could hardly have been improved on, whether as a man or in the conduct of his duties. But surely the time had come for a Canadian to take over Rideau Hall. Mr St Laurent did not need to be convinced. The question was, 'Who?' My suggestion was Vincent Massey. St Laurent was hesitant only because Mrs Massey had recently died, and he wondered whether Mr Massey alone would be able to carry the office and all that it entails. That problem, however, was easily resolved, and his appointment was greeted with a great measure of approval in the country, but not with unanimity. There were people who thought that this was one further break in the links with Britain and the throne. Some were afraid that the quality of vice-regal representation would decline; that we would go stamping into Rideau Hall in our dirty boots, waving our hats or throwing them in the air, instead of with bows and curtseys. The only change that I could detect during Mr Massey's régime from the previous régimes with which I had had some contact was that, under the first Canadian Governor General, there was an atmosphere rather more regal and rather more formal than under, say, the Earl of Athlone, a member of the Royal Family.

When Mr Massey left, Mr Diefenbaker nominated General Georges Vanier. I confess, though I never mentioned this to anyone, that I was disturbed about this. I had served under Georges Vanier when he was my senior at Canada House. I had served with him when we both were heads of missions, and when he was an Ambassador and I was Deputy Minister. Later, when I was Minister, I served over him. No one could have had a higher regard for any one than I had for him. He had, however, left his final posting in Paris in frail health, and when I saw him in Montreal shortly afterwards, he seemed an old man who had, physically, nothing left in him. I worried that his new position as Governor General might kill him and I surmised that this might be his doctor's view as well. I suspected that he had been approached to take this position as a matter of duty, and no one ever had a higher sense of duty. In a way, it is astonishing that he was prepared to accept, but perhaps he judged it a splendid challenge to be the first French-speaking Canadian at Rideau Hall. As it turned out, my worry was idle since his appointment gave him a new mission in life. His dedication restored his health and he spent many good years at Rideau Hall before that health finally waned. It is difficult for me to express the quality of his service. Until his death, I used to meet with him every week to report on the activities of Her Majesty's Canadian government. I had a few dreadful days with him at the end, in early 1967, when I knew that he was dying. He knew it too, yet he was trying so hard to stay on for the Centennial year. I wanted him to retire. I remember when Dr White, the great heart specialist, came from Boston to supplement the advice Georges had been given by his own doctor in Montreal. Dr White spent some time with him and then came downstairs and I asked: 'Well, what's the verdict?' He said: 'He will die very quickly if he doesn't leave office. He will probably die in any event. His heart condition is terrible. But there might be some chance if he were relieved of all duties.' I had to tell the Governor General this and I found it exceedingly difficult. But he agreed that he owed it to his family and to himself not to stay on when he could no longer do the job. When I left him that evening he was watching a hockey game on television. He was a great hockey fan. The next night he died. It is my belief that once told he could not carry on, that his mission had ended, his life ended. It was as simple as that.

I then had the responsibility of nominating his successor as Governor General. This could have been complicated. Fortunately, it was not. The man I nominated, Roland Michener, was as close to me personally, and in some ways even closer, than his two predecessors. We had been students together, we had played hockey and tennis together. Of course, he made an unfortunate choice of his political party! He was a Conservative and I must confess that when he was defeated in Toronto in 1962, I was glad of one more Liberal seat. Nevertheless, I hated to see him out of public life and I was able to do something about this. I invited him to become our High Commissioner in India. He certainly justified my every expectation that he would be a good one. Further, this was an experience that stood him in good stead when he became Governor General. His appointment continued my very happy relationship with Rideau Hall.

☞

My last major Cabinet change was the return of Walter Gordon in January 1967. There had been strong pressure from certain of the younger and more 'progressive' members in caucus to get Walter back into Cabinet. They felt this was absolutely necessary to counteract the impression that our party was moving to the 'right,' thus losing support which was going to the NDP. Perhaps twenty to thirty members agreed on this and they were among the brightest members we had. Some of the Cabinet shared this view. I have already mentioned Marchand; the others were Benson, Pennell, MacEachen, and LaMarsh. The feeling grew up, with some justification, that I was not trying hard enough to get Walter back.

It is well to remember that Walter Gordon's resignation in 1965 was a political decision, not based on any conflict over policy in the Department of Finance. Although his successor in that portfolio, Mitchell Sharp (who had performed very ably as Minister of Trade and Commerce), may have seemed to mark an abrupt change in our approach to economic policy, he would deny himself that he stood for an opposite viewpoint from that held by Walter Gordon. He would say that he was in fundamental sympathy with the policies Walter Gordon advocated, but was more careful and cautious in seeking their implementation. Perhaps for this reason he was considered to have a different view of finance and economics by our business and financial community. Also, Walter had made himself so unpopular with the financial community that almost anyone who replaced him would be considered as a welcome change. In fact, there was no one in Cabinet at that time whom I could have made Minister of Finance whose appointment would not have been interpreted as a departure from the ideas and the financial philosophy of Walter Gordon.

It was these differing tactical approaches of Gordon and Sharp that produced a real struggle within the Liberal party. Gordon was out of the government, but his influence remained in the caucus and in the House. The division centred on how we should deal with financial policy, banking legislation, inflation, and Medicare. Eventually, the party was said to be split left versus right, terms which have some meaning. 'Left' was applied to those who believed that a Liberal government should carry on with social security programmes, should concentrate on human welfare, and not on financial stability. 'Right' was applied to those who considered that, while these goals were good and we were committed to them, we should never put anything into effect if the expenditures would strain and weaken the financial structure of the country. This dichotomy can be found in every Liberal caucus or Cabinet. It was particularly noticeable, however, during 1966 when Walter Gordon, along with Maurice Lamontagne, managed to attract to their views quite a number within the party. Medicare became the focal issue. It was not a question of whether one was for or against Medicare. Medicare had been part of our election platform in 1962 and 1963; the Hall Commission on Health Services had said that if Canada wished to achieve its objectives in health care, a comprehensive and universal plan must be available to all Canadians. This was the goal of our party, and on 19 July 1965 I had introduced such a plan at the Federal-Provincial Conference. After consultation with the provinces the only question left was the time to implement Medicare. We had originally hoped to have our plan in effect by 1 July 1967, but in September 1966 Mitchell Sharp was forced to announce that the financial situation made it necessary to postpone it for a year. In the Cabinet there were opponents of delay. However, the Cabinet is a team where differences can and must be healed. It was the situation in caucus which worried me. There, opposition to postponement was harder to control and was gaining considerable support. The issue came to a head at our Policy Conference that October in Ottawa. Hard work resolved the crisis with a resolution accepting the decision to postpone Medicare, but with regret. On 21 December 1966 the Medical Care Act became law. I regarded it as a major triumph. The federal government was authorized to pay approximately half the cost of provincial plans which must meet four criteria: portability of benefits, universal coverage, comprehensive physicians' services, and public administration. It was to take effect, as we had decided, no later than 1 July 1968. And on that date Medicare did come into operation, without undue strain on our economic capacity. By that time I had left office, but I could still look back with pride.

It was after his defeat in the 1966 Policy Conference that Walter Gordon told me he had definitely made up his mind to resign his seat. He had called a meeting of his riding executive for the first week of November to announce his decision. He explained that he could no longer refrain in the House or in the country from expressing his own views, as a private citizen, on financial matters and on Canadian-American economic relations. Since these views would on occasion be in opposition to government policy and, as he did not wish to hurt the government, he felt he should resign his seat. He had made up his mind to leave politics permanently. I urged him not to resign at this time; that to do so would create a very real difficulty for me and for the government. He must, I said, postpone decision and consider possible arrangements for his return to the Cabinet. I would try to fashion an arrangement that would be satisfactory to him and also to Mitchell Sharp, the only Minister whom I felt I should consult on the matter. Sharp's approval of any accommodation seemed as necessary as Gordon's.

It appeared to me that if Walter went, not only might we lose a Toronto by-election to the NDP, which in itself was not so important, but we might finally split the party into 'right' and 'left,' leaving a feeling of resentment among the 'left' that might lead to a drift of some to the NDP. It would be difficult to counter the contention that if there was no room for Mr Gordon in the Liberal party, then our party had become an 'establishment' of old men on the right. Yet, if I took Walter back, I would have trouble because of the differences between him and Sharp on some matters, and certainly on the tactics related to a resolution of the Citibank-Mercantile affair. The government was running smoothly, why should I introduce a new and controversial element into it? Furthermore, Gordon's reappointment would be greeted with anger and dismay by the business and banking tycoons and by the Western free-traders in our party who had just defeated 'Gordonism' at the October Policy Conference. Despite these reservations, it seemed better to have him back in the Cabinet, with its collective responsibilities of membership, than to have him attacking our financial and economic policies from without. And, on balance, it was more important to placate the younger, more progressive elements in the party for whom Walter Gordon had become a symbol – the man who would save Canada from the Americans and big business – than it was to placate those elements in the party and the country represented by Bob Winters. So I began some 'rush negotiations' with Walter. Mitchell Sharp participated in these, having first agreed with me that unless his terms were impossible we should do everything possible to prevent Walter from resigning, even if this meant bringing him back into the government. I kept my other colleagues out of the talks.

As a final step I arranged an evening on 3 January 1967, at 24 Sussex with Sharp and Gordon, where I encouraged a frank discussion of their economic and financial views. It went very well and there did not appear to be much of a gap between them; none, for instance, in an appreciation of the dangers of US control of our economy. They did not even seem so far apart on methods for dealing with that danger. It was clear, however, that Walter would not compromise on the Mercantile Bank. Sharp and I agreed with him about making no concession to US pressure. But Gordon obviously wanted to use the situation to get the Rockefellers out of Canada once and for all, while Sharp and I would be satisfied if they complied with the law and sold 75 per cent of their stock to Canadians and became a Canadian bank. The difference did not seem so important at that time because the Citibank-Mercantile group seemed adamant in forcing our hand, relying on US official pressure to keep them in Canada as a 100 per cent US bank. Sharp and I expressed our full understanding of Walter's feelings on the matter, while he expressed confidence that we would be able to present a united front against any Citibank manœuvres. We left it at that, but as it turned out it would have been better if we had worked out a detailed arrangement. Walter felt that we had agreed to no concessions of any kind to Mercantile. Sharp and I felt we had agreed only to no change of policy but that we were not precluded from giving an extension of time, to remove allegations of unfair discrimination, if the bank agreed to become 75 per cent Canadian. Later the Bank agreed to do this, by selling shares, and Sharp in return agreed to give them more time to become 'Canadian.' Gordon felt this was a 'betrayal' of our understanding reached at this talk. Walter was also determined to do what he could to prevent US banks from being given agency concessions in Canada. Sharp agreed to discuss the matter with him before any such concessions were made.

On US control, which was the basic issue in these talks, we agreed to set up a Cabinet Committee to direct the work of a task force of experts, in and outside the Civil Service, who would make a thorough and detailed examination of the problem. A White Paper would then be issued which would include a statement of government policy which could be studied by Parliament as a basis for legislation. We agreed, Sharp only with great reluctance and against his better judgment, that Mr Gordon would be chairman of this Cabinet group, the other members of which would be picked by me. On the whole, this seemed a reassuring meeting. We were working against time. Any decision and announcement had to be made within a few days as Gordon proposed to announce his resignation unless he re-entered the Cabinet.

It now remained for me to work out the other details. Walter, with whom I had further talks alone, reiterated his desire to retire and get

out of political life for good. If he came back, therefore, he must be
satisfied that the conditions were right, that his seniority would be
respected, his views taken into consideration, and that his work in
the Cabinet would be important, not merely routine. I was determined that nothing should be done which would throw any doubt on
my full confidence in Mitchell Sharp as Finance Minister. I had to be
able to say that Gordon's return meant no change in economic or
financial policy. I therefore had to persuade him to accept a post
without Portfolio until Mr Favreau resigned, when he could become
President of the Privy Council. I also wanted him to concentrate on
party organizational and management matters as a Cabinet Minister.
All this took some doing. But, after some talks, I wrote the following
'letter of intent' to him on 5 January:

I was sorry not to have seen you before you left yesterday to tell you how
much I am looking forward to our renewed and close collaboration inside the
Cabinet and to say, once again, how glad I am that you are back.

There will, of course, be an effort by certain people, press, commentators,
etc. (it has already started) to interpret your return in the most controversial
and embarrassing way. We cannot prevent this but we can make sure that we
do not give them, gratuitously, any material which they can use for their own
purposes. They, naturally, will watch very carefully to see if they can find
some evidence of division inside the Cabinet, especially between Mitchell
and yourself. When you mentioned, for instance, 'new approaches' in policy
dealing with our economic relationships with the United States, they are
bound to say that this is an acknowledgment on the part of the Government
– consequent upon your return – that policy changes now have to be made.
Similarly, when Mitchell, on his part, says that no change in policy is required, they will misinterpret and distort that statement.

This is going to be a problem in the immediate future but I am quite sure
that we can keep it under control. The main thing is to work out, inside the
Cabinet, agreed policies which will be effective in achieving the objective that
we all have in mind, namely, securing maximum Canadian control over our
economic development and doing it in such a way that we do not discourage
the capital needed for that development.

Before you left, I had discussed with you the responsibilities which I would
like you to take in the Cabinet for the time being. These, of course, may have
to be changed, if and when you later take on new Departmental responsibilities. They are also not all-inclusive because there are many other things
that you will be doing which I will not mention in this letter; in particular,
work arising out of membership in Cabinet Committees, which, incidentally,
have not been functioning as well as they should.

Also, I would like to discuss with you the question of Ministerial responsibility for CMHC [Central Mortgage and Housing Corporation]. As you know,

this is under the Minister of Labour at the present time but is of such great and increasing importance that it needs more time and direction than a Minister, charged with heavy Departmental responsibilities, can give to it. Jack Nicholson, who has done so well at CMHC, entirely agrees with this.

A major responsibility, which we have already discussed, would be your Chairmanship of a small Committee (say three or five) to draft a report to the Cabinet which, after consideration and approval there, would become a White Paper. It would deal with problems arising out of foreign, primarily of course American, control and ownership of our resources and our industry. This problem, as you know so well, is becoming more difficult and more dangerous to our separate national existence.

Related to this problem is the necessity of taking the required measures to increase Canadian control and ownership without discouraging the right kind of foreign investment which will continue to be needed. Also related to the problem is the corporate structure of Canadian business and the development and the growth of monopolies.

An examination is now going on, of which you will be made aware, of these two problems but I would like to see your Committee give them special examination in respect of their effect on foreign ownership and control.

When the report of your Committee has been embodied in a White Paper, after Cabinet discussion, it will be made public and referred to an appropriate Parliamentary Committee for public discussion and debate. It would serve as the basis for the legislation which would then have to be introduced.

I would also like you to collaborate with me in the organizing of Cabinet business and in facilitating and expediting the decisions which are made. I am contemplating setting up a small Ministerial Committee which would meet regularly to discuss these matters. Marchand, Sharp and the House Leader would be members, as well as the two of us.

I would also like you to act as liaison between the Cabinet and the Caucus, and the Cabinet and the Federation. This does not mean, of course, that the Chairman of the Caucus and the President of the Federation would not continue to have direct access to me. But it would assist me greatly if you could maintain a continuous contact with these two bodies through their officers. We should have a talk with John Nichol and Russel Honey as to how this can best be done.

I would like you to take on special responsibility for the Chairmanship of a Committee of Cabinet, Caucus and the Federation to deal with problems of Party organization and begin the preparation of a programme for the next election.

There is now a Caucus Committee on communications and public relations. It is just beginning to operate under the Chairmanship of Bob Andras. This, you will agree, is a field in which we have been particularly weak and it is essential that we become stronger. Bob Winters is the Ministerial member of this Committee and I would like you to join it also, either replacing Bob or in addition to him.

I think you will agree that these activities will keep you more than occupied in the weeks ahead. As I indicated to you the other day, there will be some changes in the Cabinet when the present session is concluded and this will involve, I expect, your assumption of a Departmental post along the lines which we have already discussed.

The accommodation with Gordon did not work out as I had hoped. On 27 April 1967 Walter wrote me about his still being unable to take over the staff to which he felt his position as President of the Privy Council should entitle him. 'I feel I should ask you now, without further delays,' he concluded, 'to implement the various proposals and undertakings you made to me last January or, alternatively, to explain to me why you are not prepared to do so.' I responded on 16 May:

I am sorry to have been so long in replying to your letter of April 27th. I wanted to put my thoughts in writing before I talked with you and I just wasn't able to find enough time to do so until now.

I am glad that you wrote me as frankly as you did but I find it difficult to understand the basis for the concern which you so obviously feel about your present position in the Government.

In particular, I do not see why the impossibility—which I accept, as I thought you did—of transferring an important part of the administration and staff of the Privy Council to you, as President, prevents your acting effectively as a Minister, with definite and important Ministerial responsibilities. I realize you must have a base from which to operate but I thought this had been made possible by the exchange of views between you, Gordon Robertson and myself.

You would, of course, have a full Ministerial establishment. I would also be happy to transfer to that establishment any Civil Service help necessary for any work I ask you to take on, which is not supplied by the agency through which you would work in discharging a particular responsibility.

I realize from your letter that you do not feel that the conditions under which you returned to the Cabinet have been met. You refer to our correspondence of January to explain this feeling.

In our earlier discussions, and in correspondence, you asked for a senior Government post. I told you that this would be arranged and that, as soon as Guy Favreau retired, you would become President of the Privy Council. You gave me the definite impression that this was satisfactory. I am sorry if there was some delay about your appointment to the Presidency of the Council but I am sure that you appreciate my difficulties in that regard.

I am also sorry that there was a misunderstanding of the actual position and duties of the President of the Council. For that misunderstanding, I accept my share of responsibility.

But surely the important thing is the work you were to do as President and the facilities you would have for doing it.

Your main concern in returning to the Cabinet, expressed in our talks and confirmed in your earlier letter, was that the Government should take the question of foreign ownership and control seriously and that we should set up an enquiry into the problem in a form satisfactory to you.

That, I take it, has been done. As President of the Council, you are Chairman of the Cabinet Committee which is supervising the work of the task force that has been appointed and from which will come a White Paper on the subject as soon as possible as a basis for Government policy.

This is a very important undertaking. You are the Minister with the greatest responsibility for it and I assume that the facilities and staff for the work are satisfactory. This, I feel, was my major commitment to you, made before you returned to office, and I hope it has been faithfully discharged.

There are other important duties that I have suggested might be transferred to you. Responsibility for CMHC is one, where you would have an experienced and efficient staff to direct and, I believe, some imaginative new policies to implement. This would be a very important responsibility.

I thought that the CYC—and its Ottawa directional staff—might be transferred from my direct responsibility to yours. Consideration could also be given to the same transfer of the *War on Poverty* work, with Mr Phillips and his officers reporting to you.

In addition to the new policies on housing, you will recall that I discussed with you the proposed new study on the growing problems of urbanization in Canada. This was given a good deal of emphasis in the Speech from the Throne, and it is my impression that you are entirely in favour of it. It had been my hope that you would undertake responsibility for it. CMHC could have provided the base of operations, with the addition of special staff as needed.

Another problem of the future—but the very near future—mentioned in the Speech from the Throne, is the development of policy and organization with regard to satellites. No country in the world has a greater interest in this great new 'tool' than Canada—for communications, broadcasting, mapping, delineation of resources and many other applications. A special study must be undertaken to be sure we make the right policy decisions and set up the right organization for future development and control. Such a study would require a new and special staff, and I thought your qualities of mind and your organizational experience would suit you for its supervision. You will recall that I wanted you to take this on.

So there is a great deal of important work that could be done by the President of the Privy Council with, I believe, adequate staff—or 'a base,' as you call it—to assist you in doing it.

This would be available either in CMHC—by transfer of specified units from present responsibilities—or by the acquisition of special staff in new policy areas. It was not, therefore, a matter of suggesting that you should rely solely on your ministerial staff to help you. You would have special staff for special areas and I find it hard to see why this could not be made to work effectively.

Your present portfolio, with these duties alone, to say nothing of others that might develop, would certainly have become an important one and would have been far from being merely 'honorific.'

I have also very much in mind a study in depth of the operations, past and present, of the Royal Commission technique of enquiry, to see if we can't find a more effective mechanism for the future, through task forces or Senate and House Committees, or some other way. I had hoped you might supervise this.

In my letter of January 5th, I referred also to certain purely party-political assignments but I assume that we can leave this matter aside for the moment as I understand you did not have them in mind in writing your letter of April 27th.

You will recall that, in my letter of January 5th, I expressed some anxiety over the possibility that your return to the Government might be negatively exploited by some elements in the Press and elsewhere and I added the hope that no one would give them any unnecessary ammunition for this purpose.

In your letter of January 9th you agreed that we must avoid any suggestion of controversy or division between Members of the Cabinet.

In this connection, I realize that the Mercantile Bank question was one of understandable and special sensitiveness for you and I was happy about the way it was resolved by give-and-take between those in the Government who had different views about it.

I have, however, been worried about suggestions you have made publicly about 'right and left' divisions within the Cabinet and the necessity of the latter viewpoint prevailing.

Also, the press and radio reports of your speeches on Friday and Saturday last on foreign policy suggest that you went well beyond anything we have discussed—let alone decided—in the Cabinet as to what we should do about NORAD, NATO and US policy in Vietnam.

Walter never did agree to take over the additional responsibilities I suggested. I suspect he was increasingly restive inside the Cabinet, remaining only to see the completion of the work of his Task Force, which subsequently produced the Watkins Report, of which I have already written. Nevertheless, the fact that he entered and remained in Cabinet as long as he did achieved my goal: the party remained united and I was able to pass it over intact to my successor. Finally on 19 February 1968, Walter offered his resignation:

Several months ago I informed you of my wish to retire from the Cabinet. I have stayed on to see completed the work of the Task Force on Foreign Ownership and the Structure of Canadian Industry. This took considerably longer than was originally expected, but with the tabling of the report last Thursday, the time has come for me to submit my resignation in a formal way. I do so herewith, to take effect as soon as may be convenient to you, but in any event, I would hope within the next two or three weeks.

My final letter to Walter, as a Cabinet colleague, was written on 4 March. I said:

I have received your letter of February 19th confirming in writing your desire to retire from the Cabinet, about which you talked to me some time ago.

At that time, you indicated you would like to leave when the work of the Task Force on Foreign Ownership and the Structure of Canadian Industry had been completed. That has now been done and I was therefore expecting your letter which, nevertheless, I have received with much regret.

I understand from our conversation since the receipt of your letter that Monday, March 11th, would be satisfactory for your departure from the Cabinet and I am quite agreeable to that.

I know that you returned to the Government at my earnest request and, now that you are leaving, I want to thank you most warmly for the fine contribution you have made to our work since your return. The fact that I will be leaving, myself, within a few weeks does not lessen my regret at your departure.

9

NATIONAL UNITY

My passionate interest when I was in government, apart from the ultimate question of peace and war, was in the national unity of our country. In some respects this was the most important issue of my career. National unity is a problem of many facets embracing, among other factors, the constitution, federal-provincial relations, and the bread-and-butter issues of tax-sharing and equalization grants. But, in the long run, I am convinced that the problems of culture and language are pre-eminent; and I would like to think that our government made a permanent contribution to their solution.

I was convinced from the beginning, as I remain convinced now, that a prime element is the recognition of the French language. Nothing could be more important in my mind than an effort to make our French-speaking people feel that their language is an equal language in Canada. In the national capital, and in our national and federal institutions, they ought to feel at ease, and they will not if they cannot readily make use of their own language. This is, of course, an issue certain to get one into immediate difficulty. The cautious urged us to 'Leave it alone. If you start insisting that the elevator men in the House of Commons should be able to say more than "oui," you'll get into trouble.' The alternatives at the time were to work along with the Quiet Revolution in Quebec, so that ultimately we could fashion a better federal system for Canada; or to hold the line, merely keeping our thumb in the dyke, and eventually face a genuine crisis. Our choice irritated many Canadians, and among them, various members of the House of Commons. But the problem was faced and thank goodness it was! The tragic troubles we have known since then would have been infinitely worse had we not made the attempt to recognize the French fact and all it must stand for in our development. The effort, and it was a big effort, was not lost on Quebec.

I have mentioned that I took an initial step at that first Cabinet meeting after I became Prime Minister. I indicated by word and deed that any Minister who wished to speak in French should do so. If anyone could not understand, that was his misfortune. Similarly, we used French much more in caucus than ever before and encouraged its use in the House of Commons. For my own part, I decided as Prime Minister to broadcast now and then in French without simultaneous translation. I have discovered, particularly since leaving office, that however badly I may have spoken there were people in Quebec who appreciated what I was trying to do. If I did not succeed in convincing them that I was a fluent example of the bilingualism I preached, still they knew that I was trying.

I was convinced that if Canada were to be a strong, independent, and distinct state on this continent, we had to do everything in our power to extend French culture and the French language throughout Canada. Mine was a conviction often misinterpreted to suggest that we wanted to make everyone in Canada speak French. That was nonsense. We were not going to compel British Columbians to learn French. I did, however, urge that those areas of Canada where both languages were used be bilingual. I also hoped that everyone in Canada would have the opportunity to appreciate, to understand, and to learn French. In other words, I wanted French-speaking Canadians to feel deeply that they were and were recognized as an integral part of Canada. I desired a nation-wide recognition of the cultural and linguistic fact which they embodied so that they would be content to remain within confederation, and thus make Canada strong.

As a result, I have often been attacked as a believer in two nations. Our critics were trying to crucify Canada on a cross of words. It is a dreadful experience to see disputes develop over semantic differences (this time over the word 'nation'), especially when there are those who for reasons of their own are eager to distort these semantic differences into differences of substance. This misrepresentation is so easy, and has been tried so often, that one is almost afraid to use the word 'nation' at all. The French in Canada are a nation in the sense that they are a separate people. As Sir John A. Macdonald said of them: 'Treat them as a nation and they will act as a free people do—generously; call them a faction and they become factious.' There is a point, however, beyond which the federal government must not move, and I never made a speech which did not emphasize that two *political* nations cannot exist within one country. But I see no way of holding our country together unless English Canada adopts a new attitude towards the intention of our French-speaking compatriots to maintain their identity, their culture, and their language as a special fact of life within Canada. Those who persist in telling us that we must do away with this idea, that we must insist on talking about our country, race, and nation as one and indivisible—these are the real separatists.

Even though I had not had many occasions to express my views publicly before I became leader of my party, those views had undergone considerable change over the years. I remember, for instance, giving a speech about the nature of our federalism during the February 1949 debate in the House of Commons on the admission of Newfoundland into confederation. At that time my stand was, as one might have expected, more centralist than it later became. I had worked in Ottawa during the depression when the need for centralization of governmental authority over our economic and welfare policies was generally accepted. Then had followed the war, and war is always a strong centralizer of executive authority. I thought about centralization in terms of need. In those years I was in sympathy with the recommendations of the Rowell-Sirois Commission; I was convinced that in the developing areas of social security we should try to persuade the provinces to surrender responsibility to the federal government to create uniform standards across the country. Only much later I began to realize that, far from unifying, we might actually weaken our country if we did not reverse this process and return to the earlier state of affairs in which the provinces had the greater control. In consequence, I began to talk about 'co-operative federalism' in the early sixties before we took office. By that I meant that instead of trying to concentrate power in Ottawa we should try to make arrangements with the provinces for joint undertakings where the constitution allowed, while seeking always to maintain a more or less standard level of services for all Canadians.

This approach seemed to me to be particularly valuable in view of the developing national feeling in Quebec aroused by Lesage's Quiet Revolution. The intensity of that feeling made it clear that if we failed to contain and destroy separatism by coming to terms with the Quiet

Revolution, that if we failed to treat Quebec as the heart of French culture and French language in Canada, as a province distinct in some respects from the others, we would have the gravest difficulty in holding our country together. But we could not give Quebec constitutional rights denied to the other provinces. While I judged that there could be no special status for any one province, there were other ways in which the position of French-speaking Canadians in Canada could be acknowledged. I was prepared to make substantial concessions to Quebec (and to the other provinces) in the interests of national unity. My viewpoint was one of sympathy to the provinces, especially to Quebec, in their desire for more control and for more resources. By co-operative action one could encourage the devolution of power, with the provision that a province could, if it wished, restore authority to Ottawa. In this manner we might make provision for Quebec to develop *de facto* jurisdiction in certain areas where she desired it most. Although the federal government had to retain intact certain essential powers, there were many other functions of government exercised by Ottawa which could be left to the provinces. By forcing a centralism perhaps acceptable to some provinces but not to Quebec, and by insisting that Quebec must be like the others, we could destroy Canada. This became my doctrine of federalism. I wanted to decentralize up to a certain point as the way to strengthen, indeed to establish and maintain, unity. I remember being severely rebuked for suggesting that some of the centralists were the greatest separatists. In fact, I believe that our administration helped to unite the country by broadening the capacities of the provinces to discharge their constitutional powers in our federal system.

My own conviction was that national unity was the major question facing Canada. In analysing this problem I was helped most by Maurice Lamontagne. He and I talked at great length about co-operative federalism and the means of removing the impulse toward separatism, in the sense of a gradual drifting apart. As I mentioned in Chapter 3, Lamontagne had more than any other person to do with the preparation of the speech I made on national unity in the House of Commons in December 1962; this led, after our success in the 1963 election, to the Royal Commission on Bilingualism and Biculturalism. If I were asked to select the speech in the House of which I am most proud, I think I would choose that one. I made many other speeches on this subject, not only in the House but in the country and in the caucus. I spoke a great deal about the threats to confederation and the need to come out strongly as the party of national unity, based on the greatest possible constitutional decentralization and on special recognition of the French fact and the rights of French-speaking Canadians in confederation. This became a major theme of our 1963 election campaign, especially in Quebec.

I have already written of the growing lack of confidence in the government following the 1962 election. It had no strong position in Quebec and there Mr Diefenbaker was not able to make an impression. Further, he did not have lieutenants who could. This had much to do with the weakening position of his government and its defeat in the 1963 election. The following diary extract of a late 1964 meeting Mitchell Sharp and I had with Léon Balcer, Diefenbaker's Quebec lieutenant, at his request, reveals something of that Conservative weakness:

I told him that the thing that mattered now – far above politics – was to keep the country united. Diefenbaker's policy – Balcer agreed – was the greatest threat to unity because he did not hesitate to stir up and exploit anti-Quebec feeling. He must hope that by sacrificing Quebec, politically, he would return to power by securing the great majority of English-speaking votes.

This was a suicidal policy – both for him and for Canada – and we agreed that it should be defeated.

Sharp and I – far from attempting to secure Balcer's allegiance to Liberalism – emphasized the importance of having both Parties represented in Quebec.

Balcer says the die is cast so far as serving under Diefenbaker is concerned. He and some of his Quebec MP friends will form an independent group which wishes to support our Government in the legislation it is proposing for the next session, much of which is of special interest to Quebec.

I told him that we would certainly welcome such support and would keep in touch with him – privately and confidentially – through Sharp.

As soon as we were in government, we began the work of setting up the Bilingualism and Biculturalism Commission. Our aim was to implement our pledge by establishing a commission with the broadest possible terms of reference to enquire into the position in confederation of French- and English-speaking Canadians. This was to be the grand inquest into relations between Canada's two main language groups, with the purpose of recommending measures to establish a better relationship for the future. There was not too much difficulty over the terms of reference, though we did make one mistake, of which we soon learned. We failed to take adequately into account the sensitivities of citizens from other cultural backgrounds and the problems of multi-culturalism, indeed, a problem of almost multi-lingualism. We mentioned this, but we gave the impression that there were really only two elements in Canada's development, the English fact, if you like, and the French fact. The wording of the terms of reference aroused the suspicion that we were, in effect, dismissing other ethnic groups, although we did appoint a Ukrainian Canadian to the commission. What we had in mind, of course, was that while these other ethnic groups, leaving aside Canada's indigenous inhabitants for the moment, have made their own contributions, the Canadian foundation was essentially dual. Those who by choice came to Canada later were expected to fit into one or the other of the two founding groups for language purposes.

It was a difficult Royal Commission to organize. The problems were analogous to those of selecting a Canadian Cabinet. As with a jigsaw puzzle, it was imperative to put the right people in the right place. I thought that we had picked an admirable commission and I believe that the results of their work have amply demonstrated this. We had two very good chairmen, André Laurendeau and Davidson Dunton. We also had a good, yet I suspect too large, staff of experts. The work took much longer than we had expected, perhaps longer than it should have, though I, for one, was not among those who thought this kind of enquiry could be done in haste. Nevertheless, there was almost an excess of esoteric research. Academics appear to have been irresistibly tempted to get a job on the B&B Commission to get on with a research project they had been wanting to launch all their lives, but for which they could not find the funds. However, invaluable research *was* completed, which will provide a rich mine for Canadian students in the future.

Those opposed to the whole concept of the commission said that all we did was to create more problems, that rather than stopping trouble, we had provoked it. This is the invariable complaint when solutions to important and controversial national issues are sought. It may be said that one of the values of the B&B Commission was the uproar it created in revealing some of the hidden cracks in our unity. I do believe that this was true.

The first volume of the commission's report presented an important and realistic analysis of Canadian disintegration. Many thought it much too pessimistic and much too alarming. I did not. I thought it exactly right. I wanted people to be shocked, and they were. Some Canadians realized for the first time that there were differences serious enough to destroy our country if no remedial action were taken.

ℐ

The violence associated with the extremist *Front de Libération du Québec* began just before and continued intermittently during my régime, becoming somewhat more serious toward the end. This escalation reflected, of course, the growth of a violent separatist movement which in turn mirrored the extreme aspect of the Quiet, at times not so quiet, Revolution. All this was very disturbing and undoubtedly affected our attitude toward Quebec. On the whole, however, I thought it a hopeful sign that Quebec had emerged from the patriarchal society of a hundred years ago into the industrial age and the twentieth century, even though that emergence brought a good many new social, economic, and financial strains. Except for measures required against attacks on federal property, the provincial government dealt with whatever violence appeared. The situation did not then require the kind of action necessary in 1970, when the FLQ drastically increased the violence of its attacks.

I should perhaps digress for a moment to say a few words about the use of the War Measures Act in 1970. On 5 October an FLQ cell kidnapped James Cross, the British Trade Commissioner in Montreal. In return for his release they made certain demands, including the release and safe passage to Cuba or Algeria of twenty-three FLQ members charged with or convicted of criminal offences whom they called 'political prisoners.' If their demands were not met they threatened to kill Mr Cross. Three days later one of the kidnappers' conditions was satisfied when an FLQ manifesto was broadcast over the French network of the CBC. Then, on 10 October, another FLQ cell abducted Pierre Laporte, Quebec Minister of Labour, in front of his home. Rumours were rife that the civil authority in Quebec was about to collapse. In these circumstances the Prime Minister phoned me about 7:30 one evening at the York Club in Toronto, where I was attending a dinner. He was at Rideau Hall with the Governor General and wanted to bring me up to date on developments in Quebec, the seriousness of which he emphasized. He was particularly concerned at that time over the failure of the police to make any progress in tracking down the kidnappers, and told me he was now considering applying the War Measures Act to give the police greater powers. In a note of our conversation I wrote:

He believed that this move was justified in the grave situation that had to be faced. During the day he had consulted Diefenbaker and Douglas, Caouette and Stanfield. He found Diefenbaker and Douglas understanding but Stanfield more hesitant and non-committal. I told him that I was glad to be informed and I certainly appreciated the difficulties and dangers of the situation. He had my complete sympathy and understanding. I thought the governments in Ottawa and Quebec had handled things admirably. I felt that Parliament's reactions to the War Measures Act would be very important. If it backed the Government on a non-partisan basis, that would have a strong and stabilizing effect on public opinion everywhere. If, however, there was bitter debate and division, then the effect would be bad and the government's position more difficult. In any event, the earliest possible Parliamentary action on the initiative of the government was important.

I warned the PM that he mustn't assume from a private talk that either Douglas or Diefenbaker would support him publicly. I had learned from bitter experience that such private talks usually meant little when a Parliamentary debate began, and how easy it was to be deceived by them. An Opposition leader could always plead that his colleagues in the Party could override any personal views he might have.

I told the PM that if I could help him in any way during those difficult days I was always available. On 16 October the Act was put into effect by Order-in-Council, in the Prime Minister's words to 'root out the cancer of an armed revolutionary movement.' A day later the dead body of Pierre Laporte was found in the trunk of a car. Cross' kidnappers were not discovered until December, when he was released in return for their safe-conduct to Cuba. Shortly thereafter Laporte's abductors were found and arrested. Throughout these events, I had no further part in the crisis, except for an armed soldier who, for a while and much to my embarrassment, escorted me wherever I went.

The idea that difficulties with Quebec developed only in the 1960s and 70s is, of course, not historically accurate. We had, for example, a rough time in 1917 over conscription, and earlier, in 1885, over the execution of Louis Riel. But though we have had troubles ever since 1867, we have never had anything quite like those of the last decade. In the past there were isolated crises. Now there is a major political development: the emergence of a new Quebec, a Quebec determined to be recognized in confederation more substantially than in the past. The problem, as we saw it during my years in office, is perhaps reflected in a letter I wrote to a concerned citizen of Western Canada on 7 April 1964:

I appreciate the importance of the matters you mention, as I do your worry, lest it may seem that we are yielding unnecessarily and wrongly to Quebec as we try to find solutions to the very difficult problems we now face in

Federal-Provincial relationships. If we do not find fair and satisfactory solutions to these problems, our Confederation – and hence Canada – is not likely
to survive. But I want to assure you that in this search I have not, and will
not, make any concessions to Quebec or to any other Province which I do not
feel are justified or are equitable.

Quebec, and French-speaking Canadians generally, have certain rights
and privileges which are guaranteed by our Constitution and I believe that all
Canadians should insist that these guarantees are respected and made effective. This is not appeasement, but justice. I would, however, be open to the
kind of criticism you mention if our government yielded to Quebec, or to
French Canada generally, in demands which they had no right to make in the
first place. This is a matter of very delicate as well as critical balance and I
assure you it is not easy to be fair to all sides concerned.

Since the problem was essentially political, a few words are in
order here about the two men who led Quebec during my régime,
Jean Lesage and Daniel Johnson. Jean Lesage had been my Cabinet
colleague from 1953 to 1957 and before that my Parliamentary Secretary in Ottawa. He later wrote to me, on his retirement from the
leadership of the Quebec Liberal party, that his work at home and
abroad as my Parliamentary Secretary had been 'the real beginning of
a marvellous experience.' As I have mentioned, I had a good deal to
do with his return to Quebec and provincial politics, though later I
tried to get him back to Ottawa. When we were both on holiday in
Florida in January 1965, he drove over from Miami to visit me at
Hobe Sound. In our conversation, I brought up the question of the
importance of a strong federal government to protect and strengthen
the right kind of national unity. I said that I hoped he and I would
continue to work closely together to this end, and that to accomplish
this more effectively he would join me in Ottawa in whatever Cabinet
post he chose. He seemed flabbergasted, but pleased. I told him that
he had a duty to return to federal politics and that his return at this
time undoubtedly would be interpreted as indicating that he would
become the leader when I retired, as I proposed to do so as soon as
possible. Lesage said that, while flattered, he could not leave Quebec
until after the next provincial election. He did not rule out the possibility of making the change then, but he also indicated a desire to
return to private life after one more election in Quebec.

I sometimes wondered, however, whether the Lesage government
really knew what goals it was trying to reach. Perhaps this was not
unnatural; his government had to come quickly to terms with a
movement going ahead rather rapidly. There were times when we in
Ottawa judged that the Quebec government had decided the best

way to handle its problems, and particularly their extreme manifestations, was not so much to quarrel with Ottawa as to stand resolutely
against us, to show what good provincial nationalists they were. This
was quite as much a problem when Jean Lesage was in office as when
Daniel Johnson of the Union Nationale succeeded him. Such conflict
is not new in the history of federations, especially when, as with us,
the ordinary pressures of provincial against central government were
mingled with a political movement towards a greater recognition of
language, race, and culture, and indeed when a minority wished
complete separation. The provincial government had its own troubles
in keeping extremism in check.

While I knew Lesage better than Johnson, it is often easier to do
battle politically with the leader of a party other than one's own. That
Jean Lesage and I were on such good terms, and belonged to the
same party, made it at times more difficult to reject positions that he
and his government assumed. To deal with a leader from a different
party was more like dealing with an Opposition, and in some respects
more comfortable, although not necessarily so. Ross Thatcher's Liberals in Saskatchewan, for example, gave me as much trouble as any
provincial government.

And, in some ways, Daniel Johnson was easier to get along with
than Jean Lesage. Lesage was a highly strung, brilliant, rather tem-
peramental person who spoke very emotionally at times, perhaps
because he knew me so well. Daniel Johnson, who did not know me
at first, was a cool, careful, courteous man who played his cards close
to his vest. He was a most ingratiating person and at times disarming.
It was not easy, even had it been desirable, to provoke a real confrontation with him. When I was in Montreal in April 1967, Mr Johnson
called on me at my hotel and remained for almost three hours. The
purpose of the visit was to have a general exchange of views and to
get to know each other better. We succeeded, I think, on both counts,
even though our exchange of views did not result, indeed was not
meant to result, in any hard agreements. It was not easy to get the
Premier to deal with any of the detailed subjects I had studied for our
meeting. He rather preferred amiable generalities and assurances of
good will, and a desire to avoid controversies and difficulties between
Quebec and Ottawa. I felt that he was quite genuine in this, and in his
desire for a united Canada with a contented Quebec which would not
nurture separatists. I wrote, after the meeting: 'He is quite frank
about his own more extreme nationalists and is prone to excuse his
own lapses from common sense and moderation by the necessity of
handling carefully his "wilder men."'

We both agreed that it was foolish to dispute Quebec's special relationship to and feeling for France, or the renewed desire of France to develop that relationship. We did, however, discuss the difficulties and dangers to Canadian unity that could derive from this situation, especially, as Mr Johnson put it, from the tendency of 'certain people' to sound off or become too sensitive. We discussed in this context the proposed centennial visit of de Gaulle, of which I shall have more to say later. At this encounter I let Mr Johnson know that we did not desire confrontation or conflict over Quebec's relations with France; neither did he. He also tried to reassure me about the purposes and programme of his own proposed visit to Paris, and told me he would do his best to keep our Ambassador, Mr Léger, informed during the visit.

We discussed a number of other matters. Johnson was sympathetic toward the proposal which we were considering at that time for the establishment of a federal district around the national capital. He told me that he was having a provincial commission look into the matter, but he was rather non-committal about a tripartite commission of enquiry—Ottawa, Quebec, Ontario—at this stage. On the subject of Arctic Quebec, he was pleased with his contacts with Arthur Laing, my Minister of Indian Affairs and Northern Development, and with the progress that had been made for the transfer of jurisdiction from the federal to the provincial government. I noted: 'He agreed that this should be gradual and that impatience and controversy should be avoided.'

There was little discussion at that meeting on constitutional change. I emphasized that we believed a great deal of preparatory work should be done before a conference could usefully be called. I also told him about our desire to preserve the constitutional position of the provinces in any arrangements for educational television that might be made, while maintaining our own control over broadcasting in general. He did not seem disturbed by recent developments in this matter, and preferred to avoid any Quebec claim to its own broadcasting service, which he thought was unnecessary. The CBC ought to be sufficient, but he had some recent complaints about the organization, with which, incidentally, I sympathized. One area where the Johnson government (as that of Jean Lesage before it) complained quite bitterly and strongly was the federal government's share of the country's tax resources, which they claimed was too great. We had turned over more revenue than ever before, and still they wanted more.

Quebec remained throughout much concerned about what they saw as the federal tendency to develop social security programmes which encroached on provincial jurisdiction. In their view, federal grants to universities, for instance, were the thin edge of the wedge of federal intervention in education. We responded to the issues raised by Quebec with 'co-operative federalism.' Arrangements were made between the provinces and the federal government for certain shared-cost programmes but always in such a way as to allow any province to opt out. This was not discrimination in favour of Quebec, although in most of these programmes Quebec was the only province that did not wish to participate.

Perhaps I should add a few words about some of these practical features that have to be dealt with in discussing federalism. One of the major conflicts in any federal structure, especially one in which provincial responsibilities and expenditures are steadily increasing, is over the division of the taxpayer's dollar. The other basic difficulty in federalism is the sharing of jurisdiction between the two levels of government. When our Fathers of Confederation worked out the British North America Act, they were dealing with relatively uncomplicated constitutional problems. They could not possibly have anticipated the problems we would be facing a hundred years later in areas such as social security and welfare. As a result, we had to reassess and reallocate areas of revenue production and of jurisdiction.

In education, for example, the responsibility has always been solely that of the provinces (except for Indians and Eskimos), and this is one of their most jealously guarded prerogatives. This is particularly true in Quebec where provincial control over education gives some assurance that the province will be able to determine its own linguistic and cultural life. While we could perhaps in other provinces have secured a greater federal role in education, there was never any possibility of a concession from Quebec which could be interpreted as meaning that, even in the most remote contingency, the federal government might have some power over education. This sensitivity is illustrated by the reaction to our attempt to help the provinces by providing scholarships and per capita grants, in view of the greater and greater financial difficulties caused by the rising cost of university education. We never dreamed of suggesting anything to affect the primary or secondary levels (except perhaps for help in constructing buildings), and had no desire to interfere in the educational processes of the universities. Further, we were motivated by an understanding of the impor-

tance of education to the country. We planned and initiated our programme on that basis. But in a federal system such as that of Canada,
and I do not know how we can escape this, any programme or planning with the provinces inevitably and unavoidably creates circumstances which are not easy to anticipate. Quebec under both Lesage
and Johnson was adamant in rejecting federal intervention. The other
provinces were sometimes opposed to the techniques by which we
established and allocated these grants, though not to the grants
themselves. Some of the most difficult discussions I had as Prime
Minister with the premiers of Quebec arose from their insistence that
we had no right to give grants to institutions of higher education in
Quebec. If we wished to help financially, we should turn over more
sources of tax revenue to the province. If the other provinces wished
to receive these grants, and they did, then Quebec should be com-
pensated without any strings attached to the use of these funds. We
eventually worked out a compromise arrangement by which the
money in effect went to higher education, but could legally be used
by the provincial government for any other purpose if it so desired.

Another very good example of the practical complications of
federalism is to be found in the events surrounding the introduction
of the Canada Pension Plan. This also provides an encouraging illus-
tration of how a satisfactory compromise can be worked out so that
neither party abandons its principles, if there is good will on both
sides and if outright confrontation is avoided. On 9 November 1964
we introduced in the House of Commons a plan for a universal contributory pension. There had already been discussions with the provinces and we hoped, with some reason, that the plan would be
acceptable once it got through the House. Quebec, however, took
strong exception to a federal pension plan covering the whole country, even though it would be worked out in co-operation with the
provinces and in conjunction with jointly operated federal-provincial
assistance schemes. Lesage's government decided that Quebec
would have its own contributory pension programme with, of course,
financial compensation from the federal government. I was disturbed
that these views had not been made known at an earlier stage.

The Quebec government's stand was more than a question of opt-
ing out. They claimed that we had no right at all to enter this field
against their wishes. There was danger of a real rift. Quebec wanted
its own scheme and this was not to be basically the same as ours, thus
making interchangeability impossible. In an attempt to find some
solution we met with Mr Lesage in Quebec. Some of our off-the-
record discussions were frank almost to the point of brutality. Pres-

sure was on me to thumb my nose at Quebec and to go ahead on our own, but I believed that this would have been foolish. Most of my colleagues agreed that we should make a supreme effort to work out an arrangement whereby the Quebec and federal schemes would be so similar in essentials that we could provide for interchangeability and, in effect, have a national scheme. It was important that a Canadian moving from one part of the country to another should be automatically covered. In the end, we made some changes in our plan, one or two of which I think improved it, and Quebec also made some very important modifications. There was in the process a good deal of travelling back and forth between Ottawa and Quebec City, especially by some of our people: Mr Sauvé, Miss LaMarsh (who as Minister of Health and Welfare had strong views about pensions), Mr Lamontagne (who knew everybody in Quebec), and Tom Kent. In the end arrangements were worked out and our legislation was passed into law in March 1965. The important thing is that the two plans have meshed very well, providing a national pension system with substantial benefits open to all Canadians.

In these various negotiations and discussions with Quebec, federal officials and their provincial counterparts were in very close contact. Ottawa's top experts in federal-provincial and Quebec-Ottawa relations were very pleased that a group of first-class professional civil servants had begun to emerge in Quebec. Our people and the Quebec officials got along extremely well, for example, on the tax structure committee set up to rearrange the allocation of financial resources and to work out federal grants without infringing on provincial rights. This committee, incidentally, was very important, as the following extract from my diary on Lesage's January 1966 visit attests:

Lesage is very pleased with the way that Committee is functioning but appalled at the financial difficulties ahead – both for Federal and Provincial Governments. I told him no more important work, in the field of federal-provincial fiscal relations had ever been undertaken. I suggested that it might eventually lead to a basic change in those relations by which every province undertakes to discharge *all* its responsibilities under the constitution – especially in the field of social security and welfare – with the Federal Government's responsibilities restricted to:

1 Giving the provinces access to new fields of taxation.
2 Putting the poorer provinces in a position to do this through tax equalization.
3 Giving leadership in establishing standards and providing for transferability.

This change might take some years but was the direction in which we should be moving. With financial equalization, the electors of each province would insure that there was equalization in terms of social progress. Lesage was heartily in favour of this approach, but we agreed that it would take time to achieve the objective and caution and tact to move toward it successfully.

The emergence of highly qualified professional civil servants in Quebec made work on, for example, the tax sharing committee possible. There were, however, some senior officials in Quebec more concerned with the political aspects, in the broad sense of thrusting for independence, than in reaching an accommodation; and we did not much admire some of their tactics. In both Jean Lesage's and Daniel Johnson's governments there were Ministers less interested in settling problems than with using them to establish a semi-independent if not fully independent status for Quebec. We, however, had our Anglo-Saxons who were quite as stubborn as those on the other side. Often the leaders from Quebec and I would share the sentiment: 'God protect us from our extremists.'

Perhaps I should also mention here the separation of the federal and Quebec wings of the Liberal party. Before 1964 we had a common organization, which had been very convenient and efficient. Under pressure from Jean Lesage and his government, Quebec Liberals began to wonder whether it would not be advantageous to separate the federal Liberal organization from the provincial Liberal organization. The provincial Liberals believed that they would have a freer hand in their electoral manœuvrings and activities if they were not integrated with the federal organization, especially at a time when relations between Ottawa and Quebec were very sensitive. I regarded the proposal favourably (as did Guy Favreau), particularly after 1965 because we had new men in the federal party (Marchand, Pelletier, and Trudeau) who were very keen to break with the old traditions of undemocratic party management, fund raising, and selection of candidates. In the event, all turned out very well. The relations between the two wings of the party are even better, I think, since the division, and since then it has been easier to make reforms in the federal party structure.

One result of the separation of the two Liberal parties in Quebec was that I did not have anything to do with René Lévesque's departure from the provincial party. I first came in contact with Lévesque during my trip to the Soviet Union in 1955. He was the CBC correspondent for the visit. He was an amazing man, finding out where we were going and always there with that microphone before we arrived. Even when I was staying with Khrushchev and Bulganin in the Crimea he was there to greet me. I must confess that my reaction was one of impatience. I did not much like him in the Soviet Union; he was a nuisance, and I did not realize how very interesting he was. Later I got to know him and found him captivating. During the 1962 and 1963 elections when I was trying to conduct my Quebec campaign largely in French (which was not easy for me), I received assistance from him in preparing some of my French-language broadcasts. By the time he split with the Liberal party, therefore, I knew René Lévesque well enough to regret that decision. I think it unfortunate, to say the least, that it was not possible for him to remain a Liberal. The independence-minded Parti Québécois offered him only a limited horizon. I expressed some of my views on the appeal of separatism at a Liberal federation dinner in Montreal on 22 October 1967:

Yet there are those, few but vocal, inspired by a variety of motives, who would make of this land of destiny, a defeated, divided and fragmented people. They would restrict French culture, and language and tradition within the boundaries of one Canadian province, which they would make independent. They would limit the right of the French society of Canada to grow and expand, as it is now doing. They would not open Quebec to all of Canada and to the world.

On the contrary they would limit and restrict the opportunities of its people, of the working people, the business people, the farmers, the men and women in their homes and the children they are bringing up, to the boundaries of a single Province, a small part of a great continent. Is this what you want for yourselves and your children in Quebec? Is this the voice of separation which advocates this retreat to the past, to an ingrowing restrictive nationalism? It may quicken a few hearts but it dismays many, many more. It is the voice of defeatism. It is a voice which has no faith in Quebec, no faith in Canada.

It is the voice of fear, when courage is what is needed; it is the voice of despair when more confidence in ourselves will carry Canada through to great new achievements in political action, in economic progress, and cultural advancement. Separatism is a voice without hope when the times hold more hope for Canada than ever before in our history; *if* we stay together and put co-operation for the common good ahead of conflict.

ॐ

If confederation is essentially a struggle between the centre and the provinces, certainly we had more than our share of it during these years. As a consequence of our experiences, I came to the conclusion that not only should we make arrangements as palatable as possible for the provinces, giving them as much authority as we could, but also that the time had come to change our constitution. We needed to amend the constitution, to make it relevant to present-day realities. The British North America Act, which is in effect the Canadian constitution, was and is a statue of the British Parliament at Westminster. Thus, when there was agreement in Canada on amendments, our Parliament had to pass a resolution petitioning the British Parliament to take the necessary legislative action. Even though the desired action was invariably taken, I was always ill at ease at having to ask another Parliament to alter our constitution for us since we could not agree on how to alter it ourselves. We had been trying to find a formula over the years; we had made some progress but had not completed our task. At the 1964 Charlottetown federal-provincial meeting to celebrate the anniversary of the Confederation Conference held there in 1864, we thought we had reached agreement with all the provinces on an amending procedure called the Fulton-Favreau formula. I came back from that conference quite elated at the possibility that we had achieved what had been found impossible for so many years.

But during my holiday in Florida in January 1965 a complication arose, although I remained hopeful that the formula would be accepted. When Mr Lesage drove over to see me, the first thing he mentioned was his desire to have the constitutional amendment formula approved only by the Legislative Assembly, since the Quebec Upper House had a substantial Opposition majority. He later agreed, however, after hearing from me through Gordon Robertson, to forgo this plan, since this would put Quebec in a different position from the other provinces and might lead to criticism. I confirmed that this was my view, and expressed my satisfaction at his decision to respect it and to proceed in the normal way. He thought then that he could bring sufficient pressure on the Upper House to prevent a negative vote there. He told me also that he was anxious to abolish the Legislative Council in any event, as Quebec was the only province still retaining an Upper House.

But a year later, on 2 January 1966, when Mr Lesage again visited me, there still had been no acceptance of the Fulton-Favreau scheme and the prospect seemed less favourable. He arrived at Sussex Drive at 6:30 that evening, and we spent the next four hours together. He was very friendly, very cheerful and optimistic about everything, even federal-provincial relations in 1966 and beyond. Yet, to me, that evening was somehow unsatisfactory. My diary account of that visit records:

Lesage is very worried about the amending formula. He is certain that majority opinion is against it in Quebec and that, even outside Quebec, there are strong views against it—for exactly the opposite reasons to those put forward in Quebec. Perhaps, he said, we acted too quickly at Charlottetown. So what do we do now?

I replied that what he really was suggesting was that we find some device for postponing action indefinitely—or at least until the situation can be reviewed at a Federal-Provincial meeting. He agreed.

After some discussion, he said that he would send me a letter suggesting that the constitutional situation was so fluid at the moment, with important fiscal changes being considered and with increasing pressure for a fundamental constitutional revision, that perhaps the best course now would be to suspend any action on constitutional amendment until the whole position become clearer.

I told him that we, too, were embarrassed by the present position, and if the Quebec Government did not feel that they could get acceptance for the present formula, then perhaps the best course would be that which we had mentioned, but it would have to be very carefully prepared.

I was deeply disappointed that he had found it impossible to follow through in accepting the formula.

Ironically, in between these two meetings with Mr Lesage, the Quebec government finally decided that the time had come to abolish the province's Legislative Council. Abolition, however, required an amendment to the British North America Act. I reminded Jean Lesage that, at his request, we would be asking the British government, through the Governor General (for this purpose the formal channel of communication), to have the British Parliament pass an act amending the constitution of Quebec. I said, 'How will your people feel about that?' He did not like it very much, yet it was the only way this could be done. I remember when I told Harold Wilson that this question would be coming up he replied jokingly that they were tired of doing our business for us, and were not going to do it any longer. Since we were always boasting about our independence, we should take on the first attribute of independence and look after our own constitution. I was not too serious when I suggested, 'Do you know what you should do, Harold? The next time you get a request for a constitutional amendment from Canada, refuse it; tell us to look after our own business. That will create a real constitutional crisis and certainly force the issue. We will then have to work out a technique of amending our own constitution.' Of course, he did nothing of the kind. He did, however, warn me of the possibility that the British Conservative Opposition might block passage of the amendment. I raised this point with Jean Lesage. My diary records:

I told Lesage about my personal talks with Wilson on this matter and the possibility of strong opposition by the Tories. But he didn't seem too disturbed, blamed it all on Diefenbaker meddling and stuck to his view that the UK Government should introduce the measure as soon as possible after their recess, let the chips fall where they may. I asked him about the danger of an outbreak of anti-British feeling in Quebec if the UK defeated or held up the amendment. I was worried about this, but he was not.

In the event, Lesage's government was defeated before action was completed, and the Legislative Council was not in fact abolished until 1968.

As a result of the failure to implement the Charlottetown agreement, we did not make much progress with the provinces on constitutional change, though a good deal of work had been done. I was convinced that we must at least get this process started, and by stages make the alterations which I considered essential if we were going to have a federal structure appropriate to the kind of problems facing this country in the 1960s. The British North America Act must be amended; there must be new tax-sharing arrangements; there must be a new division of authority between the federal and provincial governments; there must be clarification of those responsibilities which were joint and those left ambiguous or confused in the original constitution.

We had a great deal of work to do in confidence with the provinces before we came out into the open with a further constitutional conference. And we were fully preoccupied with that work when Mr Robarts, the Premier of Ontario, hastened the procedure by calling the 1967 Confederation of Tomorrow Conference. A full-scale public conference between the provinces, summoned by the head of a provincial government, was a new development. The federal government was informed that it would be welcome, but we decided not to go. We considered the whole procedure to be out of order. That the federal government be represented at a provincially called conference, simply as one of eleven members, while still having the ultimate responsibility for constitutional change (though with the approval of the provinces in many respects) would be quite inappropriate. But, in retrospect, I would not diminish the importance of the conference. It performed a good service in calling attention to the necessity of change and in arousing public interest in constitutional reform.

Shortly after the conference, on 1 December 1967 at Sussex Drive, I met with Mr Robarts, with whom I always enjoyed working. He was in good form, happy that his conference had ended successfully. He believed that it had had a very good educational result, in exposing problems, in underlining their gravity, and in revealing the good will necessary to resolve them. The country was now more aware than ever before of the dangers of disunity. He also considered that provincial positions had been modified at Toronto, as clarification of differing points of view emerged from the discussions. He paid a warm tribute to Premier Johnson who, he was convinced, would take his stand more strongly than before in favour of confederation and against separatism.

I suggested that the test would be how Mr Johnson met the situation after he returned to Quebec; he had separatists in his own Cabinet, and René Lévesque was now gathering together a strong independence movement. Johnson, I said, would need all the help we could give him. Mr Robarts agreed with my assessment, but was optimistic about the result. He was sure that Johnson would meet and overcome the difficulties. He went on to tell me that there had also been a moderation in the viewpoints of Premier Manning of Alberta and Premier Bennett of British Columbia. Both had left Toronto more sympathetic to Quebec and to Johnson's position than when they arrived. In short, Premier Robarts was very pleased, understandably, with the way things had gone and, I sensed, with his own conduct of the conference. He had every right to be.

We then discussed the federal-provincial sequel. He thought that we should not rush things. Some of the Premiers would have educational work to do when they got home, especially Manning, who left Toronto 'rather hurt' that he had received so little support for his ideas. Also, a secretariat had been created and would wish to meet. I took the position that we should capitalize on the momentum and good will of Toronto, and transfer progress now to the federal-provincial front. We could use the subject of a constitutionally entrenched Bill of Rights to lead up to a general discussion on the whole question of unity and the new federalism and we could set up machinery for a continuing federal-provincial study of constitutional change. Robarts did not disagree. I expressed the view that we were in a much better position now to make progress than we would have been six months ago, or if the federal government had attended the Confederation of Tomorrow Conference.

During the course of our discussion, I also brought up the subject of the national capital, which I had discussed with Daniel Johnson the previous April. I explained to Mr Robarts that my reference to the desirability of a bilingual and bicultural national capital area on a recent television broadcast had been prompted by three developments. First, there had been leaks that we were beginning negotiations with Ontario and Quebec on the subject. Second, I thought that the success of the Toronto meeting and the close collaboration between Robarts and Johnson had made the time propitious for an indication that the three governments were now going to discuss the national capital project; since Johnson had indicated to me that he favoured the idea, it would be wise to strike while the iron was hot. Third, the B&B Report was soon to be made public and would contain controversial recommendations on the subject. It would be desirable that the three governments announce their plans for a discussion before controversy developed over the commission's report. We could thus remove apprehensions that we were going too far too fast, without adequate consultation and agreement between either the three governments or the municipalities concerned. Robarts accepted all this. He was strongly in favour of the idea of a bilingual, bicultural national capital area as a pilot project for a larger Canadian resolution of the problem. But he was worried about proceeding too fast. He knew from experience that Ottawa people, especially his Cabinet Minister from the city, were very suspicious of change in these matters, and that we would have to move carefully. We did. And we still do not have a federal national capital area.

We called a full Federal-Provincial Constitutional Conference for early February 1968. The cast of principal characters, starting with the West, included Mr Bennett and Mr Manning. While the British Columbia Premier always greeted me with the widest smile of any one around the federal-provincial table, and was always the most cordial when it came to slapping me on the back and telling me what a fine boy I was, I cannot flatter myself that our warm personal relationship had much effect on Mr Bennett's attitude toward the federal government when he got back to Victoria. I will say no more than that. Mr Manning, in Alberta, was the exact opposite. He was a cool, careful man, for whom we all had great respect. When Mr Bennett said something at the federal-provincial table I would think two or three times before deciding whether to take it seriously; Mr Manning never said anything that I did not take seriously. Ross Thatcher I have mentioned. Walter Weir of Manitoba I did not know well. Duff Roblin was Premier during most of my time and a very able man, fair in his approach to our joint problems, whose clarity of mind I valued. I have mentioned my very friendly feeling for Robarts of

Ontario, as well as my assessments of Premiers Lesage and Johnson of Quebec. In the Atlantic provinces, there was Louis Robichaud, a French-speaking Canadian. I was very fond of him and had great respect for his mental agility and his good Canadian common sense. I also admired Mr Smith in Nova Scotia and Premier Campbell of Prince Edward Island, and I have already mentioned in another context the special relationship I had with the one and only Joey Smallwood.

I remember, at the time, there was some suggestion that as a lame-duck Prime Minister I would not be very useful or effective if I chaired a meeting of such far-reaching importance. But I believed, and I think the members of the conference agreed, that there was no diminution of my authority or my position because I was about to leave. The conference was, I think, successful. At the least it maintained the momentum for constitutional change and made the people of this country more conscious of the need for change. That conference was my last important chairmanship as Prime Minister—one of my most difficult, but the one which I enjoyed most. This was a more interesting conference than some of our earlier sessions, and one of the first of that kind to be televised. In consequence, the entire country became the audience of our proceedings. I did most of the talking for the federal government but there was one notable occasion when Mr Trudeau had to intervene in reply to some previous interjections by Daniel Johnson. The forceful impression he made as a strong man and a quick debater, as an agile intellect with firm views, was not limited to the conference hall; his intervention was remarked throughout the country. Until then Mr Trudeau had little occasion to reveal himself to the public mind except in connection with criminal law reform. As I have noted, we wanted to focus the conference on our proposal for a Bill of Rights entrenched in our constitution (Trudeau was very keen about this and made an admirable case for it), and then continue on to more controversial questions such as the implementation of the B&B recommendations, tax sharing, and an amending formula. Our position on some of the hard issues before the conference is illustrated by certain of my remarks on the last day of our meeting, 7 February:

It seems to me that if we are to try to achieve the objective that everybody has agreed on this morning, of equalising to the greatest possible extent the conditions of life and living in our country—and that is essential, of course, if we are to work for the right kind of national unity, which depends not only on language and culture (and B&B does mean bilingualism and biculturalism, but as someone reminded us quite a long time ago, it also means bread and butter), if we are to achieve the right kind of unity on the cultural and political level, we will have to try to get a better kind of unity on the bread and butter level, and that is what we have been talking about.

This means we not only have to work to achieve greater equality of incomes among all our regions – and we have a particular responsibility federally in this regard – but we will also have to have something to equalise. If we are going to share the wealth we have got to have some wealth to share, and it is, of course, the principal function of the federal government to have the economic power and the economic wisdom to maintain stable and increasing prosperity to share. We need powers to operate in this field. Mr Robichaud said, I think, at the beginning of his statement that we cannot do that if our powers are stripped. Indeed, I don't think we can do it so effectively if our powers are strip-teased!

Now perhaps you will let me view very briefly the problem of regional income disparity as we see it and what we have tried to do federally to grapple with it in recent years. First I repeat that we must never forget that the economies of the various provinces are linked to the national economy. I have just said that if the national economy is not growing strongly and maintaining a high level of employment and investment and reasonable price stability, which is a very important aspect of progress about which perhaps we haven't said very much, and steadily increasing productivity, none of our regions are going to be strong, because the country can't be strong. Then the problem will be not who suffers most or who suffers least from a declining economy. In other words, regional and national economic objectives are inseparably linked, even if at times they are not exactly identical, with Canadian objectives. To the extent that broad economic policies are successful across the country in sustaining vigorous national growth – and we have had vigorous national growth since the early 'sixties – we will have something to equalise. In this growth since 1960-61 which has been going on in this country all regions have increased their standards and their standards of living. That is admitted by all. But what is perhaps of the greatest importance to (shall we call them) underdeveloped provinces – underdeveloped only in this sense; some have compensations of other forms of development – it is not so much the growth as the gap, and the gap hasn't narrowed as the growth has continued. That, of course, is what we are concerned with.

I remember the February 1968 conference with a good deal of satisfaction. I think that this was a good meeting and that the main paper on the federal approach to constitutional change was a fine presentation. The process has, of course, continued, although in the years since I retired it has lost much of its impetus. I regret that very much. Constitutional change can be the means to a stronger unity. We must not, of course, expect these things to be done overnight; we shall need a good many years. But I wish to emphasize once more that this is a vital problem of long-range importance. So often in a democracy the important has to take second place to the urgent. Unfortunately, there have been so many urgent problems in the last few years that we are losing sight of some of our longer-range objectives.

ॐ

I have left until the end the greatest single source of contention between Ottawa and Quebec, since this contention has a bearing on our relations with a foreign country. The point at issue was the desire of the Quebec provincial government to move into the area of foreign affairs. Both the Lesage and Johnson governments had asserted the right of the provincial government to make direct arrangements with foreign countries and to attend meetings with foreign representatives. I was convinced that the federal government could not abandon its sole right to conduct relations with other states on behalf of the whole country. If we did abandon this right, there would be the end of our confederation. Nevertheless, I also believed that we should bring the provinces much more into these external matters because so many subjects discussed at international conferences fell, according to our constitution, under provincial jurisdiction. It was, I thought, perfectly in order for the Quebec government to have special contacts with Paris, to make special arrangements, to have a special understanding and special liaison with the French government. Other provinces had been doing this for generations in London, and I was not impressed by the horror felt in certain quarters because Quebec was at last discovering France, or rather France was discovering Quebec. In no instance, however, could provincial activities be allowed to infringe upon the essential constitutional fact that only the federal government could speak for Canada abroad. It was excellent that a Quebec delegation go to Paris; but it was not excellent that a Quebec delegation go to Paris or elsewhere and sign an international treaty as between two sovereign powers. We could not concede that and we did not. This became a bitter subject, made all the more bitter because of the intervention of France in our domestic affairs.

Initially, our relations with France seemed satisfactory. I had promised in the 1963 election campaign not only to travel to London and Washington as a matter of urgency, but also to visit Paris at the earliest opportunity. In fact I did not get to Paris until January 1964. I clearly remember that our flight to Paris would have qualified as a bad beginning to any trip. There was no sleep, the cabin was hot, the lights would not go out, and the turbulence became unbearable and almost continuous around the tail of the plane. There was fog over Orly, so we, and the red carpet, were diverted to Le Bourget. We landed at 10:30 Paris time (4:30 AM ours), tired and somewhat apprehensive about the days ahead.

The welcome was friendly, but very formal: guard, salute, flowers for Mrs Pearson, dignitaries—French and Canadian, welcoming remarks by Prime Minister Pompidou over radio and television; reply by me in French with some words in English at the end. I rode to the Crillon Hotel with M. Pompidou. He was pleasant but somewhat reserved, and the fact that he understood no English made things rather constrained. I could understand his French for the most part and Baudoin of the Embassy interpreted my English and his French when needed. This was the linguistic pattern followed for the next two days in talks with de Gaulle and Pompidou. I congratulated Pompidou on the progress current in France. Evidence of this was all around us as we went through Paris, in building, bustle, and so on. I told him how well we were doing in Canada too; that the headlines about conflict between Quebec and the rest of Canada were greatly exaggerated; how anxious we were to develop and strengthen our ties with France, inside the Atlantic alliance. Lunch was at the Crillon where we had VIP accommodation. After an hour or so of rest, and a discussion with our officials, Paul Martin and I were ready for business. My report on the trip provides some of the details of what happened, and my impressions:

I went at 4 PM to the Elysée, where the Garde Républicaine was out in full regalia and I was given the full reception treatment; eventually finding myself seated across a large desk from a large President who was in a very large chair.

He is an intimidating person with a calm superiority of manner and a very dignified bearing which fitted in better with the magnificence of the surroundings than my personality does.

At first, things were rather stiff and formal but I managed to get him talking about France and the state of the world. He seemed increasingly willing to give me his views as I think I convinced him that I really wanted to hear them and that I had great respect and admiration for him and his career.

He speaks with great clarity and ease; beautiful French, slowly expressed. So I had little difficulty understanding him. He is often philosophic and historical in his comments on developments and very certain of the logic and rightness of his own conclusions. But not arrogant or aggressive in expressing them; at least to me.

From the world, we went to Franco-Canadian affairs. I was anxious to remove any impression he might have received that our country was breaking up; that Quebec alone was Canada and that the rest merely a part of the USA and that we Canadian Anglo-Saxons didn't really care much about our relations with France.

We had a very good talk of a nature which official reports do not sufficiently convey. We became increasingly easier in our exchange of views and, when I made a move to leave—as I had been told to do after an hour—he urged me to stay as he wanted to discuss his proposed recognition of Red China and Far Eastern policies generally. So we went on for another half-hour. He was pleased, I think, at my sympathetic understanding of their position as he may have thought I would react as Washington is bound to react to the news. His move is logical and, in the long run, may be of advantage to us all in breaking a log-jam but I told him it would provoke a strong adverse reaction in Washington. He should be prepared for this.

When I took my leave at 5:30 he escorted me in a very friendly way to the front door of the Palace where were photographed. It was a happy change from the first few minutes when he gazed at me seriously and silently from his throne-like chair in the office.

I found de Gaulle impressive and far more sympathetic than I had expected, but very proud, very French, very sensitive about Anglo-Saxons, and unforgetting of the treatment he had received from them during the war. He really did not believe that we English-speaking Canadians had a chance to maintain our separateness against US pressures. I determined to disabuse him on this score and convince him that the United States was not only a great but a good country.

That evening's dinner at the Elysée Palace, with a large and formal reception afterwards, was a sumptuous and glittering affair. They really laid it on and I never felt so 'royal' as in the French Republic, or so out of my natural, informal element. But the General proved to be a kind and considerate host and did his very best to make us feel welcome and at home. He introduced us to the guests, making all the right observations, and appearing to be genuinely pleased to have us as guests. His speech was short, eloquent, very friendly and even moving. I was as nervous as I have ever been when I rose to reply, in French, and before such an assemblage. But I was told that it went well and certainly our host seemed touched by what I had said about France and about him. Afterwards he was very kind and, at the end, took my wife—looking extremely handsome even in that assembly of expensively-gowned French women—and me to our car and waved us home. Paul Martin was almost misty-eyed with pleasure and perhaps relief. By midnight, we were totally exhausted.

On Thursday, 16 January, I recorded:

9:00 AM Delegation gathering–all very pleased over yesterday.
9:30 AM Wreath at the Arc de Triomphe–very impressive ceremony where the band played 'O Canada' better than yesterday.

Then a visit from the Quebec Commissioner, Charles Lussier, who accompanied me to Quebec House where I spent an hour–meeting everyone and trying to make them feel that they–as well as the Embassy–were part of the Canadian visit to Paris. They were all very kind and I was happy about Lussier's welcome as I had been told that he might be cool and 'separatist.' Not at all–quite the contrary. I had a good talk with him which should be helpful.

Then to the Matignon where I had a half-hour or so with Pompidou before the luncheon he gave us. It was a very pleasant affair and I was fortunate in having Mme Pompidou and Mme Malraux as companions. The latter, an extremely fascinating and intelligent person.

Second meeting with de Gaulle this afternoon. This time we had our colleagues with us and sat around the Cabinet table. It was much less formal than yesterday. The ice had been broken.

Afterwards a Press Conference–for almost an hour at the Hotel. Some very tricky questions.

Our dinner tonight and reception at the Canadian Embassy. Very pleasant and went off well. Many old friends there, one of whom, the US Ambassador, Chip Bohlen, got me in a corner and became very excited at the iniquity of the forthcoming French recognition of Peking. He was almost shrill in his criticism–not very good diplomacy!

On Friday, 17 January, I met and talked with the staff of the Embassy and other Canadian officers in Paris. It was the last official act of our Ambassador, Pierre Dupuy, as he was leaving for Canada the next day. I concluded, contrary to the view I had held previously, that it would not be wise to replace him by an English Canadian at that time. Since neither George Ignatieff, our representative on the North Atlantic Council (then still in Paris), nor James Langley, our representative on the Organization for Economic Co-operation and Development, were francophone and with the feeling then in Quebec, a change to an English Canadian ambassador might have caused French Canadians to regard Quebec House as *their* embassy. Thus, I decided that Jules Léger would go to Paris, even though Lionel Chevrier was High Commissioner in London.

After meeting with our Embassy people, we attended an imposing reception given by the Mayor of Paris at the City Hall–speeches, toasts, champagne and food at 11:30–followed by a tour of the place (very baroque and pretentious, and a bit overwhelming). Luncheon was at the Press Club where I spoke to about 150 correspondents of all nations and afterwards answered their questions for half an hour—in some ways, I suppose, my most important engagement, at least for Canadian propaganda purposes.

Perhaps the first indication of a diminishing sympathy in the Paris attitude to Ottawa came as a consequence of their unsuccessful lobbying in Ottawa for the sale of the Caravelle jetliner to Air Canada. The Americans and the British lobbied just as hard for their planes. I had no right to interfere in the decisions of a Crown Corporation but I did have the right to say to the Air Canada people and the Minister of Transport that there were advantages to placing this contract in a country with which we had a favourable balance of trade, rather than in one where we had an unfavourable balance. I expressed the hope that, other things being equal, we would buy a British or a French plane. But other things were not equal, and the decision was made on technical grounds that the American aircraft was best. The French government took that decision rather hard.

Further events indicated a diminishing desire even to maintain contacts between Paris and Ottawa as the desire grew to strengthen relations between Paris and Quebec. I was worried, for instance, over the French efforts to associate Quebec directly with the international francophone conferences which they had inspired, in particular the conference in Gabon. We were quite content to have Quebec make cultural arrangements with France under a general over-riding treaty between Canada and France. Within the authority of the Canadian government over all international agreements, Quebec or any other province could make arrangements with foreign countries; but to make independent arrangements for international cultural and other agreements went beyond the bounds of acceptability. The Gabon affair illustrates this. A small country in West Africa which had been a French colony and was still economically dependent on France, Gabon called an international conference for early 1968 and invited Quebec as a full participant with independent status. We could not accept this and suspended our relations with Gabon. In fact, we were more angry with France than with Gabon, which would never have attempted this ploy on its own initiative.

An earlier unfortunate incident had clouded the fiftieth anniversary of the Battle of Vimy. In planning the ceremony to be held at the Canadian Memorial on Vimy Ridge, the Department of Veterans Affairs slipped up on protocol, and protocol can be very important in ceremonies of this kind. The department invited Prince Philip to participate without clearing this invitation officially through the French government. In return, the French government showed its displeasure by refusing to have anything to do with the commemoration, even though we at once corrected our mistake. If there is one Canadian national military shrine it is the memorial at Vimy Ridge, where thousands of Canadians fell defending France; to have no French representation there was unfortunate to say the least. Happily, the situation was saved by the people of the countryside who turned out *en masse* at Vimy to give the Canadians a great welcome.

And of course there was General de Gaulle's sudden withdrawal of France from the NATO military arrangements in March 1966, with the accompanying announcement that Canadian NATO forces must leave French soil. France had the right to get out of NATO's military structure if she wished and we had to share responsibility with our alliance partners for not having dealt adequately with the circumstances leading to French withdrawal. Nevertheless, to be told to leave France and to move our troops to Germany was an ironic sequel to the history of Canadian forces crossing the Atlantic in this century. My indignation as a Canadian and as a veteran spilled over at one point while talking with a high-ranking French public servant. He was expressing his regret that Canadian troops had been asked to leave French soil. I could not refrain from asking him whether he thought we should take our hundred thousand dead with us to German territory.

De Gaulle's announcement on NATO was both unexpected and brusque. When I first heard of it, I was left with a feeling of despair and angry frustration. The country which had suffered more than any other from the absence of collective action for collective defence, the country which should have learned for all time from its own tragic and bloody experiences that there is no safety or hope in national sovereignty alone, had been so short-sighted as to reject military co-operation with NATO. True, France retained her membership, but she rejected the principle of collective organization and action that alone gave this membership any real security value.

I wrote, shortly after the announcement:

De Gaulle makes his appeal to a past that has no validity, least of all to the French. *La gloire*, 'The old guard dies but never surrenders'—all these things are relics of a nationalist society that is as anachronistic as the bow and arrow.

Is it fear of Germany that is foremost in his mind? If so, his remedy for the removal of that fear can only make it worse. NATO without France makes Germany relatively that much more powerful. She can use that power in two ways; by herself accepting the French thesis and falling back on the kind of national policy and power (this time with nuclear weapons) that has nearly destroyed France twice in this century and would have actually done so, if a system of ad hoc collective defence with integrated military arrangements had not been forced from military crisis and defeat.

Or Germany could make her own arrangements with the USA to make NATO a predominantly German-American *Bund*. This would be better than a nationalist Germany on her own; but not much better.

It may have been that de Gaulle had had enough of the Americans bestriding NATO and Europe like a colossus, that this is why he acted as he did.

The menace of Red conquest of 10 years ago had receded. Europe was again strong and confident. It was time for the USA (which had done so much to bring about this improvement) to take its troops and its Coca Cola and go home; or to Vietnam, in which it had become involved in a manner which proved its immaturity and underlined the danger of being tied too closely to Washington.

This is probably the major source of de Gaulle's decision. *Europa fara da se.* It is an understandable reaction of a proud man who had suffered indignities and now was strong again.

De Gaulle has not tried to conceal his impatience with NATO in recent years and no one should really have been surprised over his decision. It was obviously coming, even though France's allies had the right to expect a more decent procedure, some consultation and an exchange of views before the curt announcement that all had been decided and nothing remained to be discussed but the 'modalities.'

The basic de Gaulle thesis that NATO had outlived its usefulness is right – up to this point; that there should have been a radical re-examination of the whole NATO structure in the light of the changes that had occurred since the Treaty had been signed 16 years ago.

Everybody seemed to agree that changes had to be made to give the European side of the coalition greater influence and power in its direction and control. Everybody talked about the need for a new NATO, but nobody did anything about it. If we had done so, it would have been more difficult for France to move out. Indeed, de Gaulle *might* not have wished to do so.

Our difficulties with Quebec and Paris made me apprehensive about a Centennial visit from General de Gaulle. Nonetheless he was sent the same kind of invitation as was dispatched to every head of state or head of government. We were particularly anxious that his visit should be successful in every way, and after President de Gaulle accepted the invitation I felt reasonably confident that everything would go well. There would be no discourtesies or difficulties, no matter what had happened in the months immediately preceding.

On the eve of his arrival, my mind went back to the time when he entertained my wife and me at dinner at the Elysée Palace in January 1964. He made a very moving speech then: 'Our special regard for French people in Canada is natural. They interest us specially and deeply. However, there need be nothing in this particular and natural connection which would interfere with the happy relations of the French Republic with your Federal state...in which we see a faithful and courageous ally whose blood was shed on our soil in two world wars...and whose independence we wish to see assured.'

These were fine and noble words, and they gave me a certain measure of reassurance on the eve of the 1967 visit. I was not prepared for what happened, in spite of some hints that there might be trouble. During my meeting with Daniel Johnson in April 1967, the subject of General de Gaulle's visit came up for discussion. It soon became clear that Mr Johnson knew more of the plans for the visit than I did, and that he also felt strongly that it should begin at Quebec, especially as there were already four precedents for a Centennial visit beginning outside Ottawa: Ethiopia, Japan, Germany, and Austria. De Gaulle, with his deep sense of history, I was told, would never understand why he could not land, in state, at Quebec. I told Mr Johnson that we were waiting to hear whether he was coming at all, and if so, when. Once we knew, we would send him a proposed itinerary, suggesting that the usual pattern be followed, with the visit beginning in Ottawa; but we would ask for French comments, and if these asked for a change so that the arrival could be at Quebec, we would consider that sympathetically.

After General de Gaulle accepted, we did propose that he should come first to Ottawa to be received by the Canadian government. We suggested a Quebec itinerary, with a possible additional trip to the West to see a different section of our country. We were told, however, that to begin the visit in Ottawa was not acceptable to the French government. General de Gaulle wished to land at Quebec City and to visit Quebec and Montreal before coming to Ottawa. Some of my colleagues thought we should not accept this. But, as I have said, there were precedents; so we agreed.

Then there were various little matters to make the landing at Quebec unpleasant from our federal point of view. The French cruiser, for example, did not fly the Canadian flag. Governor General Michener, who was present for the landing, did not ride with General de Gaulle to the provincial Legislative Chamber for the reception. Our Governor General was not an extraordinarily sensitive person, thank goodness, and we could ignore these incidents. I remember speaking on the telephone to Mr Johnson while these arrangements were being completed, just a few days before the ill-fated visit. I kept the following note of our conversation.

He wished to discuss two outstanding difficulties about de Gaulle's visit to Quebec.

First, the ceremony at the Citadel Chapel. He would not consider riding from the dock with de Gaulle and the Governor General. Where would he be, in the jump seat, in front with the chauffeur, or perhaps—I added—he should drive the car! I told him that he could forget about this suggestion which was tentative in any event. But we didn't wish to have the Governor General leave the dock through back streets in a hurry to reach the Chapel before de Gaulle. Johnson said that they would be stopping at the City Hall first so there would be lots of time.

The next point was the reception that de Gaulle wished to give on his cruiser at the time the Governor General would be giving one at the Citadel. I said we would have to insist on the Citadel reception.

In the end, we agreed, subject to consideration by me during the night, to a compromise by which the Chapel visit would take place in the afternoon, just before the Citadel reception which should be proceeded with. This means that de Gaulle-Johnson will leave the dock reception, without any 'nauseating' federal presence during the drive through Quebec, but the Governor General will be in charge of three functions in Quebec: the arrival, the Chapel remembrance, the reception at the Citadel.

The judgment of Solomon!

So it was done, and the arrival of the French President passed without incident. The next day General de Gaulle made his historic progress and triumphant cavalcade from Quebec to Montreal. The special feeling and attention which he was receiving in Quebec was natural enough, and this did not worry me. But it was quite different when he reached Montreal. I was sitting in the small drawing-room upstairs at Sussex Drive watching him on television when he began his balcony speech. I could hardly believe my ears when I heard the words he uttered: 'Vive le Québec libre.' This was the slogan of separatists dedicated to the dismemberment of that Canada whose independence de Gaulle had wished to see assured only a few years before, when he proposed my health in Paris. This was a reflection on and almost an insult to the federal government. I have often been asked whether that phrase might perhaps have slipped out in the excitement of the moment. It is conceivable. No doubt this was a very emotional occasion for General de Gaulle. But he was not the sort of man to do or say things without careful thought. In any case, this phrase was impossible for any federal government to accept in the

circumstances and in the atmosphere of the time. Nonetheless, I was
not as distressed about that remark as I was about the analogy he
made comparing his procession on that day to his march into Paris
during the liberation of 1944. That I found infuriating. That his entry
into Montreal should be compared in any way, shape, or form with
his entry into Paris following the Nazi occupation was entirely unacceptable. I grabbed a pencil and started to write a reply. (It is always
good to get something down on paper that can be torn up later.) Then
my phone began to ring.

I called a Cabinet meeting for the next morning and told my colleagues that a statement would have to be issued very promptly. I
undertook to prepare a draft. We knew what would happen if we did
not take quick action. Public opinion would quite rightly slaughter us
if we let this incident go by default and received General de Gaulle in
Ottawa as though nothing had happened. We did not tell the General
that in view of what had happened in Montreal it would be preferable
if he went home. But I had no illusions in my own mind that de
Gaulle would come to Ottawa after he had read my statement. That
evening I went on the air to deliver it. I first made it clear that de
Gaulle's words were 'unacceptable' to the Canadian people and government. The statement went on:

The people of Canada are free. Every province of Canada is free. Canadians
do not need to be liberated. Indeed, many thousands of Canadians gave their
lives in two world wars in the liberation of France and other European countries.

Canada will remain united and will reject any effort to destroy her unity.

We also sent a copy to the French Embassy. I understand that when
General de Gaulle received a copy (after he had retired for the night),
he immediately said: 'Get the plane ready; we're going home.'

The next day, just before his departure, General de Gaulle was
entertained at a scheduled luncheon by the Mayor of Montreal. Once
more I was watching on television as Mayor Jean Drapeau made a
magnificent speech in defence of Canada. I wrote him a personal
letter to express my appreciation for his words:

I listened to you on television at the luncheon yesterday with deep appreciation and great admiration. I was very proud—as a Canadian—to hear such
moving and eloquent words which combined a broad and true Canadianism
with love for and loyalty to the traditions, culture and language of French
Canada.

You gave us yesterday a lesson in grace, wisdom and patriotism that will do much to heal the wounds inflicted on our country these last few days.

You have made it easier for us to carry on with the task of bringing about a better understanding and a greater feeling of unity among all Canadians; so that those, like yourself, who have been part of this country and its heritage for 15 generations, will be honoured in Vancouver and Halifax as you are in Quebec and feel as much at home there as you do in Montreal.

I had spent a good deal of time preparing the speech I was supposed to give at the Prime Ministerial luncheon. The last paragraph of it read as follows: 'In April 1950, speaking in Ottawa, you said that Canada is (and I quote) a state which has found the means to unite two societies very different in origin, language and religion, which exercises independence under the British Crown and forms part of the Commonwealth, which is forging a national character even though spread out over 3000 miles alongside a very powerful federation—a solid and stable state. We remember those words with deep appreciation.' What could have happened to have changed those words to 'Vive le Québec libre?'

10

SYMBOLS AND REALITIES

On the evening of Sunday, 17 May 1964, I addressed the National Convention of the Royal Canadian Legion in Winnipeg. Under the steely eyes of a hostile audience, I announced to the assembled war veterans and to the country at large that we were going to have a distinctive Canadian flag.

For me, the flag was part of a deliberate design to strengthen national unity, to improve federal-provincial relations, to devise a more appropriate constitution, and to guard against the wrong kind of American penetration. It was our purpose to develop national symbols which would give us pride and confidence and belief in Canada. The flag was a specific promise of our election campaign, specific even in terms of a time limit. We had pledged that within two years of forming a government we would submit to Parliament a proposal for a distinctive Canadian flag. I was as heavily committed to this, both politically and personally, as to any promise made. This, and the national pension scheme, loomed very large in my mind.

I recall that I had raised the question as early as January 1960, in a television talk on the CBC's 'The Nation's Business' series. In that talk I was critical of the Diefenbaker government's failure to find a solution for the problem of a distinctive national flag. Six days later I followed this up with a statement which said, in part:

The present Red Ensign has never been given formal sanction by Parliament. Furthermore (I know this from my own correspondence) it is not approved by a great many Canadians as a national flag because in design, it is the same as the United Kingdom merchant marine flag, with the Canadian Coat of Arms added. The two flags can be mistaken for each other, and there are many who think that this confusion should be removed. There is no such confusion in any other part of the Commonwealth, because each country, including Australia and New Zealand, has a flag which is easily identifiable with its country and cannot be mistaken for that of any other country. The Union Jack, a flag which every Canadian should honour and respect is not, however, acceptable to many Canadians as a distinctive national flag of Canada because it is also the distinctive national flag of the United Kingdom... The time has come, I think, when this situation should be cleared up by governmental initiative and parliamentary action.

I have not, myself, expressed any opinion about any particular design. I have merely stated that it should embody the principles I have mentioned above; namely, that the design should be such as to avoid the danger of the flag being confused with that of any other country.

It was early in 1964 when I first raised the matter in Cabinet and informed my colleagues that I wanted a resolution on a national flag to be introduced in the House of Commons. There was no opposition, though there was, I think, some hesitation and a feeling that we were perhaps sticking out our necks unnecessarily. Later, some members of our caucus brought up the matter on their own initiative. All the opinions expressed among the members of the party were in favour of our taking immediate action, though nobody had any illusions that this was going to pass through Parliament without difficulty. By this time, I knew pretty well what design I favoured myself, and even got the Post Office to put out something similar in the guise of a stamp. My first and favourite design proposed light blue bars top and bottom with a red maple leaf on a white background. But this, apparently, had no heraldic significance or any other kind of national significance, and was not acceptable to the experts.

I considered it necessary to make public our intention. It was not enough to say in Parliament, 'One of these days we are going to have a national flag.' I had to announce to the country that a resolution would be introduced proposing a distinctive Canadian flag. The problem now was to find an appropriate forum in which to state my case. John Matheson, a veteran, an active member of the Canadian Legion, and my Parliamentary Secretary at that time, was enthusiastic about the flag. Talking to him one day, I asked where I should make the speech. He replied: 'Well, you've been invited to the national convention of the Legion next week. Would you have the nerve to make the speech there?' It would not be easy. The Canadian Legion, I knew, would likely be the most violent group in opposition to a new flag.

Some members, of course, would not oppose it, but most of them would. I could make the speech much more comfortably before the Women's Liberal Association of Brown's Corners with a friendly hearing and the same attention in the news media. Yet it seemed important to take the issue before the Legion.

I had perhaps one or two friends on the platform on the night of my address but not many out in front. Nevertheless, I laid it on the line:

We are all, or should be, Canadians; and unhyphenated; with pride in our nation and its citizenship; pride in the symbols of that citizenship.

The flag is one such symbol. For Canada, it has changed as our country has grown from colony to self-governing Dominion to sovereign independence; to a nation respected among nations. Canada made this change by peaceful evolution, gradually and in a way that did not weaken the bonds with the Mother Country. That phase of our political evolution is now completed.

Our ties to the Mother Country do not now include any trace of political subordination. They are ties of affection, of tradition and respect. As a Canadian, I don't want them destroyed or weakened. But they have changed, and the symbols of Canada have also changed with them. This is an inevitable process...

In taking this position, I know there are others, as patriotic Canadians as I am, who disagree—honestly and deeply. Such an issue is bound to raise strong emotions. Symbols—whether badges, flags, or anthems—have a deep emotional meaning. That is why they help to make a nation great; help to inspire and nourish loyalty, patriotism, and devotion among those who make up the nation. An emotional reaction is roused when there is any suggestion that old symbols should be discarded or adapted to new conditions and new needs...

I believe most sincerely that it is time now for Canadians to unfurl a flag that is truly distinctive and truly national in character; as Canadian as the Maple Leaf which should be its dominant design; a flag easily identifiable as Canada's; a flag which cannot be mistaken for the emblem of any other country; a flag of the future which honours also the past; Canada's own and only Canada's...

No one would deny that we have a responsibility to the past. But we have also a greater responsibility to the present and to the future. Moreover, our responsibility to the past will be best fulfilled by being true to its real substance and meaning...

In the many letters I receive, in the debate going on across Canada today, there is a kind of yearning by Canadians for greater national unity and the pride, confidence and strength that comes from it.

I believe it is for us who knew the fervour and learned the sacrifice of patriotism when we answered the call to arms in the First World War and in the Second; it is for us to give those who follow an answer to their questioning; to give a lead to young Canada to ensure a future which will be worthy of our past, one beyond the most glowing dreams of the present; a future in which Canada will be solid in its foundations, firm in its federal unity; strong in the loyalty it receives from its citizens; a land which we are privileged and proud to serve and for which we are willing to sacrifice – as those men served and those men sacrificed – whose memory we honour tonight at this 20th convention of the Royal Canadian Legion.

When I produced the resolution in the Commons on 5 June, I could have done what Mackenzie King once did. He wished to introduce and have Parliament accept a Canadian flag, officially designated. But this should be done carefully, gradually, and with a minimum of controversy. The first step was to get the Red Ensign accepted as a replacement of the Union Jack. To that end he had it flown, on occasions that made it appropriate, over the Parliament Buildings, at Laurier House, and so on. Then the coat-of-arms should be replaced by a maple leaf 'in autumnal colours.' But the Union Jack part should be kept. In July of 1946 he told the Liberal caucus of his plans and all approved except some Quebec members led by Bona Arsenault who wanted a 'distinctive' national flag. But the majority would not consider eliminating the Union Jack from the flag. Then Mr King set up a Commons Committee chaired by Walter Harris to whom he told his preference and asked for a report proposing this design for approval. He got his report recommending the flag: 'It is the one toward which I have worked from the outset.' He was pleased and noted: 'The Committee having selected the design, the Cabinet can now proceed by Order-in-Council and accept it.' But even this was not done.

In 1964 I decided, with the support of my colleagues, that the new flag should have no trace of the Union Jack or the Fleur de Lys, and that we would produce instead a second resolution recognizing the Union Jack as the emblem of our association with the Commonwealth and as the symbol of our monarchical status. By this time we had agreed inside the government on a design with blue borders, a white middle and three red maple leaves as on the Canadian coat-of-arms. It was, of course, quite unusual to introduce a resolution with a picture attached to it. The debate which followed was one of the most bitter to arise in the House of Commons for a very long time (though not quite so violent as those debates in the nineteenth century when they threw bottles at one another).

Understandably, feelings ran very strong. During the debate – and it was a long, wearing, and at times depressing debate – an effort was made on the part of the Opposition to force me off the issue and make it impossible for us to proceed. I was determined. I did not care what happened. I was going to see it through and a flag was going to be endorsed by Parliament. Incidentally, before presenting the resolution I tried out the red, white, and blue flag on the big pole at Harrington Lake. To my amazement Mr Diefenbaker, who always seemed to have an acute intelligence service in those days, asked a question in the House of Commons the next day and gave me the devil about it.

In the midst of this debate President De Valera of Ireland came to Ottawa. In conversation after a dinner at Rideau Hall with the Governor General and our wives, he commented: 'You're having a very difficult time, aren't you, young man?' 'I certainly am,' I answered, 'I'm so politically innocent and naïve that I just don't know in advance about these things being difficult, and that's why I do them and don't think about the difficulty.' Mr De Valera continued: 'I don't think, young man, you're going to win this parliamentary struggle. It is not possible to legislate as a flag a design that has no significance and no tradition attached to it. To get a flag accepted, you have to have blood on it; you have to have waved it fighting somebody. That's how our flag became accepted. It was a badge of revolution; it was a badge of victory against the oppressors.' He added: 'You know what you ought to do, you really ought to take your flag down to the American border—it's not very far away—and get some of your friends on the other side to take some shots at it, and if you can get somebody to be mildly wounded, that will make all the difference. It will be a hallowed emblem of your independence from the United States.' I told him I did not think we could quite manage that. It would mean a little too much manœuvring on both sides of the border. Although he was only joking, his point had some merit. We should have had a flag flying in the Second World War. There was, in fact an effort made at that time to create a flag to be carried by the Canadian army into battle. But it was a ridiculous design by some heraldic expert in National Defence, with all sorts of symbols on it. Andy McNaughton flew it over his headquarters for a while, but it was never regarded as a national flag.

As the debate in the House went on and on, it became hotter and hotter, in both the literal and the figurative sense. I held a number of meetings with the leaders of the Opposition parties in search of a way out of the parliamentary impasse. The first series of three meetings, which tried to reach agreement on sending the flag question to a parliamentary committee, ended in failure. On 21 August 1964 I reported to the House that the leaders had been unable to agree. In particular, Mr Diefenbaker would not accept my insistence that the committee should be given a time limit and that debate in the House on the committee's report should be limited. I also announced, as I had informed the leaders on the previous day, that the government would call a free vote on the flag – that is to say, we would not view a defeat as a defeat of the government.

The second series of meetings began on 10 September 1964, when we met to discuss proposals put forward in the House two days before by Tommy Douglas, the NDP leader. I met with Diefenbaker, Douglas, and Thompson of Social Credit at 10:00 AM and suggested that the proposals put forward by Mr Douglas might form the basis of our discussion. The proposals as I restated them at the meeting were:

1 A parliamentary committee composed of fifteen members, seven from the government, five from the official Opposition, and one from each of the other political parties, to be assisted by heraldic experts.

2 The committee should report back to the House within sixty days (the time limit to be negotiated).

3 When the committee's report was ready, there should be another meeting of the party leaders to determine the length of time that should be devoted in the House to a discussion of the committee's report.

I asked Mr Diefenbaker to express his views on these proposals. He said that he would not, at that time, raise the suggestion that a majority of 80 or 90 per cent be needed for the committee to bring in its report, as he had proposed in the House of Commons, since there would be a meeting of the leaders after the report had been presented to decide on the subsequent debate.

Mr Diefenbaker remained adamant that there should not be a time limit in the House of Commons if there were a strong division in the committee. However, he agreed not to let the issue delay the setting up of the committee. I said that my own position on the necessity for a time limit had not changed, and that, of course, we had to consider the possibility that the committee might fail to reach a clear-cut decision. I therefore maintained my position that a time limit was essential on any debate on the committee's report, unless that report was virtually unanimous. Mr Douglas and Mr Thompson were both confident that a good report would stem from the committee's work, and that the problem of a limit on the subsequent debate would not arise. It was agreed, therefore, that the party leaders would meet as soon as the committee report had been submitted to determine the procedure to be followed in the House, and that a decision should be deferred on the question of determining the length of time to be devoted in the House to the committee's report.

Then the discussion turned to the length of time the committee should have to complete its work. I said that two months was too long and proposed three weeks, as Mr Douglas had previously suggested. We finally compromised on a time limit of six weeks. We also agreed that, recognizing that the committee was its own master, it would be better if its meetings were held *in camera*.

Mr Douglas then made a strong plea for reasonable, impartial representation on the committee, reminding Mr Diefenbaker that he had said in the House that the members selected from his party would be those who had not taken a fixed position. Mr Diefenbaker mentioned that he had said that some time ago, and that since then most of his members had spoken. However, we all expressed hope that the committee representation would be fair-minded. Finally, it was agreed by all of us that we would report to our caucuses before lunch, and that I would make a short statement in the House at 2:00 PM that day. A few days later, on 15 September, the committee was established.

The committee had sat for some weeks when one of our members on it told me that they would soon be voting. He reported that 'our design' (which the Opposition tried to degrade by calling it 'Pearson's Pennant' or the 'Liberal Flag') might get through by a majority of one or two, thanks to votes from Quebec, but would certainly not get a very big majority. I decided then that I did not want a report with a majority of only one or two. I wanted a strong report backing the design. To get that, I was told, I would have to give in to some extent. I replied that I did not mind provided they brought in a good design with the red maple leaf. The committee then came up with the red and white flag which was later adopted. While it was good, I always preferred the other with its red, white, and blue. The new flag did have the advantage of being very simple. School children could draw it easily; it stood out; it was strong. I agreed, therefore, that if there was an ample majority we would make a concession and accept it. To do this would not only justify the committee's work, it would show that we were not tied to any particular 'Liberal' design.

The subsequent report recommending the red maple leaf design was presented to the House on 29 October 1964. I met the party leaders on the morning of 2 November, as I had undertaken to do when the committee was set up. At the outset of the meeting I urged those present to give their support to the committee which had recommended by a decision of 11 to 4, or by more than a 70 per cent majority, a flag which was not the design put forward or previously supported by any one party in the House, but a design selected by the committee itself. Leboe, who was taking Robert Thompson's Place, demurred and gave a long-winded eulogy of the Red Ensign.

When Mr Diefenbaker said he wanted to discuss first the programme of business for Parliament, I mentioned it had been understood that the purpose of the meeting would be to discuss the possibility of an all-party agreement on a time limit for the debate on the flag. I asked whether we could reach agreement on a time limit for the debate on the flag. I asked whether we could reach agreement on this point, even if there could, unfortunately, be no agreement on a flag. Diefenbaker again proved obstinate, and indicated after some discussion that he could not consider this question until he knew what the parliamentary programme of the government for the rest of the year was going to be. I pointed out that no useful purpose would be served by attempting to outline such a programme until I was assured that there would be no delay in giving the government Interim Supply (which was being held up in the House), and that a reasonable time limit would be placed upon further debate on the flag. If we could not discuss this latter question, then we might as well adjourn.

Mr Diefenbaker was irritable and aggressive throughout the meeting, but backed down at once when I said a refusal to discuss a time limit on the flag debate would bring the meeting to an end. In the course of the subsequent discussion, he made it quite apparent that the members of his party were debating Interim Supply not because they felt it should be debated, but in order to bring the pressure of a minority in the House upon the government so as to influence another part of its programme. I refused to accept this tactic. Later, he did indicate that he would be prepared to ask his party to consider agreeing to a time limit on the flag debate if he could be told in advance what other measures the government wished to have dealt with as priority items before the end of the year.

I told him that the first priority was, of course, Interim Supply. After that we would go on to the Redistribution bill, then to a government resolution on the Canada Pension Plan. We would also be prepared to begin the debate on second reading of the Canada Pension Plan if an all-party agreement could be reached for a limited period of debate; otherwise we felt that this should be deferred until after the flag had been dealt with. These were our priorities; most of them should and could be dealt with before the resumption of the flag debate. I made it clear, however, that any priorities submitted to the leaders of the other parties as a programme the government would be prepared to adhere to, barring some emergency, were contingent on the Opposition parties agreeing to limiting the flag debate to one week (the time suggested by Mr Douglas). At the end of the meeting, I agreed to submit to the leaders a memorandum for a plan of work before Christmas. Mr Diefenbaker and others said they would discuss it with their 'friends.' Then, with no one committed to anything, we adjourned for four days since Mr Diefenbaker's outside engagements made an earlier date impossible.

When we met again on the following Friday, the session began badly, with Diefenbaker trying to argue ill-humouredly that a speech I had made on Wednesday in Hamilton made agreement on a program difficult. I reacted strongly and said that he must be referring to a television interview, the text of which I had and which I read. When he tried to argue that I must have said something else, I strongly denied it and he reluctantly accepted my word. Whereupon I told him that we had not come to discuss speeches, otherwise I would have some strong things to say about one he had made earlier in the week. He subsided, and the others agreed when I suggested we 'start from scratch,' not perhaps the best way of putting it.

I then read the suggested programme of work which I had submitted to the leaders. But Mr Diefenbaker said he could not even discuss this until he knew my views on a proposal he wished to make. I was surprised to learn that before Parliament discussed the committee report, he wished to have a vote on the amendments to the original flag resolution which had proposed a plebiscite. He wanted Parliament to express itself on this first. As that vote would be against Diefenbaker, and as the party positions on this matter had already been defined, I could not fathom why he insisted on something that did not seem to be of any advantage to him. My first reaction was that he wanted to resume the debate on the resolution. But he said not, he merely wanted a vote without any further debate. Then I thought that he might wish me to turn the proposition down out of hand so that he could accuse me of intransigence. I told him therefore that I could not give him an immediate answer, and would have to think about this new proposal. If he insisted on an answer before discussing a programme of work, then the meeting might as well break up at once. He said that in this case I would no doubt wish to make a statement at the opening of the House and he would certainly make one too, covering the whole ground, including my Hamilton speech. The others were alarmed at this, and Mr Douglas pleaded for further discussion.

I then asked Diefenbaker if he would accept the proposed programme if I accepted his new proposal. He eased up a little, at least
he was willing to talk on these terms. He thought the programme was
satisfactory, apart from the one-week limit on the flag debate. On that
he refused to commit himself until he knew my view on his plebiscite
proposal. He had two other requests. First, he wanted the four flag
designs on which the committee had voted tabled. I saw no reason
why this should not be done, and he seemed pleased. Second, he
wanted a single debate on the two committee reports, the majority
and minority reports. I was very happy to agree to this, on condition
that the two votes take place immediately after the debate. Again,
Diefenbaker seemed pleased, though I did not know why.

Then Tommy Douglas asked that the debate on second reading of
the Pensions bill come before that on the flag. I was expecting this,
and said I could not agree unless there was a time limit on this debate
too, say three days. Douglas agreed that there should be a time limit,
and three days should be long enough. The others did not object.
Things had become much calmer, and we decided to say nothing in
the House that day and to have a final meeting on Monday morning,
when a decision would have to be reached on the programme, with
Diefenbaker's and Douglas's amendments to it.

After the leaders had left I called in some of my colleagues and they
were as mystified as I over Diefenbaker's new proposal for a vote on
the earlier amendments, but seemed to think we should accept it and
put him squarely on the spot on the flag time limit of one week.
Before meeting again with the leaders on Monday morning, I also met
with the Cabinet. Based on the Cabinet discussion, I told Mr Diefenbaker when we met that although the procedure in his new proposal
was unusual and subject to certain disadvantages which I outlined,
nevertheless, if agreement could be reached on the rest of the pack-
age, we would accept it. In that case, there would have to be an order
of the House, establishing the new flag programme as follows:

1 Disposal, without debate of the amendment and sub-amendment
   to the original resolution.
2 If defeated, the original resolution to be dropped from the
   Order Paper.
3 Immediately after the vote, we proceed to the reports of the
   Flag Committee.
4 Debate on those reports and a decision taken within a week.

Diefenbaker then showed his hand. He wanted no agreed time
limit – a form of voluntary closure, as he called it. He was sure that the

debate would not take too long. There were only thirty Tory members who wished to speak, but he could not accept a formal agreed limitation. No one could budge him from this position. In that case, I said, the government withdrew its proposed programme and would order the business of the House as best it could in the normal way. Mr Douglas made a plea for a limitation of the debate on second reading of the Pensions bill and urged priority for it. I agreed that the House Leaders might discuss this possibility. I also agreed that a three-day limitation might well affect the time when we would introduce the Pension bill.

Finally, it was agreed that I would make a short, factual, and non-controversial statement when the House opened, merely stating we were unable to agree, without going into reasons or other details. I would then state the items of business to which we attached urgency for disposal, if possible, before Christmas. I agreed to do this provided the other leaders would not follow up with controversial debating and partisan statements. And so the flag issue went back to the House of Commons for decision.

Mr Diefenbaker was determined to do everything possible to defeat and destroy this resolution. I do not criticize him or the Opposition for the stand they took, although they prolonged the debate in a quite unnecessary way. I was pretty depressed about some of the language used in the debate. They may have thought that with the memory of the 1956 pipeline debate we would not dare invoke closure and that if they pressed me hard enough I would give in and put a Union Jack or Fleur de Lys on one of the designs. Eventually, I decided that the time had come to invoke closure. One must wait until the moment when the country is ready to accept interference in normal parliamentary procedure before using closure. By 14 December the country was quite prepared, both outside and inside the House, and there was a general sigh of relief when it was realized that the resolution was adopted by a vote of 142 to 85.

It was a raw day in the middle of February 1965, nine months after my Legion speech, when the red maple leaf flag was proclaimed as the flag of Canada. After a ceremony in the Hall of Honour, we moved out to the front of the Parliament Buildings. The Red Ensign at the top of the flagpole was lowered and the new flag was raised. There was not much of a breeze to flutter the flag in the wind, but there it was. We had a Canadian flag at last. I am very proud to have been associated with it. But I do not feel, and I have never felt, that I was disloyal or disrespectful to the Union Jack and all it stood for when I advocated and helped bring into being the new flag. The time had come to have an emblem distinctively Canadian.

I remember a few years before this, when we were in opposition, crossing the ocean on a steamer and arriving in Southampton. As we went slowly into the harbour we passed a great many merchant ships at anchor. Standing in the prow my wife said, 'I didn't know we had such a big merchant marine.' I asked what she meant. She replied, 'Look at all those ships with the Canadian Red Ensign.' It was, of course, the merchant flag of the United Kingdom. This kind of confusion would have continued to exist had we kept the Red Ensign design with minor changes. I have been very proud in my travels around the world since that time, and I think many Canadians have shared this pride, to see the Canadian Maple Leaf flying in foreign countries as the emblem of Canada, and to see Canadian athletes carrying it in the Olympic and other processions.

I received a vast volume of correspondence on this issue. There were abusive and vicious letters, and some very friendly and laudatory. Some people wrote who had been friends of mine for years to say that they would never speak to me again, that this was the end, that I had been a traitor to our traditions and background, and had sold out to Quebec. But most of those people since then have come to tell me how wrong they were. The divisions brought about by the debate have pretty well disappeared. The Canadian Legion and others now have no hesitation in honouring it as the Canadian flag. Had we taken no action and had the Red Ensign continued to be the national flag, it would never have been flown in Quebec. Now the Maple Leaf is accepted in all parts of Canada and I do not think any Canadian can fail to be proud of it.

We did not solve the question of our national anthem. I wanted 'O Canada' to be adopted as the official anthem, but only with some revision of the words. I was particularly anxious to shorten it by amending some of the last two or three lines. 'Stand on Guard' five times in four lines was, I thought, perhaps excessively defensive. Unfortunately, we never got around to a revised text; we had run out of energy by the time we got the flag through Parliament. I remember some of my colleagues saying: 'O, my God, please don't. Haven't we had enough trouble about emblems? Please don't submit us to this.' Although we also had in hand a resolution for the adoption of 'O Canada', we let it lie.

ॐ

The flag is the most noticeable but not the only example of new symbols replacing old. Other changes have appeared—the Imperial Privy Councillorship is gone, the Prime Minister is a 'Right Honourable' now by virtue of a Canadian decision, the Coat of Arms is not seen so often, 'Royal' has been widely replaced by 'Canadian,' and there are many others. This has caused more dismay, I think, in Canada than in London where it has been seen as an inevitable transition, and a transition made with dignity and grace. As I have noted earlier, the office of Governor General has also been Canadianized but still maintains a connection across the sea with the Royal Family.

The Queen is our monarch but also symbolizes our membership in the Commonwealth of which she is the Head. As Prime Minister, I of course attended a number of Commonwealth Prime Ministers' Conferences. There were more of these during my régime than in the past and they reflected the changed nature of the Commonwealth. No longer did a half dozen people gather around the fireplace at 10 Downing Street so that the Mother Country could tell us what had been going on and how we could best help her save the world and maintain herself. So skilfully and, for the most part, so agreeably were all the changes made that they seemed to conceal from the British people and others the full significance of what has happened. This, of course, also helped to make the process acceptable. As we proceeded from British Empire to British Commonwealth and Empire to Commonwealth of Nations, enough was salvaged each time from the previous order of things to continue the collective and co-operative idea, the feeling of special association, to the benefit, I think, of the Mother Country, the overseas members, and, indeed, the world. At each stage pessimists would lament: 'Ah, we are now approaching the end.' Yet the Commonwealth seems always to retain some attributes of immortality.

In this good result, we still have a sovereign whose status receives collective recognition and whose person invokes a special feeling of attachment and respect, even among the republican members of the group. The transition from empire has been made with understanding and grace; but if the imperial song has ended, the 'Melody of Downing Street' lingers on, though diminuendo. We are now all equals, but Britain is still first among equals. The atmosphere of 'empire' at Prime Ministers' Conferences in London remains and there are functions, by no means all official, helping to maintain it. That atmosphere can quickly dissipate, however, when the Prime Ministers return home to their own problems and worries. Independence within the Commonwealth has been shown, after years of uncertainty, to be not necessarily fatal to uniform policies, but certainly fatal to any general commitment to uniformity.

The first Commonwealth Conference I attended as Prime Minister was in London in July 1964. Perhaps the changes within the Commonwealth can be reflected by a story from a lighter side of this meeting. There was an amusing cartoon in a London paper handed to me during an afternoon session. It showed two African gentlemen in African clothes disappearing into a doorway, with bobbies all around and flags flying, and I was just getting out of my official car. One bobby was saying to another, 'Gor blimey, here's another new one, but he's white.'

There was, however, a very serious side to this conference. The major topic was the problem of holding this new Commonwealth together when faced with the great problem of racial discrimination in Southern Africa. This conference was very different from any I had attended in London. There was still a family atmosphere, but also a frankness of discussion which would certainly have led to a break-up at the United Nations in New York, and which, indeed, put quite a strain on the Commonwealth. The Canadian delegation actively tried to use its influence to prevent disintegration. We let the new members of the Commonwealth know that we were entirely on their side in principle; we took an active part in the discussions and a leading part in drawing up the Declaration of Racial Equality, which became a virtual charter for the New Commonwealth. Nevertheless, it was quite impracticable to do some of the things they wanted, such as enforcing racial equality on Rhodesia by military action, if Rhodesian independence were declared unilaterally.

Another proposal which some of the new African members advanced was the establishment of a Commonwealth Secretariat. At the next Conference, a year later in London, we took the major step of setting up a permanent Secretariat, and this has worked extremely well. I found this an intensely interesting development. I had been brought up in the shadow of Mackenzie King where the idea of a centralized Commonwealth Secretariat was anathema to the Canadian government: Canada would be dragged by British policy into European entanglements of which we wanted no part. Now we were instrumental in founding the Secretariat, and the first Secretary General was a Canadian, Arnold Smith.

The Rhodesian question was in fact the main topic of debate at Commonwealth Conferences during my régime. One of the first real tests for Arnold Smith and his Secretariat was to prepare for the Commonwealth Conference to be held in Lagos in January 1966, soon after Rhodesia had declared its independence. This was the first conference held outside London, and, another precedent, had been called by Nigeria specifically to discuss Rhodesia. In these exceptionally difficult circumstances I thought it wise to send a cautionary message to Mr Smith on 3 January 1966. I was concerned...

lest a conference of the nature and form now likely, as well as the advocacy at such a conference of measures which appear logically to derive from a clear perception of the issues, may serve in itself to accentuate the cleavage on racial lines already implicit in the Rhodesian situation. I am concerned, too, that during this stage of its development the Secretariat should not appear to be taking sides rather than representing whatever consensus there may be among the nations whose common interests it is designed to serve.

There are undoubtedly times when issues should be brought to a head. Equally, and perhaps more frequently in the field of international relations, there are times when the best course may be to strive to avoid a show-down. My own feeling is that, if the Lagos meeting is to serve any constructive purpose, it must find some means of re-establishing mutual confidence without forcing the discussion through to what might be counted as a clear win or loss for any given point of view...

The most important meeting of the Lagos Conference was held on 13 January 1966, and was restricted to heads of delegations and Arnold Smith. There was discussion of the situation in Rhodesia, including the possibility that the economic measures already taken, especially the oil blockade by the British, might break down. Mr Wilson thought these measures would bite more and more deeply; as the Rhodesian people became more and more anxious to return to normal conditions, they would become less enamoured of Prime Minister Smith and his policies. Mr Wilson believed that divisions were developing in the Smith government which should be encouraged, among other things, by restraint in pronouncements on our side. Business was becoming alarmed, and would be soon at a standstill. Moderate people would soon become more articulate. He said that there were divisions within the armed forces, although the police were faithful to Smith, almost to a man. Wilson concluded by saying that, if the rebellion had not ended by a certain date, the Prime Ministers would meet again to determine what measures should be taken. Later I noted in a diary memorandum: 'This perhaps was the most important meeting of the conference and Wilson handled it with masterly skill. It was the best diplomatic performance by him I have ever seen... He made the most of the "Now, this is most secret, even my Cabinet colleagues don't know a word of it" routine, and the "new leaders of Africa" were very much impressed. So Wilson got what he wanted but he made some concessions too. One of the things he wants is a Company of Canadian troops for Zambia if and when this "occupation" is arranged. He thought perhaps we could reduce our commitments in Cyprus to make this possible as they could send another company there to take our place.'

By the time of the next meeting in London in September 1966, it was clear that the existing system of non-mandatory sanctions had made disappointingly slow progress. We had been too optimistic at Lagos. The oil import embargo had not been successful, and there had been serious breaches in the export embargo on minerals. The British Prime Minister, however, presented the conference with an analysis of the impact of sanctions which indicated that these were not without effect on the Rhodesian economy. For example, tobacco was Rhodesia's major export, but by September Rhodesia had sold only about one-quarter of its crop. But progress was slow. There was no binding sanction against the import flow of oil, although there had been a specific proposal for mandatory action against oil imports at the UN. In addition, Rhodesia continued to export minerals, pig iron, chrome, and asbestos in considerable quantities.

When my turn to speak came I told the meeting that in my view we should direct special attention to stopping these exports and, if we achieved no results by diplomatic approaches to some of the main importing countries, we might consider action at the United Nations, as we had envisaged at Lagos. I emphasized to the meeting that I was discussing limited mandatory sanctions by the United Nations. There were disadvantages in applying general mandatory sanctions. These, I said, would have the effect of driving closer together Rhodesia and the other areas of Southern Africa under white minority control, South Africa and the Portuguese territories of Mozambique and Angola. To affect the important trade between these areas and Rhodesia, mandatory sanctions against Rhodesia would have to be followed by similar sanctions against South Africa and the Portuguese territories. Rather than achieve a speedy solution in Rhodesia, a general mandatory sanctions resolution, I believed, would tie that country to South Africa, and would link a satisfactory solution of the Rhodesian problem with a long and difficult economic siege of South Africa. This was a hard fact which had to be recognized in our consideration of the Rhodesian problem.

I then turned my attention to the question of the use of force against Rhodesia as urged by some who considered that economic sanctions were inadequate. I said:

Various speakers have proposed that the British Government should use force to overthrow the illegal Smith régime, saying that sanctions have not been effective and will not be effective. The use of force, of course, is primarily a matter for Britain, which has the constitutional responsibility, to decide. Up to now the British Government has decided against the use of military force and for my part I have not so far seen fit to question their decision. I still consider that strengthened economic measures are the best way of attaining our objective, even though it will take longer than we expected. Even though I can perfectly well understand the feelings of disappointment, frustration and even anger of some of our colleagues, which cause them to advocate force, I can't agree with them.

I do not consider that the use of force as part of police action, or force used under international authority with a UN mandate, or to repel an aggressor, is wrong in any way in itself. It is wrong when used exclusively for selfish national purposes, or whenever the objective can be achieved without force, or when good results are not likely to be achieved; or achieved only at a prohibitive cost. Results must always be related to the means of achieving them. So each situation must be considered on its merits.

I have had some experience with the use of force since World War II. I remember well that there were those in the United States who thought that force should continue to be used against North Koreans until their aggressor government was destroyed. Instead we got a cease-fire, armistice and a divided Korea, and I think this was the better choice.

There were those who thought that the United Nations should have authorized forces to come to the help of the Hungarian freedom fighters in 1956 against those outside forces which were destroying their revolution. This was impracticable and dangerous. It might well have provoked general war so it was rightly abandoned. On the other hand UN forces were sent to the Gaza Strip, Cyprus and the Congo... So there is no hard and fast rule on this matter as I see it; no fixed principle which must always be implemented.

But when we say, 'The Smith régime must be brought down at *any* price', I think we should remember that *any* price might result in the use of force in a way which could destroy those that we are trying to help, and have far-reaching consequences never intended or desired. There are differences of view on this, of course... However, as I presume that our consideration would be initially directed to the feasibility of mandatory *economic* sanctions, it would seem premature to discuss military sanctions before the possibility of economic sanctions had been exhausted.

Our first objective is to end the illegal Smith régime. According to most speakers, our next objective, closely related to the first, following the end of the Smith régime, is to bring about majority rule as the basis for independence. Most of those around this table feel very strongly that the grant of independence should take place only after majority rule has been ensured.

I get confused, however, over interpretations being given to majority rule. We might avoid some confusion and possible misunderstanding if we remember that this principle of majority rule, in its application to Rhodesia, goes far deeper than the expression of a formula of democratic government. That aspect of the matter is, of course, important but there is nothing sacrosanct about the right of 51% to govern 49%. When we talk at this Conference about majority rule in Rhodesia, we are really thinking about something far more far-reaching than a mathematical formula of democracy. We are concerned with something that is vital to the very survival of the Commonwealth because it involves the issue of racial equality which is the only basis on which the new Commonwealth can survive; or indeed, on which the world can remain at peace.

The idea that a minority white régime might sustain itself in office for many years in Rhodesia against the wishes of a non-white majority and might attain and retain independence on a minority racial basis, this is contrary not only to democratic principles and basic human rights, but—and this is the crux of the matter as it faces us—it violates the multi-racial character of our Commonwealth and it could destroy our association. In my experience of international affairs over the years, I have seen the unfolding drama of political and racial emancipation in Asia and Africa and in this unfolding, let us not forget, only in Rhodesia, so far as the Commonwealth is concerned, is racial equality still denied as a basis of government and of society. There is no doubt, however, that it is being denied there with a minority clinging to a concept of society with a kind of feudal obstinacy which 'is worse than a crime, it is a blunder.' This is abhorrent and intolerable to the great majority of people and must be changed.

The conference finally reached a compromise, with a good deal of effort on Canada's part, between the African desire to employ force against the illegal Smith régime and the British hope of negotiated settlement. We agreed that if no acceptable solution was found within three months, Britain would ask the Security Council to impose mandatory selective economic sanctions against Rhodesia.

I was disturbed that President Kenneth Kaunda of Zambia was not at the London conference and that he was talking of withdrawing from the Commonwealth. On my return to Ottawa I decided to write to him in support of the measures taken in London and to urge on him the value of the Commonwealth. I wrote:

As you were, regrettably, not in London, it occured to me that you might like to have one or two impressions of the conference discussions on Rhodesia.

These discussions, as you know, went on for over a week. This certainly gave everybody enough time to set out their views very clearly. There was a lot of plain talk. Indeed, once or twice the atmosphere got heated and people said rather sharp things which I hope we can now all forget. I feel that there was a really sincere attempt to reach mutual understanding and as much agreement as possible. Despite everything, the Commonwealth made a real effort to come to grips with Rhodesia last week. This type of vigorous discussion on a very difficult question like Rhodesia is what the Commonwealth is all about...

The next three months will, undoubtedly, be a difficult period for you while the British make a further attempt to persuade the Smith régime to abdicate in favour of legal government. However, in a month or two the position should be a lot clearer. If legal government has not been restored in Rhodesia, then the substantial concessions made by the British with respect both to majority rule and to proposals for UN mandatory sanctions will come into effect. I think these concessions Harold Wilson made are real and important. It was not easy for him to make them. Already I know there has been some difficulty with his Cabinet and he will undoubtedly be in for a very hard time from the opposition...

I should like to say that I think the Commonwealth, and particularly the British, have in the past ten days made a real attempt to meet the views held so sincerely by yourself and your African colleagues. I know you will keep this in mind as you think things over.

Although the United Nations Security Council did vote mandatory economic sanctions on specific goods, no final solution was found for the Rhodesian problem while I was in office. But at least no members left the Commonwealth over this issue on which feeling ran so deep.

As I wrote in the second volume of my memoirs: 'We have moved in my own lifetime from an Empire without sunset, which God had made mighty and was implored to make mightier yet, to today's mini-United Nations of equal sovereign States.' By the time I retired as Prime Minister, the meetings had a Secretariat, a variety of flags to identify the member states, an agenda and a greater formality of discussion and procedure than was required or considered in earlier days. Then, consideration of internal policies was strictly taboo, except occasionally by unanimous agreement; now, the more controversial the question, such as domestic policies that concern racial discrimination, the more vigorous the discussion, and often the stronger the language. Intervention into controversial matters of this kind has already led to the withdrawal of South Africa from the group and could lead to other departures. We know, however, that in a multi-racial Commonwealth we cannot avoid discussion and differences over controversial matters that may be domestic technically, but in their impact go far beyond national boundaries and much deeper than national emotion. The fact is that Commonwealth meetings tend now to concentrate on specific points of disagreement rather than on general areas of common concern. Indeed, discussions in the Commonwealth of today's world would not have much meaning if this were not true. Yet this kind of discussion has its own dangers for a close and continuing relationship, as we have learned in recent years.

Remote are the days when the imperial mother told her daughters or, if you prefer a more militant phrase, the lioness told her cubs what was happening in the world, assuming that they would follow where she led, even into the mud of Passchendaele or to the beaches of Gallipoli. How can one describe, or even more difficult, define this new Commonwealth of Nations? What is it? What does it mean to its members? What is its value to them?

It is not easy to answer these questions honestly and frankly without being too swayed by sentiment, which itself can be perfectly honest and honourable, or by history, which may produce opposing conclusions. We are no longer trying to claim that the Commonwealth is a political entity; Rudyard Kipling and Joseph Chamberlain are dead. It is in fact easier to describe what the Commonwealth is not rather than what it is. It is not an empire, an alliance, a power bloc, or a mutual security group. It is neither a diplomatic unit nor a trading and currency system for its members. Indeed, it is not an organization requiring formal obligations or commitments, except for those trading preferences whose importance is diminishing for some and is threatened for others. While there is no constitutional or legal relationship amongst all its members, there is a social, even a family, relationship which persists. This is not easily defined but does certainly distinguish Commonwealth meetings and discussions from other international gatherings, as I can testify from long experience with both. This feeling or sentiment permitted meetings of Commonwealth delegations to be held in the normal way at the United Nations Assembly during the Suez crisis, when the differences between members were deep and nearly fatal. It is the feeling that inspired a Nigerian statesman to say once, 'In the Commonwealth there is the quality of listening to each other with forbearance.' It is, if I may use the word, a fellowship, the great value of which stems from the fact that it is an association of peoples of every race, freely joined together as equals in the hope that they have something to offer one another and can give the world an example of inter-racial as well as international friendship and co-operation.

൲

The debate over Canada's national symbols and their meaning during the early years of my régime assumed a new emphasis through the events attending the visit of our Queen in 1964. This visit by Her Majesty was to coincide with the Centennial celebrations in Quebec and Charlottetown and was first proposed in March 1961, when the government of Prince Edward Island asked the Diefenbaker government to invite the Queen to the centennial commemoration of the first meeting of the Fathers of Confederation in Charlottetown in 1864. While the proposal was being considered by the federal government Mr Balcer proposed to Mr Diefenbaker that if the Queen did go to Charlottetown in 1964, she should also visit Quebec where, in the same year of 1864, the Fathers of Confederation had met in a second conference to work out the details of our union. I do not know whether the proposed visit was discussed with the Quebec government beforehand, but late in 1962 the Cabinet of the day agreed that the Governor General should be advised to convey to the Queen, for consideration, the hope that Her Majesty might find it possible and appropriate to visit Quebec and Charlottetown in 1964 for the centenary of the Confederation meetings. While the idea of a visit was well received at the palace, Sir Michael Adeane, the Queen's secretary, replied that the invitation could not be formally considered until a year before the event, and that the Queen would therefore like to receive the formal invitation in the autumn of 1963. By that time I was Prime Minister of Canada, and it was therefore to me that Mr Shaw, the Premier of Prince Edward Island, wrote in September 1963, raising again the question of the invitation to the Queen. After determining the most appropriate dates for a Royal visit to Charlottetown, I decided to let the matter stand until the Federal-Provincial Conference of that year met, when I would be able to discuss the matter with Premier Shaw and Premier Lesage before advising that a formal invitation be extended to visit the two capitals.

The Premiers both indicated their desire that an invitation be extended, as in every way appropriate to the important celebrations in contemplation. Mr Lesage, who heard of the proposed visit for the first time during our discussion, was insistent that the Queen should come to Quebec, and as a guest of the provincial government.

I then wrote formally to the Governor General on 5 December, to advise him of this and to ask that his office ascertain whether Her Majesty and the Duke of Edinburgh would be able to visit Charlottetown and Quebec in the autumn of 1964. The invitation was favourably received by the palace, especially as it was to inaugurate a new practice for Royal visits: to come for a specific occasion, not for a tour, and to return home when the event was over. I had been anxious to abandon the 'Royal Trans-Canada Tour' idea, and so had the palace.

The arrangements were found to be complicated; for Royal visits they always are. The problem was increased on this occasion, however, by the growing agitation of Quebec separatists against the visit as an insult to Quebec, an affront to their demand for freedom, a reminder of a colonial past and of an anglophone-dominated present. Threats against the Queen's safety and threats to humiliate her were made and given wide publicity. Indeed, these threats were blown up by certain newspapers here and abroad to a point where Quebec was linked with Dallas, and such phrases as 'awful risks,' 'flight into danger' were used to intimidate the government into advising cancellation of the visit.

All the speculation naturally gave rise to unfortunate results. It stirred up anti-Quebec feeling and created an image of Canada as a state on the verge of civil war, suggesting that the Queen was coming to a Congo or a Cyprus, to a police state or an armed camp. All of this gave priceless publicity to the separatists and played right into their hands in a completely irresponsible way. Indeed, this speculation did precisely what it was supposed to prevent: it increased the danger to the Queen by playing on the emotions of some unbalanced neurotic, inciting him to a form of violence that might not have occurred to him without all this publicity.

As a result of all this, we had to adopt more elaborate security arrangements than would otherwise have been necessary and, even more important, to reassure public opinion through emphasis on these arrangements. Even the British government and, more startling, the London *Times* were worried. In mid-September Sir Henry Lintott, the British High Commissioner, called on me to convey orally a message from his government. The important point was that the government of the United Kingdom would be greatly reassured if I could tell them that the risks of the visit had been carefully assessed by the Canadian government, and that, in my opinion, the Queen would not be exposed to undue danger. He hoped I would not think this request an unwarranted intervention on their part. I told him that I understood their preoccupation and believed that they were fully entitled to convey a message to me expressing it. I felt bound to add, however, that I did not feel similarly about some of the English newspaper comments, nor did I welcome the editorial intervention of the *Times* in the form it had taken.

I told Sir Henry that I had satisfied myself that everything possible was being done to make the security arrangements adequate, and that a few days earlier I had gone over them with the Commissioner of the RCMP. I understood that these arrangements were considered satisfactory by Scotland Yard. I also told him that, in my view, the objective of the small revolutionary terrorist group in Quebec was not to attack the Queen, but to stir up a feeling of panic by threats to attack her, which would lead to the cancellation of the visit. This would be a great triumph for the separatist movement, whereas a successful visit would be a great defeat. Therefore, they must agitate in a way to prevent the visit, and too many people, for their own different reasons, were supporting this campaign, especially in the press.

Personally, I was convinced that the terrorists would not attack the Queen because the reaction in Quebec, and even more in other parts of Canada, would be so furious as to weaken or destroy separatism. There was, I told him, a much greater likelihood of incidents and demonstrations which would not be dangerous but humiliating. I warned him that if pressures of the kind mentioned brought about the cancellation of the Royal visit, this would provoke an even stronger anti-Quebec reaction in other parts of Canada, and that it would be a long time, if ever, before there would be another Royal visit.

The next day I asked Sir Henry to see me again, to give him my formal reply to his enquiry. Thus, when I saw him on 19 September, I read him a note stating that the risks attendant to the Queen on the visit to Canada had been assessed and re-assessed by the Canadian government. The potential risks were undoubtedly greater than on previous Royal visits, but security arrangements had been accordingly increased. Therefore, in my opinion, an increase of danger had been met by an increase in security. In that sense, I believed it could be said that the Queen was not being exposed to undue danger. I went on to say that there was, of course, always a risk attached to any visit of a Head of State, and that if the United Kingdom government wished its own security authorities to make a special assessment of risks and consequent security arrangements, this could be arranged. A few days later Sir Henry called on me again to tell me that his government thanked me for the invitation to send out a security team to confer with the RCMP. However, they would not need to take advantage of this offer since they had full confidence in the RCMP.

I took a personal interest in security arrangements, attending four meetings with the Commissioner of the RCMP and many others without him. I constantly emphasized the necessity of adequate protection, which must, however, be unobtrusive. My main problem was to resist the pressure to postpone the visit. I was determined that this must not happen, though I was depressed by the certainty that the irresponsible elements of the Canadian and British press would play up and magnify every unfriendly demonstration. Every gesture of hostility would be exaggerated into a bitter incident, and the political effect of the visit would thus be deplorable, whatever the actual facts. I was also worried about the possibility that Jean Lesage would yield to pressures and advise the postponement of the Quebec part of the visit. If he had requested this, I would have had to agree but would have insisted that he put his request in writing. Fortunately, Lesage remained calm and firm.

Against this background of exaggerated danger, and in context of the Kennedy assassination, the security arrangements were made by the police. If these were excessive, and if they resulted in an unnecessary use of force on one or two occasions, this must be weighed against the atmosphere that had been created and the prevailing public opinion. (I noticed afterwards that some of those who complained about excessive security measures were among those who had been most guilty of exaggerating the dangers. Unable to report a tragedy, they seemed to get some satisfaction from noting other kinds of trouble; as they exaggerated before the visit, so they also exaggerated after the Royal departure.)

This was the situation on the eve of the arrival of the Royal party at Summerside, Prince Edward Island. We flew from Ottawa to Summerside for the arrival after lunch on Monday, 5 October. All was ready at the RCAF base. The drill, and this was true on all subsequent occasions, had been worked out in the most precise detail by the organizers. I was sure that I would never remember my own detailed orders and equally sure that this would not matter anyway. One unusual feature of the whole visit was the prominent part played by the Governor General who, according to constitutional protocol, should have gone underground, since he had no status while Her Majesty was in Canada. Mr King had always insisted that the Governor General be out of sight and given no place in the limelight, which should be directed exclusively on the Monarch and the Prime Minister. Mr Diefenbaker had followed the same practice. I changed all this, partly because I did not care so much about limelight and partly because I thought the Governor General should be on hand, especially in Quebec. I had no great regard for the protocol which required him to be non-existent during a visit, and the Vaniers obviously wanted to take part in this one, in all likelihood their last great state occasion.

My own desire and design was to break through the usual formality and stiffness to the greatest possible extent; from the beginning, Prince Philip was a great help in this relaxing process. The Queen emerged as the plane came to a stop; the door, so I was unhappily informed, was six inches beyond the red carpet. They greeted us at the carpet, and Philip poked at my tie. 'Aha, I see you are wearing a NATO tie.' 'How did you know?' I replied. 'Uncle Dickie wears them occasionally.' On this informal note, which brought smiles all around, especially when I demanded to know what tie he was wearing, the visit began and the ice broken, at least for Prince Edward Island. After a cavalcade through Summerside to the dock, the Royal couple boarded the *Britannia* for the night cruise to Charlottetown, while my wife and I went alone to the city where we had dinner with the Vaniers on their railway car. There, we examined the problem of whether the Governor General had the power to sign an Order-in-Council while the Queen was in the country, and decided to refer the question to the experts.

The next day, Tuesday, 6 October, was devoted to celebrating the Charlottetown Conference's centennial, the opening of the building, parades, a lunch on the *Britannia* (very pleasant), and a very good Canadian variety show in the new theatre that night. I noted later: 'The Queen enjoyed it and Philip enjoyed it immensely. He really had been of great value on this trip. She is shy and not as forthcoming as her mother, for instance, though friendly and very charming when you are in touch with her. He is very outgoing, seems to seek out ways of establishing a close relationship with crowds and individuals and does not wait for others to take initiatives for him. At times his quips are a shade biting—especially when he is talking about the press—but he skates very skilfully over the thin ice of protocol and royal dignity and is of inestimable help to her, even though he always seems to keep her waiting while he has just another word with someone.' The Queen and Philip were at their best in meeting the performers backstage after the show. They were to be there for five minutes but stayed a full half hour. She seemed to be quite stage struck with

Lorne Green, of TV 'Bonanza' fame, the master of ceremonies. Apparently at that time the Royal Family watched his serial every Sunday. She was very warm and friendly with the *Feux Follets* dance troupe, chatting with them in French for some time. Later, however, she told me that her favourite had been Dave Broadfoot, the satirist, who had been very clever.

As a result of all this, we did not take off for Ottawa until nearly midnight, or get home till about 2:30 in the morning, Atlantic time. The Queen, meanwhile, sailed to Quebec on the Royal Yacht. The next two days I spent back in Ottawa and Parliament where, to my surprise I was given a 'welcome home' greeting by Dief when I entered the House. I replied, 'Be it ever so rowdy, there is no place like home.' The weekend, however, and the ordeal of Quebec were soon upon us. There had been last-minute efforts from the *Britannia* and Quebec to change the Queen's speech. Lesage wanted the Governor General's insertion about King George's visit to Quebec in 1911 taken out, and the Queen wanted to remove, or alter, the sentences about her love for the French language which, I gathered, she thought were somewhat flamboyantly expressed. I advised, however, that no changes should be made. We listened on television to this impressive, well-given statement by the Queen at the legislature in Quebec, and to Lesage's more nervous contribution. Incidentally, the Queen later told me that her nervousness in the legislature was removed when she saw Lesage's hands shaking as he spoke. This made her feel easier. In any event, she showed no sign of uneasiness and was calm and self-possessed as usual. Her French, of course, is faultless and her voice was far better on this occasion than usual. Then my wife and I flew to Quebec in time to join the Royal couple for the military ceremonies at the Citadel in memory of the fiftieth anniversary of the foundation of the 'Van Doos,' the Royal 22nd Regiment.

It was cold and drizzly, quite miserable in fact, and, of course, we had to wait for thirty minutes or so at the Citadel for the Royal and Vice-Regal parties. It was tiresome to be told to be on hand so early for every ceremony, so thereafter I told Jim Coutts, my appointments secretary, to knock ten minutes or so from every one of our departure orders. I knew that this would make him and the other managers acutely uneasy, and I suspected (correctly, as it turned out) that they would do nothing about it.

The crowd at the Citadel was small and consisted only of invited guests, so everyone was polite and there was no trouble. The Van Doos did their drill magnificently in the cold, and we got a little

warmer by jumping up and down to honour the flags as they went
past. We skipped the tea in the Officers' Mess and went back to the
hotel. It was typical of the minutely organized security arrangements
that they would not let our car inside the Citadel wall to the departure
platform to pick us up because the driver did not have the pass-word,
or a key or badge or something. So we drove off in a Mountie Ford
with a Red Coat in front.

Back at the hotel I tried to get out of going down to the dock, a
fifteen minute drive, to meet the Queen and be in attendance on the
way back to the State Dinner. We had done this in Charlottetown,
had stood around for about twenty minutes, then merely bowed to
the Royal Couple, rode back in the procession, and, on arrival, got
lost in the crowd, trying to enter behind the Queen. I vowed this
would not happen again and scored a partial victory over the managers. We would not arrive at Wolfe's Cove until the exact moment of
departure, and our car would drive up to the Château Frontenac's
entrance immediately behind the Queen's, so we would enter with
the Royal Party and with the police, the security people, the staff, and
the eager populace, or at least the few of them allowed to enter the
hotel. Earlier, when all the rumours about shooting the Queen were
circulating, I had suggested that I should ride with her to show that I,
too, was willing to be a target and that I might even throw my body in
front of her, if necessary. In fact, I became quite fascinated by a
Walter Mitty phantasy of thus assuring my place in history. But the
managers would have none of it, and the Queen preferred Prince
Philip as a travelling companion in danger.

The dinner was magnificent. No hotel in Europe could have done
better. The Queen, who looks wonderfully regal on these formal
occasions, got a very warm reception from the privileged in the hotel.
I presented some of our ministers and their wives to her and also Mr
St Laurent, to whom she gave a very special greeting. It was a distinguished occasion, even though René Lévesque, a member of the host
government, boorishly boycotted it, as did one or two others.

The next day, at lunch, I sat beside the Queen and had a chance to
chat with her. She seemed, naturally, relieved that this part of the
visit was over. Her main worry was that the press would play up and
exaggerate the incidents; and Philip who successfully conceals any
enthusiasm for reporters and photographers, was even more worried
on this score. The Queen was, of course, sheltered from most of the
trouble, and what she did see did not disturb her. She was very
sensible and tolerant about strident outbursts and Canadian
nationalist excitement. Her reaction, generally, seemed to be: why all

the fuss, especially the fuss back home? Even some of her staff at Buckingham Palace, she said, had seemed to think she had had a narrow escape from a serious accident because the *Britannia*'s gang-plank at one point had been slightly out of place. 'You would think,' she said, 'that members of my staff, at least, wouldn't believe all the nonsense they read about me in the press.' After lunch we went out to the airport, and the Jetstar had us back in Ottawa in thirty minutes, and I was able to listen briefly to the World Series on radio. This Royal visit played havoc with my expert following of the fortunes of the Cards and the Yanks.

Once the Queen had escaped physical hurt in Quebec and the humiliation of demonstrations that might have actually upset arrangements, those responsible for the more alarmist predictions turned the fire on the excessive security arrangements and 'brutality' of the police, a consequence largely of their own successful efforts to alarm public opinion. The security people had a frightfully difficult task. They knew that they could not prevent a Dallas-type tragedy if some maniac had decided to attack the Queen. They did their best in Quebec but, as a result, the precautions along the route seemed more characteristic of a totalitarian than of a democratic state. Nothing, of course, happened, nor did they expect anything to happen, though they picked up one man in the crowd with a loaded rifle. He said he was going hunting. They were more worried about demonstrations which would not only lead to violence but would cause demonstrators, mostly students, to lie down on the streets and halt the Royal procession. They even occupied a house on evidence that it was to be set on fire just before the procession passed it, in the hope that the confusion and the arrival of fire engines would make a shambles of the arrangements.

In the result, all would have been relatively harmless had not the riot police tried to break up the slightest demonstration by immediate and strong counter-measures. They presumably did this under orders from the Chief of Police, who got his instructions from Lesage. The idea was to stop anything before it started. There may have been some excuse for these tactics in view of the situation created, but I think they acted with excessive speed and force. The press seized on 'police brutality' as the news of the day. Some newsmen were genuinely and understandably shocked; others, however, were more anxious to exploit and exaggerate what in fact happened. Whatever the reason, the news media gave the world a sad picture of Canada, and of Quebec in particular.

The Queen was unaware of what was going on except for what, in

some ways, was the most humiliating aspect of all – the almost complete absence of welcoming crowds. The visit was simply ignored.
The Queen, however, did not seem disturbed by the boycott. She is
calm, philosophic, and sensible, far more calm than her husband. She
told me with a laugh that she had been amused to see a group of
students with their backs to her as the car went by and then, with
backs turned, twist their heads around, 'to see,' as she said, 'what I
looked like.'

This was a black weekend for Quebec, a victory for the
separatists – but not so great a victory as if their pressure had forced
the government to cancel the entire visit. Decent Quebeckers, and
this comprised all but a few, were certain to be dismayed, I felt, when
they began to think over what had happened and why. In the meantime, back to Ottawa, we met the Royal Party once again at the
airport. Philip was quite entertained by our continuous running on
ahead to return once more to the Royal Red Carpet in a new locality.
The Uplands arrival was a great relief, with all the normal warmth of
friendly crowds. The ride from the airport to Rideau Hall was all the
happier because of its contrast with Quebec. The scene was dark and
cold, but there were thousands of cheering and flag-waving people.

And so it was the next day. Thousands of enthusiastic people
turned out, more, I suspect, than if there had not been such a cold
reception in Quebec. The security arrangements were unobtrusive;
there were no hitches of any kind. The Queen responded to the
welcome with a warm and friendly reaction to the crowds. At the
Cenotaph and at the reception at the Château Laurier, she was
friendly and informal and talked to people readily and with ease. A
luncheon at our house was really enjoyable, with no stiffness or reserve and the Queen seemed most at ease in talking to two other
young matrons, our daughter Patsy and daughter-in-law Landon
with whom she exchanged domestic experiences on children and
such matters. Treading where official persons would not dare, Patsy
even got the Queen into an exchange of views on the British elections.

We talked together at lunch about Canada's future, the Queen's
forthcoming state visit to Germany, the difficulties of a minority government, the implications of this visit for future Royal visits, the
difficulties of bringing up a Prince of Wales in a normal way. On this
last subject, which we had also discussed earlier, she regretted that
the Prince of Wales could not go to a Canadian school or university.
People simply would not let him alone, and by people she meant the

press. Therefore, it seemed inevitable that the traditional Royal pattern of upbringing had to be followed, though Philip had managed to depart from this by substituting Gordonstoun for Eton. Britishers took the monarchy more as a part of their normal national life than North Americans or Australians.

The next morning, Tuesday, we saw them off, waiting in the hangar for a half hour in cold weather for the Royal car to arrive, again an evidence of 'We also serve who only stand and wait.' So ended a memorable if controversial visit, one filled with implications for the future. Shortly after, I wrote a memorandum on certain conclusions I had reached. We were right in refusing to surrender to minority separatist pressure in Quebec to cancel the visit. And we were right to insist on unusual security arrangements, although, as Commissioner McLellan had told me, 'in this matter, the police can't win.' If there is no tragedy, the security precautions were unnecessary and unwise. If there had been tragedy or serious humiliation, or the programme in Quebec could not have been carried out because of uncontrolled demonstrations, then the security arrangements would at once have been under fire as inadequate. Nevertheless, more care should have been taken to control local police, even though the federal government had no direct responsibility for this. In future we should know, on the federal political level, what orders the provincial and municipal governments have given to the local or provincial police.

We could no longer assume that the Monarch would receive a warm, popular welcome in all parts of Canada in all circumstances. Hostility of a few in Quebec had intimidated the majority into indifference. Therefore, we would have to consider in the future, before any invitation were initiated, whether a visit would call attention to existing difficulties and divisions in our country by the contrasts in welcome between one part of Canada and another; or by going to one part of the country when it would not be wise to go to another for obvious reasons. In other words, a visit in the future to any part of Canada would have to be considered in the light of the political situation in every part of Canada. I wrote:

When we are having differences among ourselves, we cannot involve the Monarchy in those differences. But we must not draw wrong conclusions from this visit by assuming that there will never be circumstances again when a visit will bring all Canadians closer together by a common demonstration of loyalty to the Crown. The delayed reaction of chagrin and even shame in Quebec already shows how wrong such a conclusion would be. That apologetic reaction would be greater if public interest had not been diverted to the 'brutality' of the police. Criticism of them has served as an escape from a feeling of guilt.

As to the future, we shall have to wait and see; not initiating any visit, as this one was in 1962, without being certain we can follow through successfully. Because once an invitation has been formally extended and announced, then a cancellation as a result of the agitation of a pressure group could be disastrous for the position of both Monarchy and Government; as it could have been in this case.

I should mention here one other meeting with the Queen relevant to the question of the monarchy in Canada. This occurred in November 1967, after a most successful Royal visit during our Centennial celebrations. I was in London and was invited to have lunch with her Majesty at Buckingham Palace. Before joining the Queen on that occasion I had a half-hour conversation with Michael Adeane. I brought up with him the whole question of the monarchy in Canada and the changing attitude of Canadians, especially of younger Canadians, to it. I emphasized that there was still a strong feeling of loyalty to the Crown in many quarters and, in all quarters, there was great respect and admiration for the Queen. This had been abundantly shown in the visit to Expo and to Ottawa, which had gone so very well. But I thought that, apart from the general questioning of all established institutions by new generations, especially institutions that were old and seemed alien to a new and swiftly changing world, there was the anomaly that our very success in establishing the constitutional position of the Queen as the Sovereign of Canada had backfired, in the sense that people would now argue that if she were really Queen of Canada she should spend more time in Canada, should identify herself with the country in a more realistic way than by a visit every few years, or by being the object of a toast before every Rotary Club meeting or of an anthem before football games in Victoria or Halifax.

It might even be better to abandon these constitutional fictions and to consider the Queen as the sovereign of Britain, which she is, but also as Head of the Commonwealth, which she also is, rather than as an absentee monarch endeavouring, though with grace and dignity and charm, to live up to a designation which is theoretical rather than exact. This might mean that we would theoretically become a republic, with a Canadian Head of State; there would be no formal relationship to the Crown, but an association with the Crown through ties of history and tradition and through the Commonwealth. These ties would ensure that, though the formal relationship would be with the Queen only as Head of the Commonwealth (as in India), in fact it would be closer than this and would encourage the same kinds of visits that now take place. But the reception of the Queen, which while as warm as ever in English-speaking Canada, would then be warmer in Quebec.

I emphasized to Sir Michael that I was not proposing any such change and would do nothing to create discussion of it in Canada – which would undoubtedly be controversial, bitterly so in some areas. But I could see a trend toward this change, and believed we should be prepared for it. Sir Michael took all this very calmly and agreed that we should give thought to these matters. He knew that the Queen was knowledgeable about, and sensitive to, the currents of Canadian opinion.

Leaving Sir Michael, I was conducted down the long corridor to the Queen's private sitting room, where I spent a half-hour before lunch with Her Majesty and her three corgis. She was very friendly and relaxed, for we were on easy and informal personal terms and talked without Royal or prime ministerial constraint. In this atmosphere, I noted, she is a particularly attractive and agreeable lady, as well as a very perceptive and knowledgeable Queen, who certainly knew what was going on in Canada as well as the possibility of an explosion in Cyprus or an escalation of the war in Vietnam. We exchanged a certain amount of friendly gossip about persons we knew, from LBJ to Archbishop Makarios to Judy LaMarsh, and we reminisced about the July visit, of which the Queen had warm and friendly memories. I could tell her sincerely and truthfully that her visit had made a wonderful contribution to the success of our Centennial year. Indeed, I said, the whole year had been what we had hoped it would be, if only de Gaulle had not spoiled it by his malicious intervention. We shared certain views about him.

The Queen then asked me whether I would mind if she raised a rather delicate and difficult matter. I said that I would be flattered. So, on her own, she brought up the question of the monarchy in Canada as something which would, before long, have to be examined in depth. She was very anxious that the monarchy, or any controversy over it, should not become prejudicial to Canadian unity or a source of division. I was moved by her attitude and her sensitive understanding of the changing situation, and I talked with her for a time along the lines of my discussion with Michael Adeane. We left it at that, but it was very helpful to have had such an exchange of views.

I also told the Queen at that time, as I had earlier told Michael Adeane, of my plans to announce my retirement before the end of the year and to call a leadership convention at the earliest possible date. I might add that both the Queen and Michael Adeane expressed a very gratifying 'distress' at my forthcoming departure from office and from politics. I was flattered earlier when Sir Michael told me that the Queen had come to consider me not only as a most experienced prime ministerial adviser, but as a close and valued friend.

Perhaps I should add here a few words about the establishment of the Order of Canada. In Volume 1, I told of the circumstances surrounding my receiving an OBE and its delivery over the fence of the tennis court. It was not, however, until I was in Washington on 2 June 1943 that I first really gave any evidence of an interest in honours and awards. These I had never been able to take too seriously since the day when one of my friends, a private, and his officer, a dentist, had received the Medal of the Royal Household and the Order of St Sava, respectively, one for carrying the officer's instruments and the other for pulling an aching tooth from the aged King of Serbia in 1916 when the Serbs were near our unit north of Salonica. I admit that, if I had been a king and an aching tooth had been removed, I might have felt that recognition was richly deserved.

On that day in June so many years later, a list of awards to Canadian civilians for service in another war was published. This list attracted special attention since it came from Mackenzie King who had put an end to such Royal recognition some years before. It was restored in 1943, except for officials in the Prime Minister's own department, External Affairs, and for those in his office and the Privy Council. They were too close to the source of the previous policy of 'no awards' for them to be considered for recognition. Two of my colleagues in Washington, not in External Affairs, were included. For one, it could not have been more richly deserved and, for the other, more undeserved. I noted at the time: 'This is the sort of thing that makes a joke of Honour Lists. There is another defect in the list. Owing to the decision, a right one, not to permit titles, only junior decorations are available for those Canadians on the list who, if they were in England, would have received the most senior ones. It is humiliating to see the President of the University, Dr Cody, get a CMG, a decoration that is received by almost every official in the British Civil Service above intermediate rank. The only way to avoid this is to establish our own Canadian Order.'

This was, in my own mind, the origin of the Order of Canada which I had the privilege of putting before Parliament many years later as Prime Minister. Perhaps my perception of the need was also enhanced by an incident that occurred in Washington when I was there for the funeral of President Kennedy. During my stay in Washington I had dinner one night at the British Embassy with the British Prime Minister, Sir Alec Douglas-Home, and Prince Philip who were both over for the funeral. Earlier in the day Sir Alec whispered to me that he wanted to see me very much, alone, after dinner and could we get away for a few minutes. I wondered what had happened. I thought something must have gone wrong in a big way or he would not be wanting to speak to me in a corner after a dinner of this kind; he looked very solemn about this particular message. So after dinner we got into a room alone; I wondered what had happened in the Middle East or in Hong Kong or some place, but it turned out to be one of the most dramatic anti-climaxes I have ever experienced. It was to discuss a possible problem created by a certain peerage being awarded to a gentleman who had once lived in Canada!

When the time came to establish the Order of Canada I first brought the proposal before the Cabinet on 26 November 1966. I pointed out to my colleagues that nearly all countries of the world, excepting Switzerland, had some system of honours and awards. The United States had fifteen orders for civilians. Within Canada itself, three provinces were now giving awards or were on the point of doing so. It therefore seemed appropriate for the federal government to adopt a system of its own. I also explained to the Cabinet that the Canada Medal, instituted in 1943, had never been awarded and that the medal itself would require substantial revision to be appropriate for present use.

After some discussion on both sides of the question, the Cabinet agreed in principle that an Order of Canada should be established for award to Canadian citizens for meritorious service. Early in Centennial year, on 17 April 1967, I was able to announce in the House the establishment of a system of honours and awards for Canada as a means of recognizing merit, gallantry, and distinguished public service. As I told the House, 'I believe that recognition of this kind can strengthen national pride and the appreciation of national service.'

℧

As the Centennial of Confederation approached, we were heartily in favour of having a really magnificent celebration, not merely because it was our 100th birthday, but because our country was going through a difficult time, especially in Quebec. The Centennial gave us a wonderful opportunity to celebrate our Canadian identity. The decision that our hundredth birthday should be given the kind of national recognition it deserved was taken before we came into office. There was no reservation, I think, on the part of anyone that this was the time in our history when we could let ourselves go. A good deal of work had even been done before we took office, though we had a great deal more to do, and some of the legislation had to be amended. It had also been decided before we took office that Montreal would be the centre of the celebrations through Expo 67. No other city had asked to be the focus of our Centennial, and Montreal, through Mayor Drapeau, who is always looking ahead, had many years before asked the government to support him on Expo. We went full speed ahead with the celebration, with government committees, subcommittees, unofficial committees, and a very wide-ranging organization across the country. After 1965, the Minister in charge was Judy LaMarsh, as Secretary of State.

At first Judy intensely disliked the 'lace curtain' job of Secretary of State, but she soon realized that it was an important portfolio, and becoming, in Centennial year, of major importance. She is a person with some very admirable qualities, of very great talent, imagination, and progressive ideas. She was contemptuous of the red tape that might prevent her from bringing her imagination to realization. While ignoring regulations can cause a lot of trouble in the ordinary routines of government, this was a situation which often required the overruling of bureaucratic procedures. As a result, she did things which she was told could not be done. For example, she was told that her idea of publicly inviting all the children who wanted to come to the great 1 July celebration on Parliament Hill with the Queen and of serving them ice cream could not be done. She went ahead and did it. She said later that Centennial was very hard on her, and no doubt it was. But she was a very good person for this particular job at this time.

After she left office she said that she did not advise women to go into politics because politics were degrading to feminine delicacies. In the midst of masculine indelicacies, Miss LaMarsh could hold her own. Although a person of generous instincts, to her everything was black or white, with no varying shades in between. She liked to have decisive statements and decisive postures. I am sure she did not like my way of doing business by trying to find agreement rather than by standing up in confrontation. On one occasion she sent me a copy of a letter she had addressed to one of our Cabinet colleagues, referring to his 'limited intelligence' and suggesting that he had enough difficulties with his own department and should keep his nose out of hers. She ended the letter, 'Yours very truly.'

The ramifications of Centennial year went far beyond our earlier anticipation. For instance, we had decided to invite the head of government or state of every country in the world, but we had no idea what that really meant in terms of official entertaining. Fifty-nine accepted, a very large number, larger I think than for any other celebration of this sort. But it meant fifty-nine official red-carpet visitors, and every one had to be treated at the same level of ceremonial dignity. Each had to be given a dinner by the Governor General and lunch by the Prime Minister, or vice versa. It can be imagined what that meant to my wife and myself, to say nothing of the Governor General and his wife. At each official luncheon or dinner we had to go through the routine of speech-making. Then we would exchange gifts. We tried to create an easy and friendly atmosphere for each visitor, and we had every kind, from a charming Scandinavian princess to a young man and his new wife whom we had never really heard of until he turned up as the representative of the Congo. I do not think enough credit has been given to those who were responsible for arranging all these ceremonials: the arrivals and departures, and the hundred and one things that had to be done in between, with hardly a hitch from beginning to end. This was a triumph of organization. I might add for myself that I did my part with only one pair of striped pants.

A few things stand out. On the Sunday afternoon when the Prince and Princess of Monaco were on the dais in front of the Parliament Buildings we had the bands out and the troops, and a great crowd was there to see Princess Grace. It was a perfect afternoon, just too lovely, and the carillon played the theme song from one of her motion pictures. That was a high moment. I remember with great affection Heinrich Lübke, the President of Germany, and his wife. They were both past seventy and were delightful visitors. The President of Czechoslovakia was, by reputation at least, a hard-boiled Stalinist. We were told that he was unlikely to be impressed by our kind of western hospitality, and to be prepared for his saying anything whatsoever at a public luncheon or dinner about communism and capitalism. He would not be embarrassingly rude, but he would not be a very gracious guest. He in fact made one of the most moving after dinner speeches at Rideau Hall. He spoke about Czechoslovakia and its history, its roots and its traditions, and how this old land of his was so proud to be associated with this new country of Canada.

There were amusing incidents too. On each visit the Governor General and I exchanged gifts with our guests. When we got to this point during the visit of Australian Prime Minister Harold Holt, I handed him a spectacular musk-ox carved in wood. He handed me a set of beautiful silver goblets, one for each Australian state. Then I turned to Mrs Holt, who had been talking to someone, to show her this and to thank her for it. As I held it out she looked at it and said: 'Just what I always wanted. You couldn't have given us anything that would make us happier!' Her husband looked at her in despair and said: 'You're not getting it; you're giving it!'

There are other memories of Centennial year, but the important thing was what it did for our national morale. It really gave the country a lift which I thought would extend over a good many years: the canoes coming right across the country and down Champlain's River, the joyous celebrations of the little communities. In 67 Canada meant something that perhaps had not been realized before. I was thrilled and exhilarated by what was going on. And the centre of it all, of course, the climax, was Expo 67. When I was in opposition, the Mayor of Montreal came to Ottawa to see the Prime Minister of the day to get government support for Expo 67. He also came over to see me as the Leader of the Opposition one night. After dinner we talked about his dreams and his plans for Expo 67, which I thought were quite literally out of this world. He may have sensed that I was not so enthusiastic as I should have been, because he took out his plans and got down on the floor to spread them out. To my amazement, he showed me the artificial islands in the St Lawrence. I had assumed that with four million square miles of land in Canada, we would be able to find a plot some place for our Centennial Exposition, but here he had to make an island in the St Lawrence. I thought this was one of the silliest things I had ever heard, but of course he convinced me that it was a good idea. And it turned out to be perfect. As time passed, I did not see how the Expo site could possibly be ready on time. But Mayor Drapeau kept on saying: 'Don't worry, don't worry, don't worry.' Again he was right. Everything went off according to plan. The doves flew and the airplanes flew and the flags flew. It was a very moving and memorable opening day.

Of all the visitors to Canada during Centennial year, the three that should have been of most importance and should have received the widest and warmest attention were those from Britain, the United States and France. In the event, all three fell short of our hopes. I

have already written of the unhappy visit of the President of France
and of my discussions with President Johnson during his visit. But I
should say a few words here about the US President's visit itself. As
with all our official visitors, we had to work out the details well ahead
of time. To this end we were in touch with Washington to give the
President a choice of dates. But we could not get any reply from
Washington. Understandably, the President of the United States
does not like to commit himself very far in advance, but we hoped
that he would give us one or two tentative dates which could always
be changed if anything critical arose. Even this apparently could not
be done. As a result, we did not know that the President was coming
to our Centennial celebrations until almost the day before his arrival.
He decided to combine pleasure and business by going first to Expo
and then coming up to Ottawa to talk with me about the Middle East,
Vietnam, and other matters. On the social or formal side, it was not a
splendid visit; he had to be back in Washington by 5 o'clock.

We would have been proud to have given a very special welcome to
the President of the United States, but there was no time. I wanted
him to come to Sussex Drive, where we could have a luncheon, but
his security people would not allow him to come into Ottawa. So I
invited him to the Prime Minister's summer residence at Harrington
Lake. The security people agreed to that, and then headed for the
lake. When I arrived ahead of the President, they were all over the
place, on row boats and in the bushes with their walkie-talkies; a
couple of mounties could have done the job. I went into the house
and up the stairs. At the top a hard-faced chap said: 'Who are you?
Where are you going?' I replied: 'I live here and I'm going to the
bathroom.' I was pretty indignant that they had penetrated into our
dwelling to that extent. Then the President arrived in his helicopter,
brushing off the top of a maple tree, which might have had unhappy
results if the machine had been a little lower. We had a good luncheon (my wife is a good cook) followed by a good talk. Then we
went into town in the helicopter to catch his plane, and he was back
in Washington by about 5 o'clock. That was the Centennial visit of the
President of the United States. I was quite irritated about this. It was
not good enough. The visit should have been a little longer, a little
more formal, and a little more official. That would have meant more
to both countries.

As for the British Prime Minister, Harold Wilson, we also had bad
luck. He was eager to come and to take a full part. Then the Middle
East crisis made it necessary for him to cut short his stay. We have
never felt anything but regret that it had not worked out as we had

hoped. Britain, however, was also in a sense represented by the presence of the Queen and Prince Philip, and this was really a splendid visit. Their day at Expo was perhaps its climax, at least for us. It started off unfavourably. After attending the joyful Centennial celebrations in Ottawa (during which she cut the huge birthday cake on Parliament Hill), the Queen, Prince Philip, my wife, and I drove to Kingston on Sunday, 2 July, and then boarded the Royal Yacht *Britannia* to voyage overnight to Montreal. As we came down the St Lawrence in the pouring rain, I saw the Canadian Guard of Honour sopping wet in their new green uniforms and thought: 'This isn't going to be much of a success.' Also, we did not know how the crowd would react to a Royal visit after the visit of 1964.

When we disembarked, everybody had to hide under umbrellas. That morning we drove from pavilion to pavilion at Expo under very tight security with only special guests, press, and police allowed near Her Majesty. I thought it ridiculous that ordinary visitors could not get a good look at their Queen. I had wanted to take her for a ride around the grounds on the mini-rail, but the security people had said this would be impossible. Despite this and despite the fact that I was not sure whether she would want to take such a ride (although Prince Philip had grumbled about the strictness of security measures at dinner on the *Britannia* the night before), I decided to ask her on the spur of the moment just before lunch. This would be the best way for people to see her and Prince Philip. It would make the Queen a part of Expo as she would never have been, simply proceeding from one exhibit to another in a motor car. The Queen thought it a wonderful idea, even though her protectors were upset. I told them to get the mini-rail ready, for I was taking full personal responsibility. Just about this time the rain stopped, the clouds broke, and for the rest of the day the sun shone in every respect. So, after the official luncheon at which the Queen delivered an eloquent speech, half in English, half in French, off we went and had a wonderful ride. The reception given her was magnificent.

The visit was completed with a splendid state dinner of lobster tails and chicken on the *Britannia* as it began its cruise back to Kingston. The guests included the Governor General and Mrs Michener, Cardinal Léger, Mr and Mrs Diefenbaker, Mayor Drapeau, and eight provincial premiers. When we reached the Beauharnois lock, about thirty-five miles from Montreal, a cheering crowd of 7,000 welcomed the Queen as she said goodnight to her guests, except for the Pearsons and Micheners who were able to reflect on a truly successful and enjoyable day in their cabins on the Royal Yacht before falling asleep.

11

SUCCESSION

At 8:15 on the morning of 14 December 1967, with only one or two close friends and my family knowing what was on my mind, I arrived as usual at the office. A regular Cabinet meeting was scheduled for 10 o'clock. In the meantime, I told my staff of my decision to retire, telephoned the Governor General to inform him, and wrote the following letter to Senator John Nichol, the President of the Liberal Federation:

I wish to inform you of my decision, taken after lengthy and serious consideration, to resign from the Leadership of our Party. I feel that this is the appropriate time for me to take this step.

I do not need to tell you that I have reached this decision with great regret but I am convinced that it is the right one. I will soon have been in public service for forty years, nineteen of those years as Member of Parliament for Algoma East, and, for the last ten, I have had the great honour and privilege to be the Leader of the Liberal Party; and for nearly five years the Prime Minister of our country.

No Leader of a political Party could have received more loyalty, support and friendship than I have. For that, and for the opportunity to serve my country through the Party, I will always be deeply grateful.

I would like to ask you, as President of the Liberal Federation of Canada, to take at once the necessary steps to organize a national convention at an appropriate place and time. Until that convention has chosen my successor I will, of course, continue to serve as Leader of the Party.

Cabinet proceeded normally until just before noon, when we came to an item entitled 'Adjustment Assistance.' After remarking that I might soon be in need of some 'Adjustment Assistance' myself, I said, 'I've called a press conference for half an hour from now, at which I'm announcing my retirement from the leadership of the party.' It was a dramatic moment, followed by gasps of surprise and attempts to begin a discussion. I cut this short by telling the Cabinet that this was settled, and that there was no point in anyone saying anything at all. I was going out to meet the press immediately. We could consider things in greater detail the next day at another Cabinet meeting; after all, I would still be leader.

Then I left, since I did not want to be under pressure of one kind or another, and walked across to the National Press Building on Wellington Street. It was one of the memorable points in my life when I went in to the press conference and stated that I would be leaving and turning over the job to a new leader and Prime Minister as soon as a convention could be organized to select him. I had a great sense of relief, of course, and at the same time a natural feeling of sadness at giving up my political career and the responsibility of the office; but the overriding emotion was still one of relief. I was convinced that I had done the right thing in announcing my retirement, for the time had come for me to leave. My final words to the press conference were, 'Well, goodbye, *c'est la vie*.' After that I had lunch, talked to our caucus, and went home at 4:00 o'clock.

Retirement had been much on my mind. The 23rd of April 1967 was my seventieth birthday. My wife and I had discussed our future and I had already decided to retire in my seventieth year. I would have done so that April had it not been Canada's Centennial year. There was a great deal to do that summer, and I had no intention of stepping down until the celebrations were over and my obligations fulfilled. While I felt obliged to make Senator Nichol aware of my plans since I was conscious of all the work essential to organize a Liberal leadership convention, I did not intend to announce my retirement until just before the adjournment of the House on 21 December. Various factors had led me to select this particular timing, one of which deserves special mention.

Mr Diefenbaker had recently been deposed from the leadership of the Conservative party in favour of Robert Stanfield. (I might have had an easier life had he been deposed a year or two earlier.) I remember my first meeting with Mr Stanfield after his victory at the convention. It was on Tuesday, 19 September 1967, and we had lunch together at his request, at Sussex Drive. This was an agreeable occasion, and confirmed in my mind that I would be able to talk with the new leader as I never could with Mr Diefenbaker. I wrote, after the meeting:

I feel sure that he will respect confidences and will not misunderstand my desire to exchange views with him on some matters which I think should be above partisan politics in the hope of securing a maximum of co-operation and good results in Parliament, as we face so many fundamental national and international difficulties.

He is, of course, a quiet and relaxed sort of person—the extreme antithesis of John Diefenbaker—and creates an atmosphere of easy good will. I know, too, that he is a skilled politician and can play the Party game for all it is worth. He proved that in Nova Scotia, but nevertheless I am convinced that he does not wish to create the kind of atmosphere we have been bedevilled with for so many years in the House of Commons, and that his tactics will be very different from Diefenbaker's in the Party and Parliamentary conflict. In this regard, I am sure that he reflects the feelings of Canadians of all Parties who have grown sick and tired of Parliamentary bickering.

Mr Stanfield gave me some very interesting background information on the Conservative convention. There was no doubt that he and his advisers, especially Dalton Camp, had an excellent campaign plan, which proved to be very successful. I told him I thought that the critical time was on the Tuesday night when the candidates gave their statements on policies and his made such a fine impression.

There were two things in particular I wished to discuss with Mr Stanfield at lunch. The first was the date of his by-election, which he thought could be set for 6 November, the earliest possible date. I told him that I was anxious to expedite his entry into the House, but that I could not, of course, give him any guarantee that someone would not run in the by-election in Colchester-Hants. I did tell Mr Stanfield that if there were a Liberal candidate he would get no support from Ottawa.

I expressed a strong hope to him that certain matters of national importance could be discussed with a minimum of partisan prejudice. I was thinking in particular of questions of national unity and relations between Quebec and the rest of the country. I gave him my view that we were faced with a very serious situation in which the whole future of our country was at stake. I hoped that this seriousness could be reflected in our discussions in the House of Commons and that no one would try to take unfair Party advantage from it. He reacted very positively to this and agreed entirely with what I said.

I also told him that our parties should try to work together on far-reaching reforms of the parliamentary system. We had made some progress here, but it was difficult to do as much as should be done since there were members who believed that changes would hamper the rights and privileges of the Opposition. I asked him to accept my word that we were not trying to be at all partisan in this matter and, indeed, if he expected to be Prime Minister (and he indicated that he did) he would be the chief beneficiary of any changes in rules and procedures which would enable us to get more work done, while preserving all the rights of discussion and debate. Here, also, he agreed to co-operate. I concluded my note on the meeting: 'All in all, it was a very good talk, and from my point of view an encouraging one. Stanfield is certainly not going to be any push-over in these or other matters, but he is, I think, going to do his best to be co-operative within the limits of his responsibility.'

When Parliament re-assembled six days later I commented on Mr Diefenbaker's new situation: 'It is passing strange for me, indeed for all of us, not to see the Right Honourable gentleman rise, first, on the Orders of the Day and with transfixing gaze and minatory gesture, launch a penetrating question at his selected target.' I remember well the day when Mr Stanfield took his seat in the House on 15 November 1967. How very different it looked to see him across from us. It seemed to me that the change made it less likely that the Opposition would take advantage of the confused situation which my announcement would produce in the Liberal party to defeat us in Parliament and thus force an election. No one could be in a worse position to fight an election than a man who had said he is quitting, but has not yet been replaced. Mr Stanfield was new, and I thought he would not want an election until he had more time to get his bearings.

Now a very difficult situation arose. I knew it was not going to be easy for a retiring Prime Minister to conduct the affairs of state. I was quite satisfied that I could carry on in matters such as the forthcoming constitutional conference and, indeed, in some respects I was in a stronger position than if I were on the eve of an election. But the difficulty which I anticipated, though inadequately, was the disarray caused within the ranks of the Cabinet and the party as to the succession. Once I had announced my decision to resign, the campaigns for the leadership, which had been going on surreptitiously, came out into the open. Paul Hellyer, Paul Martin, and Mitchell Sharp had all set up organizations, and as for the first two, they had been operating almost openly. Paul Hellyer had been quite frank with me in November, when he told me about his ambition to succeed me and urged me to announce publicly that I was leaving, so that everything could be done openly. He considered that as long as everyone knew that I would not run again but that no decision had been taken on the date of a convention, the party would be uncertain and divided. So the sooner I made my decision known, the better. Paul Martin took a different stand. He begged me not to leave and said he had no intention of trying to succeed me. Therefore, I should make clear at once that I was staying on and would lead the party in the next election.

After my announcement in December, Paul Martin flew back at once from the NATO meeting in Brussels. I saw him at Sussex Drive immediately he returned. He bewailed my decision, was shocked and surprised, and thought that I should have warned him. Now he had to make his own decision. I suggested that he had already done that. No, now it was different. He had a duty to the country since he felt that, of all the possible candidates, he could best preserve and strengthen national unity. I demurred, telling him I thought in his own interest that he should not stand, hinting that he would not be successful, but adding that if he felt it was his duty to stand irrespective, as he put it, of all personal considerations, then I had nothing to say. He alone could make a judgment on that basis. He was, of course, disappointed at my refusal to encourage him. Later in the campaign, he reproached me for my negative neutrality, as he put it, when he had been so loyal to me. I did nothing to hinder or help his campaign. It was clear to me from the beginning that he was not going to make it. Why change a Prime Minister of one generation for another of the same vintage? The Gallup Polls, which gave him so much encouragement, meant nothing. Nevertheless, Paul certainly deceived himself in thinking, right up to the end, that he would win.

I felt that he was subordinating everything, including his work at External Affairs, to his campaign, and this I did not like. After 'Black Monday' (of which I shall have more to say later), when he was at Trois Rivières with two other MPs instead of in Ottawa to prevent our defeat, I let him know what I thought and did not attempt to disguise my feelings. But I did nothing, in any way, to hurt his chances, though there were some close to me who must have known how I felt. Toward the end I felt genuinely distressed: his campaign was obviously failing. I hated to see one who had served so long and accomplished so much moving steadily to defeat and the humiliation of rejection. I was sure this experience would crush him beyond recovery. But I was wrong. He took the blow of his poor showing on the first ballot at the convention with calmness and courage, and withdrew at once with dignity and grace. He behaved well all that long afternoon and was as cheerful on the platform, during the acceptance speech, as Mr Trudeau himself. I was glad to pay a special tribute to him in my remarks at that time; I reminded the convention that Paul Martin was a warrior who 'had been fighting the battles of Liberalism before many of the delegates here today were born.'

I asked him to have lunch with me on the following Monday. I was rather surprised when he accepted, and Maryon asked Nell Martin. We had a good talk. He showed no resentment, and faced the future with far more equanimity than he had shown during the campaign. He was wondering what he should do. We agreed that perhaps the best course would be for him to stay in External Affairs for the time being. I suggested that, in a month or two, he should then resign, be appointed to the Senate, and become Leader of the Government there (John Connolly was quite anxious to retire) with a seat in the Cabinet. This appealed to him as a very good suggestion—more so than the other I made that he should become Minister of Justice to take on the task of constitutional reform.

But I am getting ahead of myself and must return to the time of my announcement. As I have said, some of my colleagues were already openly campaigning for the leadership. In fact, there was far too much of this going on, and I wish that I had been in a stronger position to stop it. I know that this situation was, in part, the origin of the feeling that our Cabinet was divided and was leaking secrets like an old umbrella. Up to a point this had been true during those months before my announcement, and I was partly to blame. I was preoccupied with the Centennial celebrations, and failed to make clear my intention about fighting another election. Uncertainty of leadership in a minority government makes discipline within the party and in the Cabinet difficult. Whatever was going on before my resignation was announced, however, was aggravated after the decision had been taken and the convention had been called. Now everything came out into the open and, in slightly over a month, seven of my colleagues were candidates for the leadership.

I knew there would, of course, be difficulty in carrying on a government in these circumstances. While I was not conscious of any great difference at Cabinet meetings and ministerial discussions, I was aware of the great change in the devotion of these ministers to their jobs. They could not be out in the country campaigning and at the same time carry on the work they had been appointed to do in their departments. One effort was bound to get in the way of the other, though they did their best to reconcile the two. On the whole, the campaigning was civilized, in the sense that the candidates were anxious not to give the impression of disunity, nor were they anxious to make my job more difficult. There were, however, one or two unpleasant aspects, often the result of the enthusiastic loyalty of some of the candidates' supporters. In truth, I had thought that the succession would be easier than it turned out to be. My announcement was timed so that arrangements for a leadership convention to be held toward the end of January or February could be made during the Christmas parliamentary recess.

As I have said, I let John Nichol know of my decision in advance, and told him to go right at work and get the convention fixed for the earliest possible date. A few days after I announced my resignation, he came to see me with the news that we could not have the convention until early April. I said: 'April is too late; you have to make it earlier than that.' A week or so following, he made a strong case for more time. He said, in effect, that we could hold a convention at the end of February, but this would not be the kind of convention that would successfully launch a new leader who might face an election in a few months; that there was more to this convention than my retirement. He was absolutely emphatic that I would have to stay on until April. I regretted, and almost resented, that I had to do this.

More difficulties developed over the candidates. One or two of them almost begged me to tell them what they should do. It is very hard to tell a man that he should, or should not, be a candidate for the leadership of his party. If I said he should, it would probably be let out that he was my favourite; if I said he should not (and I did that once or twice), it would seem unfair to him that I was obviously not very confident of his ability to lead the party. I found this rather trying, and it went on for three or four weeks as the various candidates entered the ring.

In the middle of February I went to the Caribbean to receive an honorary degree from the University of the West Indies in Jamaica. There were a number of reasons for my accepting the invitation. The year before I had accepted a similar invitation from the university, and at the last minute had been forced to cancel it. Princess Alice, the Chancellor, was very disappointed, so I told her I would come in 1968. I hated to tell her again that I could not go. The constitutional conference with the provinces had just concluded and I was very tired. These things are a great strain. We had done a lot of work preparing for the conference, which had not been easy to manage, and I wanted to get away for a few days. Finally, there was an opportunity to see Prime Minister Shearer of Jamaica, Prime Minister Barrow of Barbados, and possibly Prime Minister Williams of Trinidad, to discuss an agreement we were trying to work out by which Air Canada would help manage the airlines in the West Indies.

My wife and I left Ottawa quite cheerfully on Friday, 16 February, for Kingston, Jamaica. The convocation the following evening was a most colourful affair. I remember it vividly because Princess Alice, most gracious and lovely, was performing with great gusto. She thoroughly enjoyed her post as Chancellor and running the convocation. I got my degree, she shook hands with me, and said: 'I declare this convocation adjourned.' She should have said: 'I now ask Doctor Pearson to address the convocation.' When someone sent her a note, she had to beat a hasty retreat: 'Oh, before we adjourn, we're going to hear from Mr Pearson.' This was all great fun, and was followed by a wonderful dinner. Then, my wife and I motored across the island to spend a couple of days with our good friends, Senator and Mrs Molson. It was beautiful weather, in a beautiful place. I was revelling in the scenery, the swimming and the warmth, and enjoying my rest.

All was apparently well on the Ottawa front. At 5 PM on Monday Torrance Wylie, my Executive Assistant, phoned from Ottawa that things were quiet and seemed likely to remain so that evening. The Income Tax bill was going through and would pass the committee stage. It never occurred to me, or presumably to my office, that the third and final reading would proceed that night. We settled down to a pleasant dinner and a game of bridge with the Molsons. If I remember correctly, the Pearsons were about five dollars and a quarter up on the Molsons, and that is something! But we did not collect, for the game was never finished. At about 10:30 PM, in the middle of a rubber, the telephone rang. It was Torrance Wylie again: 'Bad news; we were defeated on third reading of the Tax bill, 84-82.' I was flabbergasted. When he indicated the circumstances of our defeat, I was not only flabbergasted, I was furious. The Irish part of me came to the surface. Swallowing my anger and too excited to sleep, I arranged to fly back at once, while Hartland Molson, acting as my secretary, dealt with a succession of phone calls from the newspapers.

We were up at 5:30 the next morning for a twenty-mile breakneck drive up the coast behind a Jamaican police escort to a small air strip. There, a single engine plane was ready to fly us over the Blue Mountains to the Kingston airport, where our Jetstar was waiting. We touched down at Ottawa at 12:15, to be greeted by very cold weather, a flock of press and TV people, and the chastened Paul Martin and Bob Winters. I spent the lunch hour getting the grim and infuriating details of 'Black Monday' from the Cabinet and in deciding what to do. I let my colleagues know that I was more than a little disturbed about what had happened, and why it had happened.

I was not too worried about the situation politically, when I learned that it had been a snap vote. There had been no need at all to have third reading that night. Mr Sharp was both in charge of the House and, as Minister of Finance, in charge of the bill. It was suggested to him by the Opposition that they were willing to get third reading over with. That was a very tempting offer. Though our Whip assured him we would have a majority, he might nevertheless have been suspicious at the ease with which Opposition co-operation was obtained. But I cannot be too critical of Mr Sharp's tactics; had I been in his position, I might have done what he did.

It was a trap, of course, a legitimate parliamentary trick; the Tories rushed in members who were not supposed to be around, and the bill was defeated. When I heard all about this, I was concerned only with what to do. We had to refuse the demand that we resign on this vote; we had to reject it on the grounds that it was not a vote of confidence in the sense that would require a government to resign. I was comforted by the recollection that many of the people in the smaller parties had argued that the tradition whereby a government has to resign when defeated on any vote should be abolished.

The first thing was to ask for a twenty-four hour adjournment. We needed time. I phoned the Leader of the Opposition, Robert Stanfield, who agreed that this was a reasonable request and that his party would not object. From the point of view of parliamentary tactics (although some will not agree with me on this), I think he was right. I had been out of the country and had only just returned. As Prime Minister, I was asking for some hours of respite to decide the duty of the government. If the Leader of the Opposition had said: 'Your duty is to resign. We will give you no adjournment and will oppose your motion to adjourn,' I would have proceeded exactly as I did over the next two days. I knew that Mr Caouette and his Créditiste group did not want an election, and I had made it quite clear during the luncheon recess, a short time after I arrived, that rejection of an adjournment motion would mean a general election. So I was not worried. If we got a motion to adjourn, we would have twenty-four hours to work out our tactics for the next day. If the Conservatives refused the adjournment we might win it anyway, and if not, the country would be really hard on an Opposition that had forced an election by refusing a twenty-four hour adjournment. It would be pretty hard on me, too, since I doubt that I could have resigned and had somebody else conduct the campaign. All of that remained hypothetical, however. Mr Stanfield agreed to support the motion. Nor did he lay down any conditions, though later he made a fuss because he was not allowed to speak on my motion to adjourn. He should have known that this was not debatable. If the rule had been waived in his favour, others would have claimed the same privilege, and I would have had to speak to explain why I asked for a motion to adjourn. I do not know what would have happened.

On getting our adjournment Tuesday afternoon, I had another meeting with the Cabinet to decide what to do on Wednesday. I told them that I must move a specific Motion of Confidence, but there was a great deal of argument about the form of the motion. The motion which I favoured, stating that the Monday-night vote did not involve confidence, would be a little more complicated than a simple motion of confidence; but constitutionally it was quite proper and politically more palatable to any member of an Opposition group who wished to keep Parliament going. Cabinet accepted this, but Mitchell Sharp wanted something in the motion which, directly or indirectly, prepared the way for the reintroduction of his Income Tax bill.

I had been studying the precedents for such a situation. It was quite clear that a motion on third reading, which included the phrase 'The vote be *now* taken,' left the way open even after defeat for a similar vote to be taken at a subsequent date. We therefore set up a Cabinet sub-committee under Allan MacEachen to draft an appropriate motion which met both points. While we had to accept the defeat on this particular motion, nevertheless we also had to accept the responsibility of raising the necessary money by taxation to achieve our financial objective.

When I went back to my office, however, and began to think the matter over, I realized that no motion could achieve this dual purpose. No matter how correct it might be technically, it would look like a gimmick. We would be open to the criticism that we were bringing in by the back door the same bill after it had been defeated. I therefore told Allan MacEachen to work out with his group a simple motion to the effect that the vote taken on Monday night was not a Vote of Confidence. If the House accepted that, there would be no obligation to resign. If they did not, then it would be considered a straight-forward declaration of 'No Confidence,' and we would have to resign or dissolve Parliament. Before the exact form of the motion had been worked out, however, Mr Stanfield phoned me again to say that he had heard that we were going to put a Motion of Confidence on the Order Paper before 6 PM, in order that it could be discussed on Thursday. He claimed, to my astonishment, that this was a breach of 'our agreement.' I said that there had been no 'agreement'; I had merely told him in advance that we were going to ask for a twenty-four hour adjournment, and he had concurred that this was sensible. He said that this constituted an agreement not to do anything, not even to put something on the Order Paper. I told him that this was nonsense, and that I could not accept any such position. Although annoyed at his reaction, I was anxious to avoid any unpleasantness. I phoned Allan MacEachen and told him that nothing should go on the Order Paper until the following day.

On Wednesday afternoon I placed our motion before Parliament and asked for unanimous consent to proceed with it at once. This was refused. With the Opposition and the press hostile to the form of the motion, the outlook was depressing. However, we had had a very good caucus that morning, and I was encouraged by my fellow members to fight the thing through on the ground I had chosen. This I was determined to do. That evening I held a press conference and went on television to explain our position to the people. Then I started writing a memorandum for my Cabinet colleagues outlining the situation as I saw it and spelling out the tactics we should follow to meet the crisis:

Parliament in general and the government in particular were not the only ones unprepared for the failure of the government to secure third reading of Bill C-193. The public and the press were also unprepared.

Under these circumstances, the aim of the Opposition is clear:

First, it must build up now the aura of crisis that normally accompanies and, indeed, usually precedes the fall of the government.

Second, it must get across the idea that the government was in fact defeated.

Third, it must show that the defeat was on a substantive matter.

Fourth, it must establish that the defeat is not open to reconsideration.

It appears that the Opposition will try to attain all these objectives by showing the people that the government cannot govern. . .

The Opposition's hope will be that the sense of crisis thus engendered amongst the public will feed upon itself and grow and turn increasingly upon the government. By emphasizing that defeat took place on a tax measure it will hope to associate the government with higher taxes and itself with a return to untaxed affluence. Its loud-speaker will be Parliament, the House of

Commons, and the consequent upset which unusual events (such as outbursts of disorder, or frequent adjournments, or failure to make progress) will spawn. It will focus public attention on Parliament and use the circumstances there created as a pressure cooker in which to bring to bear all manifestations of public opinion against the government.

To counteract these tactics, the government must act immediately in every possible and proper way to bring the confidence motion to a vote and end that suspense. Furthermore, it must draw the focus of public attention away from the theatricals in the House and on to the issues involved, their implications and other more important matters where the national interest is more vital.

Part of this objective can be accomplished if the government in fact governs and is seen to govern normally. Inside the House, if possible, and certainly outside the House, the government should get on with important business and be known to be following its usual routine of administration...

The real battle is one of communications: to get across the government's reasons, to explain them and to win support for them. By going to the people in their homes, by radio and television and through the newspapers, the pressure can be put on the Opposition to in effect take its pressure off the government. If this can be done immediately, the debate in the House on Friday could be very different and shorter than what is now expected.

If this can't be done or isn't done, the result will be disastrous not only for the government, but for the country...

The government has a good case, if we can get it across. Reasons of commonsense as well as constitutional authority can and should be urged to demonstrate the contrary to the claims of the Opposition:

−that what happened *was* an accident;

−that the defeat of the government *was* on a technicality;

−that even if the defeat had been on a substantive matter, it would rest with the government to decide whether or not to regard that matter as an issue of confidence; and, if not, to ask Parliament to confirm or reject its view.

−that the government has a right to receive an explicit command from the House and need not be bound by a result which was not expected and which the government had no reason to take as a matter of confidence.

Of course, in putting across these points it must be clearly emphasized that, far from being arrogant, the government stands ready and willing to act immediately on the commands of the House and that, if defeated, it will resign.

By select briefings to reporters the government should also try to get across that the Opposition is using a cheap trick to try to grab power, that it is cheating by taking advantage of the leadership hiatus and the approaching convention and that all of this is shaking confidence in the dollar and in the economy to the detriment of the Canadian people as a whole.

Finally, the government must take note of allegations made against it not only by the Opposition but daily in news reports from Ottawa to the effect that it is disintegrating and that the Cabinet is split. All Ministers must make every effort to dispel this impression. Similarly, Liberal Members must be highly disciplined and this is not possible if the government does not give a lead. Not only must attendance be perfect, but good manners must be preserved so that no matter what uproar is caused by the Opposition, the Government side will appear as calm and responsible legislators. The contrast between what is bound to happen on the other side will be important. Our image must be one of responsibility in the national interest. It is the Government's most valuable asset in present circumstances.

In the last analysis, of course, the question is whether the people in fact want an election. I believe that they do not and that, in fact, they remain sick of cheap politics.

It has been said that there are not 500 people in Canada who even know what a third reading is. While this should certainly be borne in mind, it should also be remembered that there are not more than 2 or 3 hundred opinion formers in Canada and as many as possible of these should be approached by Ministers on a personal basis and their views should be rallied in support of the government. This kind of all-out effort, together with the other steps above mentioned, taken aggressively during the next 48 hours, may well prove to be decisive in the present struggle. It may well be that the Opposition committed a serious error in refusing unanimous consent. They thought to increase the pressure but they also gave the government an opportunity to act.

We must take full advantage of it or we will depart soon 'unwept, unhonoured and unsung.'

Thursday afternoon the House met again. We had agreed to move for another adjournment ourselves, as we did not wish the Opposition to adjourn the House, and it was clear that we could not proceed with the day's debate on constitutional matters, which was what I had suggested on Wednesday. Before Allan MacEachen could make the motion, the Conservatives' Davie Fulton got up on a Question of Privilege. He asked the Speaker to declare that I had breached the privileges of the House during my television broadcast and press conference by referring to the events of Monday evening as 'trickery.' I did not take the charge seriously; all I had to do in reply was to show that Mr Fulton had distorted the text of what I said in one place, read from Hansard an interjection by J.H.T. Ricard (a Conservative member) who on Wednesday had referred to our Adjournment Motion as 'a rotten Grit trick,' and quote a press report of another Conservative member (Robert Coates) saying, 'It was an organized plot by the Conservative Opposition that resulted in the government's defeat.' The Speaker had no problem in ruling against the Question of Privilege. The House then adjourned until Friday, when the Confidence Motion could be debated.

By the time the debate began on Friday, 23 February, Stanfield obviously was getting the message from the country that an election was not wanted and was beginning to look for a way out of the impasse. We expected that my introduction of the motion would initiate a violent 'pipeline' constitutional and parliamentary wrangle, but it did not come. When Réal Caouette indicated in his speech that the Créditiste group would support us, the steam went out of the debate. Finally, on 28 February, our motion that Monday's vote was not a vote of 'No Confidence' was sustained, 138-119. We had won the round, though our position as a government had been weakened by the folly of it all. When the crisis was resolved, I spoke to my colleagues in the Cabinet in terms I had never before used. From then on, they stuck pretty close to Ottawa and campaigned only on the weekends, or, if they did leave, I knew about it beforehand.

I have already spoken of my attitude towards Paul Martin's candidacy. Perhaps I should now mention the other candidates. Mitchell Sharp discussed with me his decision to contest the leadership in the autumn of 1967, and I certainly did not discourage him in any way. I thought he would be as good a Prime Minister as anyone, and I would have been happy enough if he had succeeded. My chief worry was that he seemed to be developing a certain complacency in spite of his troubles in Finance.

I saw a great deal of Sharp during the crisis after our defeat on 19 February and during the dollar crisis that developed in early 1968. I admired his general coolness and efficiency. I recall that he brought Louis Rasminsky, the Governor of the Bank of Canada, around to Sussex Drive one evening. They told me that we were losing dollars very rapidly, and that if the pressure on our reserves continued at that rate, we might have to devalue. This near-crisis put Mr Sharp, as a candidate, in a very difficult position which he discussed with me. When I told him to stop all campaigning during the crisis, even if this meant the sacrifice of his leadership chances, he entirely agreed. He fully understood my position that he had to stay in Ottawa and could not leave even for an hour to go to a meeting. In fact, I told him he should not even go to a meeting in Ottawa as a candidate. I do not think his remaining in Ottawa hurt him. He may have lost some support by not campaigning; he would have lost infinitely more if he had campaigned during a financial crisis of this kind.

In any event, for three or four days I had practically nothing else on my mind apart from this financial crisis. I knew Mr Rasminsky was in touch with other governments and other central banks, particularly in Washington and New York, seeking the support which governments and banks give one another in such situations. Canada has done this before to help other currencies. We were doing everything that could be done, but for a few days the drain continued. Mr Rasminsky and Mr Sharp were giving me almost hourly reports, and there was one moment when the Governor indicated to me he would likely have to advise drastic action – devaluation – as we could not stand the drain any longer. I knew nothing about these technicalities, this complicated international mechanism that determines our lives financially, economically, and, in some respects, socially. It always worries me that a few people have such great power in the world. There is something wrong with a society where speculators can take action which forces central banks to advise their governments to take defensive measures and force our democratic institutions and practices into abeyance. Quick action must be taken, and this cannot be done through the House of Commons. There can be no debate, because debate of that kind makes a run inevitable. I called in the Leader of the Opposition and told him what was going on. I did not want him to think that I was inhibiting his right to criticize in the House after I had taken whatever action I thought necessary. He must use his own judgment on that. But I thought that he ought to know what the situation was and how dangerous it might be. During the next twenty-four hours matters turned for the better, and we escaped the need to devalue our currency.

What a late winter and early spring that was! But we got through the dollar crisis as we had through the parliamentary crisis. From then to the convention, a few weeks later, affairs were fairly quiet on the political and financial fronts. Later, just before the convention opened, when the crisis was over and after he had travelled west, Mr Sharp came to see me again. He told me that while he had more support than the polls indicated, his position had deteriorated and he had no chance of winning. The Tax bill fiasco and the restriction of his campaigning caused by the dollar crisis had hurt him. What really shattered his chances, however, was the entry of Bob Winters as a candidate. Both Sharp and Winters had to appeal for support from the same general constituency. In my view, this in fact defeated any chance that Mr Sharp had, though I think he had a pretty good chance at one early stage. Sharp was bitter when Winters, who had first declared he would not run, entered the race on 1 March. Sharp did not wish to be fourth or fifth on the first ballot and came to tell me that he was thinking of withdrawing from the race, and to ask what I thought. I did not discourage him; indeed, I encouraged him in the plan he was considering, of throwing his support to Pierre Trudeau as the best candidate. I think my attitude was important, if not decisive, in making up his mind. I told him that if Trudeau won, he would badly need support from Sharp, who could play a very important part in the new government. I urged him not to withdraw from politics. He was needed. As it turned out, his support for Trudeau at the convention may possibly have decided the issue.

I have already briefly mentioned Paul Hellyer. He conducted his campaign as a military operation. He was single-minded in his determination to win the race and, on occasions, not only spoke but acted like a winner, and as one who deserved to win. At other times he seemed stilted and ineffectual and without any popular appeal. Just when it appeared that he might be a young, vigorous, and courageous PM, he would say or do something to make him seem quite out of touch with 1968. Nevertheless, he seemed to me to be honest and straightforward, and I shall always wonder how he would have fared had he won.

Bob Winters' candidacy, announced late in the race, was a surprise, since in January he had told me categorically that he had no intention of running, was leaving politics, and intended to return to business. He also had stated publicly that he thought any minister who was a candidate should resign from the government; that he would not take part in the ministerial circus for the succession. He changed his mind, probably because of pressure from his business friends, who urged him to save the country from the Liberal radicals. They convinced him that he could win and assured him of unlimited financial support in the effort. So he entered; and true to his word he first submitted his resignation on 28 February, but let me know that he would not expect me to accept it until the House rose.

Winters was an authentic conservative, a genuine representative of, and believer in, Big Business. Indeed, he really believed that a country could and should be run like a corporation, with the Cabinet functioning as a Board of Directors. He wanted to be the C.D. Howe of 1968, but as Prime Minister; he seemed unaware of the fact that C.D. Howe's day was over, and that government was not business. In any event, he had a lot of right-wing Liberal support; if he did not defeat Trudeau, he certainly prevented anyone else from doing so.

Next, John Turner and Allan MacEachen. They came to see me in February to get my reaction to their candidatures. I was sympathetic to both, though I told them that they would not win. A well-run race, however, would put them in line for the job in the future, since they were both young. I was pretty candid with John Turner in warning him not to appear too eager, too obviously ambitious; to play it cool and to cultivate the calmness of maturity to go with the appeal of drive and energy. His speeches were aimed at all who were impatient with the status quo and the establishment.

Then there was Trudeau, Pierre Elliott Trudeau. From the day in 1965 when he was elected to Parliament, and as a Liberal to many people's surprise, I had pushed him ahead. Though I did not know him personally, I knew a lot about him, had read much that he had written, and had acquired a high opinion of him. I felt that he, along with Marchand and Pelletier, were the men best qualified to solve the problems of Quebec and Confederation; to fight separatism and to rebuild the Liberal party in Quebec on a new foundation.

When I decided to retire, I looked on Marchand as a possible successor. While it is true that I gave no candidate any reason to think that I would support him, it is also true that I gave all the candidates and everyone I spoke to every reason to believe that I wanted to see a French-speaking candidate, and one who would make a good showing. This was the tradition of our party; this had been our advantage through the years in a party political sense over the Conservative party: we could always find good men to lead our party in Quebec, and they never could. To have a convention without a French-speaking candidate doing well, even if not successful, would have been a very serious departure from a fine tradition. So this was very much on my mind. Jean Marchand, by this time, was accepted by all as the leader in Quebec. I had a very high regard for him and had rather assumed that he would be a candidate, but he made it clear that he would not stand. He did not feel strong enough physically or sure enough of himself in English-speaking Canada. He did not feel that he had had enough national experience to be a candidate; he had been in the House and in the party for only a few years, and he regarded his English as I my French, except that his English was far better than my French; but he thought that this would be a handicap in the national campaign. He agreed with me, however, that there should be a Quebec candidate who would gather a respectable number of votes at the convention, even if he did not get a majority. He then told me that Pierre Trudeau was his candidate, and he wanted me to see him to persuade him to stand. That was the first time I had heard Trudeau's name mentioned in connection with the leadership, except in casual conversation.

I agreed to talk with Trudeau. I had talked to nearly all the others, and there was nothing to prevent his coming to see me, but I told Marchand that I did not want to see him alone. I wanted Marchand to be there when we met. For one thing, I did not want to run the risk of having matters misconstrued later on. I also knew that Pierre Trudeau was extremely reluctant to stand, and that he believed Marchand should be the Quebec candidate. I wanted Trudeau to hear from Marchand's lips in my presence that Marchand would, in no circumstances, be a candidate. We met in January, and I let Mr Trudeau know that if he were chosen it would meet with my whole-hearted approval. He was worried about his parliamentary inexperience; he regretted Marchand's decision, and wondered whether he was not too new to the party, too unconventional and non-partisan to get support. I tried to remove his fears and encourage him to run. After my talks with him, and reflecting on his performance as a member and Minister, I came to the conclusion that he would make a good leader; or rather, perhaps, that he had as fair a chance of becoming a good leader and Prime Minister as any of the others, regardless of their parliamentary and political experience.

I did not, of course, give him any support during the campaign, other than letting a few friends know that I was well-disposed toward him. This seemed to become known. As the campaign progressed, I came to the conclusion that he and Sharp were the best candidates not only to succeed as Prime Minister but also to win elections. Trudeau created an immediate and exciting impression. He was the man to match the times, the new image for a new era. His non-involvement in politics became his greatest asset, along with his personal appeal, his charisma. The growth of his support was phenomenal, and this occasioned a bitter reaction in the camps of some of the other candidates. This led to some nasty underhand efforts (not by the candidates themselves) to denigrate Trudeau, but this succeeded only in making him more exciting. He knew how to project and he knew how to impress. There was nothing banal about his speeches; their appeal was intellectual, but they were widely popular. The Trudeau campaign completely bewildered the old pros like Paul Martin, who could not understand the secret of its success. As Paul said to me: 'How can someone who knows nothing of politics or the party get so much support so suddenly, even from people like Joe

Smallwood?' The answer was simple. Canadians thought of Paul Martin, or even of Paul Hellyer, in the context of Mackenzie King. They thought of Pierre Trudeau as a man for this season, uncontaminated and uninhibited.

I had nothing to do with the convention. John Nichol and his committee were responsible, though he did come to talk with me occasionally. When he did discuss it with me, I thought one or two things were wrong and one or two things were splendid but I can take no credit for what I believe to have been a very successful convention in political terms. The drama of the convention, the tenseness, the programming, the staging, were all extremely well done. It had an undoubted impact on the country and on the election which was to come sooner than I had expected.

The Pearsons' own particular night, Thursday, 4 April 1968, was a most moving occasion. I began my farewell speech by saying:

On January 16, 1958, when I was chosen Leader of our Party, I pledged myself to do my best to justify your choice. I also said: 'I am quite sure – being human – I will make mistakes, but I can promise you that they will be honest mistakes for which I will not have to apologize to my conscience.'

Tonight, as I hand back to the Party the trust and the honour I received from it that day, I acknowledge, and regret, those promised mistakes, while I am happy and grateful for any good things I have done or good results I have helped to achieve. I am also comforted by the remark of a wise man, 'Failures are made only by those who fail to dare, not by those who dare to fail.'

Then I continued to say thanks to the countless workers who had supported my leadership during the preceding ten years:

In expressing my feelings of gratitude, I will only mention – to spare them embarrassment – those closest and dearest to me, my wife and my family. They have made my life happy and good, no matter how heavy the burden may have been.

I think also of those with whom I worked so closely, especially in those days of opposition when we had to reconstruct a defeated and shattered Party.

Then there were my Cabinet and Parliamentary comrades; my loyal and hard-working office staff to whom I owe so much; the Party workers – right across the country – so many of whom are at this great Convention. Without your selfless and untiring effort we would have accomplished little.

Nor can I omit mention of my own constituents of Algoma East, some of whom are present tonight. If they had not elected me to Parliament eight times, I would have had nothing to retire from. Indeed, I would have been retired years ago.

I went on to outline the problems that would face the party in the years ahead:

Today Liberalism must tackle problems which our grandparents never heard of; the quality, as well as the material standard of life; urban development and housing; communications on land, water and in the air, even into outer space; the constructive use of our increasing leisure, as machines do more work in less and less time with fewer and fewer people; air and water pollution and the slaughter on the roads; protection of the consumer against fraud and against 'chemistry'; greater concern with education and research and adult training; above all, the building of the new Federalism with a new Canadian unity which accepts duality and diversity as the pattern of development, and which could be the model for an interdependent world.

And I spoke for the leadership candidates: the problems the new leader would face and the qualities he would need to face them:

How to meet today's needs will be the main test of the Party in the days ahead; and of its new Leader.

As we gather to choose this new Leader, we can be very proud of those men who, having served the Party with ability, and distinction, now seek a responsibility which includes the crushing burden—I can testify to that—of directing the Government of the country; and at a time when the difficulties that face us are equalled only by the certainty of a glorious Canadian destiny if we solve them. A Party is fortunate in having among its leaders men of this calibre, all with experience, energy, high quality and a deep devotion to Canada.

Political leadership in a democratic state—I can testify from experience—and especially in a federal, continental, bilingual state like Canada—is a hazardous and demanding occupation; subject to slings and arrows; brickbats and, of course, bouquets. Its difficulties are increased, not only by the growing number and complexity of problems; not only because Government now intervenes—for better or worse—in practically every aspect of the citizen's life; regiments him before the cradle till after the grave. It is not only because of all this that the political leader grows prematurely worn and old and haggard. It is because problems are compounded by the impatient feeling, often the insistence of his masters, the people, that there is a quick and clean-cut solution to every problem; each one of which is reduced to simple terms of black and white.

The Leader has merely to find these solutions and, for this purpose, to be strong, decisive, wise, dynamic, charismatic, patient, indefatigable, kindly, and capable of inspiring unswerving loyalty, unquestioning obedience and rapturous worship.

He is expected, by the image-maker, to be a combination of Abraham Lincoln and Batman, to perform instant miracles. Then, when the poor, honest, decent chap can't live up to this image, the process of demolition begins so that another superman can be erected in the ruins.

I mention all this to give my successor courage and good cheer, as he contemplates *les grandeurs et les misères de la politique*.

I concluded: 'I hope I have achieved something along the way. If I have, it is because of the loyalty, the friendship and the support I have received in such overflowing measure, for which I shall never cease to be grateful, and which I shall never forget.'

We did a little gulping at that particular moment when I said good-bye, not only in the Liberal party, but to my political life; and I was speeded on my way by a white puppy. I have often wondered what inspired that unique gift to a retiring Prime Minister and leader, and what symbolism lay behind it. John Nichol had told me that they were going to do this, and my wife and I both thought it was the silliest thing we had ever heard of. We told him: 'We can't keep a dog; we're going to Ireland right after the convention. What are we going to do with a little puppy?' We had had only two dogs in our married life, and both had come to unhappy and tragic ends; we did not want another. Nichol was a little crestfallen about this, but he came back the next day and said: 'Well, you're going to have a dog.' I had to acknowledge that I could not stop him from giving us anything he wanted to, but I persisted in asking why he wanted to give us a dog when he knew how we felt about it. He replied: 'It will be wonderful on television.'

Nonetheless, it was a very successful occasion, quite apart from the emotion engendered in the Pearson family. This was a great evening, and it led up to the greatest moment of the convention when, on Saturday afternoon, the voting began. The tenseness of the atmosphere and the increasing and developing excitement were something long to remember. I have been through some fairly dramatic and exciting moments in my seventy-five years, but I do not believe that I have ever experienced a more heart-tightening occasion than on that afternoon. I was fairly certain that Mr Trudeau was going to win, though not on the first ballot. But there were so many other emotional aspects: Mr Sharp joining the Trudeau camp; Mr Martin getting relatively few votes, and his gallant way of taking this defeat (he was truly magnificent); the lobbying and the discussions. Then there were the adjectives thrown back and forth by Miss LaMarsh and others. There was the getting together of the candidates in full view of the spectators, and in front of the cameras. However, it all made good theatre, and a splendid show.

Even by March it had become clear that Trudeau was the man to beat, and that this could be done only if all the anti-Trudeau forces united behind one candidate. This they did not and could not do, right up until the last ballot on Saturday, 6 April. So Trudeau won, and we all gathered, weeping and laughing, around the platform, slapping each other on the back; and ultimately on to victory under Mr Trudeau. And it was all over in time to get home for the face-off of Hockey Night in Canada.

The unbelievable of January had become the acclaimed of April. Only a single outstanding opponent could have beaten Trudeau and there was none. In any event, no one in the Liberal party had so good a chance of capturing the country in the next election as he, nor anyone a greater intelligence. Experience in government he could acquire; and since there had to be some drastic reforms in the machinery and techniques of government, experience was not an unmixed advantage. I wrote at the time: 'Trudeau is also tough, resilient, and realistic. He is not likely to be mesmerized by his own triumph, or deceived by the dazzling image that his press and TV admirers have created for him.' After his selection as leader, and before I turned over the prime ministership, I saw him on several occasions to discuss policies and personnel. His approach to the frightening problems ahead was impressive and heartening. I noted: 'The choice is a gamble, of course, but a good one and worth taking. It is certainly the case of a new man for a new era.' He proceeded with wisdom and skill and tact to heal the wounds in the party, inevitably created by the leadership race.

We discussed at some length the forthcoming session, the relative advantages of prorogation or dissolution. My advice was to work toward an October election, with as long a summer holiday for Parliament as possible. The Opposition would do their best to sully his image in the Commons, and Trudeau should do his best to appeal to the country before the parliamentary hatchet-men could do their work. July and most of August without Parliament, time to get around the country, and a dissolution toward the end of August with an election in October seemed to me to be the answer. But it would be his problem, not mine.

On 19 April 1968 when we were packing, preparatory to leaving Sussex Drive (and what a job that was, trying to find room in a small house for the accumulated possessions of forty years), Trudeau phoned to say that he had almost decided to dissolve the House on the day it reassembled. I was surprised, to say the least. It seemed a spectacular beginning for his parliamentary career as Prime Minister. His argument was that he wished to use the excitement and momentum of the leadership convention to ask for a vote of confidence from the country while his image was still unsullied, before he had to do things and to make decisions that would be unpopular. He considered that this was the best time to get his majority. He admitted that there was a division in the Cabinet on the matter, but thought that this would be cleared up at the next meeting. Meanwhile, he would keep very quiet, and then on the morning before the opening of the House he would consult the caucus and try to convince them.

And this was the way it worked out. The change-over took place Saturday, 20 April, when I went to Rideau Hall to resign, as I had done once before after St Laurent's government was defeated. I went by myself for the last time as Prime Minister to greet my friend, Governor General Michener, and have a drink with him. The press gave me a great deal of attention going in; I got none at all going out. I offered my resignation, then Mr Trudeau arrived, and the three of us went through the necessary and time-honoured formalities. Mr Trudeau and the new Cabinet were sworn in, and very suddenly I was in the corner. I slipped home. There was not very far to go as I was still the occupant of 24 Sussex Drive, and did not have to stop by the grocery store as I had in 1957, when my wife told me to pick up some hamburger on my way home. I was a very happy and relieved man and would be off to Ireland for a holiday in a few days time. My departure had been arranged so as to give me a few days in the House as a private member. I did not want to take any active political part, but I wanted to see what it would be like and wondered where they would seat me.

The new Prime Minister appeared before the Liberal caucus on Tuesday morning, 23 April, before the House reassembled in the afternoon. There they were, the new Cabinet behind the table, while I was down with the back-benchers and having a great time. The Prime Minister asked if there was any business we wished to take up. I, for the first and last time, got the floor and demanded in no uncertain terms that this new government do something about the importing of American turkeys into Canada which was destroying the turkey trade on Manitoulin Island; if something was not done, there would be a question in the House. Such a speech on my part caused great merriment.

Then Trudeau spoke. He told the caucus that he would dissolve the House that afternoon and announce an election for 25 June. Gasps.

Then he very forcefully made his case for this action, and won over the doubters. It was a great performance. There was no doubt in my mind that he wanted to force a confrontation with Quebec on the national unity issue, to meet it head on. In fact, Jean Marchand had already emphasized this to me. This required courage and meant a risk. But he knew what he was doing, and subsequent events proved him triumphantly right.

That afternoon at 2:30 I took my seat in the House on the front-bench toward the end, the same place where I had sat when I first entered Parliament. The most junior Cabinet Minister was on my left and I remember very vividly that I was looking at George Hees right opposite me. Everyone was jovial and I was wondering what I should say when, as I expected he would, the Prime Minister declared this was the time to recognize the incomparable services to Canada, to the world, to the interplanetary system, of his predecessor. But I was relieved of that oratorical problem. The Prime Minister quietly announced dissolution and the Opposition were shocked into complete silence. Of course no one could speak, since there was no Parliament to speak to. The Governor General had ended it a few hours before. Stanley Knowles later complained that Trudeau had not allowed the House to pay me a deserved tribute! I noted in my last prime ministerial diary, 'Tough.'

I went home and packed. I told Mr Trudeau we would be out of Sussex Drive as quickly as possible; there was no use hanging around. All we needed was some time to move to our new house, and we had been doing that during the past ten days so we could get out almost at once.

And that same day, 23 April 1968, was my seventy-first birthday.

Then we went on our holiday. When we came back the election campaign was on. I took no part except to go up to my constituency and help Maurice Foster, who had won the Liberal nomination there. He was elected, and I think I was of some help to him, although he did not really need it as he got a good majority. I did go to Toronto for one big meeting in Jimmy Walker's constituency where the Prime Minister also appeared. This was the best political meeting I ever attended in my life. It really was magnificent and I knew then, if I had had any doubt before, that this man and his party were just going to sweep the country.

I must say that my main impression after I was out of office was a sense of great relief at being able to wake up in the morning in our own house and without things pressing in on me from all directions, knowing it was going to be like that until at least eleven o'clock that night. I missed the excitement, of course, but not nearly as much as some people assured me I would. I was very happy – happy for my family and especially for my wife. I knew that she had been looking forward to the day when her husband would no longer be Prime Minister and I was gratified to see her relieved and happy. I think she was amused at my wandering around the house those first few days like a lost soul with nothing to do. In fact, I had lots to do but gone was the urgency that had surrounded everything I had been doing for years. Of course, staying home for lunch required a little readjustment! I had no trouble, however, moving from the private car to the upper berth and I enjoyed it exceedingly.

My last personal observation on this long road will concern the night of the press gallery dinner for me. It was a very happy occasion with a good many old friends. At the conclusion of the evening, I took a taxi home. I sank back, and began dozing and wondering about the vagaries of life, about what was going to happen now, when I suddenly realized that the driver had gone by the driveway on Sussex Drive. I banged him on the back and said: 'In there, in there.' The taxi driver turned around and looked at me in a friendly but pitying way: 'Mr Pearson, you don't live there any more.'

INDEX